The State and the Social

THE STATE AND THE SOCIAL

State Formation in Botswana and Its Pre-Colonial and Colonial Genealogies

Ørnulf Gulbrandsen

berghahn
NEW YORK · OXFORD
www.berghahnbooks.com

Published in 2012 by

Berghahn Books

www.berghahnbooks.com

©2012, 2014 Ørnulf Gulbrandsen
First paperback edition published in 2014

Library of Congress Cataloging-in-Publication Data

Gulbrandsen, Ørnulf.
The state and the social : state formation in Botswana and its pre-colonial and colonial
genealogies / Ørnulf Gulbrandsen.
    p. cm.
   Includes bibliographical references.
   ISBN 978-0-85745-297-9 (hardcover) — ISBN 978-0-85745-298-6 (institutional
ebook) — ISBN 978-1-78238-325-3 (paperback) — ISBN 978-1-78238-326-0 (retail
ebook)
   1. Botswana—Politics and government. 2. Chiefdoms—Botswana—History.
3. Power (Social sciences)—Botswana—History. I. Title.
DT2478.G85 2012
968.83'01—dc23

                    2011037469

British Library Cataloguing in Publication Data

A catalogue record for this book is available from the British Library

Printed in the United States on acid-free paper.

ISBN 978-1-78238-325-3 paperback
ISBN 978-1-78238-326-0 retail ebook

For Elsa

CONTENTS

Maps

ILLUSTRATIONS

FOREWORD

This volume presents an anthropological discussion of the socio-historical emergence of the Botswana nation-state. Gulbrandsen, in the best tradition of anthropological field research, adopts a holistic perspective grounded in ethnographic experience and immersion in a diversity of social and political practices over the long-term. This is not the kind of travelogue ethnography that has begun to take a hold in anthropology, one perhaps over-influenced by postmodern cultural studies perspectives.

Gulbrandsen's observations and interpretations build from his engagement beginning in the 1970s with predominantly members of the Tswana majority, and in a great variety of contexts involving many different subject positions. The conceptual and theoretical understandings that he develops are conditional on his ethnography which is the hallmark of an anthropological approach. Here I must remark that in my opinion anthropology is not theory-driven and that this constitutes its distinction in the social sciences. That is, while anthropologists claim major theoretical significance for their work, their theoretical understanding is empirically derived (rather than merely empirically supported) and is ideally organic with the life situations examined. In this sense, anthropological theorizing does not begin in abstraction or in some transcendent authority, but in and through the grounded experience of human practice. Anthropology gives this primacy and it is in this sense that Gulbrandsen's work achieves its distinction. I say this because much of Gulbrandsen's argument – indeed its excitement – develops through a critical consideration of major conceptual and theoretical orientations in the economic, political and social sciences especially as they are applied to Africa. These have their source in European and North American contexts (in fact in the particular historical conditions of specific modernities and reflections upon them). As an anthropologist, Gulbrandsen is intensely sensitive to this fact and, more specifically, of his own Norwegian origins which bear certain assumptions that demand addressing in the Botswana context.

For example, he is concerned with dimensions of democratic practice in Botswana noting some similarities with Norway where the emphasis on local participation is emphasised especially through its commune system (not unlike that of Switzerland studied by Eric Wolf). In Norway there is a strong stress on a politics of consensus, at both local and national levels, and this attunes Gulbrandsen to similar dynamics in the Botswana context although as he demonstrates this emerges from the very particular cultural context of Tswana traditional practice. Western democracies, of course, have had considerable influence on Botswana starting in the colonial experience. But they are grounded largely in a very different history characterized by an egalitarian ethos and a comparatively historically recent culture of individualism (e.g. Macpherson 1964, Dumont 1986, Taylor 2007). The values of consensus that have been appropriated into the governing apparatus of the Botswana nation-state are grounded in a system of ranked hierarchy associated with the still persisting, though of course continually changing, clan/lineage system of the Tswana *merafe* and chiefly (*kgosi*) rule. In other words, in effect a kind of democracy, though far from reducible to the Western kind, existed in the context of a hierarchical order and continues to have effect in the altogether different hierarchical bureaucratic structures of the contemporary Botswana nation-state which nevertheless gives ideological support to Tswana kin-based chiefly hierarchical value. What to outsiders might appear to be anti-democratic in Botswana (the continuing value placed on rank) has a democratic participatory aspect which gives the general populace a marked say in events despite what may otherwise appear as anti-egalitarian features in contradiction of Western democratic ideals (themselves thwarted by what many might see as growing class inequalities).

Gulbrandsen engages his own comparative knowledge both to sharpen his understanding of processes in Botswana and to draw attention to differences that may be glossed over in superficial similarities that overlook important distinctions. Most anthropologists would argue that comparison is unavoidable and the merit of Gulbrandsen's approach is to make explicit the source of his own evaluation of the Botswana situation – and in a way which reveals crucial dimensions of it. Furthermore, Gulbrandsen's comparative orientation is not based on simple oppositions of a We/They kind and is oriented to the uncovering of differences which nonetheless contain crucial similarities at least in effect. I should note here that throughout the book Gulbrandsen is concerned to avoid an anthropological relativism whereby his discussion is merely deemed relevant to Botswana. What he achieves is to indicate the significance of the Botswana materials for wider discussion on the nature of state/citizen processes but with a strong attention to the cultural conditionality and limitation of his observations and conceptualizations as well as the tendency to universalist assessment or judgment more characteristic of other disciplines.

This work is an excellent example of anthropology as a discipline of the 'minor discourse'. The social philosopher, Gilles Deleuze (1991) – whose work constitutes a major reference in Gulbrandsen's analysis – develops the notion of the minor discourse to draw attention to arguments, orientations or understandings that are typically marginalized and not infrequently suppressed by and in the interest of ruling orientations or theories which, as Foucault also argued, support the status quo. Anthropology has conventionally worked among marginalized populations whether those suppressed in imperial expansion or those otherwise reduced in circumstance and excluded. The discipline has made important contributions in contesting dominant/dominating opinion and thought and this is especially so concerning largely Eurocentric theoretical assertions and the submerged cultural assumptions that frequently underpin them. This received further impetus from an internal critique in anthropology that questioned its colonialist or imperialist associations which for many anthropologists was an uncomfortable aspect of its specific development as a discipline of the minor discourse.

Gulbrandsen's overall conception and analytical direction in this volume is thoroughly in line with anthropology as a distinctive discipline of the minor discourse and further establishes it as such.

Throughout the book Gulbrandsen not only addresses issues central in the anthropology of Africa but also gives practices in Botswana authority and position in the evaluation of opinion and theory (particularly political science) conditioned within largely Western frames of reference. In other words, what is *made into a minor discourse* or suppressed through the hegemony of Western thought inevitably tied to imperial cum globalizing power achieves authority that it might otherwise lack. In this work Gulbrandsen demonstrates the importance of the Botswana case perhaps leading to a major reconsideration of much conventional or conventionalizing opinion.

Gulbrandsen's analysis focuses on Botswana's apparent exceptionalism. Contrary to the relatively dismal picture painted by many students of Africa, Botswana is a relative success story. The society that has taken form in the context of the establishment of the nation-state has weathered the potential hazardous effects of Colonial Rule and taken advantage of globalizing forces. The myriad 'discontents of modernity' (see Comaroff and Comaroff 1993) that have been described for elsewhere in Africa do not appear to have taken disastrous hold. The dangers of new wealth (e.g. diamonds) have not been markedly divisive (although Gulbrandsen does not rule out such an eventuality). The conflicts born of class and ethnicity have largely been avoided and the 'politics of the belly' associated with the emergence of greedy elites, although by no means outside a public consciousness, has been averted in the main. What Gulbrandsen indicates is that factors which are seen widely in Africa to be associated with political and social conflict and war in other parts of Africa are shown in the Botswana situation to be far from inevitable in their consequence. Here I should add that Gulbrandsen does not present Botswana as a harmonious exception. Antagonisms and conflicts founded in class and ethnicity are developing but they have not taken the thoroughly disastrous turn that often seems to have been taken elsewhere.

Clearly various dualisms and oppositions that continue to bedevil anthropology and other disciplines pose major difficulties for understanding, and the minor discourses of the hitherto dominated, such as Botswana, expose them. Gulbrandsen presents the Botswana situation as quashing such oppositions, and powerfully questions the reasoning behind their continuing centrality in the analysis of processes in the now post-colonial margins. Much that receives a negative value in parts of Africa, in Botswana has a more positive effect. Common dualisms that would oppose tradition to modernity or change to stasis, for example, are shown by Gulbrandsen to be inadequate to say the least.

In the Botswana context what might be conceived as tradition is a powerful force both of change and of control in contemporary circumstances. Gulbrandsen approaches the idea of tradition through the cultural orientation of anthropology that both sets it within historical processes and conceives it as a continual dynamic, always open to redefinition, within contexts of practice. In this sense the traditional is not outside contemporary forces but continually being re-created in ongoing social and political relations realizing original import and achieving often innovative effects. The traditional in this approach is not a mere product or an outcome of historical forces but is ingrained within them, vital to the various directions that societal formation in Botswana is taking as this is bound up with the structuring process of the state. In this way, Gulbrandsen goes beyond the 'invention of tradition' perspectives (Hobsbawm and Ranger 1983) that operate with a kind of hiatus between the contemporary and the past (perhaps paradoxically itself engaging in the invention of tradition) without invoking a kind of primordialism.

In Gulbrandsen's analysis there are no clear pre-colonial/post-colonial or before/after demarcations for the understanding of the formation of present-day Botswana. Prior to the advent of colonialism the Tswana could not have been considered as some kind of static cold society and a hostage, as it were, to the heat of change brought by external forces.

Gulbrandsen presents the Tswana polities before the advent of European forces as being powerfully expansive and incorporative. He shows how, as an aspect of this, Tswana socio-political processes were built on the basis of change, bringing other African populations within their suzerainty and as part of this oriented to engaging foreign would-be colonizers in accordance with their own terms. They were not the passive subjects of colonial conquest but engaged colonial interests to the pragmatics of their own cultural/political discourse. Official colonial policy of Indirect Rule (which so often through southern Africa involved the creation of political institutions that had no prior existence, see Van Velsen 1967) found a ready utility in already existing Tswana conception and practice. Different orientations towards political and social control within the colonial and post-colonial contexts were in some degree able to co-evolve in a way that was probably very different from some of the peoples in surrounding territories (e.g. South Africa). Undoubtedly this was facilitated by the fact that the territory that became Botswana, from the perspective of the colonizers, had few exploitative resources other than cheap labour. The Bechuanaland Protectorate that became Botswana effectively constituted a pool of cheap labour for the South African mines and the system of labour migration that developed itself was a structure of imperial control that even as it made exploitative use of Tswana political orders gave a degree of autonomy to the Tswana that was a crucial factor in the formation of independent Botswana. The force of Tswana cultural and social values not only persisted through changing circumstances but were vital agencies in social transformation.

In the later circumstances of the development of the independent nation-state Gulbrandsen indicates that the continuing incorporative dynamic of Tswana practice is a factor (regardless of its hierarchializing and inegalitarian dimensions) suppressing the more extreme potentials of inter-ethnic conflict. Agents of the Botswana state were concerned that tribalism (a curse in much of Africa and, as the Manchester anthropologists of Gluckman's central and southern African school insisted, more a force of modernity than of tradition) should not be encouraged. Regardless of government policy to such effect there is strong evidence that Tswana's incorporative dynamics harnessed to the interests of state formation is a major factor ameliorating ethnic tension.

Gulbrandsen's direction to overcome various dualisms that have afflicted anthropological thinking (as well as that in other disciplines) is important. For example, he records very interestingly how the centrifugal social and political effects of cattle-herding societies are not a necessary outcome of such economies as some anthropologists have asserted. On the contrary, among the Tswana concentrated, relatively permanent and dense population settlements were formed that became the core of centralized hierarchical political orders. In the terms of Deleuze and Guattari, rhizomic de-territorializing forces were bound with tree-like hierarchical centering and territorializing processes that imparted to the Tswana their particular expansive and incorporative dynamic. Here I must hasten to add that Gulbrandsen does not reduce his understanding of the Tswana to ecological or economic forces, instead demonstrating how these are not to be separated from other cultural and social institutional processes which are as constitutive of the economy, for instance, as vice versa. This is especially so in the period prior to colonialism and the forging of the independent nation-state when it could be said that strictly speaking there was no such thing as an economy in the modern capitalist sense (see Sahlins 1978, Clastres 1987, Dumont 1986). What Gulbrandsen demonstrates is how cultural forces that bear the traces of the past continue to have an influence on the political economy of the contemporary nation-state within globalizing realities. Beef exports are vital in the state economy and much of the success of the Botswana cattle industry is built on the fact of the centrality of cattle in practices of the creation and formation of social and political relations quite independently of any capital interest. In other words, the cultural importance of cattle in Tswana social life advantageously positioned Botswana in the processes of global capital.

I find fascinating Gulbrandsen's historical discussion of the relation of the various lineage-based Tswana kingdoms/nations or *merafe* and their rulers (*kgosi*) to the emerging Botswana nation-state. While they are drawn into the state order and to a large extent marginalized (and more recently losing influence as a consequence of the growth of new urban centres), Gulbrandsen suggests that the *kgosi* operate as a check on state practices. In the early period of Independence it seems that they functioned as an alternative state within the state, perhaps to play on Pierre Clastres' thesis in *Society Against the State* (1987), as a society of the state against the nation-state and its bureaucracy that in Gulbrandsen's argument is relatively exterior to society.

Overall Gulbrandsen addresses major sociological and political arguments that have developed recently with regard to Africa. I refer to the tendency to treat contemporary African states as more or less basket cases, which if so are views, in many instances, exacerbated in what would seem to be highly Eurocentric opinion: for example, arguments that discuss Africa in terms of concepts of the failed state, the politics of the belly and elite greed, radical ethnic conflict and war, intense dynamics of impoverishment and much else. The negative forces of so-called traditionalism and historically formed cultural orientations constituted outside European history, the maladaptation of African political cultural realities to rational bureaucratic orders are among some of the factors that have been stressed as well as the destructive forces of global capital in the circumstances of contemporary globalization. Gulbrandsen's work suggests that explanations of the plight of many state situations in Africa with reference to the above factors may be too easy. Traditionalism or cultural orientations refashioned within the context of modernity do not necessarily lead to negative consequences. The evidence from Botswana – and Gulbrandsen is relatively positive in his assessment – indicates that fast conventionalizing opinion and theory demands some more careful reconsideration.

This is a wonderful book rich in ethnography and every bit as rich in careful and considered thought. The book is exemplary in its anthropology and demonstrates the continuing value of an anthropological perspective across the disciplines.

Bruce Kapferer

ACKNOWLEDGEMENTS

This volume is an outcome of my long-term anthropological research in Botswana, based on a number of extended periods of field work since 1976. It relies on many conversations and observations in widespread parts of this country; from the ultra-centre of the modern state ministerial quarters to small, scattered hamlets hundreds of kilometres from the capital. Most of the time I spent in South-Eastern Botswana, in particular within the domain of one of the larger Tswana kingdoms (*merafe*) – the Bangwaketse – where I initially lived for a year and a half in a large, provincial village, composed of a majority of Tswana as well as 'minorities' of different origins. During that time I also worked closely with people living in the royal centre and with governmental employees at different levels. After numerous return trips to these and other locations in Botswana, I think back upon the years that have passed with tremendous gratitude to all the people who have engaged with me, for long hours, in conversations on all kinds of topics. Their generosity and hospitality have been important indeed for whatever merits this study might have. Beyond that, the extensive involvement with people in their everyday life – often giving rise to lifelong friendships – has, more than I can say, enriched my life. Many thanks to all of you.

There are some people in Botswana I want to mention in particular. At an early stage, the late Bathoen II Gaseitsiwe – the *kgosi* (king) of the Bangwaketse since 1928 until he abdicated and became leader of the opposition and Member of Parliament in 1969 – generously received me for a number of enlightening conversations. I also returned many times to his son and heir, *Kgosi* Seepapitso IV, until his death in 2010 and benefited always from his sharp scrutiny of my arguments and his outspokenness. Deputy *Kgosi* Gaboletswe Ketsitlile has been a close friend and a highly knowledgeable and informative conversation partner ever since I first came to the country. He has taught me much of what I know about 'how our people live and think,' as he used to say. Amongst the large number of other people in Botswana who helped me to comprehend what was going on in various quarters, I especially want to mention Edward Gabotloe-loe, Gobuamang Gobuamang, Sandy Grant, Ruud Jansen, M. L. A. Kgasa, the late *Kgosi* Linchwe, Remolefe Matiba, Otukile Masolotate, the late Tselayakgosi Motlogelwa, Kaboyamodimo Modise, the late Vance Mogotsi, MmaTebogo Mogotsi, Alice Mogwe, Macholm and Marcia Odell, Bonnie Sebonego and Pulahela Sebotho. Let me extend particular gratitude to the former state president Festus Mogae who invited me for a long evening's conversation, complementing the diversity of perspectives from which I have attempted to comprehend Botswana.

During all the years of research in which the present study is grounded, many colleagues have, at different stages, helped me to analyze and theorize my ethnographic materials through conversations as well as comments and criticisms of seminar presentations and written drafts. The present study depends, particularly, on the inspiring intellectual exchanges I have enjoyed with Bruce Kapferer for many years; I want especially to express my gratitude for his extremely helpful critique and comments on drafts of the present text. I thank him as well for writing the foreword of this book. I have, moreover, had a long-standing stimulating relationship with John Comaroff since we first met in Botswana in 1975. He has always responded generously to all the drafts I have sent him, with constructive, extensive and encouraging critique. His and Jean Comaroff's works have always provided a great source of inspiration which I hope the present volume reflects. I also want to express my appreciation for many conversations with the doyen of Tswana ethnography, the late Professor Isaac Schapera, conversations that contributed much to my comprehension of the historical developments of the Tswana kingdoms and the colonial encounter. He placed many of his field notes at my disposal which I have read with great benefit. Richard Werbner has for a long time been a challenging and thought-provoking discussion partner; he has also commented upon many drafts for which I am grateful. Similarly, Isaac Mazonde, Jacqueline Solway and Jo Helle-Valle have been most inspiring companion researchers on Botswana.

The Department of Social Anthropology, University of Bergen, has, for all these years, provided me with a highly stimulating intellectual environment. My colleagues and friends Jan-Petter Blom, the late Georg Henriksen, Olaf Smedal and Harald Tambs-Lyche have been important discussion partners at different stages. Bjørn Enge Bertelsen has recurrently commented in great detail upon my drafts for which I am most grateful.

During different phases of my research on Botswana there are a number of colleagues who over the years have been helpful, including Kirsten Alnæs, Alan Barnard, Fredrik Barth, Paul Baxter, Wim van Binsbergen,

Maurice Bloch, Ottar Brox, Jean Comaroff, Deborah Durham, Harri Englund, Vibeke Erichsen, Jean-Claude Galay, Treasa Galvin, the late Alfred Gell, Kenneth Good, the late Reidar Grønhaug, Suzette Heald, Robert Hitchcock, Edvard Hviding, Gunnar Håland, Jan Isaksen, Anita Jacobson-Widding, Judith Kapferer, Frederick Klaits, Adam Kuper, Paul Lane, Andrew Lattas, Anh Nga Longva, Christian John Makgala, Leif Manger, Monageng Mogalakwe, Peter Molutsi, Henrietta Moore, the late Leonard Ngcongco, Lydia Nyati-Ramahobo, Neil Parsons, Pauline Peters, John Peel, Jeff Ramsay, Simon Roberts, Mathew Schoffeleers, Axel Sommerfelt, Gloria Somolekae, Frode Storaas, Balefi Tsie and Pnina Werbner.

Drafts of several chapters of this volume have been presented at anthropological seminars at the Universities of Bergen, Edinburgh, Manchester, Oxford, Uppsala and the London School of Economics, in addition to a number of conference sessions. I am grateful to the participants for all the useful comments and critiques rendered me.

I thank Bjørn Brataas, Lucy Carolan and Jigger Wise for providing me with editorial assistance and Kjell Helge Sjøstrøm for helping me with maps. It has been a pleasure to work with Marion Berghahn and her staff in order to get a book out of my writings. I am also grateful for all the financial support I received from the Norwegian Research Council and the University of Bergen.

Finally, I want express special thanks to my dear Elsa for commenting unstintingly on my many drafts and for being a constant source of encouragement and inspiration. I am pleased to dedicate this book to her.

Bergen, November 2011
Ørnulf Gulbrandsen

INTRODUCTION

Botswana has often been portrayed as an oasis of peace and harmony, admired for its continuous parliamentarian democracy, esteemed for the sustainable strength of its postcolonial state and widely recognized for its tremendous economic growth. One might assume that these developments have come about due to Western ideas and practices of government, with their strong emphasis on electoral democracy and a well-functioning state bureaucracy having successfully replaced the premodern structures of power. It is my contention, however, that the postcolonial state of Botswana is best comprehended as a unique, complex formation arising dialectically from the intersection of Western ideas and practices with indigenous structures of power. On the one hand, I argue that symbolic conceptions and hierarchies of authority rooted in indigenous polities have, to a significant extent, been integral to the contemporary political processes of state formation in postcolonial Botswana. On the other hand, I shall explain how global forces have been decisive for state formation in the country, in postcolonial as well as precolonial times.

Let me say at once that my argument is not *primordial*, nor do I claim that contemporary Botswana is simply the invention of colonial and postcolonial modernism. There are significant *continuities* from the past into the present that I want to explain by examining the transformation of state processes in precolonial and colonial times with reference to a globally determined, shifting historical context. But the postcolonial significance of these continuities is the result of modern forces acting on and through sociopolitical symbols and institutions that have lengthy lineages, which are, I reiterate, both historical and in a constant state of change.

2 • The State and the Social

There is vast literature by political economists,[1] political scientists and sociologists[2] on Botswana that has contributed much to our comprehension of the development of an efficient, modern state government, a sustainable parliamentarian democracy and a forceful state-centred, diamond-driven political economy. In general, this literature presents a political economy that furnishes the state treasury with tremendous resources – financing very extensive state 'development' policies, programmes and projects that have also been massively supported, technically and financially, by international 'development' agencies. These scholars do, however, not agree on *how* successful Botswana's development has been, especially in view of escalating income differences, leaving a very substantial section of the population persistently below the official poverty threshold (Taylor 2005: 46f.). Further, the celebration of Botswana's parliamentarian democracy has been questioned, particularly with reference to all the powers concentrated in the Office of the President and the Botswana Democratic Party ruling ever since independence in 1966.[3] Nevertheless, virtually all of the literature acknowledges the successful establishment of a strong state with a forceful ruling group and an efficient government apparatus.

And so do I. However, my approach to the question of how this has come about is different. In my view, the main conditions for the formation of a strong postcolonial state in Botswana cannot be found by means of government-centred approaches, notwithstanding their significance for understanding how the political economy has evolved and governmental institutions are constructed and operate. Major conditions for Botswana's relative success in establishing a strong state with a sustainable government – seen in relation to many other African countries – have to be discovered by examining how it has progressively situated itself in the larger social context. I shall do so without restricting myself to local issues of 'state effects'[4] since I am centrally concerned how the post-colonial state has grounded itself in the larger social context, encompassing the 'local'.[5]

---

1. Key contributions include Colclough and McCarthy 1980; Harvey and Lewis 1990; Hillbom 2008; Isaksen 1981; Siphambe et al. 2005; Thunberg-Hartland 1978.

2. See Edge and Lekorwe 1998; Good 1994, 1999a, 2002, 2008; Gulbrandsen 1996a; Gunderson 1970; Holm 1985, 1988; Holm and Molotsi 1989; Maundeni 2002; Mbabazi and Taylor 2005; Molutsi and Holm 1990; Parson 1984; Picard 1985; Samatar 1999; Somolekae and Lekorwe 1998; Sebudubudu 2005; Taylor 2003, 2005; Tsie 1996; Vengroff 1977.

3. Kenneth Good has, in a series of articles and a recent book (Good 2008) represented a major, critical voice of Botswana's political development; this has cost him his residence permit and consequently his professorship at the University of Botswana.

4. E.g. Hansen and Stepputat (2001), Das and Poole eds. (2004) and Friedman (2011).

5. There is, of course, a well-established anthropological practice to approach of political systems in ways that take care of the 'the local' while also addressing assemblages of power of a

In this pursuit, I am centrally concerned with how it could be that people of power and wealth across 'tribal' boundaries joined together with other significant elites in a highly sustainable grand coalition underpinning the ruling group that took firm control over the state at Botswana's independence in 1966. Seen in a wider African context of competing elites generating weak states with notoriously unstable governments, this is a critical question. And there is no obvious answer to it, when taking into account the considerable *potential* of mobilisation amongst some of Botswana's indigenous polities. At the time of independence the large majority of the country's population was embraced by seven Tswana kingdoms (*merafe*, singl. *morafe*), including vast ethnic 'minorities'. Their ruling groups, and above all, the supreme royal authority known as *kgosi* (pl. *dikgosi*) had been strongly empowered under the British wing. What have been the conditions for these and other dominant elites' shared ambition in developing a modern nation-state, despite all their difference and conflicts? And how did they continue to prevail in the context of the *merafe* under post-colonial circumstances?

These are key questions because the dominant elites ensured, on the one hand, that indigenous institutions of jurisprudence – and thus extensive structures of social control – were, from the outset, made quite integral to the post-colonial state's administration justice. On the other hand, these elites constituted a major agency of transformation by which the conjunction of Eurocentric ideas and institutions, indigenous authority structures and distinctive global forces related to international beef and diamond trade conditioned a rapid development of a modern state. I am addressing this issue from the perspective that state formations everywhere are representing a unique assemblage of power, determined by local, regional and global conditions, by contemporary and historical trajectories.

Afro-pessimistic, Eurocentric orientations assert that the calamities of postcolonial Africa would be remedied if African governments would subscribe to human rights principles, adhere to a Christian moral code, adopt Western technology and managerial practices, practise free trade and undergo a radical political modernisation. It has often been claimed that a well-functioning modern state would naturally follow the introduction of a Western-style democratic government, operating in terms of Weberian bureaucratic virtues of universalism and separation of public

---

larger scale. What is often recognized as the seminal work on political anthropology – *African Political Systems* (Fortes and Evans-Pritchard eds. 1940) – provides early examples of such an effort, as do a range of subsequent studies, including Leach (1954), Barth (1959), Geertz (1980), Claessen and Skalnik eds. (1978), Valeri (1985), Kapferer (1988), Trouilot (1990) and Hansen (1999).

and private interests. Thus, Africa must get rid of what is conceived as its heritage of clientelism and all the 'irrational' ideas and practices arising from exercise of occult power. As other scholars have pointed out, such an outsider's view of African political life reflects a broader 'tendency in Western social scientific and popular writings on Africa to deal in stereo-types, to reduce its politics to typifying adjectives – communalist, patri-archal, paternalist' (Comaroff and Comaroff 1997b: 129). Consequently, those imbued with a Western outlook often draw the conclusion that the ideal of a sustainable, autonomous nation-state is only possible follow-ing emancipation from the ostensibly destructive influence of premodern political formations.

The case of Botswana challenges such views and demonstrates that indigenous political and social conditions do not necessarily generate un-stable strongman structures with fluctuating clientelistic networks that operate violently and destructively in relation to efforts of developing a stable modern state. On the contrary, I shall argue that however 'mod-ern' the postcolonial state in Botswana appears in its manifestation of vast modern Western-style practices and institutions of government, the development of its force is very attributable to extensive incorporation of symbolism and institutions of authority anchored in indigenous cos-mology. These are cosmologically anchored structures highly integral to people's lives and have, as we shall see, been reproduced through their own transformations and adaptation to post-colonial circumstances. One important dimension to be examined is the strong popular perception of hierarchies of authority as essential to peace and order (*kagiso*) – existen-tially critical to good health, prosperity and welfare.

Concentrating especially upon the formative and consolidating period of the post-colonial state (1966–1990) in this volume, I want to explain how agents of the state have, quite successfully, exploited this symbolic wealth in the effort to develop an imaginary of the state in accordance with people's idealising perception of authority as 'the one from whom good things come.' The considerable degree of legitimacy the ruling group seems to have enjoyed during this critical period of time – combined with the coherence of the dominant elites – has been imperative for capturing indigenous institutions of social control into the structures of the modern state. The indigenous symbolism, practices and institutions of author-ity have, moreover, been conducive to bringing people into the process of state formation by working on their subjectivities by virtue of state agents' interventions in the population, gently and with very limited use of overt coercive force. In order to come to terms with the distinctive ways in which indigenous symbolic and socio-political conditions have been important for the rise of a strong postcolonial state in Botswana, I shall trace their genealogies in precolonial and colonial state formations by an examination of their historical development.

All that said about processes and structures significant for the formation and consolidation of the modern state in Botswana, let me stress that I do not view 'the social' as solely a passive, contextual matter in which the state has grounded itself: I am centrally concerned with people's experience of the state through the discursive and material realities which the state has given raise to (cf. Krohn-Hansen and Nustad 2005: 15) and how people have increasingly reacted to repercussions of post-colonial state formation that have affected their lives adversely. In order to come to terms with such repercussions I am moving beyond the formative and consolidating decades of the postcolonial state because these repercussions are most evident after 1990.

In this pursuit I shall address two major trends. On the one hand, vast communities of ethnic minorities that have been under the domination of the major Tswana *merafe* since precolonial times, have voiced their protest in public against discrimination and demanded recognition – along with dominant Tswana – within the context of the nation-state. In view of the magnitude of these communities I shall discuss their attack on the state leadership and examine the conditions for 'minority' mobilization against the perceived dominant Tswana. On the other hand, escalating discrepancies of income and wealth have progressively given rise to social tensions and adversely affected the legitimacy of political leaders. Occasionally this development has manifested itself in popular protests entailing violent confrontations with state armed forces. I am addressing these trends in view of their apparently growing potentialities of challenging seriously the post-colonial state.

Let me then proceed to develop the points suggested so far in the pursuit of spelling out the major issues of the following chapters and how I want to address them.

Issues of Patrimonialism, Globalisation and Modern Nation-State Building in Africa

My concern with the relationship between modern state formation in Africa and indigenous ideas, practices and structures of power, links up with issues that have attracted considerable scholarly interest for a long time. In important respects this trend of research has been much inspired by Bayart's (1993) seminal study *The State in Africa*. The book's subtitle, *The Politics of the Belly*, refers to a celebrated virtue of political leadership found in many societies in Africa. Bayart (1993: 242–43) speaks of this virtue as an 'African way of politics' by which a 'man of power who is able to amass and redistribute wealth becomes a "man of honour" ... material prosperity is one of the chief political virtues rather than being an object of disapproval ... [W]ealth is a potential sign of being at one with the forces of cosmos'. This is rendered as patently a 'patrimonial' kind of political system where the accumulation of wealth is conceived by subjects as essential for their protection, support and welfare. Bayart (1993: 261) asserts its pervasive significance within the postcolonial context where the state 'functions as a rhizome of personal networks and assures the centralisation of power through agencies of family, alliance and friendship', militating strongly against a development from a 'weak' to an 'integral state'. The logic of 'the politics of the belly' under the conditions of the postcolonial state implies 'the unbridled predatoriness and violence of political entrepreneurs' (1993: 243). The heated competition for power generates notoriously political fragmentation that involves a dangerous battle – of life and death (1993: 238) – making 'the State in Africa' fragile, weak and failing.

Similarly, Chabal and Daloz (1999: 162) claim that in African postcolonial states there is 'an inbuilt bias in favour of greater disorder and against the formation of Western-style legal, administrative and institutional foundations required for development'. In such unstable states, 'political acts are played out on the market place of the various *patrimonial networks* concerned' (1999: 157, emphasis added) generating a notoriously destabilising force. They argue that 'in the absence of any other viable means needed to sustain neo-patrimonialism, there is inevitably a tendency to link politics to realms of increased disorder, *be it war or crime*' (1998: 162, emphasis added). Berman (1998: 305), equally concerned with the destructive impacts of 'patrimonialism', argues that '[p]atron–client networks remain the fundamental state–society linkage in circumstances of social crisis and uncertainty and have extended to the very center of the state'. The ill fate of African postcolonial states has in other words often been conceived in a Weberian, central-government-focused conception of 'patrimonialism', and, by extension, 'neo-patrimonialism'[6] or even 'pathological patrimonialism'.[7] (I shall question the utility of the notion of 'patrimonialism' at the end of the following section.)

Many of Africa's political disasters have thus been attributed to a contradiction between, on the one hand, ideals of the autonomous state premised on Western, bureaucratic rationality and, on the other, African realities of particularism and clientelism. It is often assumed that such

---

6. E.g. Bratton and van de Walle (1997: 61ff).
7. See Ergas 1987: 9ff.

realities give rise to monstrous leaderships and terrorist movements and stir up tribalism. The perception of such threats amongst postcolonial political leaders committed to projects of nation-state building are clearly reflected in how they in many instances tried to get rid of or reduce substantially the significance of indigenous authorities during the first era of independence. President Samora Machel of Mozambique, for example, asserted that '[t]o unite all Mozambicans, transcending traditions and different languages, requires that the tribe must die on our consciousness so that the nation may be born' (Machel 1974: 39, quoted after Bertelsen 2009: 125). Only in some very few countries 'tribes' and their leaders were officially recognized, and this includes Botswana. In this country, the status of the royal Tswana chiefs (*dikgosi*, singl. *kgosi*) had been consolidated, but by no means created, by the British and was further enshrined in the Constitution of the independent state of Botswana.[8] African postcolonial state leaders were – with obvious reason – deeply worried about the dangers of 'tribalism'. Subscribing to Western ideals of political modernisation, many made considerable efforts to curtail or eliminate traditional authority figures.

Finally, the West has, in postcolonial times, acted much as protagonists for the establishment of the modern state on African soils, yet also – in other disguises – represented major forces working contrary to their strength and sustainability. While much attention has been given to the deteriorating impacts of globalisation on nation-states all over the world during recent decades, such impacts have a long history on this continent all through the eras of imperialism and colonialism. During the latter half of the twentieth century – the postcolonial era – the rulers of many African states have maintained internal control with the support of one of the superpowers, at least until the end of the Cold War. And they did so, argues Reno (1999: 22f.), by using this support to coerce domestic 'strongmen' into structures of clientelism rather than to develop a state apparatus on the basis of bureaucratic principles. This strategy has generally created extremely shaky states, especially because as soon as the Cold War terminated, the conditions for clientelism evaporated and the strongmen turned against their previous patrons at the centre of government. In this vein of analysis of the formation of the postcolonial state, all the ostensibly destructive practices of patrimonialism reviewed above are directly related to global forces.

The consequence has, in many instances, been notoriously unstable states, often characterized by violence. It has been maintained that this

---

8. The other countries in which traditional authorities were given official recognition at their independence include Nigeria and Malawi beside Botswana.

trend has generally given rise to an unattractive image of 'Africa', militating effectively against foreign investment, effecting consequent economic stasis and excessive poverty (e.g., Bhinda et al. 1999). And when transnational capital interests have spotted a profitable opportunity on the African continent, they have operated in highly selective ways within specific areas without concern for a positive economic impact upon larger regions and without working constructively to support the state political economy of the relevant country. Also, the massive penetration of nongovernmental organisations on the continent has apparently at best played an ambiguous role in relation to the sustainability of the nation-state in Africa (e.g., Ferguson 2006: 13–14).

From Abandonment to Resurgence of 'Traditional Authorities'

The case of Botswana is important because it illuminates so well ways to avoid such calamities. A case study of this country might thus contribute to remedy what Englebert (2002: 51ff.) has identified as a major problem of theories that purport to offer continent-wide explanations: they 'fail to account for intra-African differences'. Most apparently, while diamond economies have substantially amplified violent conflicts and civil wars in countries such as Angola and Sierra Leone, Botswana's diamonds – like its cattle industry – have been successfully integrated into the state-centred political economy in ways that have, as I shall explain in this volume, contributed decisively to bringing the major elites of the country together in a persistent and strong interest in political stability and societal peace and order.[9] The state has been able to counter external forces from a position of considerable strength, which for example has enabled it to bring the various NGOs under Botswana's umbrella of government programmes and projects. In view of the often uneasy relations between capitalist corporations and nation-states (e.g., Hardt and Negri 2000: 325ff.), it is quite remarkable how the state in Botswana has managed to establish an advantageous, sustainable agreement with such a powerful corporation as the De Beers mining company. Their joint agreement has ensured that the state receives a substantial share from mining proceeds as well as direct representation on the board of the mining company, which has further strengthened the state's bargaining position (Sentsho 2005: 138; cf. Harvey and Lewis 1990: 123ff.; Leith 2005: 61ff., Chapter 3 below).

---

9. I am, to be sure, not suggesting that diamonds have caused calamities everywhere else in Africa; other cases in point where diamonds have no such consequences include Namibia and South Africa.

However, in order to come to terms with how international relations could possibly have such a constructive impact upon postcolonial state formation in Botswana, we need to address carefully another field of difference that has become ever more apparent since the late 1980s. While many postcolonial state leaders in Africa attempted at the inception of the independent state to eliminate 'traditional authorities', their force, vitality and persistence proved in due course to be considerable. For example, in such a turbulent state as Zaire (Congo), 'many chiefs *de facto* consolidated their … authority in the institutional and administrative chaos that followed independence. In an attempt to depoliticize the country after the 1965 coup, Mobutu returned to office all the chiefs that had been deposed' (De Boeck 1996: 82). Unsuccessful attempts were made to terminate this policy in the 1970s. In spite of the fact that 'the regime continues to view the traditional authorities as potentially threatening', the chiefdoms had to be restored to their full status, which 'led to a situation in which the state apparatus co-exists in various degrees of interdependence with traditional socio-political structures of varying degrees of coherence, power and autonomy' (De Boeck 1996: 82–83). The Zaire case exemplifies the kind of contradictions of, on the one hand, conflicting interests and, on the other, mutual dependency between 'state' and 'chiefdoms' that has become increasingly evident throughout most of the continent since decolonisation. Such contradictions have sponsored transformations and instabilities in many different state contexts, with, for each case, particular configurations of ambiguities and ambivalence.[10]

This trend has apparently triggered a major shift of state strategies – from abandonment to resurgence of 'traditional leaders' (e.g., see Ray and van Rouveroy van Nieuwaal 1996; von Trotha 1996). There are, to be sure, different scholarly views about what this trend actually involves.[11]

---

10. Ambiguities and ambivalence in the relationship between postcolonial state and indigenous authority figures are clearly reflected in von Rouveroy van Nieuwaal's (1999) comparative discussion of what he refers to as the 'hybrid role of chieftaincy in postcolonial Africa'. They are, moreover, reflected in a number of case studies, including Cameroon (Awasom 2005), Ghana (Lentz 1998; Rathbone 2000), Mozambique (Bertelsen 2003; Buur and Kyed 2006), Nigeria (Vaughan 2006), South Africa (Oomen 2005), Tanzania (e.g. Bienen 1970), Uganda (Karlstrøm 1996), and Zimbabwe (e.g. Ladley 1991). These ambiguities are interestingly illuminated by Western Zambia, where there has been an opposite trend: Van Binsbergen first explained that 'state and chieftainships are closely interlocking aspects of modern Zambia' to the extent that 'the incumbents of positions of the state … , in their effective exercise of popularly supported power, simply cannot do without chiefs' (1987: 191–92). Later he related that '[w]hereas in the first decades of the postcolonial era they [the royal chiefs] effectively expanded into formal administrative and representative bodies of the modern state, this process has now been reversed, largely as a result of regional ethnic conflict' (1999: 129).

11. Cf. Kyed and Buur 2007 for a recent, comprehensive review; see also van Dijk and van Rouveroy van Nieuwaal 1999.

While Skalnik (2004) argues that the resurgence of traditional leaders reflects 'failed' states' efforts to regain their strength, others place emphasis on the ability of the stronger postcolonial states to make indigenous authorities instrumental to expand their governmental controls and interventions in the population. Englebert (2002: 190), for example, claims that the legitimacy of the state in Africa would be enhanced by its incorporation of traditional institutions. In a similar optimistic spirit, Sklar (2005) makes the case for a notion of 'mixed government' and sketches a model according to which there are two distinct structures of authority whereby chiefs and state relate to the citizens through separate spheres. Such a model is, however, not unproblematic, maintain Buur and Kyed (2007: 105) with reference to the case of postcolonial Mozambique, where the state has recognized some four thousand traditional leaders as community authorities since 2002. They maintain that these authority figures 'may actually increase their access to and enlarge their scope of power' by which the state may 'run the risk of distancing traditional leaders from the communities they formally represent' (2007: 123–4; see also Englebert 2005: 54; Werbner 1996: 16).

The dilemma suggested here echoes the contradiction Gluckman identified long ago in his seminal analysis of 'the village headman' in a colonial context. He argued that 'the delicacy of the headman's position arises from conflicting principles' (Gluckman 1949: 93). In order to come to terms with this kind of conflict, we have to go significantly beyond the scope of all the scholarly works that restrict the issue of 'resurgence' by focusing narrowly on the relationships between the state governments and indigenous authority figures. As I hope the present work will demonstrate, we need to carefully examine the whole system of social relations in which such 'traditional leaders' are embedded, especially the symbolism of power grounded in indigenous cosmology and constitutive to hierarchies of authority relations.

A number of scholars have recognized the great significance of indigenous hierarchies of authority to the formation of a modern state in Botswana. Contrasting Botswana and Congo, which both are blessed with abundant, highly valuable mineral wealth but are radically different in respect of the sustainability of state leadership and societal controls, Englebert (2002: 107) argues that 'the quality of leadership and the construction of state capacity in Botswana are directly related to the embeddedness of its postcolonial state into pre-colonial patterns of political authority.' Furthermore, in search for the political foundation of development in Botswana, Beaulier and Subrick (2006: 105) claim that in this country 'political authority stems from traditional sources.' Maundeni (2002: 126) holds that the postcolonial state in Botswana 'inherited an indigenous state culture which it used to construct an indigenous development state.' Moreover, under the subtitle 'Chieftaincy and democracy as dynamic realities in Botswana' Nyamnjoh (2003: 235) asserts that 'the assumption that … [chieftaincy] is incompatible with modernity and democracy has no empirical foundation.'

In a wide ranging, critical review of scholarly usage of the Weberian notions of 'patrimonialism' and 'neo-patrimonialism' in African contexts, Pitcher, Moran and Johnston (2009: 149) argue, with particular reference to Botswana, that 'there is nothing inherent in patrimonialism to prevent creation of a democracy by leaders determined to do so.' They hold that '[f]or Weber, patrimonialism was not a synonym for corruption, "bad government," violence, tribalism, or a weak state. Instead it was a specific form of authority and source of legitimacy' (ibid.: 126). Thus conceived, they argue, '[a] more complete application suggests that Botswana – one of Africa's success stories – may also be one of its most clearly "patrimonial" or "neopatrimonial" states.' (ibid.: 150) They claim that this country's 'elites have not abandoned patrimonialism or overcome it; rather they have built a democratic state on a foundation of traditional and *highly personalized reciprocities* and loyalties' (ibid.: 145, emphasis added).

These authors argue thus that indegenious authority structures might work forcefully in favour of the development of a strong state in Africa, which I, of course, endorse. However, I reject their notion of Botswana as an example of how *patrimonialism* in the Weberian sense might constructively underpin the formation of a modern, democratic state. The authors' conception of what they call 'patrimonial legitimacy'[12] as a matter of highly personalized reciprocities and loyalties leads them to suggest that 'patron-client' relationships have been crucial for the successful grounding of the modern state in indigenous political relations in this country. In my analysis, by contrast, the post-colonial leadership in Botswana has succeeded because indigenous authorities have *not* been linked up with the modern state in relationships of 'highly personalized reciprocities and loyalties'. Rather, they were, as we shall see, from the outset incorporated in the bureaucratic structures of the modern state as civil servants by means of rational-legal provisions.

---

12. Weber did not speak of 'patrimonial legitimacy', but patrimonial domination and rule (Weber 1978 1020ff), the ruler's authority being predominantly – but not necessarily entirely – sourced by 'traditional grounds' for claim to legitimacy (ibid.: 215). Hence, it does not make sense to insist that 'patrimonialism' is 'not a regime type' but 'a kind of legitimacy' (Pitcher et al. 2009: 149). After all, notions of 'patrimonial state', 'patrimonial administration' and 'patrimonial domination' – i.e. 'regimes' – are indeed apparent in Weber's texts (e.g. Weber 1978: 1013ff.).

This means that they were effectively barred by state legislation from engaging in party politics. There have, to be sure, been some instances of informal and tacit impacts by indigenous authorities upon the modern political field. But on the whole they have been kept efficiently at bay. Furthermore, it would be far off the mark to classify the modern political practice as clientelistic. Although the ruling party has increasingly been under attack for attempting to gain support by means of allocating favours and other practices of bribery and corruption, political life in this country contrasts sharply with that of countries like Italy where my recent research has made it evident to me how the country's pervasive networks of patron-client relations work in ways highly detrimental to democratic political processes (Gulbrandsen, in prep.).

I want to show that, by incorporating indigenous authorities at different levels in the structures of the post-colonial state of Botswana, the political leadership has, quite successfully, encompassed indigenous hierarchies of authority into the process of modern state formation. These are institutionalized hierarchies that do not necessarily open up for the kind of political entrepreneurship associated with a patron's operation of personalized clientelistic networks. Although they certainly have that kind of potentiality also in Botswana, the strength of the state has depended much upon its leaderships' capacity to prevent this potentiality to manifest in post-colonial politics, especially during the formative and consolidating decades that are, I reiterate, of major concern in this volume.

Even more significantly, I shall explain, these hierarchies and indigenous governmental structures are inseparable from people's everyday lived-in-world, and are institutions right in the middle of it. We are hence faced with the complex task of coming to terms with the intricate ways in which this form of indigenous symbolism, practices and institutions of authority have interfaced with European ideas and practices in the formation of a distinctively Botswana modern state. For this purpose I question the analytical value of the notion of 'patrimonialism,' especially when conceived as a matter of 'personal connections between leader and subject, or patrons and clients' (Pitcher et al. 2009: 129). That is, a conception of reciprocal relations between ruler and subjects that focuses the transactional pragmatism-aspects of exercise of power (cf. Weber 1978: 1010ff.). Certainly, such an approach might be very beneficial to analyze particular features of pre-modern political systems, especially those of an acephalous kind as eminently demonstrated by Barth (1959). Also in the present study I have found some use of an actor/interaction perspective and, of course, the Weberian conception of sources of authority (1978: 215).

Nevertheless, I find use of the Weberian notion 'patrimonialism' problematic because it easily leads scholars' (including Pitcher et al.) attention primarily to personalized relations of power, e.g. in the form of individualized patron-client bonds. While this is a perspective that might be helpful to examine certain features of African, post-colonial politics (as demonstrated by Bayart [1993] and others), it is far too narrow to come to terms with how indigenous authority hierarchies, like the ones with which I am presently concerned, are constructed and operating in relation to modern state formation in Africa. Moreover, the highly inclusive socio-political hierarchies found in indigenous societies of Botswana are, as already suggested, constructed in ways that make it hard to distinguish between 'the governmental' and 'the social.' These points link closely up with a chief argument of the present section: The relationship between agents of the state and indigenous symbolism, practices and authority structures might be captured into modern state formation as constructive underpinnings. In this vein, it is required to go beyond Weber, who to great extent separated 'the governmental' from larger social order (e.g. 1978: 1006–1110), and to open up for comprehending how processes of state formation transcend governmental institutions. In this endeavour I now turn to presenting approaches I have found helpful for pursuing this and other issues indicated so far.

Approaching the State and the Social

Machiavelli (1977: 47) observed long ago that 'every prince' would like to be both loved and feared. And 'since it is hard to accommodate both of these qualities, if you have to make a choice, to be feared is much safer than to be loved'. Nevertheless, he asserts, 'every prince should prefer to be considered merciful rather than cruel'. This was, as we shall see, clearly a strategy adopted by the postcolonial ruling group from the outset, and I shall argue that the modern state in Botswana prevails to a great extent because the ruling group's domination is achieved and reproduced in relation to the population with a *minimal exercise of perceived violent, coercive power*. Paradoxically perhaps, the broader significance of this point is suggested by a study of authoritarian regimes as extreme as Mobuto's Zaire. Schatzberg (1988: 71–72) argues that no state can rely entirely on coercion for long: 'Although regimes may arrive in power and initially maintain themselves through force, they most often achieve stability and continuity by encouraging citizens to accept valid symbols and metaphors of authority'. Legitimacy in the population is in other words crucial for the sustainable strength of the state.

In the present case, legitimation involved, at Botswana's independence, the challenge to make such a Western phenomenon as a modern state comprehensible, acceptable and even attractive to the population. Following Taylor's (1999: 127) rendering of Hegel, this is a matter of preventing 'alienation' from arising. Alienation, in the Hegelian sense, 'arises where important ideas of man and society and their relation to nature embodied in the institutions of a given society cease to be those by which its members identify themselves'. This means that the *introduction* of all the new institutions of a modern state – as in the present case – represents a formidable challenge of ensuring popular identification. As we shall see, this is not only a matter of designing policies to meet expectations that are already prevalent in the population. From the outset the state leadership made tremendous efforts – by local encounters with people all over the country – to explain and discuss in detail the significance of all the 'development' programmes that have been recurrently launched.

We shall see that the major changes effected by this leadership did not conflict with 'tradition' in any significant respect, one important condition being that the symbolism of authority vested in Tswana kingship (*bogosi*) and anchored in indigenous cosmology has, at all times, capacitated the *dikgosi* to engage in radical transformations like changing major ritual and social practices to satisfy evangelising missionaries. This point is reflected in state agents' manifold efforts to develop an imaginary of the state that has resonance in a population highly committed to virtues of authority vested in indigenous cosmology.

At the same time, I am centrally concerned with the ways in which the modern state in Botswana, through its interventions in the population in the Foucauldian (1978) sense, works upon popular consciousness in ways that generate subjectivities with 'ideas' congruent with those vested in modern state institutions. This brings me beyond issues of legitimacy since, in my view, the development of the postcolonial state in Botswana cannot alone be comprehended in terms of popular appreciative imaginary of the state. Its strength and stability rest also upon state practices in relation to social and material realities by which the population are brought into the web of power centred in the state. This is a major problem of the social, which I shall address by an approach much inspired by Deleuze/Guattari, Foucault, and Kapferer. This approach recognizes the distinctiveness of the *dynamics* of the state yet rejects any notion of the state as a freestanding entity as its point of analytical departure. It does not, therefore, *reduce* the state to 'a fiction of the philosophers' (Radcliffe-Brown 1940: xxiii) or an ideological construction (Mitchell 1999: 95) or an 'illusion' (Asad 2004: 282), but recognizes the sociomaterial reality of any state.

I see the state as vested with inherent dynamics that, in the words of Kapferer (2008: 3), 'is oriented to achieving an exclusive and overarching determining potency in the fields of social relations in which it is situated and which state or state-related practice attempts to refine' (see also Kapferer 1997: 274ff.). The state is hence always *in the making*, which is a conception of the state that corresponds to Deleuze and Guattari's (1984: 360) notion of the state as sovereignty, yet it 'only reigns over what it is capable of internalising, appropriating locally'. Although Foucault (1980: 121) abandons the Hobbesian notion of 'sovereignty' as expressed in his famous statement of a need 'to cut off the King's head', he similarly recognizes the 'omnipotence' of the state. Not as a fixed capacity, but as an independent 'super-structural' force that dominates by virtue of its capacity to control 'a whole series of already existing power networks' (1980: 122).

Note, however, that this is not simply a notion opposite to that of Hobbes' *Leviathan*, in the sense of conceiving the force of the state as a matter of 'power comes from below' (cf. Sahlins 1999: 37). Beside the conception of the state as omnipotent, Foucault (1982: 224) maintains that 'power relations have become more and more under state control'. Such a development reflects what Kapferer names, I repeat, 'the state's overarching determining potency', which is a conception of the state as unlimited in respect to potentially engaging and exercising power in all societal fields. And it corresponds with Deleuze and Guattari's relativistic conception of 'sovereignty', as indicated above. Notwithstanding the differences that distinguish these scholars, they all render a conception of the state that transcends a restricted central-government conception; the state is, in brief, essentially vested with an omnipotent, expanding force to prevail as a superstructural or an overarching force.

The development of a strong postcolonial state in Botswana in a context where the vast majority of the population was embedded in indigenous structures of power is comprehensible if we come to terms with how the state has become an overarching force in relation to these structures. I am therefore centrally concerned with how the networks of power vested in indigenous hierarchies have been captured into the process of postcolonial state formation in ways that have not only brought them under control but contributed significantly to the strength of the state.

This analysis requires a comprehension of the character of the major hierarchical structures – Tswana *merafe* – because they inhibit, as already suggested, numerous communities that were caught into their structures of domination in precolonial and especially colonial times. The persistently hegemonic character of Tswana domination is comprehensible only by an analysis of its development in preindependence times. I start therefore by explaining – again aided by the general approach explained above – how the central power in these *merafe* grew in strength and scale from the late eighteenth century by capturing vast communities into their structures. By the establishment of the Bechuanaland Protectorate in 1885, they were subjected to British supremacy. Yet at the same time, their capacity of capture vis-à-vis other communities under their domination was reinforced.

In the Foucauldian conception, the colonial state – extensively practising 'indirect rule' – prevailed as superstructural to a whole range of power networks in which Tswana rulers of each of the *merafe* in precolonial times continued being at the apex of a hierarchy of power relations. Under British supremacy Tswana rulers lost their full sovereignty, yet were at the same time empowered by the British to transform, expand and achieve control over vast communities in the extensive, bounded territories assigned to them by the colonial power. When the British withdrew – just as peacefully as they had arrived – the indigenous hierarchies of authority, which had expanded and been reinforced under colonial conditions, were captured by the process of modern state formation in ways that again involved substantial transformations of these hierarchies.

And more than that: the state, following Foucault (1980: 122), 'consists in the codification of a whole number of power relations which render its functioning possible'. This is a notion of an intervening state that he also describes as 'a very sophisticated structure, in which individuals can be integrated, under one condition: that this individuality would be shaped in a new form, and submitted to a set of very specific patterns' (Foucault 1982: 214). This notion of the state as intervening in the population is probably best developed in his conception of the governmentalization of the state (Foucault 1978). This is a concept that, we shall see, is very helpful to come to terms with how the modern state in Botswana has expanded its network of power extensively in relation to citizens beyond indigenous authority structures, yet much aided by them.

State interventions are, however, not confined to the modern state. Under the conditions of the colonial state there were extensive state practices that Deleuze and Guattari (e.g., 1991: 434, 448ff.) have identified as 'overcoding'. For example, in the present case, the British initiated the colonial era by stating that the *dikgosi* could, with only small restrictions, continue to rule their subjects as they had always done. But, in due course, the colonial power discovered that they had contributed to empowering the *dikgosi* to such an extent that they were featuring as highly autocratic to an extent that also challenged the colonial power. As we shall see, the British overcoding of their authority made *dikgosi* capable of expanding their powers in ways that escaped the imaginaries of their overlords. They even felt forceful enough to challenge the British. In Deleuze and Guattari's (1991: 449) exemplification, 'the overcoding of the archaic State itself makes possible and gives rise to new flows that escape from it'. This suggests that even the successful formation of a strong state has repercussions that challenge states to empower themselves; there is always something exterior to states that attacks, resists or evades. I recall here Deleuze and Guattari's and Foucault's relativist notions of the state; the state being what it is actually, at any time, capable of bringing under its supremacy.

In brief, there is always an exteriority of forces to the state that might work benignly towards state formation and its agents acting cooperatively. Conversely, these forces also become frequently hostile, damaging or neutral and evasive positions vis-à-vis state-formation processes. Further, such exteriority is not confined to neat territorial distinctions and may, hence, be of local or of global origin. Thus the state formations in focus here have, at all historical stages, been surrounded by ever-changing exteriorities of forces of such diversity.

Deleuze and Guattari (1991: 361) see the exteriority as what 'escapes the State and stands against the State'. In their conception, 'the outside of the State cannot be reduced to "foreign policy," that is a relationship between states'. The outside appears, on the one hand, in the form of 'huge world-wide machines', like multinational organisations or religious formations, such as Christianity and Islam, and, on the other, 'local mechanisms of bands, margins, minorities, which continue to affirm the rights of segmentary societies in relation to the organs of State power'. These are all forces exterior to the state in the sense of being vested with *potentialities* of a particular kind of power, denoted 'war machines'. This has nothing to with armies or other institutionalized entities of violence; such forces are integral to the 'state apparatus of capture' (1991: 437). Rather, it is 'a form irreducible to the State and that this form of exteriority necessarily presents itself as a war machine ... [I]t exists in a commercial circuit as in a religious creation, in all flows and currents that only secondarily allow themselves to be appropriated by the State' (1991: 360). In the present case we shall see, for example, how Christianity, on the one hand, in the form of institutionalized missionary churches was captured into the power structures of the *merafe*, while, on the other hand, gave birth to Christian 'syncretistic' movements beyond the *merafe* with properties typical of war machines: assemblages of power of a rhizome type that are antihierarchical, deterritorializing and operating in highly unpredictable ways from the point of view of the state. These properties posit these assemblages against the state apparatus of capture that is, conversely, characterized by hierarchizing, institutionalizing and territorializing features. Further, while states are stable, stationary and in transformation, war machines operate laterally in 'nomadic' ways – in flight – and change by metamorphoses, to appear in ever-new disguises. War machines are all forms that are exterior to the state with the *potentiality* of attacking the state. In the present case, as suggested, the *merafe* are always only incompletely appropriated by the colonial – and I now add postcolonial – state, with considerable potentialities of forces challenging the state.

As suggested above, in this conception the 'sovereignty' of the state is a relative matter, being determined by the capacity of the 'apparatus of capture' to appropriate what escapes states or stands against it. In such terms, we shall see that the state forms in focus here – from precolonial to postcolonial times – can be characterized as quite successful. It seems required to expand the conceptual scheme in order to recognize explicitly that the exterior also contains entities other than those that are antagonistic or evasive in relation to the state, yet with potentials of state empowerment. For example, the expansion of Western settlers into the nineteenth-century interior of South Africa had clearly rhizomic qualities from the point of view of the precolonial Tswana states, located on the edge of the Kalahari. Although there were some ambiguities surrounding the British establishment of the Bechuanaland Protectorate, on the whole the British overlordship warded off the war-machine potentialities of the surrounding settler states as well as strengthened the apparatus of capture vested in Tswana *merafe*. In this context the British Empire – with all its war-machine potentials across the globe – manifested itself to Tswana ruling groups as an empowering force. This was, though, entirely different from the point of view of communities involuntarily subjected to the dominant Tswana *merafe*.

This brings me back to the perspective suggested at the beginning of this chapter: considering state formations as conditioned by conjuncture between Eurocentric ideas and institutions, indigenous ideas, practices and institutions of power and global markets for cattle and diamonds. For example, as we shall see, such a 'huge world-wide machine' – in the language of Deleuze and Guattari – as the diamond company of De Beers in relation to the state in Botswana has been crucial for empowering the state by supplying its treasury with tremendous revenues. However, to explain why diamonds helped to strengthen the state and stabilized its government requires comprehension of other important conditions that coincided with the discovery of diamonds. Another exteriority – that of some Western states – was highly instrumental in establishing a modern state in Botswana by bringing the whole complex of modern statecraft into the country during the process of decolonisation. That they, in contrast to many other places, succeeded quite well is comprehensible only in view of the ways in which privileged and powerful people across the country merged in support of a strong, centralized state.

The major transformations with which I am concerned in this volume – from pre- to postcolonial times – also require a conception of exercise of leadership. A conjugation of conditions for major transformations does not help much if there is no leadership. This is, as we shall see, apparent in the development of the strength and scale of Tswana *merafe* in the beginning of the nineteenth century as it developed during the years following Botswana's independence. Intriguingly, the agency of transformations can, in important respects, be personalized by, probably, the two most celebrated icons of Tswana leadership, *Kgosi* Khama III – the Great – (r. 1872/1875–1923) and his grandson, Seretse Khama, the founding president of Botswana. Their transformative agency combined, in important respects, the two modes of domination that Gramsci (1991: 12) assigns to 'civil society' (hegemony) and 'political society' or 'the State' ('direct domination through juridical or political apparatuses'). In such 'tribal' kingdoms as that of the Tswana, there is, as already suggested, no institutionalized divide between civil and political society. In fact, it is not clear either that Gramsci made any strict separation of the two as he asserted that '"State" should be understood as not only the apparatus of government, but also the "private" apparatus of "hegemony" or civil society' (1991: 261).

In scholarly literature the notion of 'hegemonic domination' is not unambiguous.[13] For the present analytical purpose I have found it useful to define it with reference to Eagleton's (1991: 115–16) rendering: 'as a whole range of practical strategies by which a dominant power elicits consent to its rule from those it subjugates. To win hegemony ... is to establish moral, political and intellectual leadership in social life by diffusing one's own "world view" throughout the fabric of society as a whole'. Following this notion, hegemony is to be conceived as always in the making and a matter of degree, always competing with other orientations.

In all historical contexts of the present case, we shall see that the 'practical strategy' of the state apparatus of capture to 'win hegemony' is characterized by an often gradualist, nonconfrontational approach. This is an approach to reach consent about submission in the spirit of peace and harmony, which is a virtue of great symbolic significance amongst communities far beyond the dominant Tswana. The approach involves extensive exercise of 'consultation', which, especially in postcolonial times with radical changes, reflects the above-mentioned Hegelian concern about alienation in relation to issues of legitimacy. In this volume we shall see how this presents challenges of 'winning hegemony' in distinctly different historical contexts, ranging from Tswana *dikgosi*'s acceptance of missionaries' requests for transforming or abandoning major rituals and other important practices, to the radical institutional change of authority by the establishment of the highly Western-fashioned, modern state.

---

13. See Comaroff and Comaroff 1991: ch.1; Crehan 2002: 98ff ; Eagleton 1991: 112f.; Scott 1990: 77ff.

The cultural construction of hegemony differs, however, in some important respects between, on the one hand, that of the dominant Tswana *merafe* in precolonial and colonial times, and, on the other, that of the postcolonial, modern state. In the former cases, leadership was constructed on the basis of a notion of the Tswana rulers and their ruling communities as anchored in a cosmological order. They were thereby indisputably authorized to govern all the subjects within their domain; their custodianship of the social order was beyond question. The hegemony of the postcolonial state leadership is certainly Tswana-biased as it has been to a great extent composed by Tswana, as indicated by the name of the postcolonial state and the selection of Setswana as the national language. But it would, of course, have been counterproductive for a political leadership in an electoral democracy to establish hegemony on the basis of a strongly pronounced Tswana orientation when a substantial section of the population do not identify themselves with the dominant Tswana but, on the contrary, often enough experience their discriminatory, repressive practices in a multitude of informal encounters. I shall argue that the establishment of the modern state reduced notably – but not eliminated – the problem of Tswana identification as the postcolonial state leadership was able to adopt extensively the virtues of 'development' in the Western sense and create what I shall call a hegemonic discourse of development which, in important respects, is ethnically neutral. Although its implementation has not always worked in that way and, in addition, accelerated very substantially inequality of wealth, the postcolonial leadership managed at an early stage to win hegemony and to capture the population into its dependency.

All this will, hopefully, bring out that the development of a strong postcolonial state might beneficially be seen as a matter of conjunctures of conditions that, at different historical stages, have been particular to this case, in accordance with Sahlins' (2000: 472) notion that '[t]he very ways in which societies change have their own authenticity, so that global modernity is often reproduced as local diversity'. Botswana, then, is, as all other African countries, special – yet in ways that are comparatively recognisable if we pursue the approaches indicated in this section, aiming at coming to terms with how the larger social context becomes significant for state formation.

Overview

The larger social context for state formation in Botswana is, I repeat, indigenous symbolism and institutions of authority, particularly in the

large-scale structures of the Tswana *merafe*. These are conditions which
have their genealogies that go back to the colonial and precolonial past.
Although I insist that my argument is not of a primordial kind, it is important to comprehend how these structures, conceived as conditions for
postcolonial state formation, have evolved historically. I am particularly
concerned with the potentialities vested in the Tswana *merafe*; for example at once giving rise to a persistent dominant class underpinning the
postcolonial ruling group and representing major repressive structures in
relation to vast groups of 'minorities'.

In order to trace these genealogies of power I start in precolonial times
(Chapter 1) in an effort to explain how the once small state formations
at the edge of the Kalahari, now known as Tswana *merafe*, developed in
strength and expanded in scale since the late eighteenth century. I aim
to show how external communities were captured into their hierarchical
order in which they became subjects to forces of assimilation in ways that
transformed the power structures radiating from the royal centre. I shall
argue that the imperial forces propelled these transformations, including
linking up with intercontinental trade, the operation of evangelizing missionaries and subjection to British colonial power. This also means that
the dominant Tswana *merafe* of present Botswana were not 'imposed' from
outside or 'created' by the colonial power (Abbink 2005: 187), although
the British overlordship had considerable impact upon their transformations during colonial times.

This is, in particular, an argument about empowerment of the ruling
group of the Tswana *merafe* selected by the British at the establishment
of Bechuanaland Protectorate (1885), enhancing their capacity to capture and keep subject communities under their domination. In Chapter
2 I pursue the issue by examining Tswana rulers' growing autocracy that
also became a challenge to the British, as the *dikgosi* were increasingly
perceived as a force ambiguously related to the colonial state, at times
exterior to it. Yet the *dikgosi* prevailed to a significant extent, indicating,
amongst other things, how dependent the British remained on their administration of the respective 'native reserves', their collection of tax and
their extensive networks of power for the exercise of social control. These
networks of power, radiating from the Tswana royal centres, are of significance to the present study because they were readily transferred from the
colonial to the postcolonial context where, as we shall see in Chapters 4,
5 and 6, they proved highly instrumental to the development of the nation-state in Botswana during the formative and consolidating decades.
The second part of Chapter 2 focuses upon the creation of an embryo
to the ruling group of the independent state in this country. I explain
their conflicting relationship to the *dikgosi* and their co-operation with

the British for the establishment of Botswana's Constitution and a highly peaceful process of decolonization.

The historical development of a ruling group and – as I explain in Chapter 3 – the formation of a dominant class is a major condition for the rapid rise of a strong, modern state in this country. I pursue this issue in Chapter 3 by invoking Bayart's (1993: 160) point that many postcolonial African states are weak and failing because of the absence of a persistent, dominant class. I shall explain that in Botswana, by contrast, people of power and wealth – across the ruling communities of the dominant Tswana *merafe* – modern vs. traditional orientation and urban vs. rural residence cohered into a dominant class underpinning the ruling group of the postcolonial state from the outset. This involved the formation that Sebudubudu (2009) has named a 'grand coalition' which prevented the development of an exteriority of what Deleuze and Guattari speak of as 'war-machines' with great potentialities of generating destabilizing rhizomic forces. I shall explain that livestock production, Botswana's immensely privileged access to the European beef market and the development of the diamond mining industry gave rise to a powerful state-centred political economy that progressively drew an increasingly diversified class of people into a privileged dependency of a progressively strong state. That is a dominant class which – despite all their conflicts and rivalries – had in common a major interest in a strong state and sustainable government.

The progressive capture of people privileged by governmental policies and programmes into the orbit of the state does, however, not help to explain the ways in which all the rank and file sections have become subjects to the postcolonial state. In Chapters 4–7 I address this issue from different angles. The overarching theme is the various ways in which the state has captured indigenous institutions of authority into its structures and become highly instrumental to control and manage the population and draw people into the process of state formation. In Chapter 4 I am centrally concerned with, first, the relationship between the state and the Tswana *merafe*, explaining how the *dikgosi* were co-opted into the state where they on the whole have been working as loyal civil servants, though not without notable exceptions. I examine two major cases of challenges to the state that perfectly illuminate, on the one hand, popular continued attachment to the symbolic wealth and sociopolitical order of the *merafe* vested in the *bogosi* and, on the other, the prevailing rhizomic potentials vested in the Tswana *merafe* in relation to the state. In the second major part of Chapter 4 I explain the significance of the dominant, everyday activity vested in these hierarchies of authority – administration of justice – and how it contributes to their reproduction under postcolonial circumstances. This examination helps to come to terms with

Nyamnjoh's (2003: 247) suggestion about 'chieftaincy' in Botswana as 'a dynamic institution, constantly reinventing itself to accommodate and be accommodated by new exigencies... [that] has proved phenomenal in its ability to seek conviviality between competing and often conflicting influences'.

I am centrally concerned with the observation that during the formative and consolidating decades, which are, I repeat, of major concern in this volume, the population was to a great extent kept in the fold without much of state policing and exercise of violence. As I explain in Chapter 5, this fitted perfectly well a state government which sought legitimacy in the population at large by attempting to build popular identification with a nation-state by envisaging a prosperous future of developmental modernity by invoking indigenous symbolism of authority – a symbolism merged with all the virtues of Western modernity. I shall explain how the state leadership attempted to win hegemony in relation to all the rank-and-file sections of the population by featuring as custodian of the common good by means of massive programmes of social infrastructures and services. That is, programmes of Western 'welfarism' which are expressed in a major, national discourse of development. To this discourse belongs also all the entrepreneur-promoting programmes I examine in Chapter 3, and I discuss the relationship between the two orientations – collective virtues of the common good versus ideals of liberal individualism – in a class-formation perspective.

Moreover, the all-encompassing character of the 'discourse of development' means that agents of the state attempt, I shall explain, to capture minorities into a process that is presented as 'national', with no relevance to ethnic or 'tribal' affiliation. In the second main part of Chapter 5 I go beyond 1990 because it is only during more recent times that minorities, despite state efforts to appear ethnicity neutral, have protested against Tswana domination and being treated as secondary citizens. I shall explain how these protests have been met by agents of the state and discuss the ongoing transformations of majority-minority relations, including questioning the rhizomic potentials vested in the 'minorities' which in sum possibly outnumber the dominant Tswana.

In Chapter 6 I pursue this issue further in an effort to explain how the indigenous authority structures, especially the discursive fields of its councils known as *dikgotla* (singl. *kgotla*), facilitate agents of state's exercise of the discourse of development in the pursuit of establishing legitimacy in relation to the rank-and-file sections of the population by making all the modern interventions familiar. With a major focus on the formative and consolidating decades, I explain how the state leadership has attempted to win hegemony by co-opting indigenous ideals of government by 'consulting with people', i.e. introducing 'democratic' practices through which opposition parties have been excluded to a great extent. These antipolitics practices are exercised by cabinet ministers and members of Parliament who, with great frequency, engage with local communities all over the country in intimate interaction within the context of the *kgotla*.

State methods to capture the population into the process of modern state formation is pursued further in Chapter 7 by focusing upon the ways in which the state intervenes in the population, especially with all its 'development' and welfare programmes. To the state leadership, these interventions have amounted to a major force for establishing hegemony by capturing the population into extensive bureaucratic practices that continuously work on their subjectivities. These are state practices that I shall consider as a matter of governmentalization of the state (Foucault 1978): a conception helpful to understand the peaceful and tacit, yet penetrating, ways 'power relations have been progressively governmentalized, that is to say, elaborated, rationalized, and centralized in the form of, or under the auspices of, state institutions' (Foucault 1982: 224). I shall discuss how and to what extent these processes have been working upon people's subjectivities to the effect of creating subjects ever more conforming with and dependent on state policies and programmes.

The state's work on people's subjectivities involves the rise of aspirations, which has, I shall argue, been nourishing the progressive conflicts between a minority of people who have risen to power and wealth and all the rank-and-file sections of the population amongst whom a substantial part has remained below the official poverty datum line. I shall address this development as an important aspect of the state-centred political economy by examining popular reactions to what they perceive as political leaders' abuse of power. These are reactions to what are perceived as rhizomic forces destructive to the idealized order of the state, finding their most profound expression in a discursive practice based upon people's imagination of political leaders' exercise of occult practices. Such an imagination of dangerous and damaging practices at the heart of the postcolonial state seems to resemble Mbembe's notion of the postcolony as 'an *intimate tyranny*' (1992: 22, italics original), which links the ruler with the ruled in ways that undermine both of them through the 'mutual zombification of both the dominant and those they apparently dominate … [meaning] that each robbed the other of their vitality and this has left them both impotent' (1992: 4). But the resemblance is only apparent because, as we shall see, reactions in Botswana to perceived hidden abuses of power are of a different kind. In popular imagination, however violent, they are patently a matter of moral condemnation of secretive practices motivated by individual greed: they are, in this conception, deterritorializing, exterior to the order of the state and hence with war-machine properties. Their opacity transgresses the indigenous ideal of political transparency and is experienced by people as detrimental to the common good. In what I shall describe as an evolving subaltern discourse, these rhizomic forces are seen as emanating from the very epitome of a modern state – state bureaucracy and representational democracy.

Geographic and Demographic Features in Brief

With a total area of 570,000 km², Botswana is about the same size as France, Belgium, Luxembourg and the Netherlands combined. This vast plateau at the centre of Southern Africa lies at a mean altitude of 1,000 metres above sea level. Approximately two-thirds of its surface area is comprised of the semiarid Kalahari Desert, the sandy soil of which supports a low, savannah-type vegetation. The rainfall, on an average less than 450 mm annually, is vulnerable to high evapo-transpiration rates.

The factors historically most determinant for people's settlement patterns have been the fertility of the soil, rainfall, and availability of water. Thus, more than three-quarters of Botswana's population – which numbered only some 2.15 million in 2010[14] – live in the east in the drainage basin area of the Limpopo, which comprises less than 10 per cent of the country's land area. Here reasonably fertile soils and higher rainfall (annual averages 450–550 mm) permit arable agriculture. With underground water technology, commercial livestock production has expanded far beyond these limits, especially since the 1970s.

As already indicated, cattle have been the major asset – economically, politically and symbolically – since precolonial times and before the diamond era. Although crucial for postcolonial state formation before the state treasury became sourced by revenues from diamond mining, livestock production – like diamond mining – is highly labour extensive. While cattle have, in addition, always been very unequally distributed, a very limited part of the population has made a living entirely from livestock production. This feature has become ever more pronounced in postcolonial times (Gulbrandsen 1996a: Ch. 10).

Since the late nineteenth century, very large numbers of men have ensured the survival of vast parts of the families in the country through circular labour migration, predominantly to the South African mines (Schap-

---

14. At Botswana's independence in 1966, there were about 550,000 people in the country; in 1975 c. 700,000, increasing to c. 1.3 mill. in 1990, c. 1.58 mill. in 2000 and c. 2.09 mill. in 2012.

era 1947a; Gulbrandsen 1996a). This employment pattern was drastically curtailed in the beginning of the 1980s with a substantial reduction in recruitment of foreign labourers. About the same time, however, the development of urban areas in Botswana accelerated, involving a building boom that recruited many of those who had previously gone to South Africa. Especially the capital of Gaborone, which was established from scratch at independence, entered a process of momentous growth, propelled by the substantial enlargement of governmental institutions and the rapid expansion of the private sector of the economy from the late 1980s onwards. Nevertheless, unemployment rates have persistently remained high (see Siphambe 2003: 481).

However massive, this demographic trend did not depopulate rural areas because Botswana had, at the same time, a high population growth rate. Moreover, and highly significant for central arguments in this volume, the capital is surrounded by five of the seven Tswana royal towns (see below) and a number of large villages, mostly within an hour's drive or less from the capital. Many people employed in urban centres have thus continued to live within the context of family and descent groups or at least kept in close touch with rural family households. The royal towns which have, from precolonial times, been – in an African context – exceptionally large with thousands, if not tens of thousands, of people (Gulbrandsen 2007), also have growth momentum as district governmental centres, service and trading centres and by some minor industries.

Map 1 displays the administrative division of the Bechuanaland Protectorate as implemented by the British upon colonization in 1885. In the eastern and northwestern part of the country, the divisions are named 'native reserves', dominated by the eight Tswana kingdoms which, as already suggested, the British officially recognized and whose rulers were subjected to the colonial administration as instruments of government. The native reserves were, as Map 1 shows, of highly unequal size, territorially and population-wise. The tremendously large areas denoted 'crown lands' were extremely sparsely populated by people living scattered in small villages, hamlets and mobile bands. The Tswana-centred native reserves, mainly located in the Eastern part of the Protectorate, were ethnically mixed to a very different extent, with the four largest ones – the Bangwato, the Bakwena, the Bangwakets and the Batawana – comprising vast groups of different origins.

The respective Tswana *dikgosi* were located in the royal towns of, respectively, Serowe (Bangwato), Molepolole (Bakwena), Kanye (Bangwaketse), Maun (Batawana), Mochudi (Bakgatla), Ramotswa (Malete) and Tlokweng (Batlokwa). The small area in the extreme southeast denoted

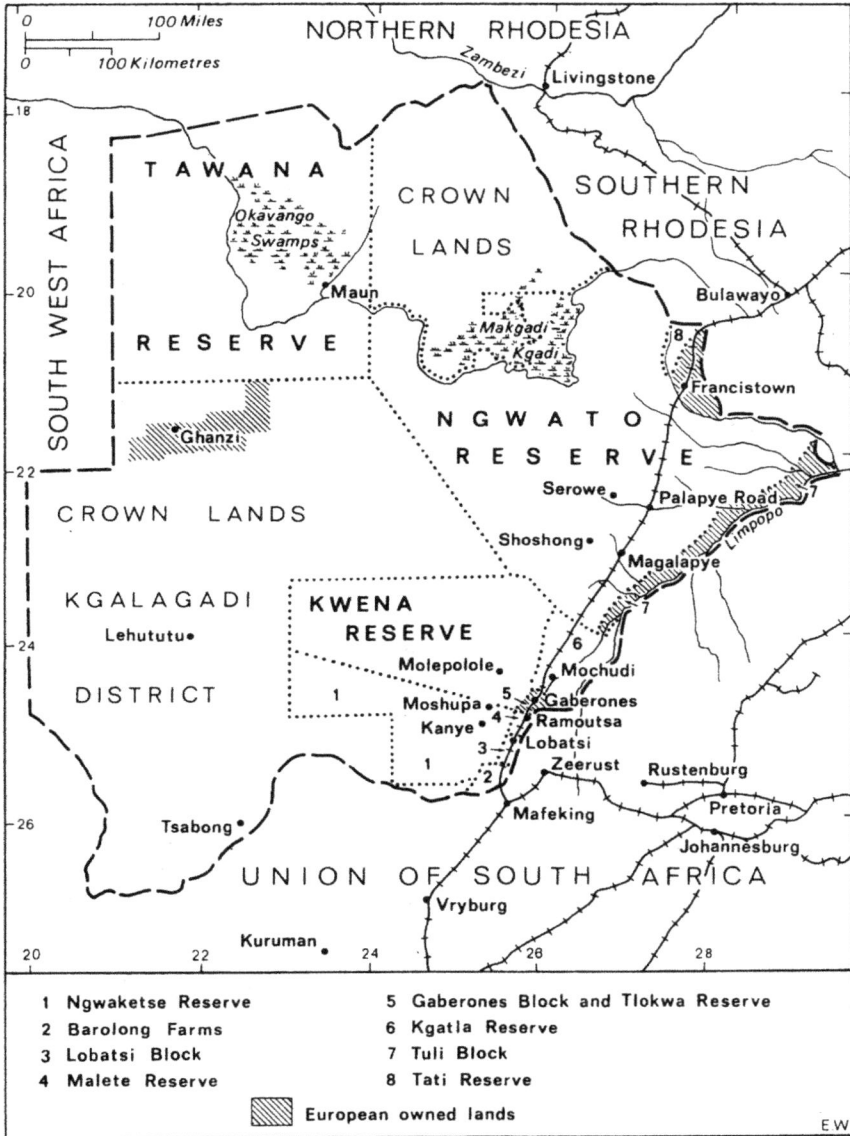

1 Ngwaketse Reserve	5 Gaberones Block and Tlokwa Reserve
2 Barolong Farms	6 Kgatla Reserve
3 Lobatsi Block	7 Tuli Block
4 Malete Reserve	8 Tati Reserve

European owned lands

Map 1: Sketch map of Bechuanaland Protectorate
(source: Schapera 1970)

Barolong farms serving as agricultural lands for the Tswana people of Barolong-Tshidi centred in the royal town of Mafeking on the South African side of the border.

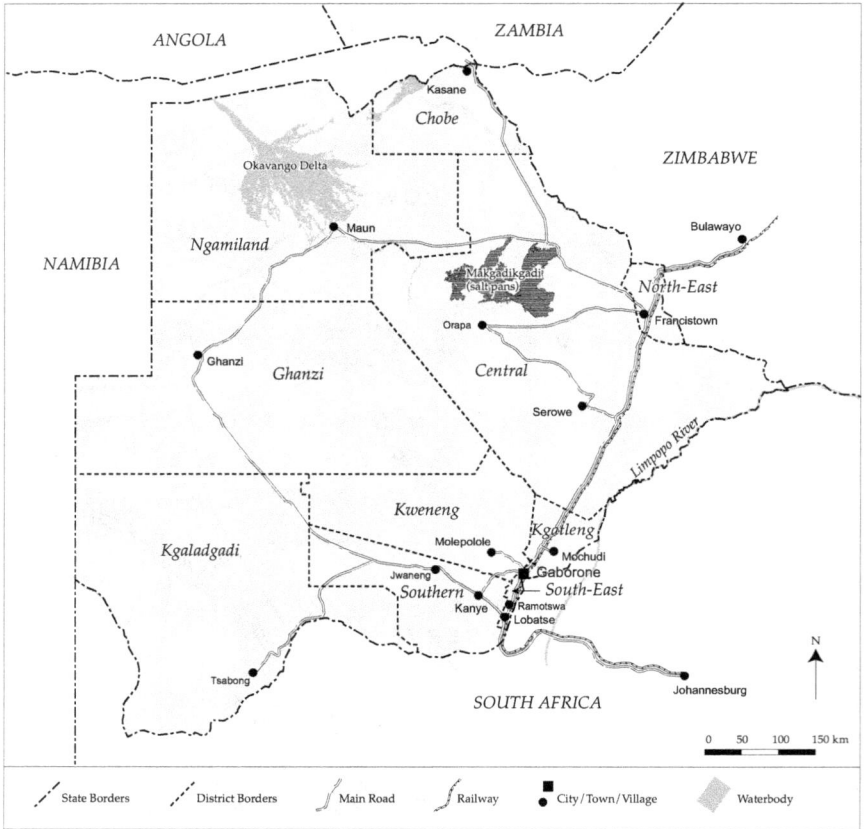

Map 2: Map of the Republic of Botswana
(based on an original map courtesy of the Department of Surveys and Mapping, Government of Botswana, Gaborone)

By comparing Maps 1 and 2 it is readily apparent that there is considerable correspondence between the colonial and postcolonial administrative divisions. This is most evident in the case of Central (Ngwato), Kweneng, Kgatleng, Ngamiland (Tawana) and Southern (which includes the Ngwaketse and the Barolong farms). The Tswana royal towns serve as district administrative centres in all these cases. The Batlokwa and the Bamalete are combined into the small South-East District, with Ramotswa as the district centre. Moreover, the Tswana royal towns host the postcolonial administrative centres – Maun (Ngamiland), Serowe (Central), Molepolole (Kweneng), Kanye (Southern), Mochudi (Kgatleng) and Ramotswa (South-East). The additional, most sparsely populated districts of Kgalagadi, Ghazi, Chobe and North-East do not fall into this pattern.

THE DEVELOPMENT OF TSWANA MERAFE AND THE ARRIVAL OF CHRISTIANITY AND COLONIALISM

On 3 October 2005 Botswana's state president, Festus Mogae, unveiled what is known as the Three Dikgosi Monument in the capital, Gaborone (see cover of this book). The monument commemorates *Kgosi* Sebele I of the Bakwena, *Kgosi* Bathoen I of the Bangwaketse and *Kgosi* Khama III of the Bangwato, renowned for their diplomatic mission to London in 1895. The president asserted in his speech, 'During the early years of colonialism these three distinguished monarchs played a leading role in ultimately ensuring our territory's independent future, by preventing its administrative handover to neighbouring white settler regimes'. In such terms the three *dikgosi* were declared the founding fathers of the nation, ostensibly preventing the subjection of their countries to Cecil Rhodes's settler regime and the racist regimes of Rhodesia and South Africa. At the time of unveiling, which amounted to no less than a state act of establishing the principal national monument, there were minority voices in Botswana which saw this as an(other) expression of Tswana domination (Parsons 2006: 680).

Neil Parsons (1998: 255) has suggested that the best way to grasp the significance of the *dikgosi*'s journey in 1895 'is to ask what would have happened if Khama, Sebele, and Bathoen had *not* gone to Britain'. Obviously, there were no other leaders in the country at that time representing polities of sufficient strength to engage with the British in efforts to prevent annexation to one of the settler regimes. In the first part of this chapter I shall approach this issue by identifying major historical transformations by which these *merafe* grew progressively in strength and scale since the late eighteenth century and appeared dominant along the eastern fringe of the Kalahari desert at the time the British decided, hesitantly, to establish the Bechuanaland Protectorate.

This approach will also serve to pursue another major issue of this chapter: the development of the Tswana *merafe* as a dominant force in relation to a substantial proportion of the population which were included in the Bechuanaland Protectorate and subsequently in the nation-state of Botswana. I shall first explain how, under changing historical conditions, ever-new groups of people were captured into the domain of the Tswana *merafe* in ways that more and more reinforced their hierarchical order, territorial control and structures of domination radiating from the Tswana royal centres. Thereafter I examine the impacts of evangelizing missionaries, before I address the significance of the British and the establishment of the Bechuanaland Protectorate. I am centrally concerned with how transformations of the major Tswana *merafe*[1] involved a progressive increase of their strength, expansion in scale and rise of Tswana hegemony in the sense I conceived it in the Introduction.

The Development of Tswana *Merafe* at the Edge of the Kalahari

The Tswana *merafe* in focus here, as Wilmsen (1989: 101) appropriately states, 'passed from a peripheral position in the region to almost uncontested dominance'. At first sight this seems surprising as one would not have expected settlements as populous as the royal towns of Northern Tswana *merafe* to exist in an area with exceptionally poor and erratic rainfall. Moreover, on examining accounts of Tswana societies in the larger region from around 1500 AD, Jean and John Comaroff found that they were characterized by a constant shifting between amalgamation and fission (Comaroff and Comaroff 1991: 127–8), centralization and decentralization (Comaroff and Comaroff 1992: 132). Nevertheless, the

---

1. I am here referring to Bakwena, Bangwaketse, Bangwato and Batawana which were at the establishment of the Bechuanaland Protectorate (1885) officially recognized by the British and assigned territories – 'tribal reserves' – that comprised the vast majority of the population. The remaining three recognized *merafe* were Bakgatla, Batlokwa and Bamalete, all much smaller both in terms of population and territory, especially the latter two. In addition a small area in the southeast corner of the protectorate achieved a special status as 'Barolong Farms' – agricultural land occupied by BaTshidi of Mafeking beyond the South African border. Map 1 indicates the location of the 'tribal reserves' dominated by these Tswana *merafe*.

Tswana *merafe* in focus here continued, with few major interruptions,[2] to develop in strength and scale from the late eighteenth century, finding their most apparent expression in very large royal towns (Gulbrandsen 2007). In this section I shall give a brief, generalized presentation of processes underpinning the formation of these small states, based, especially, upon extensive historical accounts and analysis I have published previously (Gulbrandsen 1993a, 1993b, 1995, 1996a: Ch. 3, 2001, 2007).

Since the London Missionary Society (LMS) had already been active in the region for decades, the British were well informed about the conflicts – often centred round the royal houses – that riddled these polities. On the other hand, the missionaries could also attest to the strengths of their political institutions, particularly the extent to which the Tswana rulers – and their retainers – controlled even the furthest outlying communities in a vast territory. Already in 1824 the LMS missionary Robert Moffat, on visiting the Bangwaketse, was amazed by the size and concentration of the population in well-organized, closely spaced villages: '[T]he [royal] town itself appears to cover at least eight times more ground than any town I have yet seen among the Bechuanas [BaTswana]'. He estimated the population to be 'at the lowest computation, seventy thousands' (Moffat 1842: 406).[3] The *kgosi* (Makaba, r. 1790–1824) conducted government affairs in 'a circle … formed with round posts of eight feet high … Behind lay the proper cattle fold, capable of holding many thousand oxen' (1842: 399). While Makaba was widely reputed to be a dangerous warrior, Moffat conveys an atmosphere of societal harmony. He was not struck by the barracks and military exercises but rather by civic order and the presence of adult men in the *kgosi's* council (*kgotla*). Well versed in political life among the Tswana, Moffat – clearly impressed by the manner in which they conducted their meetings in the royal *kgotla* – speaks of their 'parliament', asserting that 'business is carried on with the most perfect order' (1842: 346). The idea of the Tswana royal towns as profound manifestations of civic order is also apparent in early missionary accounts of the Southern Tswana *merafe* (see Comaroff and Comaroff 1991: 129).

These qualities of the Tswana polities were most likely conveyed to the imperial power by LMS missionary Mackenzie who represented 'a powerful voice … raised in defence of the Tswana' (Sillery 1965: 39; cf. Dachs 1972: 653f.). Mackenzie worked closely with several *dikgosi*; his

---

2. The major interruption was caused by the Matabele raids known as *difaqane* between c. 1825 and 1840 (e.g. see Tlou and Campbell 1984: 101ff.).

3. The royal town itself probably had more than ten thousand people. Another important nineteenth-century missionary source mentions its large population: 'Shoshong, the [royal] town of the Bangwato, contains a population of some 30,000' (Mackenzie 1871: 365; cf. Okihiro 1976: ch. 2; Schapera 1935; Parsons 1982).

Illustration 1. Robert Moffat, the first LMS missionary to visit the Bangwaketse royal town (1824), preaching to a Tswana local community as rendered on the title page of Moffat's *Missionary Labours and Scenes in Southern Africa* (1842).

extensive publications reveal an impressive knowledge of Tswana political institutions and practices. For example, he offers an illuminating account of the political proceedings in the royal court of the Bangwato, asserting that they were 'conducted with decorum and order' (Mackenzie 1871: 373). In 1882, during the preliminaries to the establishment of the Protectorate (1885), he went to Britain in order to make the case for the Northern Tswana on a tireless campaign for British intervention.[4] Sillery relates that Mackenzie's efforts included fostering 'public enlightenment' and enlisting 'many prominent men and an influential section of public opinion' (Sillery 1965: 39). As evidence of Tswana receptivity to 'civilization', Mackenzie could point out that – exceptionally in an African context – several of the *dikgosi* had been among the first of their people to accept Christianity and undergo baptism, with the consequence that

---

4. These campaigns should be seen in light of Mackenzie's strategy to make the country British in order to make it Christian (Dachs 1972: 652).

many of their people followed suit (Gulbrandsen 1993a, 1993b; see below in this chapter).

So how could it be that these *merafe* developed such scale and strength? I shall start examining the process of centralization in these kingdoms with the point of departure in asking how they successfully overcame the conflict-generating ambiguities and contradictions that have often permeated other 'Southern Bantu' polities (e.g. see Schapera 1956: 176; cf. Gluckman 1963: 20). Such conflicts relate mainly to succession to office and the exercise of authority once in office. They rose primarily amongst close, rivalling agnates who were able to mobilize sufficient factional support to represent a threatening challenge. However, the conditions for generating such support varied considerably amongst so-called Southern Bantu tribes (see van Warmelo 1974: 56ff, 1930; Schapera 1965: 7f.). Sansom has described how the Tswana (as a major section of the Sotho-speaking peoples) tended to have rulers whose power lay in manipulating bonds and grants concerning people's access to land. He contrasts such 'Tribal Estate' regimes (as he calls them) with 'Chequerboard' regimes, in which land allocation was decentralized and rulers depended upon 're-allocating products rather than means of production' (Sansom 1974: 251). This thesis draws attention to the fact that centralization depended on certain material resources under the ruler's control. But in order to come to terms with the centralizing forces at work during precolonial times among the three major Northern Tswana *merafe*, we need to examine the rulers' control over *cattle* rather than land (see Gulbrandsen 2007: 57–8). This notion is by no means an obvious one. Goody, for example, has stated of Africa in general that cattle 'easily become fused with the personal property of the incumbent; support of livestock is the formula for a very much looser polity ... it is difficult to centralise cows' (Goody 1974: 33). Nevertheless, it is my contention that the centralizing processes of the three Northern Tswana *merafe* were particularly powerful precisely because of their rulers' exceptional access to cattle (e.g. see Tlou 1985: 69). But note, the conundrum thus presented by the Tswana can be resolved provided we do not seek the answer in the determinist or evolutionist arguments of ecology. Instead, I shall demonstrate that the role played by cattle and cattle-based trade amongst Northern Tswana is mediated through social and political processes that favour not only state formation but a concentrated population as well.

The aggregation of cattle wealth among the ruling families may well reflect the fact that the Tswana – known as an exceptional African case (Radcliffe-Brown 1950: 55) – allow FBD (father's brother's daughter) marriages. Such marriages are practised especially among noble families (Schapera 1957). As the saying goes, *ngwana rrangwane, nnyale, kgomo di boele sakeng* (child of my father's younger brother, marry me, so the [bridewealth – *bogadi*] cattle may return to our kraal). Schapera places particular emphasis on this custom as instrumental in transforming potential rival agnates into supportive matrilaterals, arguing that 'intermarriage of royals is a means of reinforcing social ties between different (and potentially hostile) branches of the royal line' (Schapera 1963: 110, cf. 1957: 157). Whether such marriages actually work in practice, however, depends – as the Comaroffs argue – on relationships being 'skilfully manipulated' (Comaroff and Comaroff 1981: 44).

The arguments put forward by Schapera and the Comaroffs raise the question of exactly how relationships resulting from royal FBD marriages can be manipulated to amalgamate the power structures surrounding the rulers. The answer varies according to context. In the case of the Northern Tswana, vast cattle herds enabled the rulers not only to exercise such manipulations. They were also very useful in bringing potentially rebellious agnates into dependency as cattle clients.

Cattle clientship is established amongst the Tswana according to their institutions of *mafisa* and *kgamelo*. *Mafisa* is a contractual relationship by which a rich or wealthy herd owner places some of his cattle with another person who herds the cattle for the benefit of milk and some of their offspring. This practice can be found on all levels and at different scales. With the very large royal herds building up as a consequence of the *dikgosi's* monopolization of the highly beneficial trade of fur and ivory, they had the opportunity to place out large portions of the cattle, not only to potentially challenging rivals, but also a number of important *dikgosana* to ensure their loyalty. The political significance of this practice as a measure to amalgamate the power structures of the Tswana *merafe* centred in the *bogosi* follows from the fact that *mafisa* cattle could be called back at any time.[5] This powerful sanction on political clientship was further reinforced amongst the Bangwato who developed the institution of *kgamelo*; that is a contract by which the holder was compelled to return not only the cattle initially received by the *kgosi*, but his entire herd (see Schapera 1984: 249).

Although the rise and expansion of the Northern Tswana *merafe* is attributable to the fact that they were located at the edge of the Kalahari where the *dikgosi* took great advantage – economically and consequently politically – of their monopolization of the vast wildlife in their respective territories, I reiterate that I do not want to pursue a determinist or evolutionist argument of ecology. The point is that cattle wealth and cattle-based trade amongst the Northern Tswana were mediated through so-

---

5. The political significance of wealth has of course been recognized by the Tswana themselves: as an early observer noticed, 'the word *kosi* [*kgosi*] in the *Sichuana* [Setswana] language signifies *rich*, and is by metonymy therefore used to imply a *chief*, as riches seem in all countries … to have been the origin of power and importance' (Burchell 1824: 272, 347).

cial and political processes that favoured both state formation and large, compact settlements. I thus argue that there is no necessary connection between these processes and the environment (see Gulbrandsen 2007).

This point is particularly evident if we consider the ways in which these *merafe* expanded during most of the nineteenth century. At this time the Northern Tswana *merafe* were located in a region characterized by enormous unexploited pastures and hunting grounds. Further east, in the present Transvaal, by contrast, demographic and ecological pressure was building up. The consequent violence and warfare brought many groups in flight westwards where they were attracted by a resourceful environment and mostly peacefully harboured in one of the *merafe* in focus here. These peoples and the peoples who had been conquered and incorporated locally, were of such a magnitude that they in due course comprised the numerical majority (Schapera 1952: v, 1984: 5).

It needs to be explained that unlike other so-called Bantu-speaking peoples in Southern Africa, the Tswana do not form large unilineal ex-ogamous descent groups. On the contrary, the Tswana are organized in sociopolitical units known as *kgotla*; in English these units have long been referred to as 'wards'.[6] Such wards are composed of a number (usu-ally 5–7) of relatively small, agnatically structured, co-residential descent groups which may be related by marriage (and thus subsequently matri-lateral ties). But neither the descent group nor the ward has ever been endogamous. A ward has a distinct location, with a relatively dense set-tlement pattern, and is also referred to as a *motse* ('village'). Each of the agnatic segments is similarly referred to as a *kgotla* and *motse*. 'Kgotla' is, moreover, the name of the descent group's council place located in the open adjacent to the cattle kraal. This open space and the kraal are sur-rounded by family homesteads, known as *malwapa* (sing. *lolwapa*). Each ward is composed of six to eight such elementary entities which, within this context, are ranked with the ward *kgosana*'s *kgotla* as the most senior one. The wards are the basic sociopolitical building blocks of the *merafe*, 'as a basic feature of their social organisation' (Schapera 1935: 207; cf. Schapera and Roberts 1975). The ward *kgosana* – who is also the head of the most senior *kgotla* within the ward – refers either directly to the *kgosi* or to a senior *kgosana* who is assigned the responsibility of a number of wards by the *kgosi*.

---

6. Organization of the Tswana *merafe* by wards was already in operation in precolonial times (Okhiro 1976: 52; Ngcongco 1977: 34), and was described extensively during the colo-nial period (see Schapera 1935, 1984: 91ff; Kuper 1975); even now, far into postcolonial times, it remains significant (see Schapera and Roberts 1975; Kooijman 1978: 101ff; Gulbrandsen 1996a: 27).

The *kgotla* of the descent group thus constitutes the link between the everyday world of the people and the politico-judicial hierarchy of the *morafe*. In Chapter 4 I shall elaborate on these interconnections in order to explain their postcolonial significance. Here I shall give an account of the ward as an organizational tool for sociopolitical integration under precolonial and colonial conditions. As already suggested, the wards are composed of a number of agnatic descent groups which are ranked. The ward *kgosana* is either closely related to the ruler or to a particularly trusted 'commoner'.

The notion of 'commoner' is composite. It includes nonroyals of the 'original' stock as well as groups of people conquered or harboured at different historical stages. They are generally ranked according to the length of time they have stayed. Groups incorporated at an early stage were terminologically distinguished from those who could trace their agnatic descent to the founders of the *morafe*. The latter, named *dikgosana*, naturally enjoyed superior status. The former were called *batlhanka* ('commoners', lit. servants); which was an honorary matter of holding royal cattle (*mafisa*, *kgamelo*) or otherwise assisting the *kgosi* – indicated by also being titled *basimane ba kgosi* (the *kgosi*'s boys). Immigrants of more recent origin, called *bafaladi* (refugees), were in turn ranked lower than the *batlhanka*.

The dominance of the ruling dynasty is underscored by the fact that those identified as *bafaladi* might, in the larger Tswana world, be of higher rank than even the hosting *kgosi*. For example, today there are groups categorized as *bafaladi* who can trace their origin to the ruling dynasty of the Hurutshe, who are recognized as senior to all three of the *merafe* under consideration here. Such 'downgrading' in the hierarchical order is, as indicated in the Introduction, justified by the Tswana maxim of *fa tlou e tlola noka, ke tloutswana* ('when an elephant crosses a river, it becomes a small elephant').

Finally, there was a distinct 'underclass' of people (mainly San and Bakgalagadi). As the dominant Tswana groups expanded their herds – and therefore needed larger territories and more herd labour – they stripped such people of any livestock they might have and put them to work for wealthy families, either as herders or as domestic servants. People belonging to this often-despised category, called *malata*, thus became part of the *morafe* on terms that amounted to serfdom (Wilmsen 1989: 99). For example, they were 'deprived of their children or transferred from one man to another' (Schapera 1984: 32; cf. Tlou 1977; Wilmsen 1989: 285ff.), a practice prevailing at least until midcolonial times. In such circumstances, it is comprehensible that there evolved a Tswana notion of a huge contrast between the ruling group found at the *kgosing kgotla* ('*kgosi*'s court' or 'the royal *kgotla*') in the royal town – the epitome of 'civilization'

– and the mobile, 'lawless' people of the bush – hence 'bushmen'. This hierarchical order is underpinned by an elaborate code of rank and respect, reproduced in a multitude of contexts – precolonial as well as postcolonial – spanning from the elementary family group to the royal court.

Socio-politically, this means that foreigners were systematically – and tightly – incorporated into the hierarchical sociopolitical order of wards which was spatially concentrated in large royal towns or compact outlying villages (this did of course not pertain to the mentioned 'underclass' of serfs unless they were brought in as domestic servants). This was, however, not only a matter of placement in the sociopolitical hierarchical structure. The forceful apparatus of capture at work in these *merafe* involved a persistent mill of cultural assimilation through the everyday practices of litigation in the context of the hierarchy of courts spanning from the *kgotla* of single descent group to the royal *kgotla* (see Chapter 4). It was by virtue of these processes that vast numbers of conquered or hosted groups, in due course, assumed primary identification with the Tswana *morafe* in which they were incorporated.

The significance of this apparatus of capture – in the sense of Deleuze and Guattari (1991: 360) – is particularly apparent at times when larger communities were to be integrated, in which case they might be divided and distributed among various wards. In this way they were strictly subject to the hierarchy of the *morafe*, located spatially close to the political centre and always under close surveillance by the ruler's retainers. This practice gave rise to systematized power relations radically different from those of other Southern Bantu polities, where large descent groups were allowed to develop in ways that more frequently led to factionalism and succession (see Schapera 1956: 175).

In this context it is particularly important that among the Northern Tswana the division of descent groups into small sections distributed between different wards gave rise to networks of crosscutting loyalties, facilitating the ruler's exercise of checks and balances of power. The consequent strengthening of the central power was evident from the fact that the authority of ward *kgosana* and their deputies was largely a matter of *delegation* and thus subject to the ruler's control. In addition, the *kgosi* had the authority to reshuffle the distribution of agnatic segments among the various wards or – as occasionally also happened – pick such segments from different wards in the pursuit of constructing a new ward.

Nevertheless, the fact that immigrants were brought under the immediate authority of a ward *kgosana* does not mean that their incorporation automatically contributed to the strength of the ruler. That of course depended on the ruler's control of the respective *dikgosana*. Significantly, a substantial number of these *dikgosana* were members of the royal family, some of them close enough to the ruling line to represent a challenge to the ruler. This means that if the rulers lacked the measures to ensure the *dikgosana*'s support, immigration might well have aggravated rivalry for the *bogosi*.

It is in this context that the significance of cattle manifests itself as a measure to amalgamate the power structures surrounding the *kgosi* and counteract such challenges: being in control of vast herds, the *kgosi* was not only in a position to bring potentially challenging agnates into a position of dependency. By the formation of a network of cattle clientship amongst commoner *dikgosana*, the *kgosi* both gathered political support against rebellious agnates and loyalty amongst those who were delegated the authority to integrate the very large numbers of 'foreigners' into the hierarchical sociopolitical order of the *morafe*. From this position of strength, the three *merafe* in focus here expanded their respective territories and brought under their domination a number of outlying communities (Gulbrandsen 1993b). These subject communities were instrumental both in exploiting the hunting territories to the benefit of the *kgosi*, to whom they also were compelled to pay levies and tax, and to herd the large royal herds and those of wealthy, high-ranking people.

This trend of trade and accumulation of cattle centred in the *bogosi* should, however, not be taken as an indication that the rulers of these *merafe* operated in a region that was characterized by peace and harmony. During the first part of the nineteenth century the various Tswana groups of this region frequently raided each other and occasionally engaged in conflicts that amounted to small warfare (Schapera 1942a: 13–14, 1952: 21; Parsons 1982: 118). Such violence found, of course, its major culmination during the devastating intrusion of the Matebele, known as *difaqane*, by which the Tswana were conquered and dispersed for more than a decade (c.1825–1837). Yet in the long run, these aggressive actions served, on the whole, to consolidate and strengthen the three *merafe* under discussion. As so often happens in times of serious conflict, the central power, being in control of the age regiments, provided the necessary internal cohesion and thus became vitally important (see Cohen 1985: 276). In particular the *kgosi*, as commander-in-chief and recipient of booty (both cattle and people), gained considerable authority.

All these *merafe* were at times stricken by serious dynastic conflicts, occasionally to the extent that a *morafe* was temporarily separated into mutually independent sections, yet in due course reunited by one conquering the other (see Schapera 1952: 12). In the manner known from indigenous polities all over the subcontinent (Gluckman 1963: 9ff), conflicts within ruling families might lead to secession of a splinter group. In the present context, after the Bangwaketse and Bangwato departed from the Bakwena in the late seventeenth or early eighteenth century,[7] Batawana's secession from the Bangwato is the only case which resulted in a permanently independent *morafe*. There are several reasons for this (see Schapera 1952: 15ff), including reconciliation and return, hosting by another *morafe* and, most importantly, the British policy that all inhabitants of the territory – the 'native reserve' in British terms – were compelled to submit to the authority of the Tswana *kgosi* recognized by the colonial power and granted extensive credentials (see below). At any rate, on the basis of Schapera's (1952: 11–15) meticulous accounts it is evident that very few, if any, royal sections of the *merafe* here have prevailed permanently beyond their royal centres and represented a potentially challenging force.

In summary, I have argued that the strength and scale of the Northern Tswana *merafe* in focus here were in progress from the late eighteenth century, mainly conditioned by the linking up with long-distance trade, abundance of wildlife, vast unexploited pastures and incessant population increase by capturing numerous alien groups into their structures. That is, people were either searching for safe harbour in an increasingly violent landscape or conquered and subjected to one of the *merafe*. Under these conditions, I have argued, the three Tswana *merafe* in focus here underwent major transformations, the two significant ones relevant to the present argument being: (a) the amalgamation of the power structures around the *dikgosi* by the formation of cattle clientship of nonroyal leaders, including some of those of foreign origin; (b) the use of the ward system, combined with cattle clientship, which enabled the ruling groups to incorporate people conquered and hosted in ways that effectively put them into the mill of assimilation and made them integral to the hierarchal structure of the *merafe*, adding progressively to their strength and scale.

The decisive mediating factor was cattle herds which grow fast under favourable ecological conditions and the *dikgosi's* exclusive linking up with the intercontinental trade of fur and ivory and their control of trading in the region. The propelling factors were thus of a global kind – intercontinental trade and the imperial expansion into the continent that brought numerous communities and families in flight westwards from the most troubled areas. (By the way, it is a highly intriguing point that, as I shall explain in Chapter 3, cattle – in combination with global trade connections – played a similarly crucial significance in the formation of the postcolonial state in Botswana.)

---

7. There are conflicting stories about the time and circumstances of the divisions (see Schapera 1942a: 1, 1952: 9).

As for people, I have explained that the rise of the Tswana *merafe* went hand in hand with that core group in due course becoming a numerical minority. In control of *bogosi*, they prevailed as the ruling communities progressively asserted their dominant position. By means of particular practices of social incorporation and cultural assimilation, political integration of groups conquered or hosted in the royal centres worked to the effect of developing primary identification with the core group which recognized them as full members of their *morafe* (see Chapter 6). This is, however, not the whole story. Within the vast territories claimed by the *merafe*, there were always a number of outlying communities that resisted the overlordship of the rulers of the Tswana *merafe* of present concern. They were mostly of foreign origin, but also included groups seceded from the royal centre of other Tswana communities in the region. In order to comprehend how the Tswana *merafe* consolidated and expanded their domination at the edge of the Kalahari and beyond, I shall, in a subsequent section, explain the significance of being brought under British overlordship.

Anticipating that, let me point out that the transformations I have been concerned with in this section involved the development of a civic government (*puso*) very instrumental to the British establishment of a colonial state in the country, confirmed by Roberts' (1972: 103) assertion that 'the administrators of the Bechuanaland Protectorate had at their disposal from the outset a group of closely similar and already highly sophisticated judicial systems, the higher levels of which could be incorporated in the official structure almost without modification'. One of the most apparent expressions of civic order was the centrality of the *kgotla* in the structuring of social life and the settlement pattern, conspicuously manifested in the compact, well-organized royal towns of thousands of people with the royal house at the core (see Gulbrandsen 2007, cf. 1993b). The evangelizing missionaries had already impacted upon these orders for decades before the establishment of the colonial state in 1885. To their engagement with the *dikgosi* – and the *dikgosi* with them – we now turn in order to come to terms with their significance.

Strengthening Royal Ancestorhood, Receiving Evangelizing Missionaries and Establishing State Churches

Although the Bakwena, the Bangwaketse and the Bangwato were, at times, riddled by internal conflicts, they succeeded in taking control of many smaller and larger communities, either conquered or hosted. Their respective dynasties had occasionally proved their ability both to stand up to external threats and to force, if necessary, foreign groups into submission. In Tswana thought, royal authority is not only a matter of ascription by virtue of descent: it has to be asserted by a demonstration of strength and the fruits of good governance in the form of welfare, health and prosperity of the population – all proofs being supported by the royal ancestorhood (see Gulbrandsen 1995).

The authority of the ruling dynasty is cosmologically linked to a hierarchy of forces. In the Tswana imagination, this hierarchy is, in brief, projected into the realm of the ancestors (*badimo*). In this mode of thought, the ancestors of the ruling line (*badimo ba dikgosi*) constitute the supreme source of power, wisdom and morality, exclusively available to the living ruler. Furthermore, a *kgosi* is ideally in possession of the most powerful charms to protect himself and the *bogosi* against internal enemies and guard the *morafe* against threatening external forces. In addition the *kgosi* should ideally be in control of the most powerful productive medicines, e.g. for providing rain (see Chapter 8 below; Gulbrandsen 1995). A *kgosi* who acts in relation to external forces with strength and sustains internal control is spoken of as a *kgosi* who relates well to his ancestors and asserts his command of productive and protective 'medicines'.

The notion of a Tswana ruler's authority was dependent not only on descent but also on his personal strength and ability to act upon ever changing historical contexts to the benefit of his people. This is a notion – capacity and engagement – which is intrinsic to the cultural construction of the *kgosi* as a ruler with, as we shall see, considerable authority to initiate major transformations. This dimension of pragmatic assessment of a ruler's strength and ability is perfectly expressed by the mythological origin of the ruling lines of the Bakwena and Bangwaketse. As for the latter, I was told more than once, in the words of one man, that:

> Long ago, there were two brothers, Khuto and Khutwane, who were the sons of Moleta, one of the ancient *dikgosi* of the Bangwaketse. Kuto was the eldest one [as indicated by the diminutive form Kuto*yane* given to the younger brother]. However, although Khuto was the one who according to our custom [*mokgwa*] should succeed his father, this did not happen. The reason is that Khuto, in the opinion of the people at that time, was found to be too weak. They wanted Khutwane, who they thought would be a much more forceful *kgosi*. I think they were very right, because ever since the Bangwaketse have been ruled by people descending from Khutwane and they have proved to be very strong and wise, like Makaba II, Gaseitsiwe, Bathoen I, Seepapitso III and Bathoen II. The people of Khuto still live here in Kanye and much respect is paid to them, especially their seniors – although they do not have sufficient force to rule people. Their head has a very senior position in the royal *kgotla*, placed at the right-hand side of the *kgosi* among his paternal uncles and principal advisors. At the time the Bangwaketse adhered properly to the ritual practice of *go loma ngwaga*

['to bite the new year' – the first fruit ceremony], the head of the Khuto people was the one to bite the pumpkin first, even before the *kgosi*.

The LMS missionary Willoughby relates a similar myth about a 'junior' line constituting the ruling dynasty among the Bakwena (Willoughby 1928: 229). The central notion here, of strength being attributed to a genealogical line of rulers, comes out of the Tswana cultural construction of *kgosi* authority. Ideally, the *kgosi* is a *motswadintle* ('one from whom good things come'; see Gulbrandsen 1995: 421), ensuring societal order and thus social harmony (*kagiso*). As I shall elaborate in Chapter 4, *kagiso* is imperative to health, fertility, prosperity and welfare. In popular imagination, a powerful *kgosi* is a *kgosi* who provides *kagiso* for the *morafe* at large because he is perceived as being on good terms with the principal custodians of the *morafe*'s moral order, the royal ancestorhood (*badimo ba dikgosi*). A *kgosi*'s authority – as the incumbent of the *bogosi* – thus springs to a significant extent from his exclusive access to the royal ancestorhood. Yet, I reiterate, it also depends on his actual ability to act with strength and determination to the benefit of the *morafe* as proof of ancestral support. In terms of Tswana cosmology, if he does well, he will, at his death and subsequent inclusion in the royal ancestorhood, add to the popular perceived strength of the ruling dynasty (see Gulbrandsen 1993b: 566ff.).

The preceding section illuminates how Tswana *dikgosi* attempted to amalgamate the expanding networks of power that enabled them to prevail as forceful rulers of a *morafe* that expanded in strength and scale. For example, the Bangwaketse extraordinarily powerful hero-king Makaba II features, even to-day, prominently in popular consciousness about the force vested in the ruling dynasty's ancestorhood. His great significance is currently most apparent in the symbolism in the royal *kgotla* of the hierarchical order of *bogosi*: the senior living descendants of the senior male line descending from each of his wives are, in ranked order according to the ranking of the wives, situated on the right-hand side of the *kgosi* in the royal *kgotla*, with the most senior descendant next to the *kgosi*.

Tswana *dikgosi* are not to be classified as 'sacred kings' (e.g. of the kind analyzed by de Heusch (1982) in Central African contexts). But their responsibility for their people's overall health, prosperity and welfare instilled them with major tasks that could not easily be taken care of solely through the stratagems of amalgamating and expanding networks of power. Their spiritual leadership is required for providing rain and preventing the influx of pests and plagues, depending on a range of ritual practices. That is, practices which are, on the one hand, directed towards satisfaction of the royal ancestorhood (see Chapter 4) and, on the other hand, involving deployment of powerful 'medicine', ideally provided by the strongest doctors/diviners (*dingaka*, singl. *ngaka*) available. They are often of foreign origin, reflecting a belief in their capacity to convey constructively highly potent, potentially dangerous spiritual forces prevailing beyond the limits of the *morafe*.

It is in the light of this obsession with empowerment and fortification by spiritual means as well as more tangible forces that we should understand why a number of Tswana *dikgosi* were, unlike many other African rulers, amongst the first to be baptized, engaging extensively with evangelizing missionaries who were often attracted to establish a church in the royal town and subsequently in outlying villages.[8] David Livingstone of the London Missionary Society was the first to be stationed in what would become the Bechuanaland Protectorate. The Bakwena (see Map 1), amongst whom he worked and lived for about ten years from 1842, were at that time under repeated attack by the Boers, and missionaries were ostensibly helpful both with strategic information and arms (Sillery 1954: 110).

On the other hand, missionary requirements that the *dikgosi* impose radical changes in several important ritual and social practices[9] gave raise to major conflicts at the royal centres (see Gulbrandsen 1993a: 50 ff). For example the missionaries obliged the *dikgosi* to abandon all but one of their wives, famously illuminated by the aftermath of Livingston's baptism of *Kgosi* Sechele I of Bakwena (r. 1831–92) in 1848 involving major conflicts with some of his senior *dikgosana* (see Livingstone 1857: 13ff.; Schapera 1960: 298ff.). Amongst the Bangwato, tension and conflicts emerged in 1860 when *Kgosi* Sekgoma – who was highly ambivalent, if not hostile, to the evangelizing missionaries – and his son and heir Khama became bitterly divided as the latter refused to participate in the initiation ceremony (*bogwera*) after having been baptized. There were violent confrontations around the royal town of Shoshong between Sekgoma's and Khama's supporters (see Illustration 2), before a process of reconciliation (*tetlanyo*) started and ultimately led to the enthronement of *Kgosi* Khama III (r. 1872, 1875–1923, see front cover of this book).[10] However serious, these conflicts were in due course resolved; after Khama had taken full control of the *bogosi*, he was never seriously challenged by anti-Christian or anti-missionary factions.

---

8. Because of limited space, I refer the reader to the archival and other sources I rely on in matters of evangelizing missionaries and the Tswana in my previous publications Gulbrandsen 1993a and 2001.

9. As a condition for baptism these Tswana rulers were required to abandon some of their central rituals such as initiation (*bogwera* [male], *bojale* [female]) and rainmaking. They also made it unlawful to marry more than one wife without the *kgosi*'s consent and they put an end to the practice of levirate and sororate.

10. See Mackenzie 1871: 423 ff., 1883: 238ff.; Gulbrandsen 1993a: 52ff.

Illustration 2. 'Battles outside Shoshong' as rendered by LMS missionary John Mackenzie (1883: 246)

While it is true that the missionary–*kgosi* relationship could, at times, become tense and even conflict ridden, in some important respects the *kgosi* was the stronger party because the evangelizing missionaries depended on his permission to establish a church in his *morafe*. Usually, the *dikgosi* allowed only one missionary church to be established (Schapera 1970: 122), which they attempted to capture into their polity. That the *dikgosi* and their close retainers functioned as the church elderhood epitomizes the extent of their engagement. As I have argued elsewhere (Gulbrandsen 1993a: 49ff.), this meant that the missionary churches tended to take on the character of a 'state church'. Landau (1995: 51) emphasizes the missionaries' dependency on the *dikgosi,* one of whom pointed out that '[i]n a very true sense Khama is head of the Church as well as head of the State'. Likewise, during a celebration in the royal *kgotla,* a prominent man asserted that *Kgosi* Khama 'reigns through the Church. His reign is established by God' (Landau 1995: 52). Echoing European notions of church–monarchy relations, Khama himself declared that '[t]he Lord Jesus Christ … made me a chief, and He knows how I try and have always tried to rule my people for their good'.[11]

---

11. Chief Khama to Rev. Cullen Rees (4 Aug. 1890), Chief's Papers, Folder 4, Selly Oak Public Library, Birmingham.

By these constructions, several *dikgosi* hence attempted – to a great extent successfully – to add a new spiritual dimension to their respective *bogosi*. For example, when *Kgosi* Bathoen II of the Bangwaketse (r. 1928–1969) played the organ during church service, he was both asserting his divine connection and naturalizing Western idioms of eminence into Tswana hierarchical thought. This did not conflict with the *kgosi's* centrality in indigenous cosmology which was continuously reproduced in the discursive field of the *kgotla* – the locus of ancestral morality – into which also the missionaries were drawn, e.g. in the conduct of Christianized ritual practices, like praying for rain (see Gulbrandsen 1993a: 68–70).

The consequent close relationship between *dikgosi* and the evangelizing missionaries was the prevailing pattern amongst the Northern Tswana – to the extent that the missionary church assumed the character of being a 'state church'. To a very limited extent 'the spiritual aspect of the chieftainship' drew a wedge between 'religion and politics, chapel and chieftainship' as Comaroff and Comaroff (1986: 4–5) report in the case of the Southern Tswana. But there were a few exceptions, as for example in the case of *Kgosi* Kgama who ran into a serious conflict with the missionary resident in the royal town that instigated the formation of a challenging faction (in 1894), entailing a major controversy which involved the protectorate administration (Chirenje 1978: 35ff.). However, Khama prevailed as a Christian *kgosi*. Amongst the Bakwena a controversy over the initiation ceremony of *bogwera* also entailed factionalism and a major conflict at the royal centre that implicated the missionaries; I shall discuss this case in the following chapter.

In the case of the Bangwaketse, an indigenous LMS priest, Mothowagae, came acutely at odds with the resident missionary and he established an independent church – King Edward BaNgwaketse Church. This gave rise to a major divide amongst the Bangwaketse, revealing itself in a serious conflict between *Kgosi* Bathoen I (r. 1889–1910, see front cover of this volume) who was attached to the missionary, and important *dikgosana* who supported Mothowagae. Their support was largely influenced by an emerging rivalry between Bathoen and his younger brother, Kwenaetsile. As I explain extensively elsewhere (Gulbrandsen 2001: 44ff.), the *dikgosana* were unhappy with the *kgosi's* close association with the resident missionary and his consequent reform and abandonment of important ritual and social practices. Mothowagae exploited this rift by expressing adherence to Tswana cultural practices. This he allegedly articulated in a charismatic manner that prompted the missionary to accuse Mothowagae of having brought 'Ethopianism' to the Bangwaketse. At the same time the *dikgosana* exploited this development to build up a second political centre. *Kgosi* Bathoen prevailed, though, because Kwenaeitsile died. But there was also a perceived threat emerging toward *bogosi* represented by independent church movements to which the *dikgosana* felt equally vulnerable as the *kgosi*.

Apart from capturing Christianity in the effort to adding another spiritual dimension to the *bogosi*, it became increasingly evident that the *kgosi*'s control over the missionary church was highly conducive – from the point of view of the royal centre – to sustaining spiritual control within the *morafe*. During the latter part of the nineteenth century an increasing number of young men migrating to industrial and mineral centres of South Africa were exposed to indigenous church movements, lead by people who had departed from a missionary church. Some of these church movements also attempted to expand into the Tswana *merafe*, where they were fiercely rejected as potentially disruptive to social order and a major challenge to *kgosi* authority (see Gulbrandsen 2001: 49ff. for an extensive account).

Thus, by granting a missionary society a monopoly on evangelization and taking firm control over the church and its congregation, the *dikgosi* virtually gave rise to state churches. Quite pragmatically, virtually all the Tswana *dikgosi* recognized by the British (see below) privileged the missionary churches with a monopoly since they represented a powerful instrument preventing syncretistic movements – as dangerous exterior forces – from generating rhizomic attacks. Especially the provincial communities represented potentialities of such forces (Gulbrandsen forthc.), the supervision of which was tacitly conducted by the network of clergies extending from the royal centre. In particular, to keep at bay forces giving rise to challenging independent church movements was at least as much in the interest of the missionary church as the ruling groups of the Tswana *merafe*. Before the *dikgosi* lost their control over the establishment of churches at Botswana's independence, there seems to have been only one instance (in the 1930s) when one such movement temporarily became of some significance in a dynastic conflict at the Bakgatla royal centre (Morton 1987: 88f.; Gulbrandsen 1991: 52f.).

Negotiating Protection: Threats of Annexation and the Establishment of a Colonial State

The formation of the Bechuanaland Protectorate cannot, however, be characterized as entirely a matter of 'love at first encounter'. Negotiations with each *kgosi* were conducted by a colonial officer – Charles Warren – who was met by the Bakwena with some reluctance, but shown considerable appreciation by the Bangwato (see Ramsay 1998: 66ff, on whose excellent account much of the following relies). Scepticism was only to be expected in view of British expansion into the region over the past decades. Indeed, this expansion was at one point perceived as such a serious threat that initiatives were made to unite various Tswana *merafe*, including the Bakwena and the Bangwaketse, into a confederation to resist what they considered British aggression. Such a confederation never materialized, however. The Northern Tswana rulers Gaseitsiwe (Bangwaketse) and Sechele (Bakwena) remained spectators to the violence perpetrated by the British in order to safeguard the diamond fields in and around Kimberley.

When they eventually welcomed the British offer of 'protection', their acquiescence should be understood against a background of other colonizing forces at work which was perceived by Northern Tswana as an indeed dangerous threat. These were settler communities – British as well as Boers – which were by no means under British control and which pushed for expansion into the territories of the Northern Tswana *merafe*. This led to some violent interactions in the early 1880s (Ramsay 1998: 65).

In the context of such dangers, and given that they had no chance of resisting the British if the latter really had wanted to gain the Northern Tswana land, the three *dikgosi* consented to the establishment of the Bechuanaland Protectorate. The deal was after all quite acceptable, since the British had promised that 'the chiefs ... might be left to govern their own tribes in their own fashion'[12] and, very significantly, the colonial power firmly restricted the establishment of white settler communities within the tribal territories. The Northern Tswana's geopolitical location had worked to their advantage: the decision to establish a British protectorate was triggered by increasing German activity in what was then South-West Africa. Was there now, the British asked themselves, a 'danger that the Germans might join hands with the hostile Boers, or with the Portuguese, or even with other Germans who were in East Africa, cut the road to the north and thus permanently bar the Cape from access to central Africa?' (Sillery 1974: 75). As Maylam (1980: 25) states, being 'in danger from three sides: South African Republic, Germany and Portugal' the establishment of the Bechuanaland Protectorate served the British imperial interests in blocking South African and German expansion. These interests were more than 'political' (Parsons 1985: 29) as the control over the vast territory of the protectorate helped significantly to secure economic interests further north, especially by the construction

---

12. BPP C.4588, Stanley to Robinson, 13 Apr. 1885, quoted in Ramsay 1998: 68.

of a railway through the country which remained the only direct link between South Africa and Rhodesia until the 1960s.

That the British considered negotiating the establishment of a protectorate was also due to the existence of somebody to address. That is, somebody in sufficient control of the country and people to be recognized as a partner with enough local authority and political control. Hence the significance of the strength and scale of the Bakwena, the Bangwaketse and Bangwato *merafe* to be brought under the British wing in order to avoid annexation to the neighbouring violent states.

The negotiated agreement proved, however, not to be watertight. After only a few years the British saw the protectorate as a base for imperial expansion into central Africa. Meanwhile Cecil Rhodes emerged as a leading figure capable of imposing colonial rule on the protectorate. Queen Victoria paved the way for his British South Africa Company (BSACo) to take control, which encouraged the British to push for more than mere 'protection'. In an Order-in-Council the British denied the sovereignty of the *dikgosi* and gave themselves absolute power over all the territories of the Bechuanaland Protectorate. This set in motion a power struggle between the *dikgosi* and the colonial agencies during which the former's strength was severely tested. On at least one occasion, the British and the Tswana were on the brink of war. Aware that the *dikgosi* might join forces, the high commissioner decided to give in, and this particular confrontation was resolved peacefully. But the British had not abandoned their plans to transfer the protectorate to the BSACo. Rhodes at this time was at the height of his power: 'For him direct control of Bechuanaland was the stepping stone to the realisation of his greater ambition – to seize the gold-rich Transvaal' (Ramsay 1998: 75).

Alarmed by the possibility of annexation, the *dikgosi* of the Bakwena, Bangwaketse and Bangwato embarked on the famous journey to London (September–November 1895) mentioned above. Not only did they take their case to the British government, they mounted a lengthy – and successful – campaign throughout Britain against the BSACo, accompanied by missionaries and presenting themselves as model Christian rulers. Asking what would have happened if Bathoen, Khama and Sebele had not travelled to Britain, Parsons suggests, I recall, that the protectorate would have been taken over in October–November 1895. Instead, the *dikgosi*'s effect on the electorate made Prime Minister Chamberlain 'obliged to make partial concessions to the chiefs' and held him back from 'throwing his lot completely into the Rhodesian camp' (Parsons 1998: 255). Perhaps most significantly, their lobbying in London had such an impact on the Colonial Office that it complicated a plan by Rhodes to attack the Boer government. Since this venture subsequently failed to the extent that it became an international scandal, Rhodes's political standing was significantly reduced. The British government abandoned its plans to leave his company with most of the Bechuanaland Protectorate and renewed its promise to protect Bechuanaland. Having apparently defeated Rhodes, the *dikgosi* were celebrated as heroes by their followers.

And yet, the ostensible promise of 'protection' represented no definite guarantee against annexation. In the wake of the South African war, the British government 'began to press for the transfer of the Protectorate to the control of the nascent Union of South Africa' (Ramsay 1998: 82). Once again the *dikgosi* headed campaigns against such plans, and in 1909 they made a second journey to London, where 'the Batswana leaders' views had an immediate, if immeasurable, effect on public discussions'. The *Times* remarked on their 'skill in elocution', concluding that '[t]he speeches of these barbarian chiefs ... are far better reading than the speeches of most European statesmen'.[13]

Although the success of the Tswana *dikgosi* certainly owes considerably to their personal capacity, it must be stressed that their endeavours were decisively conditioned by the conjunction of particular historical circumstance. First, the strength of their respective polities, centred round large, well-organized royal towns and their extent of control over many outlying communities perfectly matched the British strong desire of running the protectorate at minimal cost by implementing extensively practices of indirect rule from the outset by leaving 'the traditional organization very much alone' (Ashton 1947). Second, the *dikgosi*'s development of a close, supportive attachment to the London Missionary Society facilitated the development of the British-Tswana relationship. Third, the new orientations emerging amongst ruling groups of the Bakwena, Bangwato and Bangwaketse underpinning the *dikgosi*'s efforts to ensure British protection, was conditioned by the threat of being captured into the violent domains of the expanding settler regimes immediately east and north of their own territories.

Finally, despite their capacity of incorporating and assimilating foreign groups, these processes were, however, not complete: during the latter part of the eighteenth century a number of communities, some of which large and strong, were located within the territory claimed by one of the three Tswana *merafe*. As we shall now see, with a privileged position within the colonial state, the dominant position of their ruling communities in relation to other communities was progressively reinforced.

---

13. The *Times*, 28 July 1909, quoted in Ramsay 1998: 91.

Expansion of the Dominant Tswana *Merafe* under the British Wing

After the Bechuanaland Protectorate had been established in 1885, the eight Tswana *merafe* officially recognized by the British were each designated a distinct, demarcated territory, known as 'native reserve' (see Schapera 1943a: 7ff.; Motzafi-Haller 2002: 86ff.).[14] A *kgosi* was established as the 'native' authority in charge of all the peoples living in each of them. Furthermore, during the three *dikgosi's* visit to England in 1895, the British made it clear that they would be given full backing, if required, to prevent junior sections of the ruling dynasty from branching off and forming separate establishments. The rulers of these *merafe* were hence installed by the British as the supreme authority of all those communities living within their respective reserves. This also meant, as suggested previously, that groups that had seceded from the royal centre and taken residence elsewhere, were now subjected to the overlordship of the Tswana *kgosi* recognized by the British (Schapera 1952: 17). The *dikgosi* were assured full support in case subject communities should challenge their overlordship. In this section I shall explain how the dominant Tswana expanded the network of power within their respective reserves and how the increasingly repressive structures were countered by resistance.

As suggested in the Introduction, there were huge differences among the eight 'native reserves', both in territorial range (see Map 1) and population size (see Schapera 1952). Moreover, they differed sharply in the extent to which foreign groups were assimilated into a recognized *morafe*.[15] The three smallest ones – the Barolong, the Malete and the Batlokwa – occupied minute areas and were quite homogenous, with no unassimilated groups of any significance except for a small category of servants (*batlankha*). The Bakgatla were also relatively homogenous, small in number and confined to a relatively small territory, yet, as we shall see, with one distinct Tswana community with non-Kgatla identification. Of the four larger territories – the Bangwaketse, the Bakwena, the Bangwato and the Batawana – the first two included some sizeable communities which identified themselves as Tswana, but originated from sections different from the three 'hosting' *merafe*. In addition, a considerable number of people were scattered around in small villages or hamlets: as discussed earlier in this chapter, these consisted partly of small groups originating from

---

14. Morton et al. (1989: 105) relate that 'Proclamation 9 of 1899 established five reserves: Bangwakerse, Bakwena, Bakgatla, Mmangwato, and Batawana. Three others were later created Bamalete (1909), Tati (1911) and Batawana (1933).'

15. For a comprehensive account of the features summarized in this section, see Schapera 1952.

Sotho-speaking communities in the Transvaal, and partly of people who had 'always' been living in the area and who were classified by the ruling Tswana groups as Makgalagadi or Masarwa.[16] When the dominant Tswana communities increased their cattle wealth from the eighteenth century onwards, the latter categories constituted a source of free labour and consequently were exploited as herders. This was particularly the case among the four large *merafe*. The Bangwato and the Batawana were granted the most extensive 'native reserves'; they also were assigned overlordship of great numbers of people who had retained their non-Tswana cultural identities.

By the exercise of their dominant position, all communities within the confines of each native reserve were captured into the hierarchical structure of authority radiating from the royal centre of the officially recognized *merafe*. The Tswana ruling group exercised their power by means of this network: formally on behalf of the Crown, they administered the allocation of natural resources, collected tax and exercised jurisdiction. The heads of provincial communities were recruited either from the local group or from members of the royal centre who were placed in provincial communities to embody the authority of the *kgosi* officially recognized by the colonial state. During the colonial era such delegation by the *dikgosi* increased, with a system of 'chief's representatives' originating from the royal centre and also an extensive intelligence service.

This system worked more efficiently in compact communities, especially those closer to the royal centres, than in peripheral communities in large 'reserves' such as those of the Bangwato and Batawana. On the other hand these peripheral communities, composed mainly of hunter-gatherers and horticulturalists, were politically inactive and thus represented no threat to the Tswana rulers. Moreover, although the majority of the population in the reserves lived in compact villages, being agriculturalists and pastoralists they operated over a wide area: a family's arable land could be located 5–10 kilometres or more from their village and their cattle post even further away. As all land resources were 'communal', and under the trusteeship of the *kgosi* access to land could be obtained only with the consent of the *kgosi* or one of his deputies, by appointing 'overseers' to administer all the areas used for agricultural and pastoral purposes (see Schapera 1943a: 143, 224ff), the *dikgosi* kept control of this particular part of the hierarchical network.

It needs to be stressed, however, that communities foreign to the Tswana *merafe* were brought under their domination to a highly different extent. This had partly to do with space. For example, while one Kalanga

---

16. The prefix 'Ma'(kgalagadi) – in contrast to Ba(ngwato) – is degrading and was by Botswana's independence made unlawful.

group was so closely connected to the royal centre of the Bangwato that it constituted a separate ward in the royal town, other Kalanga groups were living far away at the fringes of the territory which the Bangwato attempted to control, allowing them considerable de facto autonomy (Werbner 2004: 37; cf. van Binsbergen 1994: 156; Schapera 1952: 65ff). Partly this was a matter of power: while most 'foreign' Tswana-speaking communities were tightly integrated with the royal centre, there were some large Tswana communities which, as we shall see subsequently, were not located far from the royal centre yet always challenged the supremacy of the ruler of the 'hosting' *morafe*.

In any case, the domination of the Tswana *merafe* recognized by the British prevailed. The force of the processes and structures of subjection is testified by the fact that during the colonial era – spanning some eighty years – there were very few rebellions or serious conflicts between the dominant Tswana groups and their subject communities. It also reflects the fact that the leaders of these subject communities often perceived some benefit in submitting to the dominant *morafe*. For example, in 1922 a large contingent of Herero (originating from the present Namibia) sought refuge among the Bangwato and were accommodated by the establishment of a separate ward in 1922 (see Durham 1993: 72, 130–31). Furthermore, among the sizeable, composite population designated by the Tswana as Makgalagadi, who were mostly scattered among small hamlets, there were groups which gathered under the leadership of a *kgosana* and formed Tswana-style settlements, centring on compact villages divided into units known as *kgotla*.

I lived for a year in such a village in southeastern Bangwaketse that had been established at a small lake in the southern part of the 'reserve' and brought into the political order of the Bangwaketse at the time of *Kgosi* Seepapitso III (c. 1915). In 1946 his son, *Kgosi* Bathoen II, moved the people of this community some 15 kilometres towards the north and placed it under the authority of one of his *dikgosana* who were located there in a separate ward with five descent groups from different wards in the royal town. They were, without question, compelled by the *kgosi* to move in order to give the *kgosi*'s representative a substantial support group. The group of people brought from the south were identified by the Bangwaketse of the royal town as X; their actual name I do not relate for reasons that will be obvious shortly. This group met this reorganization with considerable ambivalence, if not resistance.[17] On the one hand, it

---

17. The *kgosana* who was sent by *Kgosi* Bathoen II to the place claimed to me in 1977 that he had repeatedly been victim of occult attacks by women of the X community.

linked them more closely to the hierarchical order of the Bangwaketse, thus clearly ranking them above those who were, as one of their elders put it, still living in the bush. Moreover, the position of their leader (to whom I was able to speak shortly before he died in 1977) was strengthened within his own community, and he asserted that he worked well with *Kgosi* Bathoen's *kgosana*. On the other hand, the Bangwaketse group from the royal centre – constituting the senior ward in the village – never accepted X as Bangwaketse 'proper'.[18] When I came to the community thirty years after it was established, there had been – with one exception – no intermarriage between the X and those who claimed to be bona fide Bangwaketse. Yet the X insisted to me that they were Bangwaketse 'just like everybody else in the village', and they made every effort to appear indistinguishable from them. The story of the X offers a perfect illustration of how the dominant Tswana group had inculcated their holistic ontology of an all-embracing hierarchical order – there was nothing else to aspire for than belonging to the dominant Tswana.

Similarly I have come across other groups of 'Bakgalagadi' Tswana in a number of small provincial communities in Eastern Botswana who were hiding their perceived stigmatized identity and asserting their belonging to the dominant Tswana (see Solway 1994; Chapter 5 below). This aspect came out in an intriguing way at Botswana's independence when the ruling group of the postcolonial state embarked on constructing a 'nation' principled upon nondiscrimination and other virtues of equality (see following chapter). It became a matter of offence that could be prosecuted to address minorities by the degrading prefix of 'Ma', as in Makgalagadi and Masarwa, the stigmatising Setswana label of Makalaka for Kalanga, or even by the use of their distinct group name if they themselves perceived it humiliating, as in the case of the X above. This and many other communities insisted on being identified by the name of the *morafe* that claimed ownership to the territory in which they were living.[19] I was told

---

18. Schapera and Merwe (1945: 9–10) have classified this group as 'emancipated Kgalagadi' which distinguishes them from those living under the direct authority of a Mongwaketse authority 'to whose immediate ancestors they were formerly attached as serfs'. On the other hand, their lack of recognition by the Bangwaketse make them distinct indeed from those communities amongst the Bangwaketse who are also categorized as the 'Kgalagadi' but thoroughly assimilated and accepted as full-fleshed Bangwaketse to the extent that some of them have established conjugal relationships with the royal family.

19. It is not like this everywhere, however. For example, communities located in the north-western Botswana at the Tswapong hills within the territory over which the *kgosi* of the Bangwato claims supremacy identify themselves as Batswapong and hence distinct from the Bangwato. Intriguingly the Batswapong are – just like people of Tswana royal towns – of mixed origin, or as Motzafi-Haller (2002: 110) asserts, they have 'never been a uniform group with distinct historically rooted ethnic boundaries'. Wherever I have travelled in Botswana a similar statement might have been appropriate, but there are considerable differences in re-

by people who identified themselves as Bangwaketse proper in the village in which I was living that 'if you call them X, they might hit you or take you to court!' Tswana hegemony had obviously been forcefully at work. I shall pursue the issues of domination and pressure for assimilation in Chapter 5.

While many groups thus submitted rather quietly to Tswana overlordship, there were some occasions on which ambivalence, tension and uneasiness turned into open conflicts and confrontation. Although not so many in number, they are significant because they show that the *dikgosi* of the colonial era began to rely less on amicable incorporation and more on coercion. A case in point is the Kalanga, living scattered in a number of small communities in a region of northeast Botswana into which the Bangwato expanded. Werbner has compared the Kalanga to the Tswana, describing both as 'super-tribes': having 'neither political community nor territory, [they] emerged as the broader category of culturally related people, widely spread in tribes and their diasporas, both rural and urban' (Werbner 2002b: 733). In addition, both contained peoples of diverse origins from the outset (e.g. Ramsay 1987: 74). Sociopolitically, however, the Kalanga and the Tswana appear to have differed radically from one another. During the nineteenth and twentieth centuries, the northern Tswana were organized in increasingly centralized polities while at the same time expanding their territories; Kalanga-speaking groups by contrast formed small 'headmanships' scattered throughout the northeast of present-day Botswana.[20] In the Tswana manner of expansion, these settlements were incorporated into the Ngwato *morafe* in the latter part of the nineteenth century as a result of refugee movement and conquest.[21] They thus came under the rule of the Ngwato *kgosi* Khama III (r. 1872/5–1923), who accommodated them peacefully for a long period of time (van Binsbergen 1994: 675) and included their leaders in his government.

A major shift came with the regency of Tshekedi (r. 1926–1949). Whereas *Kgosi* Khama III had allowed the Kalanga a measure of self-government, Tshekedi installed his own retainers as governors of the re-

---

spect of people's willingness to identify themselves as distinct from the dominant community. This feature reflects issues of domination, assimilation and stigmatization which I shall address in Chapter 5.

20. An important condition for sociocultural integration during this period and later was the *Mwali* cult (see Werbner 1989: 245ff).

21. They were allegedly under pressure from an Ndebele ruler who 'sent his impis to collect cattle, grain and other items' from the Kalanga living in this region. When gold was discovered in 1867, the British brought the territory under the control of a private company (the Tati Company), which divided the land up for European settlers and also marginalized and exploited the Kalanga in other ways (see Mgadla 1987: 134ff.).

gion and diminished significantly the existing Kalanga authority figures. This move initiated a protracted struggle, during which the Bangwato ruling group used considerable violence in their efforts to subjugate the Kalanga. Indeed, their treatment of the Kalanga was so harsh that at times British support was given only reluctantly (see Ramsay 1987: 77ff.). The British saw all too well that continued resistance by the substantial Kalanga minority[22] within the Bangwato-controlled *morafe* threatened the interests of the colonial state and, especially, their practice of indirect rule.

The shift by the Tswana ruling groups to exercise more coercion while under British protection, engendered resentment among many subject communities. But the vast majority were too small and weak to react by resistance.[23] Even the larger ones reluctantly submitted to Tswana rule – for example the BaKaa, who were located in the 'native reserve' ruled by the Tswana community of BaKgatla (baga-Kgafela). Kooijman (1978: 13–14) explains that '[a]lthough they felt resentment, the Kaa feared the consequences of ignoring the Kgatla chief's call too much to demur openly', except on one occasion in 1927 when a young man, Phesudi, was installed as their leader. During the ceremony he wore a leopard skin, a true symbol of supreme authority, and expressed his intent of claiming 'full independence from the BaKgatla'. However, shortly afterwards Phesudi died, and this was perceived as an occult attack effected by the personal involvement of the BaKgatla *kgosi*: 'to the Kaa it was a stern warning that they were to obey Kgatla authority or otherwise suffer consequences of dire misfortune' (Kooijman 1978: 15).

These events substantiate the growing strength of the ruling Tswana communities during the colonial era. Calls for British intervention were required only in a few special cases such as the Kalanga-Ngwato conflict mentioned above. Another such case involved the BaKgatla-baga-Mmanaana in the Bangwaketse 'native reserve'. This large Kgatla community had moved around the region for many decades without being able to gain control of a separate territory. Finally they were taken in by

---

22. According to the 1946 census, of the total population of 100,987, the Kalanga numbered 22,777 (c. 23 per cent) and, note, the distinctively Ngwato 17.850 (c. 18 per cent) (Schapera 1952: 65, see also p. v).

23. Some of these groups tried to evade the orbit of the dominant Tswana by escaping to the fringe of the reserve or even beyond. This was particularly the case amongst the Bakwena, whose central power was weakened as a consequence of a long-term dynastic dispute (see Chapter 2). This is illuminated by what was reported in 'law-less' Bakgalagadi community in the extreme western part of Kweneng (see Makgala 2010). Yet this tendency of evading the colonial state and the dominant Tswana *merafe* represented no potentiality of rhizomic forces and, on the whole, it represented only a marginal problem from the point of view of their point of view.

the Bangwaketse and installed at Moshupa some fifty kilometres north of the Bangwaketse royal town (Kanye). A series of conflicts between their leader and Kgosi Bathoen II of the Bangwaketse, initiated in the early 1900s, culminated with the senior section of the Bakgatla ruling dynasty and many followers being exiled in 1933 to the neighbouring Kwena 'native reserve' when the British intervened with physical force (see Schapera 1942a: 21 and 25, cf. 1942b; Tselaesele 1978: 35). This particular intervention was no doubt due to the tenacity of the Kgatla leader at the time. However, the progressive polarization that brought the relationship to the brink of physical violence (Tselaesele 1978: 40) also reflects a growing tendency towards authoritarianism among Tswana rulers (see the following chapter).

A third case is that of the Babirwa whose leader tried, in the 1920s, to challenge the authority of *Kgosi* Khama III to remove them from their area, the background being that Khama had given this area to the British for sale of land to white farmers. The Babirwa resisted, only to experience that a Bangwato regiment (*mophato*) forced them out of their area and put fire to their houses. Their subsequent efforts to bring the case to court were jeopardized by the British who co-operated closely with Khama in a process that was concluded with the Babirwa leader being banished from the protectorate (see Ramsay 1987: 64ff.). This case illuminates that the British were quick to support the *dikgosi* when harsh physical violence was seen necessary, but there were very few occasions of this kind.

The *dikgosi*'s heavy-handed behaviour was not only a matter of imposing their will on the subject communities within the *merafe*. It also owed a great deal to the authoritarian style and structure of the colonial state, which made the *dikgosi* responsible for extracting taxes and enforcing British rules and regulations. These were responsibilities they willingly took on since they were given a percentage of the tax collected. Imposed colonial state rules and regulation only reinforced their dominant position in relation to subject communities (see following chapter). Although these measures, perceived as oppressive, originated from the colonial state, subject communities reacted against the *dikgosi* rather than the British. In fact, the Bakgatla-baga-Mmanaana, the Bakaa, the Bayei and others wanted to eliminate Tswana *kgosi* domination by obtaining a direct relationship with the colonial power. The British always refused to accept such requests.

In conclusion, under the circumstances of the colonial state, the repressive character of the dominant Tswana intensified. Despite subject communities' resistance, the Tswana rulers prevailed because they could always appeal for British support and were provided violent measures if required. A multitude of – often tacit – repressive practices that developed during colonial times have, as we shall see in Chapter 5, been sustained in important respects under postcolonial conditions and have become integral to the modern state structures of social control. However, under these circumstances, I shall explain, major conflicts are emanating from contradictions of, on the one hand, Tswana domination and repressive practices in relation to minority communities, and, on the other hand, the modern state's virtues of equality and liberalism.

Reinforcing of the Tswana *Merafe* within the Colonial State

That the domination of the Tswana *merafe* triggered minority protest as late as some thirty years after independence, I take as an indication of how forcefully Tswana hegemony has been working at all times. The ways in which these protests manifested and were countered by agents of the state are a major issue of Chapter 5. Here I am concerned with the ways in which the dominant position of the ruling communities of the Tswana *merafe* recognized by the British was reinforced during colonial times by virtue of extensive delegation of power. The British had after all promised at the inception of the protectorate that the selected Tswana *dikgosi* 'might be left to govern their own tribes in their own fashion'.[24]

Always wanting to run the protectorate at minimal cost, the British established a very small colonial administration, headed by a resident commissioner whose office was in fact located outside the country – in the township of Mafeking, some twenty kilometres beyond the South African border. (The resident commissioner was referring to the British High Commissioner residing in Cape Town.) This meant that the day-to-day government of much of the country was left with the *dikgosi* and their respective 'tribal administration'. The British authorized, I recall, the *dikgosi* to govern all the peoples (except Europeans) in their 'reserves'. Moreover, in several official statements (see Schapera 1970: 51–52) the British asserted from the outset that the colonial administration should 'respect any native laws or customs' regulating 'civil relations'. The secretary of state actually instructed the high commissioner to 'confine the exercise of authority and the application of law, as far as possible, to whites, *leaving Native Chiefs and those living under their tribal authority almost entirely alone*' (Schapera 1970: 52, italics added). When the colonial administration wanted to establish laws and other regulations, the high commissioner had the power of doing so in the form of 'Proclamations'. Crucially, however, the British rather preferred to encourage the *dikgosi* to frame laws for

---

24. BPP C.4588, Stanley to Robinson, 13 Apr. 1885, quoted in Ramsay 1998: 68.

their subjects (see Schapera 1943b: 9; 1970: 53). It is true, as we shall see in the following chapter, that around 1930 the British took a more active and critical line in relation to the *dikgosi*, being worried about their os-tensibly ever-more-autocratic style of rule. Nevertheless, throughout the colonial era the British depended much upon the executive power of the *dikgosi* in relation to the population within their respective 'reserves' and continued to feature as authorities with wide-ranging executive powers.

The increasing array of activities undertaken by the *dikgosi* and their respective governments is reflected in systematic written records of their decision making. For example, *Kgosi* Seepapitso III of the Bangwaketse (r. 1910–1916) compiled comprehensive accounts that later on were published by Schapera (1947b) and examined by Roberts (1991: 173). Roberts has identified the various fields in which *dikgosi* exercised their authority, including: 'the agricultural cycle; control over access to agri-cultural land; the regulation of population densities in residential areas; the regulation of family life; the management of education; the organisa-tion of public works such as roads and construction, and the eradication of noxious weeds; attempts to control Christian sects; regulation of the activities of the Ngwaketse medico-religious specialists (*dingaka*); control of money-lending; and the management of stray cattle'.

As this suggests, many of the *dikgosi* readily operated as agents of West-ern modernity, extensively confirmed by Schapera's (1970) 'Tribal In-novators'. In the *dikgosi*'s effort to conduct the administration of their respective 'reserves', they also developed a small administration, staffed with clerks who, amongst others, made written records of political deci-sions and court judgements. This was, however, not a radical break with the past. As Wylie (1990: 55) states, the northern Tswana *dikgosi* changed to 'govern with the aid of salaried bureaucrats who were accountable to him alone'. The point is that the *dikgosi* could only operate powerfully in the interest of the British (and themselves) by *maintaining their authority* in relation to the *morafe*. This meant that they had to *exercise* author-ity continuously in the context of the *kgotla* and cultivate networks of political support amongst powerful *dikgosana* and other authority figures. A *kgosi* who repeatedly acted in disagreement with his subjects would not last long (see Chapter 6). That the two most prominent indigenous rulers during the colonial era – *Kgosi* Bathoen II of the Bangwaketse and the regent Tshekedi of the Bangwato – developed particularly forceful leader-ships did not depend upon British support alone. As we shall see in the following chapter, the relationship between these two *dikgosi* and the Brit-ish was at times ridden by serious conflicts and was always ambivalent.

Of course, it is questionable the extent to which the popular meetings in the *kgotla* (*lebatla*, *pitso*) under the presidency of the *kgosi* – with a highly inclusive assemblage of the adult male sections of the population (see Schapera 1984: 82) – were operated in a 'democratic' way in a modern, Western sense (see Chapter 6). It is nevertheless crucial that vast sections of the population were regularly gathered in the royal *kgotla* and exposed to the exercise of *kgosi* authority as the apex of the hierarchical structure of royal councillors (*bagakolodi*, singl. *mogakolodi*) and *dikgosana*[25] of all the wards comprising the *morafe*. This exercise of authority was, to missionaries and other Westerners, readily conceived as mundane, secular practices of public debate ended by the *kgosi*'s concluding statement. But, as I shall explain in Chapter 4, the process itself – in the discursive field of the *kgotla* – had significance far beyond resolving pragmatically the issue at hand in a straight forward Western sense. In brief, the debates in this discursive field – which often go on for hours and even days – ritualized the rich symbolism underpinning the hierarchical order of the *merafe*. They hence asserted the eminence of the Tswana ruling group surrounding its apex – the *kgosi* – who, as the incumbent of the *bogosi* and the principal custodian of ancestral morality, gave this particular hierarchy a cosmological anchorage.

The consequent reenforcement of the dominant position of the Tswana was gaining further momentum by the ever-more-present, larger world that impelled the *dikgosi* to secure societal control by means of legislation. Prior to legislation the *dikgosi* consulted extensively with their *bagakolodi*, *dikgosana* and the *merafe* at large in the context of the *kgotla*. Schapera's (1943b) extensive survey of the laws (*melao*) framed by Tswana rulers since the mid-eighteenth century shows how legislative activity intensified progressively during the colonial era. This development had a significant bearing on the dominant Tswana groups' exercise of authority in relation to subject communities as the legislative debates in the royal *kgotla* also included their leaders. Patently, they were brought into a discourse governed by the dominant Tswana which was leading up to the *kgosi*'s decision, anchored in the Tswana royal ancestorhood.

The intensified exercise of Tswana domination in the discursive field of the *kgotla* was even more pervasive in the conduct of jurisprudence in the *merafe*'s hierarchy of courts according to *mekgwa le melao ya Setswana* – the highly inclusive normative repertoire of 'Tswana custom and law' (see Schapera 1984; Comaroff and Roberts 1981: 70ff; Chapter 4, this volume). The gradual commoditization of the economy and, in particular, the extensive labour migrations to farms and mines in South Africa which took off with the exploitation of the diamond mines in Kimberley in the early 1870s (Schapera 1947a: 25), had a profound impact on family

---

25. A *mogakolodi* might or might not be a *kgosana*, vice versa.

and community life and increased progressively the number of disputes and other conflicts. Such cases were usually initiated at the lowest court level – that of the descent-group *kgotla*. If unresolved there, the case was appealed to the ward level and, if still unresolved, ultimately to the royal *kgotla* where the *kgosi* made the final judgement.[26] As I shall explain in Chapter 4, people's recognition of the *kgosi* as supreme judge follows from being perceived as the ultimate, living custodian of morality vested in the royal ancestorhood.

The everyday exercise of jurisprudence at all levels involved a mill of cultural assimilation that worked most powerfully in relation to immigrants distributed on wards in the royal towns. By the British instalment of the Tswana *dikgosi* as supreme authority of the various 'reserves', the Tswana royal *kgotla* also became the court of appeal for all lower-ordered courts, including those of outlying subject communities. Seen in retrospect, this practice had certainly a strong impact upon the establishment of Tswana domination in the sense that members of minority communities – without question – have become very accustomed to bring their unresolved cases forward to one of the Tswana *dikgosi* (see Chapter 4). This goes even for people in Kgalagadi communities beyond the Tswana *merafe* in western Botswana who still – some thirty-five years after independence – call upon the *kgosi* of the Bangwaketse to judge their appeal cases. In view of the existentially important issues involved in many of these cases, minority communities' readiness to appeal their cases for judgement by a Tswana *kgosi* is obviously a major confirmation of how Tswana domination took hold during colonial times amongst people far beyond those incorporated in the royal towns.

In conclusion, the British wide-ranging authorization of the Tswana *dikgosi* to deal with all vital issues evolving amongst their respective subjects, perfectly matched the ways in which relations of authority are generated and reproduced amongst the Tswana: through the exercise of authoritative leadership in the discursive field of the *kgotla* under an imaginary cosmological guidance of the royal ancestorhood. Virtually obsessed by dispute settlements and very devoted to debating rules and notoriously concerned with social control and order, the British had at hand practices and structures that proved highly instrumental to implement principles of indirect rule. Just as the missionaries saw the *kgotla* as a secular field, the British had probably little idea about the extent to which their authorization of the *dikgosi* gave the latter prerequisites conducive to strengthening their authority and expanding the domina-

---

26. The British opened up for further appeal to their district commissioner, stationed in each of the royal towns, but this option was very rarely used.

tion of the officially recognized Tswana *merafe* in accordance with their cosmological centrality.

Conclusion

The Tswana *merafe* of present Botswana is not a colonial creation; their strength, structure and practices were in many respects well established at the arrival of the British (see Comaroff and Comaroff 1991: ch. 4 for a corresponding account of the Southern Tswana within South Africa). I have explained with a particular focus upon the three major *merafe* – the Bakwena, the Bangwaketse and the Bangwato – that their growth in strength and scale resulted from transformations propelled by interaction with global and regional forces at succeeding historical stages. The external forces seem to have been so decisive that their growth in strength and scale might be seen as culminations of regional processes (see Gulbrandsen 1993b). As I have explained in this chapter, royal cattle herds that grew fast under the favourable ecological conditions and immense benefits from fur and ivory trade involved aggregation of vast symbolic and material wealth. By virtue of the ruler's agency these conditions proved highly conducive to major transformations by which the *bogosi* was fortified by the amalgamation of power structures at the centre.

In particular, the Tswana practices of ward organization, I have explained, were instrumental in capturing a huge number of foreign communities, potentially challenging exterior forces, into mills of assimilation. Their consequent incorporation in the hierarchical order of the *merafe* was reflected in, on the whole, submitting to the overlordship of the Tswana ruling group. The capacity of these *merafe* to expand in strength and scale by capturing exterior communities into their sociopolitical structure is indicated by the fact that in due course, 'about four-fifths of the Ngwato tribe … consists of what were originally foreign peoples, and among the Tawana the proportion is still greater' (Schapera 1952: v).

Although this did not mean that all communities conquered or hosted were brought fully under the control of the Tswana *merafe* in focus here, their rulers were receiving the evangelizing missionaries and incorporated their churches in their respective *merafe*. They were granted monopoly to the exclusion of 'independent' African Christian movements. This venture added, in important respects, both a spiritual dimension to the *dikgosi*'s authority and structures of societal control which meant they virtually assumed the character of 'state church', although there were occasionally rifts between missionaries and the *kgosi*. And despite the fact that the evangelizing missionaries required major shifts in some central ritual and societal practices that at the time set in motion processes that led to serious – but temporal – political divides in the royal centres, they were met with limited resistance (see Gulbrandsen 1993a, 2001). On the whole, they added strength to the *bogosi*, in spiritual as well as secular respects. In particular, the privileged missionary churches were very instrumental for the Tswana ruling group's efforts to control people's spiritual life to prevent their engagement with all the African Christian movements in progress on the subcontinent.

In precolonial times the Tswana ruling groups managed only partially to capture outlying communities of different origins into their process of state formation. Brought under the British wing, they were able to fully assert their dominant position and to subject these communities to the Tswana hierarchies of authority. The immense significance of British overlordship to the selected Tswana *dikgosi* is underscored by the fact that any section of the royal families seceding from the royal centre and residing elsewhere within the 'native reserve' was by the British placed firmly under the authority of the *dikgosi* to whom the British had assigned supreme authority over the respective 'native reserves'. There was thus no scope for creating an independent *morafe* or a second centre after the establishment of the colonial state. Although all the threats of annexation to one of the highly repressive, neighbouring European regimes were the apparent motivation of the three *dikgosi*'s journeys to London to have the queen's protection asserted, the British empowerment of the *dikgosi* was probably also a significant factor underpinning their acceptance, if not appreciation, of being brought under the British wing.

Although the relationship between the *dikgosi* and the British was, as we shall see in the following chapter, progressively riddled by ambivalence, tension and, at times, serious conflicts, this relationship was nevertheless a matter of mutual dependency. Especially because of the British determination to govern the protectorate at minimal cost and maximal implementation of principles of indirect rule, the Tswana *dikgosi* were substantially empowered. And their respective ruling communities manifested increasingly their positions as judicial authorities and political leaders in respect of a steadily wider span of issues throughout the different *merafe*, also in relation to subject communities.

This development under the British wing lasted for no less than eighty years and naturalized to a great extent Tswana leadership. Through a gradualist, often nonconfrontational approach, the ruling Tswana groups were, moreover, winning hegemony in relation to subject communities and hence capturing them, to some extent, into their structures of domination by consent. However, as I stressed in the Introduction, to win hegemony in the sense of leadership by virtue of consent (*dumela*) is always a matter of degree. In the present case it is patently evident that Tswana domination relied upon coercive measures as well. And these measures were not only exercised within the limits of politico-jural order. They were also exercised in a wide range of social relationship through which dominant Tswana, often by means of subtle and tacit discriminatory measures, prevented minorities from rising against their overlords. Thus, only very rarely they represented openly challenging forces during colonial times. The extent to which Tswana repressive forces had been at work before the independent state of Botswana was established with declarations of social equity and liberal individualism, is perfectly confirmed by the fact that it would, I reiterate, as we shall see in Chapter 5, take some thirty years after the independence before minority voices gained significance in the public sphere (see Chapter 5).[27]

27. The only important deviation from this pattern is the Kalanga (see van Binsbergen 1994; Werbner 2004; Chapter 3 below).

Chapter 2

Tswana Consolidation within the Colonial State
Development of a Postcolonial State Embryo

In view of the ways in which the British established supremacy as a rather distant power, it is not surprising that the peoples of the Bechuanaland Protectorate did not develop any strong notion of a repressive colonial power. Of course, the imposition of tax and levies and other requirements were received negatively. Yet many of my old friends and acquaintances on labour migration to South Africa (which was very substantial for almost a hundred years, until the mid-1980s[1]) recalled a strong contrast between the protectorate and the repressive, racist regime of South Africa. This difference finds one of its most important expressions in the fact that while peoples of the surrounding states had to engage in violent freedom fights to get rid of the respective racist regimes, the peoples of the protectorate received independence long before the others in a highly smooth and nonviolent way. The colonial state faded out in 1966 as nonviolently as it had captured the population into its realm some eighty years earlier.

This disparity illuminates that, as John Comaroff (2002: 126) reminds us, there is nothing like *the* colonial state in Africa: 'colonial regimes contrasted widely'. He argues that instead of conceiving such regimes in terms of 'generic properties', we should envisage 'an ensemble of generative processes' (2002: 124). Such a processual approach will help to iden-

---

1. See Schapera (1947a) for most of colonial times and Gulbrandsen (1996a) for the post-colonial period.

tify, with a much higher degree of specificity, the diversity of colonial regimes. Within the present limits I shall pursue this approach from the point of view that the colonial state in the Bechuanaland Protectorate was not reducible to the British Administration, although it relied, as we have seen, on some dominant coercive powers under its command. Rather, the colonial state should be seen as an assemblage of interrelated regimes in which the officially recognized *dikgosi* held a key position.

As shown in the preceding chapter, each of the *merafe* might be seen as a hierarchy of regimes, centred in the respective *kgotla*, with the royal office *(bogosi)* at its apex. The royal office was in turn subject to the British Administration. However, the latter depended on the chain of command vested in the hierarchies of authority within the *merafe*. At the same time the former depended on the British should their authority ever be seriously challenged. In what follows I shall first pursue the argument initiated in the preceding chapter: that on the whole this situation had the effect of strengthening the structures of authority relations and domination within each of the *merafe* recognized by the British. In fact I shall identify significant processes that worked to amalgamate the power structures of the *merafe* – structures that proved, as we shall see in the following chapters, also to be very sustainable under the conditions of the modern, postcolonial state of Botswana.

But this is not to say that consent and harmony prevailed throughout the eighty years of the protectorate's existence. In this chapter I shall explain how conflicts and tensions evolved both between the *dikgosi* and the British and between the *dikgosi* and their subjects. These conflicts and tensions developed greatly under the impact of Western modernity and raise a major conundrum: under these circumstances, how could a quite unified group of people emerge, often at odds with the *dikgosi*, which was capable of negotiating decolonization and establishing firm political control over the postcolonial state? Furthermore, I want to address this question: how could such a group, strong adherents of Western liberalism, the market economy and electoral democracy, succeed in curtailing the powers of the (mostly resistant) rulers of the Tswana *merafe* and incorporating them into the structures of the postcolonial state, far more tightly and powerfully than the British had ever attempted to do?

Colonial State Transformations: Conflicts and Mutual Dependency between the *Dikgosi* and the Colonial Power

It is true that with the establishment of British overlordship the rulers of the Northern Tswana *merafe* lost their absolute sovereignty, since some limitations were placed on their judicial and legislative powers. Nevertheless, Schapera has asserted that 'the events of 1895–96 greatly enhanced the personal powers of traditional rulers in the Bechuanaland Protectorate' (quoted in Parsons 1998: 254). The long-term significance of these developments has also been noted by Gillett, who maintains that 'under the Protectorate the Tswana chiefs [*dikgosi*] enjoyed almost unchallenged power' (Gillett 1973: 180).[2] Such statements reflect the British policy of leaving the *dikgosi* to govern their respective *merafe* with minimal interference until some forty-five years after the establishment of the colonial state.

The extensive practice of indirect rule over such a long period of time amply demonstrates the capacity of the *dikgosi* and the hierarchies of their respective *merafe* to keep the population in the societal fold. Nevertheless, in due course the relationship between the *dikgosi* and the colonial administration became more and more ambivalent and at times riddled by serious conflicts. Although the authority of the *dikgosi* and the strength of their polities still enabled the British to run the protectorate at minimal administrative and financial cost, the *dikgosi* were increasingly perceived by the British as dictatorial, operating highly autocratically in relation to their subjects. The trend on the British side in relation to their possessions was, by contrast, to introduce Western principles of legal rationality and state of justice. These strongly conflicting orientations came out fully around 1930.

For example, in 1929 an important resident commissioner stated in his diary: '[The *dikgosi*] practically do as they like – punish, fine, tax and generally play pay hell. Of course their subjects hate them but daren't complain to us; if they did their lives would be made impossible' (Parsons and Crowder 1988: 4). Other contemporary statements by representatives of the colonial administration similarly portray these rulers as rather autocratic. For example, a resident magistrate stationed in the Bangwaketse capital of Kanye reported that *Kgosi* Bathoen II of the Bangwaketse (r. 1928–69)

> is very obstinate and inclined to be antagonistic in matters connected with the Administration ... Morally, Bathoen is rather a low type of native ... being legally married to an educated woman, and at the same time living openly with his concubine. He is disinterested in matters beneficial to the tribe unless he, personally, can benefit thereby, and considers everything from his own pecuniary standpoint. His councillors are young and inexpe-

2. This is patently testified to in all the accounts I have collected among the Bangwaketse about the long reign of *Kgosi* Bathoen II (r. 1928–68). *Kgosi* Khama III and his son, Tshekedi Khama, are the other two most outstanding examples of the growth of royal power in the context of the protectorate (see Parsons 1973; Crowder 1987; Wylie 1990).

rienced headmen of the Communist type; he takes little heed of his older and more reasonable men.[3]

Furthermore,

he is very selfish. If he requires labour for his own work, such labour is forthcoming, but if for the benefit of the Tribe he is apathetic.[4]

The autocratic tendencies of the *dikgosi* were of course very much a product of their privileged and protected position within the colonial state, reflecting indeed the British dependency upon the ways in which they had expanded their networks of power and captured vast subject communities into the structures of the colonial state (see preceding chapter). Furthermore, the range of executive powers of the rulers of the Tswana *merafe* selected and privileged by the British increased steadily as the political economy of the protectorate developed. Since it 'was an explicit policy that the British Government had no interest in the country north of the Molopo ... except as a road to the interior' (Sillery 1974: 77), the Tswana were informed that they would have to bear the costs of the protectorate themselves. A hut tax system was thus enforced,[5] from which the *dikgosi* benefited substantially since they received a 10 per cent share of whatever they collected, over and above funds received from a number of other sources.[6] Significantly in the present context, the *dikgosi* retained their 'customary' privileges, including the mobilization of age regiments

---

3. Report on Chief Bathoen from Resident Magistrate to Ag. Resident Commissioner (Mafeking), Kanye, 4 June 1935 (BNA: S. 433/11).

4. Report on Chief Bathoen from Resident Magistrate (Kanye) to Ag. Resident Commissioner (Mafeking), Kanye, 9 January 1936 (BNA: S. 433/11).

5. Such a 'hut tax' system was commonly imposed in Central and Southern Africa as a measure to create a local demand for cash sufficient to attract black labour to European farms and to the mines. Although it has been argued that taxation in the Bechuanaland Protectorate was primarily imposed to cover government expenses (Schapera 1970), in effect it propelled large numbers of men in their prime to work in South African mines and farms. In other words, there was a close connection between extensive labour migration, and the generation of government funds for the running of the protectorate. Schapera quotes official sources, which state, for instance, that 'the wages earned by these [mine] workers are by far the main source of income in the district and without this money trade and tax collection would be almost at a stand-still' (Schapera 1947a: 157).

6. These sources included various payments from Europeans. 'The most lucrative were annual "subsidies" for prospecting and other concessions ... [plus] "stand rents" for traders and blacksmiths' (Schapera 1970: 76). Moreover, the *dikgosi* imposed taxes on the migrant workers, and occasionally levied charges for particular purposes, such as the financing of public buildings (Schapera 1970: 75). On several occasions, Tswana *dikgosi* exploited the system of labour migration more directly. For instance, 'according to Kgatla tradition, chief Lentswe, who was then at war with the Bakwena, actually sent a newly-formed regiment of young men to Kimberley to work for £8 each, the money being spent on arms and ammunition for the tribe' (Schapera

(*mephato*, singl. *mophato*) and draught power for the cultivation of their large fields, as well as the receipt of hunting spoils (*sehuba*), 'thanksgiving' corn after harvest from every household (*dikgafela*) and, most important- ly, all the unclaimed stray cattle collected in their respective territories (*matimela*).

All the wealth thus aggregating in the royal household was customar- ily justified by the virtues associated with the *kgosi* as *motswadintle* ('the one from whom good things are coming', see Gulbrandsen 1995 and Chapter 5, this volume). By right, therefore, he should be rich – ideally as the guarantee of everybody's welfare. His wealth was also seen by his subjects as a major condition for his independence and incorruptibility as a ruler. However, as the British contributed strongly to reinforcing the *dikgosi*'s powers, the *dikgosi* were not dependent on extensive networks of power by dispensing cattle widely for establishing cattle clientship (cf. Chapter 1). At most, their resources were used to ensure the support of their especially important political retainers in relation to the royal cen- tre. Moreover, as labour migration to South Africa provided most ordi- nary families with a stable source of basic subsistence requirements (see Schapera 1947a), there was less need to dispense grain from the royal granary during times of poor harvest.

All this meant that the *dikgosi* retained a number of economic sources throughout the colonial era which facilitated the accumulation of wealth – mainly in the form of cattle – that progressively attained the *de facto* character of private property. The British became increasingly disturbed by the *dikgosi*'s expropriation of funds considered by the colonial power to be destined for 'tribal' purposes. They first attempted to separate the *dikgosi*'s 'purse' from that of the tribal treasury by establishing what was known as the Native Fund. In a major administrative reform dating from 1934, it was stated that '[the] chief could no longer impose tribal levies without written approval from the Resident Commissioner and without agreement of the tribe in the *kgotla*' (Colclough and McCarthy 1980: 25). Nevertheless, although this proclamation managed to a certain extent to separate public resources from those to be held by the *kgosi* personally, considerable uncertainty remained over what belonged to the tribe and what was the *kgosi*'s property. I shall pursue the issue of the *dikgosi*'s appar- ent avarice in the subsequent section.

The institution of a 'Native Fund' reflected a broader British concern about the *dikgosi*'s alleged abuse of power, a concern which should be seen

---

1947a: 26). Bathoen I sent an age regiment to the Transvaal, because many of them had noth- ing to pay tax with (Schapera 1947a: 153).

in the context of the colonial empire. First, after World War I, the British initiated a revision of their previous methods of indirect rule that was extended to the Bechuanaland Protectorate in the 1930s. Secondly, at this time there appeared very critical reports in Britain attacking prolonged neglect on the part of the Protectorate Administration that had resulted in stagnation, extreme backwardness and highly autocratic chiefs. It was argued, for example, that 'colonial authorities had failed to bring traditional institutions in Bechuanaland into conformity "with the essential requirements of a modern civilized administration"' (Picard 1987: 49). In addition to such broader concerns, the administration had experienced difficulties with *dikgosi*, seen to be incompetent or otherwise unsuitable for their office: the most serious of these concerned *Kgosi* Sebele II of the Bakwena, who was, as we shall see in the following section, dethroned by the administration and exiled to Ghanzi in the extreme west of the protectorate.

This was the beginning of a long-term process, lasting through most of the colonial era, by which *dikgosi* and agents of the colonial state repeatedly confronted each other over attempts to check the *dikgosi's* powers by means of radical changes in the principles of government of the *merafe*. I shall review some of the most important ones in order to identify processes and structural conditions that explain why the *dikgosi* nevertheless largely maintained – even in certain respects enhanced – their position as supreme authority figures and strengthened the structures of their respective polities.

The determination of the British to make radical reforms found a major expression in two proclamations issued by the high commissioner in 1934. These proclamations were both introduced by reference to the Order-in-Council of 9 May 1891 whereby 'the High Commissioner is empowered on His Majesty's behalf to exercise all powers and jurisdiction which Her late Majesty Queen Victoria at any time before or after the date of that Order had or might have within the territory of the Bechuanaland Protectorate'. It was conceded that proclamations issued by the high commissioner 'shall respect any native laws and customs by which civil relations of any Native Chiefs, tribes or populations under His Majesty's protection are now regulated'. There was, however, one important caveat: respect was to be accorded only insofar as native laws and customs were not 'incompatible with the due exercise of His Majesty's power and jurisdiction'.[7] Motivated by the experience of allegedly autocratic,

---

7. This and the preceding quotations are extracted from p. 1 in Proclamations No. 74 and No. 75 of 1934, by His Excellency the High Commissioner, the Bechuanaland Protectorate Native Administration Proclamation.

incompetent or otherwise unsuitable *dikgosi* – the most obvious case being the deposition of *Kgosi* Sebele II of the Bakwena, mentioned above (see Ramsay 1987: 39f.) – the resident commissioner argued that 'it is essential that we should legalise the position of the chief ... there must be provisions for the Government to recognise the Chief and his suitability for the chieftainship in the interest of the whole tribe'.[8]

The first proclamation (No. 74 of 1934) stipulated channels through which 'the tribe' might articulate dissatisfaction with their *kgosi* as well as proper procedures to hear the *kgosi*'s defence before the administration made its decision in such matters. The *dikgosi* rejected this and other provisions in the proclamations on the grounds that these provisions fundamentally disagreed with the Order-in-Council of 9 May 1891. As described above, this document authorized the high commissioner to legislate by proclamation; however, he was restricted by the condition that he should, I reiterate, respect *any* native laws or customs regulating civil relations (see Schapera 1970: 51). Thus, the new rules for the recognition and instalment of a *kgosi* were perceived as being in basic disagreement with the Tswana maxim *bogosi bo a tsalelwa, ga bo lwelwe* ('a man should be born for the kingship, not fight for it'). In cases of abuse of power or misconduct in office, it was argued, they had their own procedures: *Kgosi ke kgosi ka morafe* ('The *kgosi* is king by virtue of the tribe').

The *dikgosi* feared that they had now been relegated to the lower end of the colonial state hierarchy, supervised by and committed to report to the local resident magistrate. This was obviously intolerable for powerful figures who were accustomed to being recognized by their people according to the dictum *Kgosi ke modingwana, ga e sebjwe* ('The *kgosi* is a little god, no evil must be spoken of him') and whose authority was sustained by another important maxim: *Lentswe la kgosi ke molao* ('The *kgosi*'s word is law'). They had also been accustomed to relating directly to the high commissioner. In one of my conversations with *Kgosi* Bathoen II he stated that to him the resident magistrate was a foreign representative and 'not my superior' (cf. Picard 1987: 51).[9]

Furthermore, when the proclamation of 1934 mentioned above required the *dikgosi* to establish 'Tribal Councils' comprising named members with whom the *dikgosi* were obliged to consult, it conflicted both with a *kgosi*'s customary privilege to consult whomever he wanted and with his commitment to give due importance to the views of his subjects as expressed in the public sphere of the *kgotla* where the 'entire *morafe*' (i.e. all adult men) were entitled to participate. Both proclamations, if

---

8. Resident Commissioner C.F. Rey to the Bechuanaland Protectorate Native Advisory Council, Minutes of the Fifth Session, Mafeking, 10 July 1933, 12.

9. Conversation at Bathoen Gaseitsiwe's home in Kanye, January 1983.

fully implemented, would probably have undermined the popular forum of the *kgotla*, idealized by people as the place where all authority figures should make their operations transparent (see Chapter 8). The administration, however, saw the *kgotla* as patently open to manipulation by the *dikgosi* and thus conducive to their alleged exercise of autocracy.[10] They wanted to establish identifiable and thus accountable bodies that were less dependent on the *dikgosi*.[11]

The aim of ensuring legal-rational accountability was particularly apparent in the 'Natives Tribunal Proclamation' (No. 75 of 1934), which established that the courts of the *merafe* were to be divided into two classes of tribunals, designated as Senior Tribal Tribunals (presided over by the *kgosi*) and Junior Native tribunals. According to this system, ward and descent-group courts were no longer judged competent to pass legally binding sentences. The tribunals were to be composed of identifiable councillors selected from the Tribal Council and nominated by the *kgosi*, and the councillors were to be paid a fixed salary. The *dikgosi* refused to comply with the requirement to elect named members to the tribunals, rhetorically asking: 'If anybody is to be paid are we going to pay all the Chief's Councillors, which implies the whole tribe?'[12]

The *dikgosi* were obliged to ensure that written records of their proceedings were available for inspection by the local magistrate, in part to ensure adherence to the principle of equality before the law. It had been a common practice for quite some time to keep written court records, so the request was not in itself controversial. What provoked the *dikgosi* was the underlying intention to facilitate the appeal of cases from the Senior Tribunals, over which the *dikgosi* should have presided, to the local resi-

---

10. This need for ensuring a body thus militating against autocracy might well have had some justification in view of Crowder's rendering of *Kgosi* Tshekedi's ostensible motivation: 'Tshekedi's bitter opposition to the Proclamations was in part inspired by the implied limitations they would place on his power. He was most reluctant to share power on a formal basis with named councillors and judicial assessors. Apart from the resultant diminution of his authority he feared that his opponents would gain positions on the Council and the Tribunals. And indeed the new dispensation was to find favour among those members of the elite who had long sought to obtain a share in the governance of the Bangwato state, especially Simon Ratshosa and K. T. Motsete. But by effectively abolishing the *kgotla* as an administrative and judicial organ, the ordinary people would be excluded from participation in their own governance, a point Tshekedi made only too clear to them'. (Michael Crowder, *Black Prince: A Biography of Tshekedi Khama 1905–1959*, unfinished typescript, 1988: http://www.thuto.org/schapera/etext/classic/blpr.htm.)

11. In the words of the Resident Commissioner Rey: 'We wish to encourage a sense of responsibility among those who administer the affairs of the tribe generally or who administer justice in the tribe'. (Minutes of the Fifth Session, the Bechuanaland Protectorate Native Advisory Council, Mafeking, 10 July 1933, 12.)

12. See Minutes of the Fifteenth Session of the Bechuanaland Native Advisory Council, Mafeking, 10 July 1933, 13.

dent magistrate court. These provisions, which went together with the recognition of 'native laws and customs' only insofar as they did not contradict the legislation of the colonial power, epitomized the subjection of the *dikgosi* – both as legislators and as judges – to the administration.

Behind the strong resistance towards the proclamations lay also the fear of annexation: in the last session of the Native Advisory Council[13] at which the two proclamations of 1934 were debated, the following resolution was addressed to the high commissioner: 'This meeting of Chiefs and Councillors present on behalf of their respective Tribes of the Bechuanaland Protectorate records its protest and objection to the incorporation of their Territory into the Union of South Africa'[14] (see preceding chapter). *Kgosi* Tshekedi, regent of the Bangwato between 1926 and 1949[15] and always on the alert in relation to the question of annexation, had evidently been 'particularly alarmed by the similarities between the proclamations and the South African Native Administration Proclamation No 38 of 1927' (Wylie 1990: 113). Similarly, *Kgosi* Bathoen II of the Bangwaketse indicated in several of our conversations that 'we all saw the writing on the wall', but could do nothing at this stage except stating objections, since the council was advisory only.[16] The resident commissioner and the *dikgosi* (with the Tswana councillors) failed to reconcile their differences on the matter.[17]

The two most forceful *dikgosi* at the time, *Kgosi* Bathoen II of Bangwaketse and *Kgosi* Tshekedi of Bangwato, were the leading figures in further efforts to have the proclamations abandoned. In the typical Tswana

---

13. The Native (after 1949, African) Advisory Council was established in 1920 by the Colonial Administration in order to discuss the use of the recently established 'Native Fund' and to enable the *dikgosi* to articulate their views and discuss matters of common concern with the administration. At the same time the administration created the European Advisory Council on matters affecting the Europeans in the protectorate (see Schapera 1970: 57–58). In 1950 the Joint Advisory Council brought together the members of the two councils.

14. Bechuanaland Protectorate Native Advisory Council, Minutes of the Fifth Session, Mafeking, 10 July 1933, 34.

15. See Wylie 1990 for a very illuminating and comprehensive account of this 'African patriarch' and an analysis of the Bangwato during colonial times.

16. Especially conversations at Bathoen Gaseitsiwe's residence in Kanye, January 1980 and March 1985.

17. The resident commissioner closed the issue by stating disappointingly that 'the Chiefs have not understood either the purport of the proclamations or the intentions of the Government ... [That is,] to introduce an advance in the state of affairs as they exist to-day; they were not intended to perpetuate everything that existed, good or bad, merely because they happened to be Native custom' (Minutes of the Fifth Session, the Bechuanaland Protectorate Native Advisory Council, Mafeking, 10 July 1933, 33.). In his diary the resident commissioner wrote: 'the Chiefs put in a lot of damned silly proposals and fresh amendments which if accepted would have had the effect of killing the Proclamation. So I made them a short speech telling them how disappointed I was' (Parsons and Crowder 1988: 123).

manner, they brought their case to court, suing the high commissioner by invoking, among other things, precisely the same Order-in-Council of 1891 with which the proclamations had been introduced (see above). In particular, they claimed that the high commissioner had legislated in contradiction of the rights accorded their respective tribes by treaty with Great Britain. But the judgement lay in the hands of the British themselves: a special court was set up that ruled against the *dikgosi*, stating that a treaty could not prevent His Majesty from legislating, and that as a result the administration had 'unfettered and unlimited power to legislate for the government and administration of justice among the tribes of the Bechuanaland Protectorate'.[18] Thus although the *dikgosi* invoked the 'treaty' their ancestors had made with the British in support of their claim that the 'protection' was a matter of partnership,[19] the judgement made it utterly clear that the rulers of the Tswana *merafe* in the protectorate were subject to the orders of the colonial state.

However, as Wylie has observed (1990: 115), '[t]he administration's victory was symbolic' in the sense that it was never really implemented. For example, tribal councils and tribunals were only partially established; the *dikgosi* kept on the customary practices of consultation (*therisanyo*), particularly in relation to their selected councillors and the *kgotla*. The people at large did not experience any significant changes: they continued to respect the judgements made in descent-group and ward courts, which were occasionally appealed to the royal court, but indeed very seldom further to the British Magistrate Court.

This meant that the *dikgosi* continued to run their *merafe* in autocratic ways. Also, even though the colonial power had now firmly established that the *dikgosi* were under the full legislative authority of the colonial state, the British rarely interfered with their rule. In fact, 'the chief's right to legislate independently was still officially recognised; and, as in the past, the Administration often preferred to advise, not to order, him to enact measures it favoured' (Schapera 1970: 63, see also Jeppe 1974: 138). Furthermore, the minutes from the Bechuanaland Protectorate Native Advisory Council leave the strong impression of a generally cooperative relationship between the resident commissioner and the *dikgosi* (see Gabasiane and Molokomme 1987: 162–63). The controversies surrounding the proclamations of 1934 stand out, in many respects, as exceptional.[20]

---

18. Quoted in Picard 1987: 51–52.

19. Thus, during the Special Court proceedings, '[p]arallels were drawn between the roles of an ambassador (district commissioner) and head of state (the chief)' (Picard 1987: 51).

20. It might be argued that this notion of a rather laid-back administration is contradicted by its heavy intervention in the dynasty-centred turmoil among the Bangwato in 1949 when

It is therefore difficult to agree that 'a series of colonial proclamations and ordinances ... undermined the institution of chiefship' (Vaughan 2003: 28) or that 'the cumulation of multiple acts of British authority and the pervasive influence of commercialisation served to undermine the *morafe* as a system of rule' (Peters 1994: 42). As long as such claims are not substantiated by an examination of the real political impact of the proclamations on the authority of the *dikgosi* and the hierarchies of authority relations over which they presided, we cannot simply assume that the British right to issue proclamations had an undermining effect. First, the British often preferred, I repeat, to let the *dikgosi* legislate (see Chapter 1), and if they wanted to legislate themselves, the *dikgosi* were usually thoroughly consulted in the Native/African Advisory Council (see Makgala 2010: 60), as is abundantly evidenced by the extensive minutes from the meetings. Secondly, it can also be argued that proclamations might increase the *dikgosi*'s authority since they expanded the field of their exercising jurisdiction – an activity central to the reproduction and strengthening, as I argued in the preceding chapter, both of their authority and of their respective *merafe*'s sociopolitical order.

It is tempting to suggest, therefore, that in the long run the *dikgosi* triumphed in important respects. This point is underscored by the arrival of two new proclamations in 1943 by which both the tribal councils and the tribunals were abandoned. Moreover, 'the list of offences excluded from the jurisdiction of the Courts is now reduced to cases in which a person is charged with an offence punishable by death or imprisonment for life' (Hailey 1953: 226), a change which largely restored the authority of the *dikgosi* to its original form (cf. Ashton 1947: 239).[21]

The increasingly relaxed attitude of the British to implement reforms stipulated in the proclamations of 1934 which might be seen as the background of the prevailing uncertainty – virtually throughout the colonial era – about whether to hand the protectorate over to the Union of South Africa, militated against implementing a reform that would have implied substantial costs. More basically, as reflected in a British official assessment, in due course the British recognized that it was not a straightforward matter to impose radical changes on the indigenous institutions of

---

Seretse Khama, the heir of the *bogosi*, returned from England with an unexpected English wife. I take this case, which I shall address later in this chapter, to indicate how much was actually required before the administration exercised its power. This point is supported by their much more relaxed attitude in another case, also during the 1950s, in which the administration let *Kgosi* Molefi (allegedly a notorious alcoholic) misconduct the *bogosi* for years without applying the provision it now held for disposition (see e.g. ka-Mbuya and Morton 1987: 157–58).

21. Hailey (1953: 227) relates, for example, that the courts of the *dikgosi* have 'unlimited civil powers' and also impose severe sentences in criminal cases.

authority. In view of the colonial state's heavy reliance on these institutions, it is no surprise that it was criticized in a major review of 'native administration' in the British African Territories: 'in insisting on the establishment of a formally constituted Tribal Council and of Tribunals of a fixed composition to take the place of traditional trial by Kgotla, the law made a radical change in some of the most characteristic institutions of the Bechuana people … the people saw a menace to a system of trial to which they were as deeply attached as is a Briton to the procedure of trial by jury' (Hailey 1953: 222).[22]

With some important exceptions, which I shall address subsequently in this chapter, the pragmatics of extensive indirect rule lasted virtually to the end of the colonial era as suggested, for example, by a highly critical observer of *dikgosi*'s rule during the final decades of the colonial era, Botswana's former state president, Quett Masire. He clashed with *Kgosi* Bathoen II at several occasions (see below) and came to realize how protected *Kgosi* Bathoen actually was by the British, reflecting their need 'to reinforce the powers of the chief in their method of controlling, or ruling, the people' (Masire 2006: 259). That there was a mutuality of dependency – despite the ambivalence, tensions and conflicts over the years – between the *dikgosi* and the British is curiously demonstrated in Illustration 3, where the two major Tswana figures of the colonial era – Bathoen and Tshekedi – are expecting the British royal family in British uniforms.

Finally, this also means that in relation to the conflicting relationship between the distinctive Tswana principles of politico-jural practice and the ideals of Western bureaucratic rationality, the British made great concessions to the Tswana mode of exercising authority. Their rationale for considering another line – that of reconstructing indigenous institutions in line with modern principles of bureaucracy – was obviously reflecting a sense of losing control of the *dikgosi*, being perceived as increasingly autocratic and even exterior to the order of the colonial state.

Yet, in due course, they certainly came to realize that to challenge these authority figures more than necessary might well make them – and their institutions – less integral to the colonial state, creating potentialities of forces of a rhizomic kind. The central point is that the strengthening of the authority of the *dikgosi* under the British wing was, as I have explained, much a matter of the progressive expansion of the power structures radiating from the *bogosi* of the officially recognized Tswana *merafe*. As suggested by Hailey's statement above, the British came to realize how strongly these

---

22. In fact, the administration itself, when revising the proclamation in 1943, had already recognized and accepted the fact that it was unfeasible to give effect to these particular provisions (Hailey 1953: 222).

Illustration 3. Regent of Bangwato, *Kgosi* Tshekedi (left) wearing a uniform of Royal House Guards Blue acquired by his father (*Kgosi* Khama III) during the three *dikgosi*'s visit to England in 1895 (Parsons 1998) and *Kgosi* Bathoen II (right) of Bangwaketse wearing the scarlet uniform of the Dragoon Guards presented to his grandfather (*Kgosi* Bathoen I) by Queen Victoria on the same visit to England. They are seen waiting for the arrival of the British royal family in the Bechuanaland Protectorate on 17 April 1947. Courtesy of Associated Press.

structures – which they had themselves contributed much to reinforce – were anchored in the indigenous cultural construction of authority, upon which the British always remained dependent. In other words, the British had to realize that with the extensive practice of indirect rule, they had given rise to a colonial state highly dependent on instruments of government of mainly a pre-modern kind, whose major agencies fiercely resisted transformations towards modern, legal-rational institutions. However, at the same time, the *dikgosi* depended upon the colonial state as a source of power – a mutual dependency prevailed in important respects (Ashton 1947: 238). Only in some few instances did the colonial administration intervene with harsh measures in relation to Tswana royal centres, examples of which we shall see in the following sections.

Issues of Modernity vs Traditionalism at Tswana Royal Centres

The *dikgosi's* distaste for Western, 'rational' principles and practices of government and administration of justice does not mean that they entirely held on to customary practices and resisted modernity in all respects. On the contrary, as already suggested in Chapter 1, in their actual political practice within the frame of their institutions, many of them represented driving forces in implementing many smaller and larger reforms in positive response to the progressive arrival of Western modernity. The three *dikgosi* on the cover of this volume – Bathoen I, Khama III and Sebele I – featured already before the turn of the century in Western suits which soon became the daily dress of men of authority in the *kgotla* context. This practice was adopted under the impact of the evangelizing missionaries as a prominent sign of being a civilized (*tlhabologo*) person. And in such guise the *dikgosi* took, I recall, Britain with great positive surprise when traveling across the country for gaining popular support for their cause (see Chapter 1, cf. Parsons 1998). The acceptance of many aspects of Western modernity became even more apparent as the succeeding *dikgosi* acted upon the European impacts in ways that are reflected in Schapera's (1970) notion of 'tribal innovators'.

Nevertheless, in Tswana parlance there is a distinction between *Setswana* (Tswana ways) versus *Sekgoa* (the ways of the white people). Comaroff and Comaroff (1991: 212ff.) have examined thoroughly the complexity of the *Setswana-Sekgoa* interface in the case of the Southern Tswana in the South African context. In the present case I am concerned with the significance of these categories in terms of distinct and conflicting political identities at the royal centre of Tswana polities. That is, conflicting political identities entailing factionalism challenging the ruler.

In the preceding chapter I discussed the conflicts surrounding the *dikgosi's* acceptance of Christianity and the presence of an evangelizing missionary, forming a church congregation. At an early stage, I explained in Chapter 1, there was clearly a Christian vs. non-Christian divide surrounding the royal office. This was particularly dramatic in the case of Kgama III and his father Sekgoma I before Kgama defeated his father and initiated his long reign in 1875. At such an early stage, there were also serious conflicts related to the arrival of Christianity at the royal centres of the Bakwena and Bangwaketse (Gulbrandsen 1993a: 49ff.) as well as the Batawana (Tlou 1973, 1985: 99ff.). Moreover, there then emerged conflicts between missionary churches and so-called independent Christian church movements that appealed to many people because of their greater tolerance toward indigenous ritual and social practices. These movements were often fiercely rejected by not only the *dikgosi* but also to a great extent the ruling elites because of, I recall, the perceived threat represented by these movements to the order on which they all basically depended. For these elites, it meant that they in due course had to comply with and impose the missionary requirement of abandoning important ritual and social practices.

However, popular resistance towards the abandonment of polygyny, *bogadi* ('bridewealth') and *bogwera* (initiation ritual) as well as prohibitions of alcoholic drinks prevailed as an undercurrent in many contexts. These changes had thus to be enforced continuously by Tswana rulers (Schapera 1970: Ch. 9). But in a few instances the *dikgosi* did not readily comply with missionary requirements of doing so. One intriguing case is that of *Kgosi* Sebele II of Bakwena (r. 1918–31).

Sebele inherited a major conflict from his father (*Kgosi* Sechele II, r. 1911–18) who came seriously at odds with a major section of the Bakwena elite, including members of the royal family, who were closely associated with the church of the London Missionary Society when he allowed the Anglican Church into Kweneng. In a bid to replace *Kgosi* Sebele a faction of the Bakwena elite made every effort to portray him as a reactionary 'traditionalist' whose rule would impede progress in the *morafe*. In addition to accepting the Anglican Church *Kgosi* Sechele II had, shortly before he died, restored polygyny, rainmaking and the initiation ceremony of *bogwera* in 1916.[23] When *Kgosi* Sebele II succeeded him in 1918 he went further and encouraged circumcision (Schapera 1970: 209). This won him sufficient popular support to quash the combined efforts of the LMS-associated elite and the British to get rid of him.

Yet the conflict remained. Sebele was not a unifying person, but rather provoked reactions in the Kwena elite and became increasingly at odds with

---

23. This faction was also attacking Sechele II and his heir for breaking the monopoly of the London Missionary Society and welcoming the establishment of an Anglican church.

colonial officials. Charles Rey, the heavy handed Resident Commissioner (see above), was, as soon as he was in office, determined to have him replaced. So he did in 1931 and Sebele was exiled to Ghanzi in the remote western part of the protectorate (Parsons and Crowder 1988: 71f.). While the rebellious faction, LMS and the British had many grievances against him, according to Ramsay (1987: 40) *bogwera* featured at the end as the central issue. It was alleged that boys had been forced to participate and 'Rey greatly exaggerated the bogwera disorder in his reports [to London] and gained permission to banish Sebele. His younger brother, Kgari was installed which initiated tensions and conflict in the royal office which, in fact, still prevails.'

On the face of it, at least, this case reveals highly different cultural orientations. In one particular respect *Kgosi* Sebele might be identified as a neotraditionalist, as the LMS-faction considered him to be. Nevertheless, like other *dikgosi* of the time he imposed a number of laws and regulations and other 'modernising' initiatives inspired by the colonial encounter, which would place him squarely among those *dikgosi* whom Schapera has called 'tribal innovators' (Schapera 1970). Ramsay (1987: 35) explains, for example, that Sebele

> imposed strict standards on the building of houses and fences and had streets kept clean and well maintained. Rubbish pits replaced garbage heaps. He told his people to bury their dead in the graveyard rather than their lolwapa. New roads were built, and dam constructions were attempted.... [H]e welcomed the establishment of the Scottish-Livingstone Medical Hospital... [H]e also wanted Molepolole [the capital of the Bakwena] to be a source of entertainment for the BaKwena. Sebele's reign was marked by many public events, some traditional and some not. And on such occasions, Sebele was apt to show off his skills as a pianist, singer and ballroom dancer.

Moreover, Sebele was not at all opposed to Western knowledge, being well educated and indeed the first Bakwena *kgosi* to be literate in English. For the LMS-faction – and subsequently the British – these aspects of his person were not significant. He was obviously under fire because he had marginalized politically that faction and sustained his father's decision to take away the church monopoly from the LMS – it had virtually featured as a state church.[24] But, note, neither Sechele nor Sebele permitted the

---

24. As I explained in the previous chapter, several dikgosi gave a missionary church monopoly because it was instrumental for keeping spiritual control over the population, especially in the context of socalled independent churches. But, in some instances, a second missionary church was permitted as, for example, in the case of the Bangwaketse, where the Seventh-day Adventist Church was accepted when it was promised to build a hospital in the royal town of Kanye, which they did (1921). But 'independent' churches were always rejected until Botswana's independence when freedom of religion was declared.

establishment of socalled independent churches, sympathetic to ritual and social practices condemned by missionaries (see previous chapter). What is more, Sechele's and Sebele's acceptance of the Anglican Church had obviously secular reasons: in order to balance the pressure they felt from the senior *dikgosana* who were closely attached to the LMS, they promoted junior *kgosana* and commoners as their advisors. To undermine the LMS church monopoly was obviously seen by these rulers as conducive to this end (Ramsay n.d.: 1).

The general point I want to make is this: apart from the time after the first arrival of evangelizing missionaries, it is hard to trace any clear-cut traditionalist-modernist divide amongst the Tswana elites. That is, there was no enduring 'traditionalist'-faction of political significance amongst Tswana elites that prevailed by virtue of taking a principal – and persistent – stand against European ways (*Sekgoa*). It is true that in some very few cases – the present one probably being the most significant – missionary requirements spilled into elite politics where such a divide was construed by people identifying themselves as 'progressive' and enlightened. But only with temporary political significance. Thus, although the Bakwena have been riddled by dynastic conflicts and succession disputes ever since *Kgosi* Sebele II was exiled and his younger brother, Kgari (r. 1931–62) enthroned, the factions have not taken the form of a permanent traditionalist-modernist divide despite the fact that *Kgosi* Kgari ruled the Bakwena autocratically for some thirty years with substantial British support (Ramsay n.d.).

One important condition for this is, as I shall elaborate in Chapter 4, to be found in the discursive field of the *kgotla*. While the *dikgosi* were fiercely rejecting the British request to modernize Tswana judicial and political practices and institutions, the content of cases brought to court and political issues debated in the *kgotla* required more and more acquaintance with *Sekgoa* ways. In order to boost authority and gain respect as speakers in the *kgotla*, it was always important to be eloquent and demonstrate command over 'deep' Setswana, especially in order to invoke convincingly the normative repertoire of *mekgwa le melao ya Setswana* ('*Setswana* custom and law'). But the substance matter of court cases and political issues increasingly required also knowledge of the larger, modern world, which an ever increasing part of the elites gained by secondary education in South Africa. Competence in *Sekgoa* ways was important for being recognized as an enlightened (*go sa matlho*, litt. 'with eyes') and civilized (*ba rutegile* – 'with knowledge') person. This kind of competence was – and still is – crucial because *Sekgoa* ways involved categorization and valuation significant for processes of hierarchization in the discursive field of the *kgotla*. This has, of course, been an important aspect of the reproduction of Tswana elites' hegemonic domination under changing historical circumstances.

In other words, the discursive field of the *kgotla* encouraged cultural orientations that often combined *Setswana* and *Sekgoa* in mutually reinforcing rather than conflicting ways. I propose that this trend was of considerable significance to the high degree of unity amongst the dominant elites in the country at the time of Botswana's independence in 1966. There is, however, one important exception to this: during the two decades preceding the independence, major conflicts and tensions developed in the royal centres which were apparently a matter of a traditionalist-modernist divide. But only apparently. To this we now turn.

Contradictions of Power, Rank and Wealth: Towards the Formation of a Postcolonial Ruling Group

If the relationship between the *dikgosi* and the British was ambiguous, the *dikgosi's* relationship to certain sections of their subjects was no less so. I have not in mind their relationships to subject communities of ethnic minorities, which often remained unambiguously repressive. I am referring to their relationship to people of power and wealth located at the royal centres. With the emerging prospect of decolonization and the establishment of an independent nation-state, it became increasingly clear that opinion was highly divided as to what kind of nation-state was desirable. This disagreement manifested itself most profoundly in the relationship between the *dikgosi* (together with some of their retainers) on the one hand and an emerging category of educated and commercially oriented people on the other.

I have already argued that the authority of the *dikgosi* and the structures of the *merafe* were strengthened in important respects during the colonial-era transformations. The question here is how these developments can be reconciled with the emergence at Botswana's independence of a ruling group which not only assumed full control of the postcolonial state but also absorbed most of the power thus far vested in the *dikgosi*. In this section I shall explain how particular interfaces between the internal dynamics of the *merafe* and certain external forces during the latter part of the colonial era caused transformations resulting in a gradual reduction of the *dikgosi's* dominant position and gave way to people who took a leading role in the formation of a post-colonial state.

These transformations were, I propose, propelled by two major contradictions. On the one hand, market forces now started working more powerfully, giving substantial momentum to the formation of a category of commercially oriented people. Although this group can be traced back to the nineteenth century (see Parsons 1977), it took off after World War II in ways that gave rise to a major contradiction between the *dikgosi* for whom 'wealth is power' and the up-and-coming young entrepreneurs. On the other hand, these young men were often among the best educated. They were well informed about African liberation movements and the prospect of decolonization, exposed to Western liberal ideas and ultimately spearheaded a postcolonial ruling group in a republican democracy: that is, a political order that contradicted the patrimony of the Tswana *merafe* in most respects, and in which the *dikgosi* could envisage no positions of political importance. Nevertheless, the relationship between the two sides was always ambivalent since, across the divide, the hegemonic significance of 'Tswanadom' prevailed: although occasionally seriously at odds with the *dikgosi*, most of those who challenged them and ultimately assumed full control over the nation-state in 1966 were to a great extent firmly anchored in the discursive field of the *kgotla* and attached to their natal group in the hierarchical order of the *merafe*. These post–World War II transformations will subsequently be examined in the context of the larger world: the expanding political economy of South Africa; the changing policies of the British ('development', 'democratization' and 'decolonization'); and the ever-present threat of annexation to either of the neighbouring racist regimes.

Despite the fact that the British contributed little to economic development in the protectorate, after World War II there emerged (as mentioned above) an extremely important category of people with a commercial spirit which formed an important part of the embryo of a postcolonial ruling group. This group recognized two major sources of power, both rooted in Tswana culture: knowledge and wealth. They were not only quick to take advantage of the emerging possibilities for secondary education; above all, they saw the potential of cattle to generate wealth. Cattle possess the unusual property of being at once the means of accumulation, production and exchange. In 1954 an abattoir opened in Lobatse, which allowed Batswana livestock producers to enter the then expanding world beef market (see Hubbard 1986: 118f., 250f.). The establishment of the abattoir in turn sowed the seed for the eventual arrival of a group of people motivated and strong enough to stand up to the *dikgosi*. In the following chapter I shall argue that the commercialization of cattle production and trade was the major condition for the formation of a coherent postcolonial ruling group.

During the 1950s there thus emerged industrious individuals who did not necessarily begin with a large herd but started converting education and subsequent salaried employment or profit from commercial arable farming into cattle wealth. Commercial arable farming was now supported by a small agricultural extension service and the introduction of tractors, which substantially increased productivity; the surplus from this activity could easily be used to buy livestock. With investment in the drilling of underground water sources (see Gulbrandsen 1996a: Ch. 10), good pastures in virgin areas could support large herds.

Let me, at this point, briefly relate the following politico-economic context: the protectorate was at this time a labour reservoir for the South African mines and farms. The large majority of families were short of essential productive means (especially cattle) in order to work on a subsistence level of farming. And with demands for tax and other levies, they depended heavily on labour migration (see Schapera 1947a), yet their income rarely gave any surplus to enter such spirals of accumulation as indicated above. This pattern in fact continued until foreign labour migration declined substantially in the 1980s (Gulbrandsen 1996a: 195ff.). The political significance of this pattern of adaptation is apparent: the vast majority of the population was linked up with an economic source which sustained – irrespective of recurrent droughts – their subsistence and contribution to the tribal treasury.

As I explained in Chapter 1, the Tswana make a close connection between power and wealth which attempts to make sense of the highly unequal distribution of cattle as corresponding to inequality of authority in the hierarchical order of the *morafe*. This emphasizes the perception of the *kgosi* as the wealthiest individual – as I was often told, 'the *kgosi* should have most of everything'. By contrast, people who managed to increase their herd substantially were generally met with suspicion, even to the extent of being accused of occult practices damaging to other people (Gulbrandsen 1996a: 182).

The rise of commercially oriented young people who successfully exploited new opportunities to enlarge their herds through the entrepreneurial ventures mentioned above presented a particular challenge to authority figures, the *dikgosi* in particular. I explained in Chapter 1 how *Kgosi* Khama III of Bangwato (r. 1873/1875–1923) implemented measures to counteract potential conflicts arising from the contradiction between rank and ascribed authority on the one hand and the emerging opportunities for commercial ventures on the other. Yet by the late 1940s these measures seem to have had only a limited effect. This was particularly apparent in the attempt by the Bangwato royalty to monopolize trade, transport and such industries as grain milling. However, royal privileges were challenged more and more by the category of educated people, mentioned above, who now attempted to use their income from teaching, or from employment as clerks, shop assistants, mechanics and so on, to finance self-employment – and, further, the acquisition of cattle herds. There followed further resentment against their ruler – the acting *Kgosi* Tshekedi – owing to his alleged exploitation of regimental labour to benefit his own economic endeavours (Parsons 1987: 125; Wylie 1990: 200). In the following section, we shall see the political consequences of the progressive rift among the Bangwato, which manifested itself in conflicts between *Kgosi* Tshekedi and this emerging 'middle class' who increasingly subscribed to liberal virtues of Western democracy.

I had not lived with the Bangwaketse for long before I was regaled with stories of *Kgosi* Bathoen from people who had achieved financial success. The following case is illuminating:

> Radiputi was a senior member of his *kgotla*, a person who people recalled as extraordinarily hard working, good with cattle and open minded: 'He always wanted to try new things'. In the 1950s he bought a bus and wanted to start a bus service between Kanye and the railway township of Lobatse. What then followed was told to me by many different people, and I relate it in the words of one of his friends: 'Then *Kgosi* Bathoen became angry – he became in fact very jealous towards Radiputi. He wanted to have the road for himself. And Bathoen just told him to keep away, starting a bus service himself. Radiputi had to retreat and start a far less attractive service between Kanye and Mafeking. Bathoen said that "this is my road, so just get away". You know it was not really right of him to say that, because although in a certain sense we say that everything in the *morafe* belongs to the *kgosi*, this does not mean in such a personal sense – in the sense that he could take the advantage of it and run his own business. That was not right!'

Asking why Radiputi did not complain to the British magistrate, I was told, 'Oh, no, then life would have been made impossible for him here in Kanye. To be sure, the *kgosi* could have made tricks on him or influenced other people secretly to do damaging things towards him. That would have been to play with fire!'

And even if he had dared to approach the magistrate, he might not have got any support from that quarter if we are to believe the former state president, Quett Masire, who devoted a full chapter to his troublesome relationship with *Kgosi* Bathoen in his memoirs (Masire 2006). As mentioned in the previous section, the magistrate apparently acted protectively towards the *kgosi* in order to uphold the authority on which the magistrate himself depended. Masire was an industrious individual who attempted to install a mill where people could purchase his services, 'only', I was told, 'to find that Bathoen was secretly trying everything to get people to keep away from it'. I received detailed accounts from a retired senior agricultural officer of the difficulties *Kgosi* Bathoen allegedly made for young people who wanted to engage in commercial farming. Yet he himself took a keen interest in adopting more productive farming techniques. I was told a story – which I subsequently received in many versions – about how *Kgosi* Bathoen had taken a huge piece of land away from Masire. As the first master farmer in the Bangwaketse, Masire bought a tractor and got hold of a large piece of land for cultivation, which allegedly 'Bathoen took … away from him – just because he was very, very jealous, he could not bear anybody else ploughing large fields and getting more crops for themselves'. Masire gives his own version of the incident in his memoirs (Masire 2006: 27) and offers other examples of how Bathoen allegedly punished him for his 'impudence'.

Along with such stories of *Kgosi* Bathoen's apparent attempts to take advantage of his royal trading privileges, there were complaints that he exploited age regiments for his own benefit. The group of people I am referring to here told me how he 'could command us to cultivate his fields without any compensation'. His supposed appropriation of tribal wealth is substantiated by the specific allegation that he 'grabbed tribal boreholes, actually belonging to the people'.

Masire concludes his chapter 'Chief [*Kgosi*] Bathoen and my views on chieftainship' with the following statement:

> Time after time he had frustrated me and my fellow tribesmen in our daily lives. He tried to control us and our commercial activities and prevent individuals from innovating unless he personally approved. All this had a profound effect on how I saw the future of the country. If Batswana were to really experience freedom to develop their own potential, I felt that we had to find ways of democratising the society at the local as well as the national level. (Masire 2006: 29)

As this suggests, the endeavours pursued by Masire and other young, commercially minded and often educated people across the country reflect a strong desire to engage in politics. It is these individuals whom Adam Kuper identified as the 'new men' (Kuper 1970: 54ff.). They took an interest in the spending of public resources and confronted the *dikgosi* in the *kgotla* about the use of tribal funds. They were also strongly opposed to the *dikgosi*'s extensive exploitation of regimental labour and people's draught animals for the cultivation of their fields (the proceeds of which were then used to enlarge the royal herds, which *dikgosi* still treated as their private property rather than a tribal resource). People like Masire were well informed and eloquent speakers in the *kgotla* and called for transparency in decision making. Their criticism was thus pronounced in the *kgotla*, to which they sincerely adhered. They made a fundamental distinction between the discursive field of the Tswana *kgotla* – which in its authentic form they idealized as 'democratic' despite the exclusion of women – and the perceived autocratic rule of the *kgosi* (see Chapter 6).

It is important to stress here that these people's engagement in the *kgotla* was not mainly a matter of confrontation. They were well acquainted with the rules of the *kgotla*, and with its ideals of harmony (*kagiso*) and efforts to reach consensus (*dumela*). In order to win their case, their arguments had to be both substantial and unprovocative. Hence their differences with the *dikgosi* did not mean that they were regarded by everyone else with disapproval. The nationwide significance of their combined adherence to Western modernity as well as indigenous political virtues is confirmed by the presence of such 'new men' even in small and remote villages. Writing about the village of Kule in Western Botswana, Kuper relates that there were people

> who command the respect of the villagers as men-of-the-world and people who take daring economic initiatives, buying lorries or setting up stores. These are men who left the Kalahari for long periods in South Africa or South West Africa [Namibia], returned with capital which they invested in new ways, and who began to deal with the outside world in new terms. In the 1960s they organised some communal cattle-drives to the Lobatsi abattoir, so that the villagers would not have to sell at low prices to local buyers … They brought the Democratic Party to the Kalahari, and with the election of District Councillors from the villages in 1966, their political role was institutionalised. They were now the main mediators between district authorities and the villagers. This immediately gave them positions of greatly enhanced authority in the villages. (Kuper 1970: 62)

Kuper's account anticipates the issue which springs from the present section and to which I now turn: how did this category of 'new men' come to front the major transformations of decolonization and the establishment of a ruling group that took control of the postcolonial state? The question is intriguing for two main reasons. First, while the *dikgosi* preferred a federal state in which the *merafe* retained much of their political integrity, the new men made the case for a democratic nation-state in which the *dikgosi* would be stripped of most of their executive powers. With reference to the question raised at the end of the previous section, this might well be seen as a political divide between 'traditionalists' and 'modernists' – or better: between *Setswana* and *Sekgoa* political ideas, practices and institutions. Secondly, however, although the emerging political-cum-economic elite were often at odds with the *dikgosi* and certainly represented a force for political and economic modernization, they retained the very close adherence to the *kgotla* already described. This pattern suggests a considerable ambiguity in the relationship between the modern state and the Tswana *bogosi* which, as we shall see in subsequent chapters, still prevails.

The Ngwato Political Crises and their Repercussions

The transformations that ended in decolonization and the establishment of a democratic republic were of course driven by diverse processes. Yet there is one famous event which did much to trigger these transformations, namely, the crisis among the Bangwato following the return from England of the heir to the *bogosi*, Seretse Khama, with a white wife. Since the story is so well accounted for in many publications,[25] I shall only recapitulate those aspects that are particularly relevant to the present issue.

When Seretse's father, *Kgosi* Sekgoma II, died in 1925 after a three-year reign, Seretse was an infant. The person next in line, Tshekedi,[26] therefore assumed the *bogosi* as regent (*motshwareledi*). Seretse was in due course sent to England for law studies, where he fell in love with and married an Englishwoman, Ruth Williams. Preparing for his return, he informed his uncle Tshekedi about the marriage. This was shocking news, and Tshekedi reacted furiously. To select a wife and marry without even consulting the acting *kgosi* and his *rrangwane*[27] was unheard of. Tshekedi ordered Seretse to explain himself in the royal *kgotla*. In a series of meetings he was confronted with an audience of thousands,[28] coming from all over the *morafe*. Tshekedi complained that

> [t]he thing that cuts deep into my heart is that this tribe of ours is heading for disintegration … My work in the past twenty two years, the plans I have for the tribe's future welfare, all now go overboard because of a white woman 6000 miles away who has never seen Africa in her life … A chieftainness who could not speak the language would be completely stumped. The coming of a white woman can lead only to chaos and disintegration.[29]

---

25. See Parsons et al. 1995: 75; Williams 2007; cf. Robins 1967; Dutfield 1990.

26. See Wylie (1989) for a beautifully written account of Tshekedi, examining in depth and context his long reign.

27. All the agnatic descendants of his grandfather *Kgosi* Sekgoma I referred to as *rrangwane* (classificatory junior paternal 'uncles') constituted the senior elderhood of headmen (*dikgosana*) of the *morafe*. (For a genealogical charter of the royal descent group see Parsons et al. 1995: xv.)

28. The accounts range from 3,500 to 10,000 (Parsons et al. 1995: 81).

29. 'Tshekedi Tells of Duties Awaiting White Chieftainness', Johannesburg Star, 4 July 1949, Ellenberger Papers, quoted in Wylie 1990: 186.

During the first series of meetings, which lasted for five days, there was substantial support for Tshekedi's hardline requirements: divorce and submission to the customary procedures of royal conjugality. However, during the subsequent weeks and months, when discussions about the matter continued in most quarters, support for Tshekedi diminished considerably while several factors in Seretse's favour became evident. Tshekedi's self-serving, autocratic regime had made him unpopular among much of the population, who now began to harbour suspicions that he had a hidden agenda. For example, it was alleged that he had made secret attempts to gain control of the royal wealth to which Seretse, the actual heir, was entitled (cf. Parsons et al. 1995: 80). There was even speculation that Tshekedi had used 'witchcraft' to induce Seretse to marry the English-woman. Such suspicions, along with people's fear that they would lose their rightful heir and be forced to remain under Tshekedi's rule, succeeded in turning the crisis into factional politics. Secret meetings – according to customary practice – were held during the night. Sections of the aristocracy changed sides, apparently seeing this as an opportunity to become makers of the new *kgosi* and thereby to regain the prominence they had lost under Tshekedi's autocratic regime.

All this meant that 'popular allegiances had shifted massively' when thousands of men assembled in the royal *kgotla* again in June 1949 (Wylie 1990: 185). The split within the aristocracy – and the translation of the issue into a dynastic dispute – became evident once a major figure among them told the *kgotla* that 'The talk is no longer about the wife but about chieftainship [*bogosi*]. Sekgoma's son,[30] not Khama, is the chief. Seretse is the chief. I say, let the woman come and their children shall succeed'.[31] At this point Tshekedi responded with what has been identified – probably correctly – as the greatest blunder of his life: he asked the 'sons of Sekgoma' who rejected the marriage to come forward. This produced the support of precisely nine royal *dikgosana*. His mistake was to introduce a practice that appeared to premise the decision in the *kgotla* on a vote. Seretse was quick to exploit this radical break with custom and made a similar appeal. First he asked all those who supported him to sit quietly and those opposing him to stand. Only forty persons stood. He then appealed to those in support of him to stand. The vast majority of the gathering of thousands of men rose up and declaimed in unison the major Setswana formula of blessing: '*Pula! Pula! Pula!*' ['rain!']. This concluded the matter as far as most of the Bangwato (including many among the elites) were concerned. Clearly, Seretse had won overwhelming popular support as

---

30. Referring to Seretse's father, the late *Kgosi* Sekgoma II.
31. Ellenberger, report on June 1949 *kgotla*, Ellenberger Papers, Rhodes House Library. Quoted in Wylie 1990: 184.

the rightful *kgosi* of the Bangwato, despite his marriage to an Englishwoman.[32] Tshekedi and the tiny group of senior *dikgosana* remaining loyal to him sought refuge in the neighbouring (and senior) *morafe* of Bakwena.

Yet, although the people had made it abundantly clear that they wished to see the rightful heir to the *bogosi* enthroned, Britain chose to intervene, thereby setting in motion one of the less admirable episodes in its imperial history. Alarmed by the possibility that the South African government would be provoked by such a mixed marriage – especially when it involved such a high-profile person as the heir to the largest kingdom in the protectorate – the Labour government in London decided to banish Seretse and his wife (see Parsons et al. 1995: 80ff.). They were exiled to England during the years 1950–1956.[33]

The Bangwato *bogosi* was thus left without an incumbent; the district commissioner acted as a representative for about four years. Thereafter the administration forced through the appointment of Rasebolai Kgamane as regent. Rasebolai, second in rank after Tshekedi and a close ally of his, was associated with the anti-Seretse faction and failed to gain popular support. As indicated above, the conflict was apparently a dynastic one from the outset. However, there is no doubt that the pro-Seretse faction benefited greatly from the fact that Tshekedi had antagonized different sections of the population over the years. First, as I explained in the preceding chapter, he had taken punitive measures against minority groups (the Kalanga in particular) in various outlying villages. Second, his rule was considered repressive by most sections of the rank-and-file population – especially the women, who broke with 'their ancient political exclusion ... [and] were prominent in the massive demonstrations in Seretse's favour' (Wylie 1990: 200). Third, a substantial section of the aristocracy had been alienated by Tshekedi's autocratic exercise of power, which had denied them their rightful political influence. Fourth, as already described, the young educated men were strongly opposed to Tshekedi's perceived authoritarianism.

Now, from the composite pro-Seretse camps there crystallized a group of people whose aim was to have Seretse returned and installed as the

---

32. It is noteworthy that except for *Kgosi* Bathoen II (Tshekedi's close ally), 'the representatives of the other Bechuanaland "tribes" all accepted Seretse as a kgosi', and so did the representative of the Resident Commissioner (Parsons et al. 1995: 83).

33. This decision was made against the recommendation of the resident commissioner. Moreover, the British set up a Judicial Inquiry, which concluded that the *kgotla* procedures had been conducted correctly and that Seretse himself was a 'fit and proper person' to be installed as *kgosi*. The Labour government in London, which ostensibly had hoped for a different outcome to the inquiry, could not reveal in public the real reason for the banishment (the objections of the neighbouring racist states), and kept the report secret (Parsons 1987: 127).

kgosi. These were mostly educated young men: Seretse's age-mates, many recruited from his own age regiment (*mophato*). After their experience of Tshekedi's harsh regime, Seretse's fearless rejection of his uncle's demand for divorce amounted to a major act of liberation. Seretse's advocacy of his case in the *kgotla* did not constitute an attack on 'true' Tswana values; rather, it targeted the abuse of power by Tshekedi and his retainers. There are no detailed records of his speech, but probably it already addressed the theme that would become so important in his mature political rhetoric: the attempt to bridge 'authentic' Tswana virtues and Western liberal ideas.

At this time, Seretse's banishment had become world news and attracted particular attention in England. A pro-Seretse group went to London and appealed in public to have the banishment lifted. The Conservative government reacted by stating that the banishment was permanent and subsequently ruled that Seretse, Tshekedi and their descendants were to be barred from ever succeeding to the chieftainship of the Bangwato. This triggered a violent response, with gatherings of the royal *kgotla* breaking out in bloody riots.

In subsequent years the British made a number of unsuccessful attempts to restore peace and order. In 1956 they finally gave in and permitted Seretse to return. The official capitulation undoubtedly reflects a major change in the British attitude to South Africa after a tough apartheid government had taken over. Moreover, the era of decolonization was under way and it was time to 'democratize' local government. The Bangwato remained uncooperative as long as Seretse was kept in exile. Shortly before Seretse's return, he and Tshekedi met in London and made peace. Their reconciliation (*tetlanyo*) was manifested during the public reception of Seretse on his arrival in Francistown, from where he went on a parade of triumph to Serowe with thousands of people along the route to celebrate the homecoming of their *kgosi*. Allegedly, '[f]lashes of lightning followed each other and clouds erupted ... "Seretse's home and it's raining," screamed the mob. "Seretse has brought the pula [rain]"' (Parsons et al. 1995: 150). A more powerful symbol of the blessings brought by the presence of the senior grandson of *Kgosi* Khama III (the Great) could hardly have been imagined. Yet Khama was to become only the *de facto* and not the *de jure kgosi* of the Bangwato, since the British had made it a condition for his return that he, his children and Tshekedi should renounce the *bogosi*.[34]

34. At this time Rasebolai Kgamane was to be installed as an African Authority (1953–1964); he was followed by Leeapetswe Khama (1964–1974) and Mokgatsha Mokgadi (1974–1979) (both denoted Tribal Authority). In 1979 Seretse's eldest son, Ian Seretse Khama, was enthroned as the *kgosi* of Bangwato – enthusiastically received by the people. However, he has

The British were amazed by the effect of Seretse's presence on political and social life, which quickly moved into more peaceful waters (Parsons et al. 1995: 159). However, this change was also attributable to the reconciliation of Tshekedi and Seretse, their renunciation of the *bogosi*, and the establishment of the tribal and area councils[35] (in which uncle and nephew took the leading roles, as chairman and vice-chairman respectively). The turmoil following Seretse's marriage had given rise to electoral bodies that assumed much of the power previously vested in the *bogosi*.

The drive towards independence was of course increasingly influenced by the pan-African anticolonialism so recently nourished by all the traumas surrounding Seretse's deportation. As mentioned above, Seretse was seen as a symbol of liberation; his marriage to a white woman and his antiracist rhetoric added a further dimension to the symbolism. This dimension was undoubtedly reinforced by the international attention given to the reaction of the neighbouring racist regimes. The marriage – as a love marriage – had a further significance which should not be underrated: Bangwato women celebrated him as a force against the undesirable patriarchal controls to which they were subject.

Nevertheless, the contradictions which triggered all the conflicts among the Bangwato preceding Seretse's return had not evaporated by the time of his reconciliation with Tshekedi. Although the latter took up leadership in the tribal council, he was against electoral democracy. While both Seretse and Tshekedi were determined to be emancipated from Britain and to establish an independent state, the former pushed for a republican democracy in which the *merafe* had a clearly subordinate position. Tshekedi (along with most of the other *dikgosi*) wanted a federal state in which the *dikgosi* retained most of their power, thus leaving each of the *merafe* with considerable autonomy.[36] These differences correspond significantly to the prevailing conflict between, on the one hand, the roy-

---

not yet assumed the *bogosi* on a daily basis, as he was the lieutenant-general of the Botswana Defense Force and has been Botswana's vice-president since 1998.

35. The establishment of 'tribal councils' had been on the British agenda since the 1934 Proclamation discussed above. As we have seen, for a long time they declined to impose it because of the resistance of the *dikgosi*. The British raised the issue once more in the early 1950s; this kind of council was first established among the Bangwato as a result of the turmoil which I explain in this section.

36. *Kgosi* Bathoen had proposed as early as 1952 to establish a legislative council which, he argued, 'would ensure continuity in policy in the Protectorate, where colonial officers with different ideas kept coming and going. A legco [legislative council], he said, would also give the general population a feeling that through their representatives, they were involved in framing laws which applied to them' (Gabisiane and Molokomme 1987: 164–65).

al privileges fiercely guarded by Tshekedi and his retainers[37] and, on the other hand, the new men's vocal demand for commercial freedom.

Owing to the composite character of the anti-Tshekedi camps, they never formed a coherent political movement. During the period without recognized leadership, the *morafe* descended into chaos, to the extent that popular protest found its expression in violent riots (Wylie 1990: 196). On the one hand, the various camps were united in their desire to have Seretse return to the throne. In the eyes of his aristocratic supporters he held out the promise of a new role for them as *kgosi* makers and, as already suggested, a return to prominence and power in the royal *kgotla*. To the growing number of educated people of the younger generation caught by Western ideas, on the other hand, he exemplified the *modern* man who spoke of freedom, democracy and antiracism as essential to development and progress. Such achievements depended on Western 'rational' knowledge and thus formal education. Among these new men Seretse was celebrated for daring to challenge authoritarianism and thus came to be seen as capable of curtailing patriarchal controls on their entrepreneurial endeavours. For example, as soon as he returned in 1956, he involved himself in the commercialization of livestock production, which he attempted to construe as 'popular' by speaking of 'a cattleowning democracy' (Parsons et al. 1995: 204). His rhetoric on development, addressed to 'all the people', emphasized his identity as 'our true *kgosi*': one who fulfilled the ideal of the *motswadintle* ('the one from whom good things come', see Chapter 5).

Intriguingly, Tshekedi might also be seen as a Janus-faced figure embodying both 'modernity' and 'traditionalism' but in a highly different sense. For example, he too was eager to engage in commercial enterprises, simply because they offered new possibilities for him to accumulate wealth in order to remain the wealthiest and most powerful person in the *morafe*. And, as we have seen, he did so by exploiting his 'customary' privileges: he manipulated 'tribal' politics and funds, exploited regimental labour and applied repressive measures to his personal advantage. For the subject communities within the 'reserve' who had been ruled by Tshekedi with a heavy hand, Seretse's antiracist and antitribalist stand had attractive connotations of liberation from the dominant royal centre of the Ngwato. Finally, it should be noted that the Tswana concern themselves greatly with the specific attributes of their authority figures. In a 'praise' poem Tshekedi was portrayed as 'a man-eater ... [who] swallows people'

---

37. Among others, they defended as their hunting territory a vast area into which upcoming commercial cattle owners want to expand by drilling boreholes.

(Schapera 1965: 242). Seretse, by contrast, was seen by most people as an exemplary person with a particularly good character (*botho*) with great impact on people because of his *seriti* ('dignity', 'charisma').

The Development of Party Politics:
Towards the Formation of a Postcolonial State Embryo

Although the contradictions examined in the preceding section were present in all the *merafe*, nowhere else did they manifest themselves with such profound consequences as among the Bangwato. This is best illustrated by the contrasting example of the Bangwaketse. Their ruler, *Kgosi* Bathoen II, guarded his privileges jealously yet largely maintained legitimacy among his people (see Chapter 6 below). His main challenge came from the 'new men'; even so, he managed quite successfully to isolate them and their ventures. Early in his reign *Kgosi* Bathoen had shown his muscles against a faction that had gained power in the royal *kgotla* of his predecessor. His exercise of authority in the *kgotla* – especially in his court judgements – was recalled with great appreciation by very many of my interlocutors, according to whom he was unbiased towards people of power and wealth yet at the same time protective towards the rank and file. His wide-ranging support, at least among all the people of the royal town of Kanye, was, as we shall see, testified to after he abdicated in 1969, joined the major opposition party, Botswana National Front (BNF) and stayed for election to Parliament – through which he defeated none other than the epitome of 'the new men': Quett Masire (who at this time had become the vice-president of Botswana).

With the time for decolonization rapidly approaching, there was as yet no strong *popular* drift away from the *bogosi* and towards a republican state based on Western principles of liberalism and democracy. What little determination there was to get rid of the *bogosi* or at least to adapt it to republican requirements was in evidence only among those with strong entrepreneurial ambitions or adherents of Western-style enlightenment, democracy and liberalism. However, even in these circles there was, if not approval of the extensive *executive* powers of the *dikgosi*, then certainly considerable respect for them as authority figures, considerable appreciation of the *bogosi* and, in particular, a recognition of the *kgotla* as central to people's lives. As we shall see in subsequent chapters, this ambivalence still prevails – some forty years after the *dikgosi* were stripped of their executive powers – among supposedly 'modern' elites.

Against such a background it is understandable that the postcolonial status of the *bogosi* and its incumbents turned out to be the single most difficult issue in the preparations for a new state constitution. The critical nature of this issue was clearly recognized by the high commissioner, who stated at a final stage of the constitutional negotiations that 'the Chief's power could not continue on the same basis as in the past' and that it was up to the *dikgosi* to decide whether they would participate fully in terms of the capacities now assigned to them: 'the future welfare of the country depended upon their decision'[38] – nothing less. That the high commissioner was not overstating the case is amply confirmed by the biographies of two of the key Tswana figures in these negotiations, Seretse Khama and Quett Masire.[39] The resident commissioner at the time has recently asserted that the precarious relationship between *dikgosi* and political leaders proved to be 'the most difficult of all' the conflicts to resolve before agreement about the new Constitution could be reached (Fawcus 2000: 130). It was in this context that political developments in the Bangwato *morafe* became critical, affecting in particular the subsequent career of Seretse, whose importance had become clearer after the death of Tshekedi in 1959.

The situation in the Bangwato proved to be a breeding ground for political parties. In 1959 the first of these, the Bechuanaland Protectorate Federal Party (BPFP), was founded. This party recruited a number of prominent teachers and other intellectuals in addition to some 'traditional' elite members. Ideologically, echoing the wave of nationalism sweeping across Africa, the BPFP wished 'for the unity of the tribes of Bechuanaland and to promote political, economic and social emancipation'. The BPFP was also critical of certain aspects of traditional rule and the power of the *dikgosi* (Nengwekhulu 1979). Nevertheless, the 'party tried to link the evolution of a parliamentary system with a strong but non-partisan traditional administration … [it] called for a chamber of chiefs with the entrenchment of "traditional" authority as a part of a federal system of government' (Picard 1987: 136–37). In this vein, its leader Raditladi – who until then had been a trade union leader in the small township of Francistown and also a central figure among the younger generation of the Bangwato elite in Serowe – drew on young militants from peripheral urban areas as well as those associated with the discursive universe of the *kgotla*. In the context of such apparent contradictions, Raditladi alienated potential supporters in both constituencies and a number of key people withdrew their support; the party soon dissolved.

---

38. Notes on a meeting between Her Majesty's High Commissioner and the Chiefs at Lobatsi on 14 April 1964 to discuss constitutional and political developments related to the role of the Chiefs. (BNA, I/6/2986, H. 145 II, reproduced *in extenso* in Parson 1990, the quotations extracted from p. 434)

39. See especially Parsons et al. 1995: 212ff., Masire 2006: 72ff.

Whereas the BPFP constituted a fairly moderate movement, the Bechuanaland People's Party (BPP), founded in 1960, had a much more radical agenda. Ideologically, the party was rooted in South African antiracist movements, particularly the African National Congress (ANC) and the Pan-African Congress (PAC); it was widely recognized as a liberation party that enjoyed the support of the Organisation of African Unity (OAU). In fact, the party established several branches within South Africa in an attempt to win the support of Tswana migrant workers temporarily resident in that country. For obvious reasons, this was fertile ground for their ideology, which advocated nationalism and a transfer of power to the indigenous people. Migrant workers suffered so much under the harsh apartheid regime that many of them 'took an active part in the politics of the ANC ... and later of those of the PAC' (Nengwekhulu 1979: 54). Furthermore, 'internally, the returning migrant workers also had a profound effect on the birth and the growth of political parties. They formed the nucleus of the budding working class which was in turn the major driving force and mainstay behind the formation of the BPP' (Nengwekhulu 1979: 55). However, this working-class nucleus did not give rise to any class movement beyond the small railway shantytowns of Francistown and Lobatse. The vast majority of those who clearly constituted a proletariat went to the mining and industrial centres of South Africa to find work. But when these migrant workers returned to the protectorate, they almost always settled with their families in their natal villages. Here they found themselves once more subject to the hierarchical order of the *morafe* and the authority of the *dikgosi*.[40] The leaders of the BPP, composed mainly of radical intellectuals of the younger generation, took a strong stand against 'traditionalism', denouncing it 'as a narrow, exclusive, totalitarian outlook, communal chauvinism, stagnating conservatism, nepotism, patronage, belief in mythical hereditary divine right of precedence.'[41]

Since the BPP had declared that they wanted to abolish the institution of the *bogosi*, the *dikgosi* and their retainers mounted a strong counterattack. In this effort, the *dikgosi* were supported by the British, who were alarmed by the radical nationalism of the BPP on the grounds that it would seriously antagonize South Africa and thus militate against a smooth transition to independence. They therefore 'instructed the chiefs to deny the BPP permission to hold meetings and rallies in their areas. This had the effect of denying the BPP the opportunity of popularising its policies in those areas, with the result that the party was not popular in the rural areas' (Nengwekhulu 1979: 63).

---

40. See Schapera 1947a. This pattern still prevailed in the 1970s (Gulbrandsen 1996a).
41. Quoted by Parsons et al. 1995: 190.

It was in this context that Seretse felt himself compelled to enter party politics. Seretse and his associates naturally had no quarrel with the BPP's strong antiracist line. Neither were that party's attacks on the *dikgosi* and the *bogosi* discordant with Seretse's vision of a republican state. But he did not approve of their uncompromising and confrontational approach. Like the British, he had no wish to provoke the South African government at this critical stage. Moreover, people like him felt no solidarity with a party that was associated with socialism and even communism; in particular, the emerging class of entrepreneurs did not see how such a party could ever be conducive to their interests.

The activities of the BPP in the Bangwato triggered a series of debates in the royal town about the desirability of party politics in the *kgotla*. Whereas those associated with the 'traditional' camp did not want this kind of activity in the *kgotla* at all, Seretse believed that 'the only way to fight the party is … to form ourselves into a body which would expose the falsehoods put out by the People's Party'. Alarmed by the BPP's progress, he saw the need for 'a political party to guide [the nation] down the pathways of parliamentary democracy'.[42] In due course he started exploring the possibilities of forming a new party. Seretse had at this time developed relationships with people like Quett Masire within the context of the Advisory Council and the Legislative Council (Legco),[43] of which they were both members. Masire (2006: 48ff.) relates in his memoirs that the growing concern about the BPP among the African members of these councils manifested itself in November 1961 when Seretse called upon them to discuss the matter. They soon reached a unanimous agreement about establishing a new political party. Early in 1962 the Bechuanaland Democratic Party (BDP)[44] was founded with Seretse as its leader.[45] He attacked the BPP's alleged 'radicalism' and advocated Western principles of liberal democracy. This made him and his party particularly attractive to the British, who now saw him as an important – if not indispensable – ally in their struggle to secure a peaceful journey towards independence (see Fawcus 2000: 87).

---

42. Quoted in Parsons et al. 1990: 194.
43. The Legco had been created by the British in 1960 after long-term pressure for a legislative body with indigenous representation. As suggested above, in 1952 *Kgosi* Bathoen II had already raised the matter of establishing a council with legislative authority which the British, dissatisfied with the slow progress of establishing Tribal Councils, rejected as 'premature'. The demand for establishing such a council gained momentum in the late 1950s, at which time the British were more sympathetic to the idea (see Gabisane and Molokomme 1987: 167ff.).
44. At Botswana's independence it was renamed Botswana Democratic Party.
45. See Parsons et al. 1995: 194 ff.

Marginalising the *Dikgosi*:
Paving the Way for a Modern Nation-State

In 1963, during the run-up to decolonization, the resident commissioner invited the *dikgosi*, the political party leaders, and European and Asian representatives to a conference in order to review the Constitution. It was at this point that the respective positions of the *dikgosi* and the elected politicians became a major issue. At this time the BPP was riddled by internal conflicts. The party therefore participated with representatives that were divided amongst themselves and did not play any significant role during the proceedings.[46] It was Seretse and Masire, backed by the British, who took the lead in the negotiations. The debates centred on two major issues: the choice between a tribal/federal state and a centralized republican one; and the status of the *dikgosi* in a putative republican state.

As mentioned above, Tshekedi had proposed a federal state. After his death this option, which the other *dikgosi* favoured, was persistently advocated by Bathoen. Their rationale was obvious: in a federal state composed of the Tswana *merafe* most of the executive powers would remain on the level of the *morafe*, and their own position would be less vulnerable to marginalization. Those who proposed a centralized republic were equally concerned to transfer executive and legislative powers from the *dikgosi* to elected parliamentary members. With the establishment of the BDP, there were now prospects of political developments at the state level and hence also of republican state institutions. The British strongly supported these aims. Among their concerns was a purely financial one, namely, the disproportionate expense of maintaining a federal state given the poverty of the country. Furthermore, without a strong centralized government, potentially hostile neighbouring countries were perceived as posing more of a threat (Fawcus 2000: 131–32). But this kind of government could not coexist with a structure that retained most of the autonomy of the *merafe*, since the latter would readily promote 'tribalism' – indeed, it was even likened to the development of Bantustans in apartheid South Africa (Parsons et al. 1995: 238) – and thus hinder the creation of a strong nation-state.

With both the British and the elected members of the Lecgo totally against their preferred solution, the *dikgosi* eventually recognized that the battle for an all-encompassing federal state had been lost. The *dikgosi* of

---

46. In due course, the BPP sidelined itself by boycotting what it alleged to be the *dikgosi*-cum-British-controlled Advisory and Legislative Councils. Its further destiny was as a marginal political party, 'embroiled in major internal conflicts ... resulting in the breaking up of the party into factions in 1964' (Nengwekhulu 1979: 65).

the southern *merafe* then proposed a federal development in the southern part of the protectorate that would be separate from the northern part (the stronghold of party politics). This alternative was presented in a meeting between the resident commissioner and the *dikgosi*, who had been invited to present their concerns about 'the role of chieftaincy in the process of constitutional development'. Once again the British rejected their suggestion, apparently for the same reasons as they had vetoed the previous proposal of a federal state.[47]

Having had to give in on the issue of federation, and already frustrated by their participation in the advisory and tribal councils, where the elected members formed the majority, the *dikgosi* were naturally deeply worried about their potential status in a republican state. Well aware of the strong position the *dikgosi* still held in the *merafe*, both the British and the BDP took pains to argue carefully with them. The two positions were in many ways fundamentally irreconcilable, reflecting the contradiction between a premodern polity and a legal state. This contradiction was stated clearly by the resident commissioner:

> [i]f they wish to retain their influence as Chiefs it seems essential that they remain aloof from politics and reasonably neutral. As Chiefs, they are required constantly to arbitrate and settle various sorts of disputes and problems and to do this effectively they must be seen to be fair and impartial. If they go into politics they will get into a position perhaps of violent dispute with some of their subjects and immediately the image of the Chief as an impartial arbiter will be obscured. I remain of the opinion therefore that the Chiefs should keep out of politics.[48]

In other words, the customary authority of the *dikgosi* had to be restricted to fit a Western legal state system based on the principle of division of power. In the attempt to resolve this conundrum the commissioner ruled that, on the level of the *morafe*, the councils should replace the *kgotla*, but the latter could still be used for 'the expression of Tribal opinion on one or two large issues'. At the same time, the *dikgosi* must 'come to terms with their Tribal Councils and Executive Committees ... they must work with them'. Nevertheless, the frustrations of the *dikgosi* remained. According to *Kgosi* Bathoen, '[t]he Chiefs were forced to defend themselves all the time in that Council but their voice carried no weight ... The way the Chiefs had been treated in the Council had been most surprising and painful'. *Kgosi* Bathoen – highly critical of the elected members of the

---

47. Extensive records of this meeting are reproduced in Parson 1990: 407–14.
48. Referred to in ibid., 419–20.

councils ('new and young men'), who he alleged were out of touch with people – argued that '[t]hey had not emerged from the *Kgotla* and they wanted to do away with the *Kgotla*. They had emerged from behind the scenes. One could see the writing on the wall for the Chiefs'.[49]

The humiliation experienced by the *dikgosi* reflects the gulf between decision making based on the recognition that those involved are of unequal significance and decision making by majority vote in which each vote carries an equal weight. As I shall elaborate in Chapter 6, there were two radically different discursive fields: one highly consensus oriented and reconciliatory, the other competitive and conflict generating. This inherent contradiction was aggravated by the fact that many of the *dikgosi* did not always satisfy the discursive requirements of the new political arenas, because they were not as knowledgeable as the young educated men about the 'modern' issues being brought up in the Advisory Council. Paradoxically, perhaps, the reverse was not true: the politicians had no problem in engaging in the discursive field of the *kgotla*. Indeed, the latter still draw first on the symbolic wealth of this field to enhance their legitimacy (see Chapter 5); the ruling party uses it manipulatively to depoliticize policy issues (see Chapter 6).

If this contradiction was manifest in the context of the protectorate, it became acute at the level of the prospective independent state. In this context the *dikgosi* made their case for a privileged position within the Legislative Assembly of the Parliament. Their initial proposal was that the *dikgosi* should constitute the senate: this was rejected. They then put forward the idea of a House of Chiefs with the power to block legislation, much like the British House of Lords (see Proctor 1968: 61ff.). This proposal was equally unworkable because it contradicted the basic tenets of a republican democracy. The Constitutional Conference finally resolved the issue by proposing that Parliament should include a House of Chiefs composed of the *dikgosi* of the eight recognized *merafe* as members ex officio and four subchiefs of districts outside these *merafe*. This house would have an advisory function vis-à-vis the Legislative Assembly on matters 'concerning tribal affairs, including customary law, tribal organisation and tribal property'. The House of Chiefs would thus operate separately, with no legislative power; the *dikgosi* were 'not ... eligible for election to the legislative body' (Fawcus 2000: 123).

Despite consenting to this proposal at the 1963 Constitutional Conference, the *dikgosi* were still unhappy and appealed to the British to have the Constitution revised. Fawcus, who by then had become the queen's com-

---

49. Referred to in ibid., 411.

missioner, gives an extensive account of his discussions with the *dikgosi* in April 1964, when he tried to convince them that their participation in politics would quickly undermine their authority as *dikgosi*. He argued that 'even if they all were elected they would have only eight members of an Assembly of thirty-one. They could not therefore form a government, and their position would be dangerous because they could frustrate the majority party. If they did so, the majority party would be determined to destroy the chieftainship as it had done in Nyasaland. The resultant friction between the chiefs and political leaders would do great damage to the country' (Fawcus 2000: 138ff.). An agreement was ostensibly reached whereby 'the chiefs recommitted themselves to the constitutional white paper ... abandoned their claim of standing for elections to the Legislative Assembly and accepted their obligations to serve in the House of Chiefs ... A serious crisis had been averted' (Fawcus 2000: 144–45). In the process, however, the *dikgosi* had exacted concessions in the form of an amendment that permitted the House of Chiefs to interact more fully with the Legislative Council, the president and cabinet members. The issues to be dealt with should not be restricted to 'tribal affairs': the House of Chiefs should be authorized to comment on any draft bill, to consult any minister on any matter, and also to discuss any issue within the executive and legislative authority.[50]

Nevertheless, shortly before the final constitutional talks in London in 1966, the House of Chiefs (which by then had come into operation) passed a vote of no confidence in the new Constitution. As Masire relates, the *dikgosi* were 'planning to sabotage the London talks'. This prompted Seretse to approach all the *dikgosi*, asking: 'So, could we hear the views of your tribes on the draft constitution?' One by one – according to Masire, who was also present – they admitted that 'they had not consulted their tribes' (Masire 2006: 75). It was then suggested that they should carry out such a consultation among their respective people and report back. Still concerned to stop the *dikgosi* from finding their own allies and hence undermining all the efforts to gain support for the new Constitution, Seretse reacted by offering the presence of his ministers at the *kgotla* meetings 'to explain to people how the new constitutional proposals were going to work' (Masire 2006: 76–77). This proposal was accepted, and he sent his ministers on a nationwide tour of the *dikgotla* in order to explain the new Constitution. To all appearances, they received broad popular support.

50. See Bechuanaland Constitutional Proposals, Presented to Parliament by the Secretary of State for the Colonies by Command of Her Majesty, June 1964 (London: Her Majesty's Stationary Office), 12; Fawcus 2000: 144.

Always careful to present their arguments in a nonconfrontational and conciliatory manner,[51] they managed to avoid conflicts with the *dikgosi*, who finally gave in.

The last major transformation of the colonial era was thus to subject the authority of *dikgosi* to the republican state. As I shall explain in Chapter 4, in addition to being constitutionally recognized as *ex officio* members of the House of Chiefs, the eight *dikgosi* were subject to the state president by virtue of the Chieftainship Act, in which their duties were stipulated as being those of civil servants.

Intriguingly, these legislative measures meant that the potentially disruptive *dikgosi* were now co-opted and subject to the structures of a nation-state just as previous *dikgosi* – the epicentre of Tswana polities – had 'always' attempted to co-opt and subject potentially disruptive forces (cf. Chapter 1). Masire recalls the efforts made by the new government 'to set the minds of the chiefs in the right direction … and [make them] feel part of the whole process'. Much later, when Nelson Mandela came to talk to Batswana political leaders during South Africa's debates on a new constitution, he was urged to give Bantustan leaders their due just as the Batswana politicians had done with the *dikgosi*: 'you should not drive them into the hands of the Nationalist party' (Masire 2006: 76).

That the doctrine of inclusivity was central to the new political regime is testified by Seretse's attempt to recruit *Kgosi* Bathoen to the BDP. The latter declined, but after he had abdicated in 1969 and then defeated Masire during the 1969 election, 'Bathoen wanted Seretse to form a "Government of National Unity" and include him' – an offer which Seretse rejected (Masire 2006: 53). For some years Bathoen was one of two MPs of the opposition party (Botswana National Front); nevertheless, in due course he was offered the position of president of the Customary Court of Appeal, which he accepted, thus becoming a civil servant under the rule of Quett Masire (who by then was state president).[52]

In fact, Bathoen was now virtually the only force for the opposition among the *dikgosi*. Since Tshekedi's death, Seretse had become the unchallengeable authority among the Bangwato (and thus among a sizeable

---

51. Although there were certainly many BDP members who wanted to 'put the chiefs down as soon as possible' (Masire 2006: 49), a careful gradualist approach was persistently applied, in the expectation that they would in due course 'die a natural death'.

52. Curiously, it might be noted here that at an early stage Bathoen realized Masire's personal capacities; albeit identifying him as a young 'radical', Bathoen 'co-opted' him as his deputy in all matters relating to agriculture. Their working relationship continued until Masire annoyed the *kgosi* severely by bypassing the cattle trade monopoly controlled by the Bangwaketse Tribal Administration (see Morton and Ramsay 1994: 34–36).

section of the protectorate's population). After *Kgosi* Kgari's death in 1962, the Bakwena had only a weak regent, Neale. The British apparently kept the succession pending in order to prevent a Bakwena *kgosi* from emerging as a political force: since the Bakwena are recognized as the most senior of the eight Tswana *morafe*, 'a strong Bakwena chief would have a legitimate claim to national leadership' (Vengroff 1977: 56–57). The rulers of the three smallest *merafe*, Barolong, Batlokwa and Balete, had no potential for mobilization. Pulane, the female regent who ruled the Batawana under the threat of a hostile faction, would hardly have come out against a constitution proposed by the British because it was largely thanks to their support that she remained in office (Murray 1987: 116ff.). The only exception was the young Bakgatla *kgosi*, Linchwe, who had been installed in 1963. Allegedly, Linchwe soon 'sensed that the BDP was an "anti-chief" party' (ka-Mbuya and Morton 1987: 159) and was therefore attracted by the BPP. However, at this time the BDP had got a strong footing among the Bakgatla, and *Kgosi* Linchwe backed out. He continued for some time to contemplate party politics – until the state co-opted (and 'exiled') him by appointing him as Botswana's ambassador to the United States.

The successful co-optation of the *dikgosi* is intriguing in view of the authority which most of them still held, yet quite comprehensible if we examine the prevailing conditions. Perhaps most importantly, by this stage what Makgala (2006) has appropriately denoted 'the Khama-factor' had come into force. During the first national election in 1965, the BDP manifested itself as a tremendous political machine – which ran campaigns by visiting virtually every village in the country – in the powerful hands of Masire (now the BDP secretary general). He worked very closely with Seretse (the chairman) to develop a didactic approach in order to convey their vision of development and universal welfare to the entire population. A particular case was made for national unity and a strong centralized state government (Masire 2006: 56ff.).

It was in this context that Seretse played a vital role as an agent of transformation. Since Tshekedi was dead, Seretse remained as the uncrowned *kgosi* whom the BDP-based ruling group readily accepted in his new role as leader of the whole nation. The House of Chiefs was not an issue here. Rather, the enormous symbolic wealth attached to his royal ancestorship – he was the eldest grandson of *Kgosi* Khama III (the Great) – had a significance extending far beyond the confines of his own *morafe*. With his distinguished lineage, his remarkable charisma and his bravery in standing up to Tshekedi and the British, he possessed a nationwide appeal which no other Tswana person of authority could rival.

The complex symbolism attached to Seretse proved to act as a transforming and unifying force. For although he represented virtues of liberation, modernity and progress, he still remained the big *tautona* (the big lion); he soon 'learnt to exploit the essential ambiguity of his position in politics and society – as a mediator not only between modernity and traditionalism and (through his marriage) black and white, but also between aristocrats and commoners' (Parsons et al. 1995: 162). When he appeared all over the country in the context of the *kgotla*, his rhetoric of progress and universal welfare evoked the notion of the idealized *kgosi* as selfless custodian of the common good (see Chapter 5). We should recall that in Tswana thought, this custodianship grants a *kgosi* considerable freedom to abandon outdated practices and to act pragmatically within a changing historical context, as long as people perceive his actions as conducive to the common good, progress and prosperity. As we have seen in Chapter 1, it was by virtue of this special concession that some of the *dikgosi* introduced Christianity and discontinued some of the most central ritual practices.

Finally, it was much due to Seretse's outstanding authority, in particular amongst the Bangwato, combined with his dedication to establish a centralized nation-state that he became the key figure in a process that retrospectively should be decisive for Botswana's postcolonial development: achieving state control over all the mineral resources in the country which were mainly vested in the *merafe*. This has, of course, been a major condition of state control over the tremendous wealth which the diamond industry started to generate only some few years after the independence (see following chapter).

Significantly, the issue of mineral rights featured very low on the agenda prior to decolonization. Although a number of small mines had been opened during the colonial period, they were in operation only for limited periods and very few of them were in operation at independence. These mines were run with capital provided by foreign interests, generally based in the Union of South Africa, and they were closed as soon as the short-term profits dropped (Gulbrandsen 1996a: 78). Masire (2006: 199) recalls that during the preliminaries to independence, 'there was not even a rumour of any possible minerals other than in the Bangwato area'. He relates that Seretse went to 'his tribe in 1965' and presented the view 'Let us share any wealth we find underground with the whole nation, irrespective of where it is found'. They fully consented to this matter. He subsequently achieved the consent by the other *dikgosi*, although hesitantly by *Kgosi* Bathoen II (Masire 2006: 199–200). Parsons et al. (1995: 255) assert, highly intriguingly, that by independence (1966) '[t]he discovery of the Orapa diamond pipe [in the Bangwato territory] was known in great secrecy by a few individuals, including Harry Oppenheimer, the head of De Beers-Anglo American Corporation and Seretse himself'.

As Leith (2005: 60) points out, Khama made his choice between the nation and his *morafe* which 'was made clear in the BDP Election Manifesto for 1965' where it was stated that 'it will be the policy of the BDP Government to negotiate with all parties concerned the take over of the country's mineral rights by the Central Government'. The 'parties' were predominantly the *merafe*, the 'owners' of all the 'tribal' lands that were kept in custody by the *dikgosi*. The president set in motion a political debate on the issue and together with his ministers toured the country, meeting *dikgosi* and addressing *dikgotla* on the subject. He appealed to national sentiments and argued that the government was the body best able to encourage and control mining development. All of the chiefs and tribes in the *kgotla* agreed to the president's proposal in the course of 1967. The formal negotiations of transfer of mineral rights from the tribes to the state were concluded as 'the tribes signed vesting agreements with [Seretse Khama] on behalf of the government' (Masire 2006: 200). A milestone was reached when the Parliament, with full support of the House of Chiefs, passed the 'Mineral Rights in Tribal Territories Bill' (29 September 1967).

Conclusion

Thanks largely to the way in which the British had operated the Bechuanaland Protectorate, Botswana at its independence in 1966 ranked among the twenty-five poorest countries in the world, largely in lack of the most basic infrastructure. The fact that the 'capital' of the colonial state, Mafeking, actually lay beyond the South African border was clearly an expression of the marginality of the protectorate within the British Empire. The new capital, Gaborone, was erected from scratch in southeastern Botswana, where a neutral site beyond the borders of all of the three major *merafe* had been found. The energy and industriousness of the ruling group surrounding the first state president soon manifested itself in the construction of ministerial quarters and the development of a small city centred on a shopping mall. The shopping centre was surrounded by villas with pleasant gardens (all designed in an utterly Western style), housing the mounting stream of Western expatriates, overwhelmingly white, who were recruited to fill ministerial and other government posts. The story of the capital's early years reflects one of the major drawbacks of a ruling group with tremendous aspirations towards 'development': a domestic population with a very low level of education.

Nevertheless, only ten years after independence, Botswana had become among the most successful countries in the Third World. The expansion of government institutions and the development of welfare services and public infrastructure spread progressively throughout the country. As I indicated in the Introduction, it is well established in numerous publications that these developments also went hand in hand with the radical transformation of the country's state-centred political economy. This was driven by the livestock and subsequently the diamond industries. It was further supported by foreign aid and an advantageous customs union with South Africa through which Botswana received a handsome share of the gross customs income (see Colclough and McCarthy 1980 for a comprehensive and illuminating analysis of Botswana's political economy, especially during the first decade of independence). Another major contributing factor was of course the aforementioned influx of foreign expertise to develop and run ministerial bureaucracies and most other government institutions. Both the rapid expansion of Botswana's state finances and the easy access to numerous foreign specialists help to account for the fact that the ruling group managed to put in place an efficient government machine that soon began to realize its promises of welfare and prosperity. In particular, its ability to negotiate highly beneficial cattle-trade agreements with Europe, together with revenues from the diamond industry, gave tremendous impetus to the national economy, explaining why within a decade Botswana was ranked among the wealthiest states in the Third World (see next chapter).

In this chapter I have been concerned with the historical conditions for these postcolonial developments, in particular the crystallization of a strong ruling group that managed to establish a republican state by co-opting the *dikgosi* of the eight (recognized) Tswana *merafe* and subjecting them to the state president. The significance of this achievement cannot be fully comprehended unless the strength of these polities and their *dikgosi* is given due recognition.

I started out by explaining how in the colonial period the three major *merafe* were already showing themselves as powerful negotiating partners with the British. This strength, which only increased under the British wing, was at once attractive and challenging to the colonial power. The selected Tswana *dikgosi* and their respective ruling communities in important respects governed most of the protectorate's population on an everyday basis for some eighty years, which patently met the British wish to run the protectorate at minimal cost and implement extensively principles of indirect rule. In this perspective, the colonial state captured extensively into its network of power major structures of societal control. Structures that, by virtue of the force of expansion vested in the Tswana *bogosi*, expanded and were reinforced through the colonial era.

But at the same time, this left the *dikgosi* with great potentials of expanding their respective realms by capturing vast subject communities into their structures of domination. In consequence, from a British perspective some of the *dikgosi* were perceived as operating autocratically in relation to their subjects and as a force exterior to the order of the colonial state. Their rhizomic potentials were particularly evident in challenging the British desires of modernizing the politico-jural structures of the *merafe*.

In this chapter I have illuminated all the tensions and conflicts consequently building up between the *dikgosi* and the colonial administration. In retrospect, this was perhaps not more than what was to be expected under the circumstances of a colonial state. And it easily overshadows the fact that the two parties always found themselves in a relationship of strong mutual dependency, characterized by a high degree of pragmatism which is abundantly testified by the detailed minutes of the Native Advisory Council and the African Advisory Council. This is not to say that the British did not occasionally intervene with repressive measures and progressively sidelined the *dikgosi* in the process of decolonization. But from the early beginnings of the colonial state to the declaration of the independent state of Botswana, exercise of violence was kept at a very low key.

This also means that the peoples of Botswana – in stark contrast to the neighbouring countries – experienced no major struggle against the colonial power and, above all, were never engaged in freedom fights.

In the second half of this chapter I have been centrally concerned with how a postcolonial state leadership developed after World War II in relationship to the struggle between *dikgosi* and the 'new men'. In particular, I have shown how this struggle worked itself out in the largest *morafe* – the Bangwato – in ways that created the embryo of a republican state. I have focused my examination on Seretse Khama as an agent of transformation, mediating between internal dynamics and external forces. This transformation ultimately led to the creation of a powerful ruling group that in important respects was winning hegemony (see Introduction) – and subsequently took control of the postcolonial state.

First, Seretse's marriage marked a major shift from peace and order under Tshekedi's harsh rule to a crisis that resulted in the realization of elected political institutions and subsequently the formation of political parties. Second, faced with the challenge of political radicalism, Seretse found himself compelled to found a 'moderate' political party, which – thanks to his own efforts – made party politics increasingly acceptable within the context of the *merafe*. Third, the British shifted allegiance from the *dikgosi* to Seretse and his retainers, with whom they carefully negotiated in order to marginalize the *dikgosi* politically. As a result of these manoeuvres, the *dikgosi* were co-opted into the House of Chiefs in an advisory capacity and subsequently into the government as civil servants.

During the final stage of the colonial era, Seretse operated with British support and maintained a sufficient working relationship with the *dikgosi* to promote the Botswana Democratic Party within all their respective *merafe*. It was in this context that the conflict between 'traditionalism' and 'modernity' (which had played its part in the rise of Seretse and his retainers) virtually evaporated. Merged together, the two qualities gave a tremendous impetus to Seretse's political movement.

As I have explained, both Seretse and Tshekedi appeared as idealized images of Tswana authority, the true descendants of *Kgosi* Khama III (the Great). But in contrast to his uncle, who had claimed royal privileges in order to exploit commercial opportunities, Seretse – with his rhetoric of progress and modernization in the pursuit of the common good – appealed to the population as a caretaker (see Chapter 5 for the esteem in which this role was held). In addition, his call for democratization – and his corresponding attack on autocracy – had a deep resonance among people who celebrate open and transparent politics and who subscribe to the maxim *kgosi ke kgosi ka batho* ('the *kgosi* is *kgosi* by the grace of the people').

Against this background I want to comment on Frank's (1981: 187) assertion that 'the successful efforts of Seretse Khama and the Botswana government to establish legitimate rule have rested upon an ideology of legal-rationalism'. To be sure, the extensive (and successful) development of government structures was based on Weberian ideals of legal-rationalism, manifested in the practice of universalism in bureaucratic decision making and the division of power between the law-making, executive and judicial bodies. However, this was certainly not what made the postcolonial state 'legitimate' in relation to the population. After all, as I shall explain from different perspectives in the following chapters, the rulers of the postcolonial state drew significantly upon indigenous ideas, practices and institutions of authority.

These conditions satisfied, as we have seen, no such ideals of rationality. Nevertheless, the symbolic wealth and institutions of authority constituted major continuities between the past and the present, representing major conditions, as we shall see in Chapters 4 and 6, for the postcolonial state's development of an apparatus of capture that progressively brought the population into the process of modern state building. But, note, this was not, in all respects, an unambiguously successful process. The repressive indigenous practices and structures centred in the Tswana in relation to minorities, reinforced under the circumstances of the colonial state, were not eliminated by Botswana's independence. They continued to work in discriminatory and exteriorizing ways, also in relation to the postcolonial state, generating, as I shall argue in Chapter 5, considerable rhizomic potentials.

Chapter 3

CATTLE, DIAMONDS AND THE 'GRAND COALITION'

The development of a strong state in Botswana is closely linked to what Bayart (1993: 155ff.) has identified as critical for a sustainable government in post-colonial Africa – 'fusion of elites'. He was, as indicated in the Introduction, centrally concerned with how powerful people operate in predatory and violent ways in relation to postcolonial states on the continent, making them notoriously fragile, weak and failing. This is a matter of forces, in Deleuze and Guattari's conception, exterior to the state – 'war-machines' that generate rhizomic attacks on the state. My chief aim in this chapter is to identify major conditions underpinning the formation of elites in Botswana that – despite all their conflicts and rivalries – have prevented such forces to gain significance. Furthermore, I ask, what were the particular circumstances in Botswana during the first decades following the independence that constrained the development of the kind of 'politics of the belly' which Bayart has attributed to state failures elsewhere in postcolonial Africa? The question is important, of course, because of all the wealth generated by the diamond industry in postcolonial times. I am pursuing these issues here with a particular concern with the formative and consolidating decades (1966–90) of the modern state in Botswana.

Picard (1987: 271) has attributed the development of a strong state to Botswana's government being 'led by a cohesive group of elites who see themselves as modernising agents'. Parson makes a similar case for elite cohesion. He suggests that although certain factions were evolving within the ruling party after the death of President Khama in 1980, they managed to agree on 'a mineral-led strategy in which government would play a leading role ... Thus there was a good deal of unity among this, rather tightly knit, group of bureaucrats, cattle owners, and politicians' (Parson 1984: 90). In a later publication, Samatar (1999: 181) asserts the existence of a 'dominant class's unity' which was sustained by an 'unchallenged leadership that had legitimacy with the elite and the general population'. Werbner (2004: 21), however, attacks Samatar and rejects that 'there was a unified dominant class throughout the move from one postcolonial phase to the next' and goes against the notion of elite cohesion. This is an argument that might find support in Makgala's (2006) illuminating review of elite conflicts, which reveals numerous instances of confrontation among 'elite' groups, leaving the impression of considerable animosity – amply confirmed by an autobiographic insider account of a former minister, MP and senior civil servant (Magang 2008).

But such conflicts and rivalries as narrated by these authors are no more than what to expect where people compete for power and wealth within contexts of multiparty politics, state government and business enterprises. These are, after all, conflicts and rivalries typical in modern, Western contexts where antagonism amongst elites prevails at certain levels, yet, crucially, without undermining their consent about basic issues of major state policy orientations and, of course, the state constitution. Hence, in the present context of modern state formation, people of power and wealth might well disagree on various issues related to state policies and compete severely for benefits of government projects and programmes. But they do agree to a great extent on the direction of policies and the orientation of projects and programmes. In the conception of Deleuze and Guattari (see Introduction), amongst such people there has thus been no significant breeding ground for rhizomic forces attacking the order of the state. On the contrary, they were from the outset captured into the process of nation-state formation. A chief task of the present chapter is thus to explain, in the words of Sebudubudu (2009: 4), the development of a 'grand coalition [of elites] that enabled the new state to take control of key resources such as land, minerals, wildlife and ultimate political authority across the country without alienating, antagonising or even abolishing traditional institutions'.

The embryo of such a coalition was, as we saw in the preceding chapter, created during the final stages of the colonial era. Patently, in the debates which led to the Constitution for the postcolonial state – as related by former president Quett Masire (2006: 36), who was a central participant – 'there were seldom divisions of whites versus blacks, tradition-alists versus modernists, northern versus southern'. Significantly also, the highly peaceful decolonisation of the country prevented the development of cleavages between sections of the population. Yet, however important these conditions have proved to be for postcolonial developments in Bo-tswana, it does not follow by necessity from the formation of a 'grand coalition' in support of the state ruling group under Seretse Khama's leadership.

The key to resolving this issue is to ask what many people of power and wealth across the ruling communities of the Tswana *merafe*, modern po-litical leaders and senior state bureaucrats had in common at the time of independence and the first decades that followed. The blunt answer to this question is obsession with accumulation of cattle, for all its symbol-ic, political and commercial value. I am certainly not the first to suggest this. Leith (2005: 55), for one, holds that at the time of independence, 'the interests of the political majority, the old and new political elite, and the economic elite all largely coincided' which he relates to the 'joint economic interest of all those involved in the cattle sector'. The task at hand is then to come to terms with the ways in which cattle contributed to uniting the politically significant elites of the country into a common desire for a strong state with a sustainable government.

The focus here on the cohesive significance of cattle does not imply that other conditions were unimportant for the establishment of a nation-state government, such as the existence of networks established amongst people who went to the same institution for higher education (see Se-budubudu 2009: 3), or the recruitment of well-educated people not ob-sessed by cattle accumulation to senior positions in government. But these were conditions that became significant for the development of a strong state only because the postcolonial ruling group was underpinned by a grand coalition which also included people of power and wealth beyond the modern spheres of the postcolonial state government. That is, the 'new men' with an entrepreneurial spirit who I presented in the previous chapter, as well as people of high rank who possessed large herds of cattle and occupied positions of authority in dominant Tswana hierarchies.

In the following section I want to explain that across 'traditional' vs. 'modern' and rural vs. urban divides the state soon manifested itself as cru-cial and indispensable for connecting people obsessed by herd accumula-tion and highly beneficial European beef markets. I shall then discuss the relationship between the symbolic and commercial significance of cattle, explaining how their mutual reinforcement accelerated the obsession with herd growth. Subsequently, I want to show how the state captured, into its network of power, people beyond bovine obsessions – people of authority in certain contexts with apparent potentialities of rhizomic attack on state formation.

I shall argue, moreover, that with the acceleration of revenues from diamond mining a decade after independence, the institutionalized ways to dispense state resources expanded significantly and then in ways favouring the 'grand coalition'. This expansion drew ever more people into a dependency on the prevailing state order, thus diversifying and enlarging the 'grand coalition'. When vast revenues from diamond mining started to flow into the state treasury, a system was already in place ensuring the privileged, dominant class a lion's share of this wealth. Legally established governmental projects and programmes hence made, in Bayart's sense, 'politics of the belly' quite redundant, especially during the formative decades (until the late 1980s).

This is not to say that I am pursuing an argument of the state in Africa as entirely 'a powerful and lethal instrument in the hands of repressive and dominant elites' (Blom Hansen and Stepputat 2005: 28–29). However dominant the various categories of people of power and wealth have been in the sense of underpinning a ruling group responsible for programmes and projects of which they have been the privileged beneficiaries, this is not a case of a cattle-owning elite *dictating* state policies. I shall explain how the state gained considerable autonomy in relation to 'bovine interests', embarking on extensive financial and technical assistance of off-farm commercial and productive enterprises. In addition, as we shall see in the following chapters, major welfare programmes have been launched in efforts to generate electoral support amongst all the rank-and-file sections of the population.

Obsessed by Cattle: On the Cohesion of Dominant Elites

It did not take me long after my first arrival in Botswana in 1975 to realize the immense symbolic, economic and political importance of cattle in this country. Their importance was not limited to peoples living in places remote from the capital, which is often the case elsewhere in Africa. In fact it was some high-ranking government officials who first told me of their enthusiasm for raising cattle, which was vividly demonstrated by the various complicated arrangements such people had to make as they rushed to their cattle posts after office hours on Friday afternoons. The Monday-morning chats closely resembled conversations one might encounter in any typical Norwegian office after a nice weekend in the mountains. Life at the cattle post[1] was romanticized to such an extent that, as one permanent secretary (who was about fifty at the time) explained, 'the only thing I am now looking forward to is to quit this job that overloads me with paper, and move to the cattle post where I can look after the herd boys and just sit under a tree and drink milk'. On a more practical note, they discussed various 'improved methods' of breeding, problems of getting boreholes drilled, ways to obtain good prices for cattle, the challenge of getting hold of a good bull, and other measures to enhance herd productivity. When I moved to the royal town of one of the major Tswana *merafe* (Kanye of the Bangwaketse) and became acquainted with cattle owners there – people of high rank in the *morafe* as well as nouveaux riches – I was exposed to exactly the same obsessions. In many places I went in Botswana, I encountered this passion for cattle. And it was by no means limited to those who already had hundreds of head: people without large herds would put their money into cattle when they were earning enough, and many of them – whom I have followed over many years – now own very large herds.

One major condition for this development is an ecological one. Botswana is a large country, I recall, equal in size to France and the Benelux countries combined. Most of this vast tableland is suitable – or adaptable – for pasture. This is predominantly common land, which in practice means that wealthy people obtain *de facto* exclusive rights to huge grazing lands by being given permission to drill a borehole.[2] That this translation of common property into individual wealth has had significant sociopolitical repercussions is evident when we consider that at that time (1975) some 5 per cent of Botswana's households owned about half of the national herd (about 3 million head of cattle in total); 37 per cent had no cattle. This highly skewed distribution, the significance of which I shall discuss in various contexts in subsequent chapters, has been steadily increasing since Botswana's independence. Elsewhere I have examined in considerable detail how state programmes and projects have facilitated a tremendous herd growth amongst a privileged minority, leaving the large majority with small herds or nothing at all (Gulbrandsen 1996a: Ch. 10).

---

1. They customarily divided their life between the village, their arable land and their cattle post. This division corresponds to the zoning of each 'tribal' area into villages (some of which comprise thousands, or even tens of thousands, of people), arable land areas where people are allocated fields for cultivation and pastoral areas where people graze their cattle on a permanent basis (see Schapera 1943a; see also Gulbrandsen 1986a; Werbner 1980). In a single household, these locations might be tens of km apart.

2. Boreholes are, of course, extremely important in this country with poor and erratic rainfall – making the livestock production regimes quite drought resistant.

As already indicated, I am centrally concerned with the connection between two characteristics common across most of the elite spectrum, especially its powerful and wealthy members: on the one hand, their strong drive to accumulate large herds of cattle, and on the other hand, their acceptance of – even enthusiasm for – the development of a strong, sustainable state. I shall address this issue by explaining the indispensable role played by the state in relation in the development of a modern and immensely profitable livestock industry in Botswana.

At its independence, Botswana had, in addition to a very high livestock population and huge areas of common pasture, a relatively advanced veterinary care system. As early as the mid-1950s, I recall, Seretse Khama was speaking in public about the fantastic economic possibilities of cattle raising. And he was increasingly surrounded by people – 'the new men' – to whom it was particularly easy to appeal in this matter. These were people with whom he worked during the process of decolonization and in particular the establishment of the Botswana Democratic Party. It is therefore no surprise that 'nationalisation [of the Lobatse abattoir] and fair prices became a major election platform' for this party (Hubbard 1986: 146). For reasons I shall now explain, no people with large herds would subsequently be disappointed, especially as they soon received prices for their livestock which exceeded those of the world market.

The new government immediately engaged in developing the beef industry. Crucial to this endeavour was a small abattoir and canning factory in Lobatse nationalized by the state. The state established a para-statal company, known as the Botswana Meat Commission, whose board was effectively under the direct control of the state president. By means of this venture, the state also monopolized beef production and constructed a technically highly advanced abattoir, satisfying all Western standards of hygiene and with the capacity to slaughter 1,500–2,000 cattle per day. At the time it was said to be the largest modern abattoir in the Southern Hemisphere. In Botswana this large construction was much appreciated as a significant step towards modernity. The abattoir soon became a national attraction that received, on a daily basis, a stream of visitors – primary school classes as well as international delegations – who were guided along the production line.

No one but the state had the finances, know-how and not least the international support to embark on such an enterprise. The ruling group proved extremely capable of showing the international credibility necessary to attract large amounts of foreign development aid, in the form of financial resources as well as 'experts' with technical, administrative and managerial skills. For all those involved in commercial livestock production, the abattoir was the gateway to the high-price market of Britain and later the larger European market of the European Economic Community (EEC), which subsequently became the European Union (EU). Botswana was virtually the only African country which had access to this very profitable market, with prices beyond those of the world market level. However, dealing with it was not always a straightforward matter, and much depended on the negotiating capacity of state officials. Negotiations were recurrent and became particularly tough when the British entered the EEC, at which time Batswana beef had to satisfy more stringent standards than member producers are required to meet (Samatar and Oldfield 1995: 652).

Batswana livestock producers had enjoyed a significant rise in prices as soon as Botswana reached an agreement with Britain in 1966. Moreover, prices paid to producers continued to increase and by 1976 were already 150 per cent higher than what they had been in 1966.[3] This meant that, as already suggested, Botswana's privileged market access continued to guarantee beef prices beyond the world market level.[4] What is more, owing to the close links between cattle owners, the state and the Botswana Meat Commission (BMC), 'state legislation stipulated that *the BMC should forward any profits to the livestock producers*' (von Massow 1983: 218, italics added).

The importance of these trade agreements for the stability of the state in Botswana was well recognized in Europe. For example, when Britain entered the EEC, there was considerable resistance to allowing Botswana access to the larger EEC market. But resistance was overcome after considerable diplomatic activity prompted by 'the likely politically destabilising impact of a predicted halving of producer prices if access were not restored' (Hubbard 1986).

However, everything depended on three major conditions in relation to Britain and the EEC/EU. First, the abattoir had to meet their requirements for high-quality meat. Second, strict standards of hygiene had to be satisfied (inspectors from Europe continuously monitored the BMC performance). Third, Botswana was virtually the only African country that had been granted this privileged access to the European markets, because of its exceptionally good veterinary conditions virtually throughout the country. These veterinary conditions had to be kept up.

---

3. Colclough and McCarthy 1980: 121, see also Hubbard 1986: 258; Hewitt and Stephens 1981: 121–22.
4. Hence Botswana achieved beef prices in the European Community which were 'generally 20–50 percent above the prices in other BMC markets from 1972 to 1981' (Harvey and Lewis 1990: 79).

To maintain the required veterinary conditions in Botswana, however, was a formidable task that once again made state intervention indispensable. Botswana's vast grazing land was therefore divided into zones by so-called veterinary cordon fences extending over enormous distances, constructed and maintained by the state. Livestock movement between these zones was strictly controlled, requiring a state apparatus with the necessary strength to ensure nationwide compliance with the regulations. The state also expanded the network of veterinary extension workers throughout the country, made certain vaccines compulsory by law and ran vaccination campaigns in all areas inhabited by livestock.

Besides negotiating access to the European beef market, the state managed to obtain substantial aid from Britain and the EEC/EU to 'develop' the livestock production sector. Although universally available to livestock owners, these development programmes have benefited the large-scale cattle owner much more than anyone else. Owners of large herds have received all kinds of support to enhance productivity. For those able to maintain a degree of financial security, the state has offered very favourable loans for investment in breeding stock and other capital purchases such as lorries and tractors. Of particular importance has been substantial financial support for drilling private boreholes. This has created privately owned, permanent water points and consequently exclusive access to favourable pastures within Botswana's vast common land. The *de facto* privatization of communal land by wealthy cattle owners has gained momentum from what is known as the National Policy of the Tribal Grazing Lands (see Gulbrandsen 1996a: 337ff.). This was a state policy allowing the establishment of very large fenced-off, private ranches. Once again it was accompanied by state livestock programmes that included massive technical support and loans on very favourable terms. These state initiatives epitomize the government's focus on the large herd owners, because ranch allocations and loans set very high requirements as to the size of herd and other assets.[5] Moreover, as I shall explain below, when money started to flow into the state treasury in the form of revenues from the diamond mining industry in the early 1970s, an additional source was in place to subsidize a wide range of 'development' programmes that were *de facto* directed towards the wealthy – and the powerful.

---

5. The development of this wide-ranging policy confirms, moreover, that the close connection between cattle-owning interests and the operation of bureaucrats had great impact on policy-making processes, as substantiated by Picard who asserts that '[t]he evidence suggests that both the policy-making process and the coalition building that followed it were intended to formulate a new land tenure system which would increase the economic prosperity of those administrators who made and who would later implement the policy'(Picard 1980: 349).

Finally, for owners of large herds the state played an indispensable role in ensuring their security. Livestock production in this large country was potentially extremely vulnerable to the kind of violent conflicts affecting many other African countries. High crime rates, including stock theft, would have been very damaging to cattle raising. In fact it goes without saying that peace and order were of critical importance to a production system that requires the exploitation of huge areas of pastures and grazing land in remote areas, the implementation of measures to enhance productivity, and safe conditions for bringing cattle to the abattoir over extremely long distances.

Hence, what might appear to be the perfect conditions for state-destructive Bayartian 'politics of the belly' – a swelling state treasury – works, in the context of Botswana, to the effect of strengthening the state. Elites obsessed by accumulating cattle wealth have taken a strong interest in supporting state policies by which the vast wealth of the nation has been translated into private property (cf. Good 2008: 69ff.). They were, for reasons explained in this section, operating basically as a unified force in relation to the state by virtue of their class-based interest in a strong, sustainable state. Consequently, the state became a major instrument in the hands of a ruling class, cohering most of the dominant elites in the country that shared an obsession with accumulating cattle – and power. These state resources were distributed so generously that corruption in the Western sense was kept at a very low level for more than twenty years after independence (Gulbrandsen in prep.).

The pervasive nature of these forces is epitomized by the fact that no political party developed an agenda contradicting the elites' privileged access to benefits organized and distributed by the state. However biased Quett Masire may be on political issues, he is obviously right in arguing that '[t]he opposition parties may talk about the BDP being the party of cattle owners, [yet] most of their leaders are quite happy to own cattle. Kenneth Koma's[6] father was said to have been a cattle baron, though Koma claims to be a socialist. K.T. Motsete, a founder of BPP, was reputed to be a major cattle owner, and Chief Bathoen, of course, had many, many cattle' (Masire 2006: 198). Nor was there any political protest against

---

6. Dr Koma was the founding leader of the Botswana National Front (BNF). He was educated in the Soviet Union where he received a doctorate in political science. He appeared to be a 'socialist' in his rhetoric, but he was never able to formulate a radical political agenda appealing to the Batswana. After former *Kgosi* Bathoen took over the party leadership, the party attacked the BDP also from a traditionalist section. Yet, under Bathoen's leadership the BNF represented no major challenge to the cattle-oriented elites of the ruling party as Bathoen, with his vast herds of cattle, indeed shared their elite interests.

policies favouring cattle accumulation.[7] Equally importantly, these state policies found strong support among the dominant groups of the major Tswana *merafe*, and also among the leaders of large minority communities such as the Bakgatla-baga-Mmanaana (in the Bangwaketse), Bakaa (in the Kgatleng) and Herero (in the Batawana). As for the principal political body – Parliament – nearly all its members were large- or medium-scale cattle owners (Samatar 1999: 106).

I agree with Samatar's criticism of Gundersen's 'administrative state' thesis, which argues that the country was governed by bureaucrats rather than politicians (Gundersen 1970). Samatar relies on Isaksen's seminal work in this area, qualifying Gundersen's thesis in asserting that 'the autonomous bureaucrats making policy [did so] within the framework set by the political elite' (Samatar 1999: 67).[8] And according to Isaksen the political elite was 'overrepresented' by big cattle owners who had substantial policy leverage. The fact that '[w]ithin this limit there exists an area for the bureaucracy and bureaucratic politics' with which 'the formal political system … seldom interferes' (Isaksen 1981: 32–33) does not conflict with the view that 'cattle interests' had an immense impact on government policies and their implementation. As already indicated, many of those citizens of Botswana in important bureaucratic posts during the first formative decades had strong interests in cattle – or, as we shall see in a subsequent section, were more or less forced to be loyal to the interests of the dominant elites.[9]

Finally, I also agree with Samatar (1999: 106) that 'dominant class unity' was a major condition for the establishment of the key institution in Botswana's livestock industry – the BMC. However, Samatar fails to grasp the larger dynamics in which this connection was just one factor. The full significance of this factor only becomes evident when seen in the

---

7. The only exception was former *Kgosi* Bathoen's rejection of the Tribal Grazing Land Policy. The reason was that he had rejected the transfer of all the tribal lands to the state by the Tribal Land Act. This was one of the major reasons why he abdicated and joined the major opposition party, BNF, and became its president and a member of Parliament. He was strongly committed to sustaining the tribal lands as commonages and fiercely rejected the new policy which opened up for fencing off vast sections as de facto private holdings.

8. That the ruling party represented a major policy-directing force is most apparent in view of the detailed statements in the party's 'Election Manifesto 1974 – Build Botswana' (Gaborone: Printing & Publishing Co.).

9. There is evidence that this pattern has not persisted. As we shall see in a subsequent section, a law was passed in the early 1980s which permitted civil servants to engage in commercial activities beyond crop farming and livestock production. During this decade they gradually moved into 'modern' sectors of the economy; by the late 1980s the majority of permanent secretaries no longer had cattle in significant amounts and instead 'held shares in private companies and parastatals' (Molutsi 1989a: 111). I shall discuss the significance of this later in this chapter.

context of the systemic interdependencies which I have tried to reveal in this section. These interdependencies are basically conditioned by the conjuncture of particular structural conditions: (1) the culturally and materially determined obsession with cattle among virtually all politically significant elites in the country; (2) the existence of vast pastures where veterinary healthcare was of a very high standard; (3) the possibility of extremely profitable sales contracts with Britain and the EEC/EU accompanied by substantial aid to 'develop' cattle raising in Botswana.

It was within this context that Seretse Khama and his people soon convinced the dominant, cattle-obsessed elites that only a strong nation-state could create the necessary conditions to take advantage of the highly profitable beef market in Europe. To succeed in establishing a beef trade agreement required, in particular, that Botswana could ensure Britain the capacity to develop high veterinary standards throughout the country, to establish a countrywide livestock marketing system, and to construct and manage a large scale, modern abattoir, satisfying strict European conditions of hygiene. It became clear to cattle-obsessed elites that only a centralized, strong state government could handle this matter in relation to Britain (and then the EEF), and to ensure satisfaction of the highly demanding requirements. In this particular sense, cattle was a critical factor underpinning cohesion of the dominant elites, as a state-carrying class during the first decade and a half of Botswana's independence.

The Politico-Cultural Significance of Cattle as a Force for Elite Integration

It is by no means my aim to reduce obsession with cattle to a matter of mere cultural inclination. As I explained in the preceding section, the tremendous attraction of increasing one's herd is grounded in rational economic decisions. Nevertheless, I want to consider the politico-cultural significance of cattle because it helps to explain how cattle ownership has contributed significantly in bridging the gap between the urban-based state leadership and the people of power and wealth located in rural areas of the *merafe*.

Let me first raise the question of the commoditization of cattle in view of its symbolic importance. I take as my point of departure Ferguson's notion of 'bovine mystique' in Lesotho. This mystique ostensibly involves a contradiction between cattle as commercial commodity and cattle as signifier in kinship and community relations: such a conflict places considerable constraints on the commercialization of livestock production (Ferguson 1990: 135; see also Comaroff and Comaroff 1992: 152 on the

Southern Tswana). Such notions are certainly not unknown among the Northern Tswana. Cattle may embody 'social biographies' whereby they personify, for example, relations of affinity – and subsequently matrilaterality – generated by the transfers of bridewealth (*bogadi*), reinforced by gifts of cattle between a mother's brother and his sister's son. Nevertheless, where the number of cattle in the herd exceeds around fifty, any 'socially significant' members of the herd start to represent a minor proportion. Here, cattle have crossed the line from being part of a small-scale exchange and substinence economy to become units of commodity production. They no longer stand mainly for interpersonal relations but are predominantly valued for their marketability. Consequently, in the present context, there is no contradiction between a highly individualized cattle entrepreneurship and engagement in political and social relations, whether it be in the 'traditional' context of the *kgotla* or at the political centre of the state.

As indicated in Chapter 2, the *dikgosi* themselves privatized and ran commercial cattle operations at an early stage, and they had no reservations about adopting Western technology to increase productivity. Given the relatively close correspondence between cattle wealth and position in the hierarchy of the *merafe*, the Botswana Democratic Party's emphasis on utilizing the new state as a means of promoting beef production and trade was attractive not only to the 'new men' but also to *dikgosana* and other senior people whose authority was largely based on cattle wealth. Consequently, the evolving cattle-centred political economy found favour among the various elites, ensuring wide-ranging consensus about the Constitution of the state, its institutional development and its policies and programmes. This consensus existed among people in control of the state apparatus itself as well as amongst dominant elites of the *morafe*.

Nevertheless, the integration of the various elites was determined by more than a pragmatic coherence of commercial interests. There were also processes of sociocultural integration at work. As I have already explained in Chapter 2, however much the 'new men' might appear to have been agents of modernity during the colonial era, they adhered closely to the *kgotla* and thereby achieved recognition in that context, gaining 'positions of greatly enhanced authority in the villages' (Kuper 1970: 62). It is important to point out that these men did not become esteemed members of the community because of their successes elsewhere. Rather, it was the fact that they submitted to the local authority structures that enabled them to bridge the gulf between their commercial ventures and an engagement in the 'traditional' discursive field of the *kgotla*.

Such cases bear some resemblance to a much more pervasive trend throughout the most populous eastern parts of the country. In this region people who had successfully accumulated substantial numbers of cattle came to prominence as members of a particular social rank known as *bahumi* (person of wealth), a position closely associated with the affairs of the *kgotla*. Up to the present time these 'persons of wealth' have continued to enjoy their social rank because the *kgotla* has remained a highly meaningful social and political context attributing the established symbolic values to cattle and cattle ownership. I was always assured that 'a man who has got a large herd of cattle is a man who can speak freely in the *kgotla*'. The significance of this has, as we shall see in the following chapter, become no less during postcolonial times as the *kgotla* has retained much of its centrality in many people's lives. In particular, the *kgotla* has remained as a major public discursive field in which material wealth is translated into rank, recognition and respectability and has thus often a bearing upon social identity in the deeper existential sense.

Non-Cattle-Oriented Elites

So far, I have given the impression that the elites underpinning the postcolonial ruling group during the formative decades were all obsessed by cattle, and that the most successful elite members combined bureaucratic or political careers with the accumulation of considerable wealth. Although this is true to a great extent, we need to account for the fact that some important people had other orientations. Even among Tswana there were people who had prominent positions in the royal court, but very little interest in cattle rearing and owned few or no cattle. Some of them were what I would call intellectuals: people who mastered the rhetoric of the *kgotla* and who were generally recognized as wise and knowledgeable. Some of them became clergymen and teachers within the context of a missionary church.[10] The *dikgosi* often attached such people to their *bogosi* for consultation; they were also entrusted by the *kgosi* to express his views during debates in the royal *kgotla* (see Chapter 6).

In due course, quite a number got a secondary education and were either recruited as senior civil servants by the colonial administration and then the postcolonial government or joined party politics (usually opting for the ruling party). Rather than being driven by a desire for wealth, they gained satisfaction from success in politics or the civil service. Their ambitions might include a large and well-appointed house in the capi-

---

10. Among the Bangwaketse, in the Kgasa family, father as well as sons being prominent *baruti* (priests) in the local church of the London Missionary Society, were of this kind. They were among the closest personal advisors of *Kgosi* Bathoen II and thus had high standing in the royal *kgotla*. But they had no interest in cattle rearing and accumulation.

tal and the best available education for their children. Any surplus from their salaries might be invested in property or might enable their wives to establish small businesses such as dry-cleaning shops.

There were, moreover, some large non-Tswana communities – not strongly integrated in the dominant Tswana *merafe* – who were cultivators rather than herdsmen. Nor did their leaders show much interest in the new opportunities to accumulate cattle. The most significant of these communities were the Kalanga and the Wayei, both of which had developed a rather antagonistic relationship towards their respective Tswana overlords – the Bangwato and the Batawana respectively – during the colonial era (see Chapter 1). At the time of independence, the Kalanga had the potential to develop an elite capable of forming a dissident movement that might have challenged the Tswana-dominated ruling group of the postcolonial state, because they had been quicker than the Tswana to 'recognis[e] the link between education and social mobility' (Werbner 2004: 72) and by independence they had comparatively a much greater proportion of well-educated people. Among concerned Tswana they were thus perceived as a potential destabilizing force after the withdrawal of the British.

This fear was by no means unfounded, since there were also a number of other minorities within the domain claimed by the Bangwato whose leaders might have allied themselves with the then rurally based Kalanga leadership. Always concerned with the threat of 'tribalism', Seretse Khama adopted a strategy which was, as we have seen, extensively practised by precolonial Tswana rulers: that of capturing potentially challenging leaders of 'alien' communities with potentialities of rhizomic forces – into the hierarchical structure of their kingdom (see Chapter 1). Some of the well-educated Kalanga were accordingly recruited into the ruling party, serving as members of Parliament and even as cabinet ministers. Many of them were employed in central government, where they outnumbered the Tswana at the more senior levels. The president's strategy of capture was epitomized by his incorporation of some of these Kalanga into his inner circle. The significance of this was very apparent to me when I first came to Botswana in 1975: at this time Khama's actions came in for criticism in many encounters I attended with prominent Tswana. Not only did they object to the increased competition for high positions; they were anxious about the influence the Kalanga might wield. Such conspiracies allegedly gave impetus to 'a secretive brotherhood for Tswana known as *Lefatshe Larona*, Our Country, as if to say in an assertion of autochthony, "The Land Belongs to Us not Them"' (Werbner 2004: 79). There was, in other words, a widespread *perception* of the Kalanga's, in Deleuze and Guattari's conception, war-machine potentialities (see Introduction).

However, neither at this early stage nor later did the Kalanga manifest any serious threat to the cohesion of the Tswana-dominated ruling group or to that of the various Tswana elites underpinning this group. On the contrary, I propose, their perceived challenge had the effect of uniting rather than splitting the Tswana. This is due to the fact that the Kalanga were co-opted by a political apparatus or a state bureaucracy which was after all in the hands of President Khama. There is no indication that the Kalanga even tried to exploit whatever divisions there might have been among Tswana elites. As Werbner has substantiated in a thorough account of their behaviour, they consistently showed great loyalty to the state leadership. I have already mentioned that several of them became cabinet ministers and were thus strongly committed to government policies defined by the Tswana-dominated ruling group. More significantly, as a minority their power lay not only in knowing the rules of the game thoroughly but also in their ability to play with the rules (see Werbner 2004: 108). And when the Kalanga played with rules, the rules were both internalized and reinforced.

There was, though, another institution associated with the better-educated Kalanga: the Bakalanga Students Association, which in 1980 gave rise to the Society for the Promotion of Ikalanga Language (known as SPIL). SPIL also recruited some of its members from the established Kalanga urban elite. However, according to Werbner, this is an association which is characterized by 'something of the erratic flow of student enthusiasms … [with] very real ups and downs'. Nevertheless, the Tswana majority apparently believed that it was 'an effective agency with its networks and tenterhooks everywhere that matters; that *it is able to plan a political "takeover" on the national scene*; that it conspires successfully to keep jobs for Kalanga through discrimination against others, on a tribalistic basis' (Werbner 2004: 54, italics added).

Again, we see how, in Tswana imaginaries, the perceived war-machine potentialities of the Kalanga featured in new disguises. This notion of a Kalanga 'takeover' threat reflects the contradiction that Khama built into the central government by co-opting the leaders of a potentially rebellious community, as the Tswana perceived it. On the one hand, he used this strategy to bring the Kalanga elite under tight control, which – as suggested above – may have prevented the rise of a challenging minority movement. Moreover, as part of this strategy, he attached to his office people whose positions were particularly dependent on their personal loyalty to the president. Just as the Tswana *dikgosi* bolstered their positions against challenging agnates by granting leaders of alien communities a prominent position in the royal *kgotla* (cf. Chapter 1 above), Khama deployed several Kalanga in (for him) strategic positions.

On the other hand, in the context of a modern state with all its career rivalries, such power games tended to exaggerate ethnic conflicts, because the up-and-coming Tswana faced stiff competition for high-ranking
positions. Having attained such positions, well-educated Kalanga were
strongly empowered and – most importantly, according to Tswana conspiracy theories – constituted a growing network of hidden power which
progressively infiltrated and gradually would replace the existing Tswana-
dominated state order with that of the Kalanga. This conspiracy of the
Kalanga as, from Tswana point of view, a force exterior to the order of the
state, with apparent potentials of operating in hidden, lateral networks
as rhizomes attacking this particular order, has never materialized in any
attempt to challenge openly the dominant Tswana.

As Werbner (2004) explains, the Kalanga elites have identified themselves as successful, urbanized bureaucrats and, more recently, as businessmen. There is no indication in his account that they saw themselves as
leaders of a rural Kalanga peasantry. Actually, in his account their rural
roots and connections are given very little significance, which is intriguing
in view of the close and sustainable urban–rural relations among Tswana
elites. The Kalanga elites appeared to be of a strong modern, urban inclination, and not much in touch with those Kalanga peasant communities
among whom they might have fomented a dissident movement. Instead
their focus was very strongly on the aspirations of Western modernity –
an attitude which indeed they shared with the dominant Tswana elites
in urban contexts. During the first decades of independence, the life trajectories of urban Kalanga elites were entirely dependent on an expanding, strong and stable state. More recently, the cross-ethnic coalescence
of elite orientations has developed into successful commercial ventures
in which former high-ranking Kalanga bureaucrats have engaged with
Tswana as well as Indian and Afrikaner businessmen (Werbner 2004: 84).
This means that the Kalanga elites have been fully integral to the rise of a
dominant postcolonial class in Botswana: the development of the private,
off-farm sector of Botswana's economy has been – and still is – entirely
diamond-driven and thus highly dependent on a strong state and a stable
political leadership.[11]

The monolithic character of these processes of elite integration in urban contexts during the formative and consolidating era of the postcolonial state is testified by the fact that it was not until the latter part of the
1990s that the Tswana elites were openly challenged by leaders of minori-

---

11. The majority of the Kalanga have never been associated with any political party, while
some Kalanga elites were prominent members of the ruling party as cabinet ministers and members of Parliament.

ties in (often bitter) confrontations. These confrontations stemmed to a great extent from contradictions inherent in the eight Tswana *merafe* that developed under colonial conditions (Chapter 1). In Chapter 5 I shall explain how the state leadership has attempted to temper majority–minority tensions in their efforts to sustain national unity.

Transformations of the Cattle-Centred Political Economy: The Impact of Diamonds

A 'grand coalition' – including people of power and wealth located in senior positions of authority in the Tswana – evolved, as I have argued, as integral to the cattle-centred political economy during the first independence decade and formed a dominant class underpinning a strong, sustainable ruling group. The question is what happened to this class as massive revenues from diamond mining started to fill the state treasury in the late 1970s (see Harvey and Lewis 1990: 120 ff.).

Before pursuing this issue, let me briefly explain that the first diamond mine was opened in Orapa in the Central District in 1971, while production in the second one, Jwaneng in the Southern District, commenced in 1982. They both depended on surveys conducted by what was established in 1969 as the De Beers Botswana Mining Company (Debswana), a joint venture by the De Beers and the state (see Jefferis 1998: 301). Through tough negotiations in 1974 the state reached a favourable agreement with the De Beers which entailed such a substantial flow of revenues into the state treasury that 'from 1965–80 [Botswana] had the highest rate of GDP growth in the world at 14,2% and from 1980–90 it had the third highest increase in the world at 9,9%' (Edge 1998: 337). The Debswana was closely linked to the De Beers Group, which in the 1970s controlled '80–90 percent of the world diamond production which reaches the open market' (Colclough and McCarthy 1980: 151–52).

It has been a common assumption that the state leadership was particularly successful in its negotiation with De Beers as the country got direct representation on the board of Debswana Mining Company, highly exceptional in view of the country being categorized, at the time, amongst the least developed countries in the world (Sentsho 2005: 140; Harvey and Lewis 1990: 123). This assumption goes with the recognition of the extensive revenues that have persistently flowed into the state treasury ever since.

After 1980 revenues from the diamond industry gained further momentum, and diamonds have made a major contribution to Botswana's economy ever since (see Jefferis 1998: 303; Sentsho 2005: 141). This is an intriguing state of affairs, since in other African postcolonial states with a significant diamond industry – such as Angola and Sierra Leone – diamonds have, as I pointed out in the Introduction, been the source of and amplified major divides within these countries, causing serious violence and even civil wars. So why did the discovery of diamonds have such different consequences in Botswana? In the previous chapter I explained how the state gained control over all the mineral rights in the country, significantly due to Seretse Khama's engagement in this matter. Already a year before the Mineral Rights in Tribal Territories Bill passed Parliament (29 September 1967), he had been secretly informed about the discovery of the Orapa diamond pipe in his own 'tribal' territory – the Bangwato. This did not affect his strong commitment of nation-state building; apparently it was never in his mind to make the Bangwato special beneficiaries of this wealth.

However, it is hard to believe that Khama's commitment alone – albeit indeed strong – was sufficient to avoid such disastrous developments as reported from other African countries where diamonds play dangerously into politics. In such contexts, any legislation on mineral rights would not have been worth the paper it was written on. In order to come to terms with the fact that elite cohesion across the Tswana *merafe* did not break up when all the revenues from the diamond industry started to flow into the state treasury in the early 1970,[12] it is important to take into account that the Bangwato elite had a strong sense of control over the ruling party as well as the state. The state president was, after all, their man, and the ruling party had overwhelming support in their district which was by far the largest in the country. Above all, at this time the state had already asserted itself as indispensable for the development of the livestock industry and trade, setting up a most generous system of distributing resources – financial and technical – to those who had sufficient initial resources to enter a spiral of wealth accumulation.

And this is a crucial point: when revenues from the diamond industry started to flow into the state treasury, a system was already established that ensured the Bangwato and other dominant elites the lion's share of the wealth. This was so first through the existing and new programmes and schemes directed towards the livestock industry and commercial crop

---

12. Revenues from the diamond industry grew slowly from the early 1970s and started to accelerate in the mid-1980s, especially after the second mine (Jwaneng) had come into operation (see Sentsho 2005: 142; Harvey and Lewis 1990: 120–21). The significance of this is apparent from the fact that already by around 1976 'the real national income per capita [had] tripled' since independence in 1966 (Colclough and McCarthy 1980: 74; see also Jefferis 1998: 302–3; Samatar 1999: 146).

production. Subsequently, old and new entrepreneurs, in the Bangwato and elsewhere, enjoyed extensive financial support through new 'development' programmes to promote off-farm commercial enterprises.

A new major policy was launched whereby the state could once again disseminate resources to people taken by an entrepreneurial spirit: the Financial Assistance Policy (FAP). This policy was launched in 1982, about the same time that the state abandoned a legal bar preventing civil servants from off-farm commercial engagement. The lifting of the bar was justified by the need to counteract an invasion of foreign investors: '[t]op civil servants, in particular, were explicitly given great encouragement to become investors and shareholders' (Werbner 2004: 78).

The FAP provided the financial backing for a huge number of enterprises all over the country; by 1993 it had supported over 4,000 projects of different sizes at a cost of 160,439,000 pula (Samatar 1999: 150) and had generated some 11,000 jobs. Along with other government development programmes and policies, the FAP directed many people with initiative and energy towards a market economy that was highly dependent on the market demand represented by the state government, directly or indirectly. Many of them were people well established in the livestock sector who diversified their economic engagement into off-farm sectors. Significantly, as already suggested in the case of the Kalanga, a number of well-paid civil servants and political leaders started to engage in private enterprises; hence also they were caught into the process of dominant class formation. In addition, many political leaders – including people who had no basis in the livestock sector like the recently retired state president, Festus Mogae – started to engage in commercial enterprises (see Good 2008: 69ff.). With very limited experience in off-farm activities, many of these people established simple retail shops – above all dry-cleaning and bottle stores were favoured. The wealthiest also bought shares in larger companies run by Indians or foreigners.

Therefore, the diamond-derived state wealth strengthened a political economy that privileged the dominant elites and *reinforced their shared class interests in a sustainable state under the rule of a strong ruling group* that perpetuated programmes and projects which greatly privileged those who had the required initial assets to take advantage of them. Of course, with the expansion of state programmes that provided financial and technical support for productive and other entrepreneurial activities, more people were caught up in a dependency on the state, including an increasing number of people beyond the dominant elites which at the early postcolonial stage ensured the ruling group a solid political platform. They became no less dependent on a strong state that generously supported, directly and indirectly, entrepreneurial activity of different kinds. And note, this development meant that people across the party political spectrum were progressively caught up in extensive dependency on the state, meaning that there were, as I shall elaborate in Chapter 8, poor conditions for the creation of a political elite with a political agenda breaking away from the dominant elites of central concern in this chapter.

The central point is that a diamond-sourced political economy expanded a state system of wealth distribution that was basically institutionalized, as I have explained, with the development of the state's livestock-centred political economy. While the proceeds from diamonds in countries like Angola and Sierra Leone played into political situations in ways that vastly exaggerated existing conflicts of civil wars and excessive violence, revenues from diamond mining in Botswana was caught into a state treasury that was controlled by a unified political leadership. In this context, the diamonds served to consolidate and expand a political economy that only reinforced the dependency on the existing order of the state amongst the increasingly diversified dominant class and also increasingly a spectre of small entrepreneurs and petty traders.

It goes without saying that however unquestionably favourable this order was amongst people of power and wealth, state resources were not unlimited and hence invited considerable competition and rivalry. People who were in a position to engage in commercial ventures were drawn into competitive games, as epitomized by the scramble for arable land and, especially boreholes, pastures and ranches.[13] Moreover, the heated competition for residential land in the wake of the rapidly expanding urban centres from the mid-1980s onwards found one of its major culminations in Botswana's first major corruption 'scandals' involving high government officials, including the vice president (see Good 1994: 502). Furthermore, however generous the government's financial assistance from FAP and the National Development Bank, such assistance was not readily available to everybody. The consequent competitive situation gave rise to much conspiracy which spilled into political life, causing an ever-more-apparent concern that people with a BDP affiliation were preferred. It is not easy to determine to what extent this was the case. Yet it seems justified that key opposition politicians have been brought into dependency on the ruling party by receiving handsome loans and other forms of financial support (see Makgala 2005: 321). In fact, many of them are as engaged in off-farm enterprises as are those of the ruling party.

---

13. There is a substantial literature that addresses these issues from different angles, including Comaroff 1977; Hitchcock 1978; Werbner 1980, 1993; Gulbrandsen 1986a, 1996a; Mazonde 1994; Peters 1994; Makepe 2005.

In other words, however competitive people aspiring for power and wealth have been, they have readily gravitated into a basic dependency on the state as the sustainable, generous source of resources and, importantly, a reliable protector of private property. They have all been attracted by the state's tremendous financial, legislative and technical facilitation of individual commercial or manufacturing activities. These attractions and aspirations have given rise to an emerging class of 'bourgeois' capitalists and petty traders that are integral to a state-centred, diamond-driven political economy

Internationally, the image of Botswana has nevertheless featured as one of the least corrupt countries in the world, according to such ratings as that of Transparency International.[14] But in more recent times it has become increasingly evident that the expansion of Botswana's private sector of the economy from the late 1980s – with the state as a major customer and with the fall of a legal bar between government employment and commercial engagement – the ground has been well prepared for corrupt practices. The most recent of a series of corruption cases culminated in September 2010 by the resignation of the minister of defence, security and justice, Ndelu Seretse (of the Bangwato royal family and a close relative to President Ian Khama). He had then been charged with corruption by the Directorate of Public Prosecutions because 'between June 17 and 18, 2008 in Gaborone, whilst he was a member of the cabinet of the Republic of Botswana, wherein he served as the minister of defence, justice and security, and as such responsible for the Botswana Police Service, minister Seretse is alleged to have entered into contract with the Botswana Police'. Reportedly, he had a direct interest as shareholder and director in a company with which the Botswana Police Service, a department under his ministry, proposed to enter into a contract for the supply, delivery and commissioning of aviation ground support equipment.[15]

That there are a number of skeletons due to fall out of the closet is illuminated by a case directly relating to diamonds and the relationship between De Beers and the state: while it has seemed obvious that Botswana made a quite favourable deal with De Beers, David Magang (2008), once a cabinet minister, relates that he, as responsible for the Ministry of Mineral Resources, questioned why Botswana had not been even tougher in their negotiation with the diamond mining company. His colleagues, including Quett Masire (at the time the state president), were

---

14. On the Transparency International ranking list for 2008, Botswana was identified as number 36 amongst 180 countries around the world.

15. Mmegi, 1 September 2010.

allegedly evasive and unwilling to pursue the issue, the reason being, suggests Magang, that Masire had received financial support by this company for his private enterprises (which, in fact, Masire himself has subsequently confirmed).[16] As this had ostensibly happened some twenty-five years ago, the diamond mining company's recent public declaration that these practices had been brought to an end has nourished conspiracy theories that considerable diamond money has found its way into the pockets of state officials, softening them before negotiations.

However much the dominant class in Botswana has been privileged by very generous, state-sponsored projects and programmes, these resources have, I recall, been predominantly distributed according to legitimate political and bureaucratic decisions. The cases referred to here are radically different, of a rhizomic kind operating in hidden ways laterally beyond the hierarchical order of the state, patently undermining the strength of the state by causing damage to the legitimacy of the state leadership. In Chapter 8 I shall pursue this issue further by explaining how such 'war-machines' – in popular imagination – operate in occult ways.

All that said about use and abuse of diamond-sourced state wealth, let me finally stress that this does, of course, not mean that the state treasury merely sponsors private entrepreneurships. While these distributions have been essential to sustain the legitimacy of the ruling group amongst people of power and wealth, it goes without saying that the state has deployed quite different measures to gain legitimacy amongst all the rank and file sections of the population. For, as I shall discuss in Chapter 5, parallel with preaching how critically important liberal individualism and private entrepreneurship are for the development of the nation, it is asserted that the overall objective of the state is social justice and other virtues of the 'common good'.

Expansion of State Bureaucracy and Reinforcement of the Dominant Class

During the first decade and a half of independence, Botswana's central government as well as its district administrations were to a very great extent populated by European and American 'experts' and 'volunteers'. This guaranteed the ruling group a very competent and indeed loyal civil service. Although many of the expatriates – especially the volunteers – were at times critical, even highly critical, of government policies and programmes because so many of them favoured the privileged sections of the

16. Mmegi, 25 February 2010.

population,[17] the fact that they were on temporary contracts compelled them to keep a low profile. They were also constrained by government restrictions, imposed on all civil servants, which barred them from engaging publicly in what could be defined as 'politics'. On a more positive note, the vast numbers of often enthusiastic and very qualified people, accustomed to Western government practices and eager to preach the virtues of bureaucracy, meant that the government machinery in Botswana operated with considerable efficiency and force from the beginning.

Most positions became localized from the late 1970s onwards. As a result, young, educated Batswana were gradually socialized into a professional bureaucracy. On the one hand, they followed careers that gave them a handsome salary, which in many cases meant resources to raise cattle and off-farm enterprises, thus sympathizing strongly with major state policies and programmes. On the other hand, for reasons already explained, they were barred from engaging in political activities and challenging the political leadership. The state bureaucracy has always represented the driving force behind the development and implementation of government policies. But, as was often asserted to me by experienced bureaucrats in the Ministry of Finance and Development Planning and other important ministries, they were always aware of the political limits set by the political leadership.[18] Hence, despite how critical some of them might have been to government policies, senior civil servants have operated much as a force integral to the state-building efforts directed by a ruling group. On the whole, the civil service has been highly instrumental in implementing policies in the interests of the state-carrying dominant class which also includes policies aiming at bringing large sections of the unprivileged sectore into the process of state formation (see Chapter 7).

In needs to be added, however, that the political leadership wanted more from its senior civil servants than loyalty to the major policy objectives, which largely remained uncontroversial across the party political spectrum. They also wanted civil servants' political support which could be expressed, not through active political engagements, but through membership and other legitimate signals of adherence. In widespread conspiracies amongst civil servants I recorded in the late 1970s, such adherence was rewarded by resources like permits to drill boreholes for

---

17. For example, the establishment of the National Policy of the Tribal Grazing Lands (see above) in the mid-1970s caused much critical debate among expatriates, especially Peace Corps volunteers, who rightly saw it as a policy favouring the wealthy cattle elite.

18. Charlton 1991: 237 (quoted after Samatar 1999: 67) asserts, for example, that the ruling party of 'the BDP has the power and the ability to intervene decisively and definitely … at any or all stages of a policy-making process'.

watering cattle, extensive *de facto* private land in the form of ranches, favourable loans for purchasing breeding animals, tractors etc. These conspiracies were strongly stimulated when the first corruption scandals featured in the late 1980s and accelerated in the 1990s, probably responsible for a substantial decline in the support of the ruling party in the 1994 election.

Rewarding political loyalty with public resources and corruption are both practices exterior to the order of the state with rhizomic property in relation to state organs. Nevertheless, even at present late postcolonial times, Botswana continues, I reiterate, to feature amongst the less corrupt countries, especially in an African context, but also in the larger world. Yet, the question is, as suggested, whether many more skeletons are due to fall out of the closet.

Conclusion

In this chapter I have tried to come to terms with why Botswana has not been faced with the problem of 'fusion of elites' which, I recall, Bayart attributes to state failures in postcolonial Africa. On the contrary, a sustainable ruling group has been underpinned by the formation of a 'grand coalition'. That is, an assemblage of people of power and wealth which encompasses not only those directly engaged in the processes of establishing a modern state government but also people beyond these limits, in particular people with large herds of cattle and persons of authority well positioned in the hierarchies of the Tswana *merafe*. These are people who alternatively might have challenged the establishment of a centralized nation-state, for example through an organized effort to implement what some important Tswana *dikgosi* wanted – a federal state. That is, I recall from Chapter 2, a construction within which, in particular, the rulers of the Tswana *merafe* would have been left with much more executive authority than what has been granted them within the republican constitution of Botswana. The following chapters will discuss the rhizomic potentials represented by the symbolic wealth and politico-juridical institutions that are still controlled by people of authority, power and wealth within the Tswana *merafe*. Without capturing them into the process of state formation, these indigenous conditions might have created the kind of exteriority to the state which Deleuze and Guattari have conceptualized as breeding grounds for war-machines (see Introduction), detrimental to all the efforts of building a strong nation-state.

The key to comprehend the initiation of a 'grand coalition' is, in my analysis, the symbolic, political and commercial significance of cattle, bridging, in particular, the elites of Tswana royal centres and modern political leaders of the post-colonial state, educated people making careers in government service and people engaged in indigenous political and judicial practices at superior levels in the hierarchies of the Tswana *merafe*. I am, of course, not arguing that all elites that contributed to developing a modern state government were obsessed by accumulating cattle, the Kalanga being, as explained, a case that underscores this point. Moreover, although not all elites obsessed by cattle entrepreneurship were caught into the Seretse Khama–led political movement that materialized in the ruling party (see Chapter 2), they were, I have argued, captured into a process of state formation where they saw a strong state with a sustainable government as indispensable for establishing all the conditions required to develop a prosperous livestock industry and highly profitable beef trade with Europe.

In explaining that postcolonial development in Botswana had a unique trajectory owing to the impact of the commercial livestock industry, I do not simply relate the formation of a 'grand coalition' to the coalescence of interest across such divides as indicated above. This coalescence would not have gained such a tremendous political significance unless it had conjugated with other crucial conditions, the most significant being the British – and subsequently the EEC's – acceptance of beef imports from Botswana. I have explained how critical the establishment of a strong, centralized state in Botswana was for this conjugation of conditions to manifest. Notably, this was a conjugation of local and global conditions within which the symbolic and political as well as the material significance of cattle was indispensable, just as in the formation of precolonial Tswana *merafe* (see Chapter 1). The contexts were, to be sure, very different, yet both cases are ethnographically intriguing as cattle wealth is predominantly associated with acephalous political orders – 'it is difficult to centralise cows' (Goody 1974: 33). In the larger context of precolonial as well as postcolonial state formation across the world, such a political significance of the symbolic and material value of cattle is hardly found anywhere.

That the state-centred development of Botswana's livestock industry involved major programmes and projects that progressively captured people of power and wealth into the process of state formation involved the creation of multiple structures for the state's dissemination of public resources. I have thus argued that the tremendous revenues from the diamond industry that accelerated from the mid-1970s onwards entered the state treasury in a situation where institutionalized ways to distribute privileges to people of power and wealth were already in place. In other words, diamond-derived resources entered a political landscape radically different from that of those in countries where diamonds powerfully amplified major political divides, entailing civil wars and other violent calamities.

In Botswana, by contrast, diamonds have enabled the state to expand projects and programmes that brought ever more people engaged in off-farm enterprises into dependency – directly or indirectly – on the state (see Molutsi 1989b: 124–25). Significantly conditioned by the abandonment of legal constraints on civil servants' engagement in off-farm commercial ventures in the early 1980s and facilitated by new state financial and technical assistance programmes, a major process was sparked off in the mid-1980s that represented a momentous expansion of the private sector of the country's economy. And, note, the state – which sourced this economic development (Edge 1998: 334f.) – continued to feature as superstructural, in the Foucauldian sense, to ever-more-diversified networks of power.

This involved a major transformation of the always highly state-dependent, dominant class. First, by a progressive differentiation of inequality amongst people of power and wealth, and the crystallization of a super-elite of people who have been particularly successful in exploiting the private, off-farm sector of the economy. Second, in a short time these elite people have developed a kind of urban, Western-oriented bourgeoisie culture of nouveau riches, residing in a posh, suburban area near the capital in grand mansions or luxury villas in proximity to a golf club. They epitomize a modernist kind of orientation that gradually impacts on customary practices, most apparent, perhaps, in recent changes in wedding ceremonies that such people conduct in spectacular parties at their mansions or fashionable hotels with hundreds of people – always by invitation. Heavily dependent as they are on the diamond-driven political economy, they remain, to be sure, within the 'grand coalition' underpinning the state, despite all the competitions and conflicts amongst them – as amongst state-carrying bourgeoisies everywhere.

This trend has thus represented a further reinforcement of the state, as it had developed and been consolidated up to 1990. In the conception of Deleuze and Guattari, the state apparatus of capture continued also after that time to bring into the order of the state an ever-more-diversified assemblage of people of power and wealth. Yet, at the same time this development created new spaces of exteriority to the state where hidden exercise of power threatened its order, occasionally revealed to the public in the form of major corruption scandals. This involved a development which has, as I shall explain in Chapter 8, progressively affected negatively the legitimacy of the political leadership, especially amongst all the poor and unprivileged sections of the population.

On the whole, the networks of power that keep the ever-more-diversified, privileged sections of the population in dependency on the prevailing order of the state have, I reemphasize, expanded and been reinforced. Although the dominant classes have been more and more diversified, and, as I have explained, conflicts and rivalries within them intensified, the state prevails as superstructural in the sense of being constitutive to their dependency on the order of the state and will most likely continue to be so as long as the state treasury receives all the wealth from the diamond industry or other sources. To phrase it in Poulantzas' (1978: 127) general terms, 'the State constitutes the political unity of the dominant classes, thereby establishing them as dominant'.

This means also that however significant cattle 'interests' were initially to the creation of a dominant class – or grand coalition – that persistently underpinned the ruling group, this was not a matter of a 'bovine elite' dictating governmental policies (cf. Holm 1985: 174–75; Molutsi 1989b: 125f.). With huge foreign aid and revenues from diamond mining, 'a typical developmental state [occurred] where the bureaucracy and the ruling party mesh' (Taylor 2005: 52). In this intercourse, a 'development'-oriented civil service, for a long time populated by Western, aid-sponsored 'experts' and 'volunteers', represented a driving force behind not only diversifying programmes and projects favouring commercial enterprises beyond livestock production. All these projects that favoured the privileged were 'balanced' by major welfare programmes directed towards the vast rank-and-file sections of the population. For the ruling party, one thing was to establish legitimacy among people of power and wealth; another critical matter has, of course, been to ensure electoral support amongst all the poor and unprivileged sections of the population.

In the following chapters we shall see how the modern state in Botswana evolved as an autonomous force in the sense of operating in ways that cannot be derived immediately from any simple notion of it being an instrument in the hands of a dominant class. This is a case in point to testify to Badiou's (2005: 105) general critique of such a notion and his assertion that '[t]he State is simply the necessary metastructure of every historico-social situation, which is to say that the law guarantees that there is Oneness, not in the immediacy of society – that is always provided for by the non-state structure – but amongst the set of its subjects' (see also Clastres 1987: 203). In this conception, notwithstanding how important the state might be perceived to be by those included in the dominant class as instrumental to their interests, the postcolonial state is not *of* this class, in which case the state would simply have been what was there already (Badiou 2005: 106).

Chapter 4

THE STATE AND INDIGENOUS AUTHORITY STRUCTURES
Ambiguities of Co-optation and Confrontation

However crucial, the development of a grand coalition has, of course, not been a sufficient condition for the post-colonial state in Botswana to prevail as strong and sustainable. In accordance with what I indicated in the Introduction about the Foucauldian notion of the state as 'superstructural' in relation to a wide range of power networks, I shall show how the establishment of the postcolonial state involved a major transformation through which the Tswana *merafe* and other indigenous authority structures became highly instrumental to the state for the exercise of societal control without overt exercise of coercive power.

The establishment of a strong postcolonial state in Botswana has not only been a matter of bringing the Tswana *merafe* and other indigenous authority structures under control. The strength of the state and sustainability of its government have, from the outset, depended upon state agents' extensive engagement with the symbolism, practices and institutions of indigenous authority hierarchies at all levels. This is the overall issue of the present and the two following chapters where I am centrally concerned with how the population has gradually become integral to the development of the modern state during the formative and consolidating period (1966–1990). Although there were voices at the time of Botswana's independence predicting that the *dikgosi* and the structures of which they are the apex would die a silent death, and despite the fact that there has since then been considerable ambivalence amongst the postcolonial state leadership towards the *dikgosi* (and vice versa), these chapters will show how instrumental the symbolic wealth and sociopolitical institutions of the Tswana *merafe* and other indigenous authority structures have been for capturing the population into the process of state building.

In Chapter 2 I explained some of the *dikgosi's* resistance towards being subjected to the nation-state of Botswana and how the matter was finally resolved by co-opting them into the structures of the state by subjecting them – along with all significant indigenous authorities in the country – to the state president as civil servants. Through particular provisions in the Constitution the *dikgosi* were granted *ex officio* membership of the House of Chiefs, an advisory body to the nation's Parliament. This meant that they lost virtually all the *executive* powers they had enjoyed within the colonial state. Since the *dikgosi* and other indigenous authorities were in control not only of 'polities' in a narrow Western sense but the all-encompassing sociopolitical hierarchies of the *merafe* in which the vast majority of the population was embedded, this transformation meant that the state captured into its domain major institutions of societal control. In particular, the hierarchy of customary courts still prevails under the *dikgosi's* precedence, albeit – as in colonial times – people may, as I shall explain, appeal their cases to courts within a Western court system. In this chapter I am centrally concerned with what it meant, in the words of du Toit (1995: 91), that 'the customary law and the *lekgotla* became formal extensions in the modern state.'

The hierarchies of customary courts are not simply a matter of top-down, imposed state system of social control, captured by the state and made instrumental to control the population. The indigenous authority structures are, as we shall see, to a great extent reproduced from below by virtue of popular, positive engagement, virtually as an aspect of their everyday life. An everyday life that has, to a great extent, resonated positively with the superior authority that people still ascribe to the *dikgosi* and *dikgosana*, despite their extensive loss of executive power at independence some thirty-five years ago. Note that although *dikgosi* are recognized in the Constitution and granted *ex officio* membership of the House of Chiefs (*Ntlo ya Dikgosi*), an advisory chamber in the nation's Parliament, they are entrusted with far less power by the state than 'chiefs' in some other postcolonial African states such as South Africa (Sklar 2005: 21; cf. van Kessel and Oomen 1999). This means that the *dikgosi* are, on the one hand, quite marginalized within the context of a modern state government. On the other hand, they prevail as the much respected apex of hierarchical orders – as the custodians of the symbolic wealth vested in the *bogosi*. The *dikgosi* thus continue to feature in indigenous cosmology as the 'link of mediation' with the royal ancestorhood (see Chapter 1).

This chapter is divided into two major sections where I address the post-colonial Tswana *merafe* because, apart from encompassing vast sections of the population, they are cases in point for pursuing the issues indicated above. In the first major section I am concerned with the ambivalent relationship between the state and the *dikgosi* just indicated. On the one hand, I observe that, on the whole, the *dikgosi* submit to the state, which is, of course, one important condition for the smooth incorporation of the *merafe* in the post-colonial state formation. On the other hand, ambivalence prevails and I shall examine two major cases in which Tswana *dikgosi* and their people have been challenging the state in ways that gave rise to the most serious confrontation during postcolonial times in the relationship between the state and a *morafe*. These confrontations have not only been very serious but also highly exceptional, begging an answer to the question of why most of the *dikgosi* have, after all, readily submitted to the postcolonial state as loyal civil servants. Although exceptional, these cases are important because they so evidently demonstrate the *merafe's* potential to mobilize the people, even against agents of the state. What is more, the cases bring to life the existential importance of *bogosi* and the centrality of the *kgosi* in people's lives. These issues actualize the question of the limits of the state's interference in the affairs of the *bogosi*. This question I pursue by examining another major conflict – still in progress – where the *kgosi* deploys age regiments (*mephato*) in violent campaigns to instil discipline and respect for the *bogosi*.

Importantly, both case studies substantiate the criticism I made in the Introduction of current scholarly works elsewhere in Africa that address the relationship between the state and indigenous or 'traditional' authorities without examining the structures within which these figures are only the apex. I pursue this issue further in the second main section where I want to come to terms with what the conditions have been for the reproduction of symbols, practices and institutions of authority anchored in indigenous cosmology. I want, amongst others, to substantiate the point already suggested – that this order is in important respects reproduced from below by examining the *kgotla* as a discursive field at all levels, from that of the descent group to the royal centre. While I am centrally concerned in this volume with the formative and consolidating decades (1966–90), I shall finally explain that the processes and structures I am identifying are also of considerable significance after the massive movement of people to urban areas from the late 1980s and onwards.

Merafe vs. the State

The seven Tswana *merafe* – Bakgatla-baga-Kgafela, Bakwena, Bamalete, Bangwato, Bangwaketse, Batawana and Batlokwa – that were officially recognized by the British within the context of the colonial state (see Chapter 1), plus Barolong, were named in Botswana's Constitution where their respective *dikgosi* were, as suggested, recognized as *ex officio* members of the House of Chiefs[1] in the National Parliament. The communities beyond the territories claimed by these *merafe* have been represented by four elected members. In addition, the *ex officio* and elected members selected three 'specially elected members' (Constitution of Botswana of 1966, Sec.77 and 78). The Tswana *dikgosi* were thus in a majority in this house, and, significantly, they represented all the communities within the territories they were assigned by the British, including those of ethnic minorities. As I explained in Chapter 1, larger *merafe* – Bakwena, Bangwato, Bangwaketse, Batawana – are composed of a substantial number of 'minority' communities that have not been assimilated into – or do not identify with – the respective dominant Tswana communities. In the next chapter I shall examine the extensive (and partially successful) mobilization of those minority communities against the state which started in the mid-1990s, with the request for recognition in line with the recognition of the dominant Tswana and the elimination of clauses in the Constitution of 1966 heavily criticized as discriminatory (see Chapter 5). Very recently the Constitution has been revised to ensure broader representation.

In actual practice the *dikgosi* and other indigenous authorities rarely appear in public as spokespersons of their *morafe* in relation to the government, and they hardly ever call for meetings in the *kgotla* in order to consult the *morafe* on matters on the agenda in the assemblies of which they are *ex officio* members. Of course, they are expected not to do so by state officials who always emphasize that the *dikgosi* and other indigenous authorities are, as civil servants, barred from engaging politically. Interestingly, I have never registered that they have been expected to do so by individuals or groups within their respective *merafe* either. These authority figures are themselves certainly comfortable with acting independently and seeking advice informally. Their engagement in the House of Chiefs,

---

1. By the establishment of the *Bogosi* Act in 2008, this house was renamed in Setswana *Ntlo ya Dikgosi*.

where they are entitled to call upon cabinet ministers to answer questions and debate current political issues, occasionally appears in newspaper headlines. But it is very hard to tell if it has any impact upon political processes within a political system where the legislative assembly of the Parliament has often been heavily dominated by the state president and his ministers (e.g. see Good 2008: 28ff.). In the District Councils the *dikgosi* have mostly held a low profile. One apparent exception is the charismatic *Kgosi* Linchwe II of the Bakgatla (r. 1963–2007) who enjoyed tremendous authority amongst his people, at least during the first decades of his reign (see Chapter 8 and below). As an *ex officio* member he was elected chairman of the District Council where he had great impact – as he also had on the Tribal Land Board. The other high-profile *kgosi* in postcolonial times, *Kgosi* Seepapitso IV of the Bangwaketse (r. 1969–2010), found himself ignored[2] in the District Council, while he was able to have some influence on the Tribal Land Board.[3]

This also means that the *dikgosi* and other authority figures very seldom mobilize people in the context of the *kgotla* in ways that provoke state officials, an exceptional case in point being the recently enthroned *kgosi* of the Bakgatla, Kgafela II. In this section I shall examine his neo-traditionalist efforts to mobilize the Bakgatla for the purpose of instilling discipline and reinforcing the hierarchy of indigenous authority, especially the position of the *kgosi*.

From the point of view of the state, the *dikgosi* and *dikgosana* should conduct their offices according to what is stipulated in Botswana's legislation, notably the Chieftainship Act of 1966 that was replaced recently by the *Bogosi* Act (of 2008). The Chieftainship Act establishes that the 'dikgosi, sub-chiefs and headmen shall be paid' by government (Sec. 16(1)), the limits of their power and their duties are in very broad terms – 'to promote the welfare of members of the tribe' (Sec. 18). In practice, the most important task of the *dikgosi* and *dikgosana* is to make available to the state their respective *kgotla*. Here they are, on the one hand, expected to act, according to customary principles, as judges in the hierarchy of the indigenous courts, which is incorporated in the state's judicial structure as 'customary courts' by virtue of the Customary Courts Act. On the

---

2. So he repeatedly complained during our many conversations. This probably reflects that the Council was dominated by Botswana Democratic Party while Seepapitso was associated with his father who had, I recall, abdicated to join party politics and became a leading figure in the major opposition party, Botswana national front. However, Seepapitso who, after all, was not on good terms with his father, did not associate with this party, at least in such ways that the government could accuse him of being engaged in party politics.

3. Several members have, over the years, often complained about his overt exercise of authority as *kgosi*. For example, while frequently being absent in meetings ('without apology'), he might appear in one meeting only to require reversed decisions made in his absence.

other hand, whenever agents of the state require communicating with a community, they should call for and conduct a meeting in the *kgotla*. Indigenous authority figures live up to these expectations to a very great extent; in the subsequent major section and the following chapters I shall discuss the significance of this in relation to post-colonial state formation in this country.

There are, however, two major cases of confrontation and conflict between the *merafe* and the state which perfectly demonstrate that this state of affairs should not be taken for granted. What is more, they reveal that the popular attraction of the symbolic wealth vested in the *bogosi* has not deteriorated in the wake of massive movements to urban centres since the late 1980s and as a consequence of the Batswana's intense and massive exposure to Western modernity. This means that the hierarchical structures of the *merafe* are intact and, above all, that considerable potential for mobilization is still vested in them. To this we now turn.

State Suspension of a *Kgosi* and *Bogosi* in Crisis

The series of events I shall examine was initiated in April 1994, when the minister of local government and lands, Chapson Butale, appeared in the royal *kgotla* of the Bangwaketse and accused their *kgosi* – Seepapitso IV – of grave negligence of duty. He presented a number of allegations, prompted by the most recent one: *Kgosi* Seepapitso's failure to prepare for a ceremonial reception in the Bangwaketse royal *kgotla* for the president of Zambia, Frederick Chiluba, who was on a state visit in the country. In summarizing all his complaints about the *kgosi's* misconduct in office, the minister declared: 'Now Bangwaketse, I say you that *Kgosi* of Bangwaketse *Kgosi* Seepapitso IV is beyond my control, and I have found it necessary to suspend the *Kgosi* of the Bangwaketse'.[4] The minister concluded by appointing *Kgosi* Seepapitso's eldest son, Leema, to act in his place. This is, to be sure, a most serious and a highly exceptional way to call a *kgosi* to account. In postcolonial times only *Kgosi* Seepapitso himself had been suspended (in 1973) before 1994.

My Bangwaketse friends and acquaintances immediately perceived the suspension as state intervention into matters that lay at the heart of their *bogosi*, to be handled by the most senior members of the *morafe*. Of course, it made matters still worse that *Kgosi* Seepapitso was absolutely opposed to the idea that Leema should act in his place. Leema was, however, apparently tempted by prospects of permanently replacing his

---

4. In Setswana: 'Jaanong Bangwaketse ke rola ame ke re *Kgosi* ya Bangwaketse *Kgosi* Seepapitso IV o mpaletse ka jalo ka re ke seegela Kgosi ya Bangwaketse fa thoko'.

father. *Kgosi* Seepapitso approached Leema in a letter, requiring him to step down, which Leema rejected, stating, '[o]ur relationship has been a healthy one until I received this letter from my father … instructing me to quit as a chief'. Leema refused to obey, arguing, 'I was appointed by the government, and it's only the government which is going to remove me'.[5] Bangwaketse elders were careful not to abandon Leema at this stage because that might have made it more difficult to reconcile him with this father. The fact that he was offered a house by the government and was driving a Mercedes Benz gave rise to suspicion that the government was bribing him.

In popular conception, the fact that Leema had not been fortified by *dingaka* of the royal *kgotla*, and hence left vulnerable and weak, readily turned him into an instrument for agents of the state. The blame was thus put on government officials for pursuing their case by means of dirty methods, only to cause great damage to the *morafe* and destroy 'our culture'. In a meeting in the royal *kgotla*, one elder appealed to Leema: 'Come over to our side; the government is just damaging you!' The matter was delicate because Leema was, after all, the heir to the *bogosi*. There was a sincere concern that the intervention of the state would give rise to a major dynastic conflict by drawing a line between father and son. I was repeatedly told that the ground was prepared for such a development, because the most senior elders of the *morafe* – the paternal uncles (*rrang-wane*) of the *kgosi*[6] – kept a low profile in the conflict. It was conspired, they were siding with the state and supporting Leema due to their poor relationship with *Kgosi* Seepapitso.

The group of concerned parties (of which the senior elders – at odds with the *kgosi* – were not a part) conducted a highly successful money-collection campaign amongst the Bangwaketse to hire an attorney who, on behalf of 'the Bangwaketse tribe and *Kgosi* Seepapitso', addressed the minister in a letter.[7] The claim was, specifically, that the allegations were without substance and 'provided no justification for the provisions of Section 12 of the [Chieftainship] Act to be brought into play'. The attorney general responded immediately on behalf of the state, defending the decision of the minister as lawful and proper and pointing out that a commission of inquiry was due to be established, addressing 'the fitness of the subject to be a Chief'. On this basis, 'depending on the outcome, either

---

5. *Mmegi (Gaborone)*, 20–26 May 1994.
6. These are recognized as the *dikgosi*'s most senior councillors, always seated at the right-hand side of him in the *kgotla* and each of them being the senior descendent of each of the houses of the hero *Kgosi* Makaba II (ruling 1790–1824) and ranked in the same order as the houses of *Kgosi* Makaba's wives.
7. Letter from Modisanyane & Co. to The Hon. Minister of Local Government, Land & Housing, 17 May 1994.

the suspended Chief will be restored to his position, or proper steps will be taken under the act to fill the position'.[8]

The public debate soon reached a national level as reflected in the most important newspapers. It was observed, for example, that '[t]he suspension … is indeed spiralling into an inferno … the calls for Seepapitso's reinstatement have tapped into the depth of tribalism, which the government has been trying hard to ignore'.[9] In several editorials the state intervention was attacked and condemned, e.g. as 'autocratic and capricious'. There was a deep concern among the Bangwaketse that the *bogosi* was in the hands of a man who had, in most people's view, betrayed his own father and their *kgosi*. The perceived disorder was linked to the absence of rain, seen by people as a most critical indication of the destructive impact of the heat (*mogote*) building up in the *bogosi* by the state's intervention. Significantly, a discourse developed that more explicitly than before had as a theme the idea of the value of 'our culture' as anchored in the *bogosi* – 'if the state kills *bogosi*, the state kills us'. This was a notion I recorded in all Bangwaketse quarters I visited, in urban centres as well as remote villages, amongst senior elders as well as rank-and-file youngsters.

It was in this atmosphere of anger and frustration that the state president, Quett Masire, arrived in the Bangwaketse royal *kgotla* on one of his routine visits of 'consultation' (a practice I shall examine extensively in Chapter 6). His agenda was to inform the people about an entirely different matter – Botswana's foreign reserves. Leema, now acting as the *kgosi*, chaired the meeting; Seepapitso was absent. While the state president commonly attracts substantial numbers of people to the royal *kgotla* during a visit, on this occasion the *kgotla* was packed by hundreds of people.

As soon as the president had finished his speech, an elder (Rabotho Sebonego) – known as a particularly forceful and brave speaker – stood up and addressed the president in the typical ironic (*nonola*) style of Bangwaketse rhetorical practice, filled with understatements:

> I know I am speaking to a gentleman of the Sealetsa descent, whose totem is *phiri*. I must let you know that you find us still living because of God's grace. There were disturbances such that I expected this village of yours, the Ngwaketse village, would have been the first issue of concern and discussion, which would have also come as consolation to us [clapping of hands]. At times you leave us for lengthy periods and we feel very neglected … My fellow elder, I must tell you that you almost found us not here. Something that has never happened here before came up in this vil-

---

8. Letter from Attorney General to Modisenyane & Co., 19 May 1994 (Ref. LX/18 (21)).
9. Editorial, *Mmegi*, 13–19 May 1994.

lage. Let me say, the situation almost brought bloodshed. You know, you are a Mongwaketse – I am not relating anything new to you.[10]

Mr Sebonego started here by indicating the president's identity as a Mongwaketse – one of their own. By making a reference to Masire's totem *phiri* (hyena) Mr Sebonego alluded to the president's rather inferior position in the hierarchy of the *morafe*;[11] which he repeated several times. This was to say that here, amongst us, you are just an ordinary somebody – from an inferior ward of immigrants (see Chapter 2). In other words, the state president was required to subject himself to the hierarchy of the *morafe* rather than prevailing as the apex of the state. Albeit designated as being of low rank, he was taken to task for ignoring his responsibilities as a Mongwaketse elder. Named as 'my fellow elder', Mr Sebonego went on to reprimand the president for not having terminated the state intervention in the *bogosi*, the heart of the *morafe*. Instead he had made the Bangwaketse highly vulnerable to serious disaster – 'you almost found us not here'. Mr Sebonego was repeatedly saluted; the atmosphere became increasingly nervous.

Several other speakers joined him in a series of similar attacks, much in the same rhetorical style, while Leema and some state officials supported President Masire. The former were frequently interrupted by indeed articulate support from the large audience. People's expression of anger and hostility toward the president culminated in a very tense atmosphere; the president's bodyguards and the police gathered around him. Afterwards people spoke of this as a shocking experience, very contradictory to what is imperative to the *kgotla*: a cool atmosphere (*hola*) of peace and harmony (*kagiso*), as I shall elaborate on in the second part of this chapter.

Before the apparently humiliated president left,[12] he defended himself by asserting all his responsibilities as the leader of the whole nation and the fact that he had left the issue with a particular commission of inquiry whose work was in progress. The Bangwaketse retreated in anger over a president-cum-elder of the *morafe* who was still evasive in relation to the perceived dangerous situation caused by his government's intervention in the *bogosi*. All the 'heat' (*mogote*) said to be generated during this meeting in the royal *kgotla* only added to popular fear and frustration.

---

10. Transcribed from a full video record of the meeting (in the archive of the author).

11. The reference to totem *phiri* significantly indicates Masire's foreign origins (see Schapera 1952: 43).

12. Although this was certainly one of his worst experiences as a political leader, he is silent about it in his recently published memoirs (Masire 2006).

With strong moral and financial backing from the *morafe*, *Kgosi* See-papitso took the state and his son, Leema, to the High Court where he applied for the court to declare his suspension and the appointment of Leema to act as a *kgosi* as unlawful. The application challenged the state's use of the Chieftainship Act, meaning that the government's exercise of power was attacked, not with reference to *mekgwa le melao ya Setswana*, but with reference to state legislation.

Furthermore, in response to all the wrongdoings claimed by the government, it was argued that the *kgosi* had performed entirely adequately and could not be accused of misconduct, according to the criteria set by the government itself. In other words, it was *not* denied that the agents of the state had the right, in principle, to require the *kgosi* to take on a number of duties as a civil servant. Rather, the claim was that the government's judgements of his performance were biased, partial and affected by the malaise of a free-speaking *kgosi*. More than that, it was alleged that the case was set in motion by an anti-Seepapitso conspiracy, centred in ministerial quarters. The court announced its judgement on 22 February 1995, stating:

(a) The application to challenge the suspension of the Applicant from the position of Chief is refused;

(b) The appointment of the 2nd respondent to act as Chief of the Bangwa-ketse pending the inquiry instituted by the Minister is unlawful.[13]

This was taken as more than half a victory. Although the suspension was sustained (also by the High Court of Appeal), the High Court's verdict that the state's temporary appointment of Leema was unlawful established that state intervention in matters of the *bogosi* without consulting/ or without reference to the Bangwaketse was against the law.

This also meant that, by now, the Bangwaketse *bogosi* had no incumbency, and that the state depended upon the Bangwaketse's nomination of a candidate to temporarily fill the royal office during the suspension of Seepapitso. But the Bangwaketse refused to co-operate in this matter. After the perceived disastrous confrontation between the state president and the Bangwaketse, and deeply worried by its political repercussions, senior Bangwaketse members of the ruling party decided behind the scenes

---

13. High Court of Botswana: Chief Seepapitso vs. Attorney General and Leema Kwena Gaseitsiwe (Misca. 229/94 & Misca. 310/94), Judgment in Open Court 22 February 1995. *Kgosi* Seepapitso subsequently appealed the High Court's acceptance of the suspension, but the High Court of Appeal dismissed the appeal by accepting all the allegations made by the state of Seepapitso's unfitness to serve as *kgosi* in respect of the first (1973) as well as second (1994) suspension, see http://196.211.206.107/bw/cases/BWCA/1996/9.html.

to bring the conflict to a halt. The state subsequently gave in.[14] Again the Bangwaketse were collected in large numbers in the royal *kgotla* to receive Minister Butale's vindication for an unconditional reinstatement, referring to 'the courteous manner in which members of the royal kraal and senior of the tribe pleaded for reinstatement. He claimed to have received assurances from the chief's paternal uncles that they would ensure that Seepapitso treads a proper path'.[15]

The Bangwaketse were satisfied that order was restored: By the end of the year the *merafe* was blessed with plenty of rain that was taken as a true sign of the *bogosi* being in proper conduct. I often heard stated 'when the *kgosi* was suspended, there was a lot of crime in the village. Now, when he is back in office, everything is much more calm – now we live in peace [*ka kagiso*]'.[16] The significance of this notion came home to me during a *lebatla* in the royal *kgotla* some months later where many speakers expressed strong appreciation for *Kgosi* Seepapitso, to whom was also dedicated a praise poem (cf. Schapera 1965) in gratitude for all the rain that had recently fallen. This notion of peace and order (*kagiso*) thus found its expression at the overall level of the *morafe*, in the form of rain (*pula*) – the perceived major source of life and the principal symbol of longevity and prosperity for everybody. And it underscores the main point of this section: popular appreciation of and attraction to the symbolic wealth of the *bogosi* and readiness to challenge the state to protect it. This is, above all, a question of sovereignty which is epitomized in the case to be examined in the following section, where a *kgosi* challenges the state's monopoly of violence.

Before I proceed, let me note that after the series of events following the suspension, *Kgosi* Seepapitso approached Masire's successor, President Festus Mogae, in the pursuit of obtaining a more attractive state post than that of a *kgosi*. It says a lot about the pragmatism of politics in Botswana – which has, as we have seen, long genealogies – that the president responded indeed positively: he sent this man – who had been repeatedly accused by state officials of bad performance as *kgosi* and suspended twice from office[17] – as Botswana's ambassador to the two major political powers

---

14. Ostensibly, members of Parliament from the ruling party, worried about the tremendous reactions amongst the Bangwaketse against the suspension of their *kgosi*, levelled pressure upon the minister to resolve the case by reinstalling Seepapitso.

15. *Mmegi,* 28 April–4 May 1995.

16. It belongs to this story that not only was the minister replaced: upon the reinstatement the district commissioner was moved to another district. Moreover, the suspicion of governmental bribing of Leema was, in the Bangwaketse eyes, evidenced by the fact that he was appointed court president of the urban customary court in Jwaneng.

17. The allegations are comprehensively listed in the High Court of Appeal Judgement of *Kgosi* Seepapitso case against the State and his son Leema, see http://196.211.206.107/bw/

on earth, first to Washington and then to Beijing.[18] After some six years in the diplomatic service he was, in November 2004, officially reinstalled in *bogosi* by the state president in the presence of hundreds of enthusiastic Bangwaketse in the royal *kgotla*. Ironically perhaps, this case represents an example of the way in which the Tswana exercise domination: as a process of reconciliation in the pursuit of co-optation.

Nevertheless, again revealing the ambivalent relationship between the *dikgosi* and the state, *Kgosi* Seepapito continued to the end[19] to blame the state for undermining *bogosi*, complaining that the president and cabinet ministers were belittling the *Ntlo ya Dikgosi* and that the president nullified *bogosi* because he had asserted that he had always been a republican and hence he thought that *dikgosi* should be elected like all other leaders. But, as in the past, Seepapitso never attempted to mobilize the *merafe* to put pressure on the government or to support his attack on political leaders. He limited himself to expressing critical statements on particular issues, mainly when government officials appeared in the royal *kgotla* to address the Bangwaketse (see Chapter 6) and in the *Ntlo ya Dikgosi*.[20] Although he was suspected of sympathizing with the major opposition party, the Botswana National Front (BNF) of which his father was, I recall, the leader for many years, his critical views on the government did not necessarily coincide with those of that party.

It is also significant that it was a group of elders that mobilized the *morafe* against the state in the suspension-case examined above and that

<hr>

cases/BWCA/1996/9.html.

18. The former state president Festus Mogae (1998–2008) told me in a conversation (17 January 2008) that *Kgosi* Seepapitso had approached him asking for a senior position within the government, referring amongst others to *Kgosi* Lentswe of Bakgatla who had become the president of the Customary Court. The president's positive response might have been motivated by a desire to get rid of an often-outspoken critique of government. However, it was allegedly Seepapitso who took the initiative, which is comprehensible in view of what I have indicated about the *kgosi*'s frustrations of being side-tracked in relation to senior civil servants, rising to power and wealth. Interestingly, the president also suggested that the transfer to Beijing was much due to Seepapitso's dismay at not being treated with due respect as an aristocrat by Americans. The Chinese, by contrast, treated him to his full satisfaction, which Seepapitso himself had already expressed to me in an earlier conversation (17 December 2005).

19. *Kgosi* Seepapitso became seriously ill in 2008 and was incapacitated until his death on 24 March 2010.

20. Let me suggest here that the relationship between *Kgosi* Seepapitso and the state leadership was always ambiguous in the sense that he tacitly engaged with them in the pursuit of personal interests, like approaching President Mogae. He co-operated with the then vice-president Masire and his brothers in getting hold of certain ranches, leading to the matter being set under investigation by a presidential commission appointed by President Khama shortly before his death. Upon President Khama's death and the taking over by President Masire of the commission, the commission's report was never released for the public and its recommendations never implemented.

the case was concerned with the *bogosi* much more than the *kgosi*. However, they were not attempting to generate political gains, albeit a number of them had affiliations to the BNF. They furiously rejected allegations about that because they knew that bringing party politics into the matter would escalate the conflict surrounding the *bogosi*, contradicting their major argument about the potentially disastrous consequences for the Bangwaketse of such conflicts.

Flogging in Support of *Bogosi*

Recently, there has been in progress a case of a *morafe* challenging the state in ways which might be significantly more consequential than the, after all, isolated confrontation between the Bangwaketse and the state in 1994. After the death of *Kgosi* Linchwe II of the Bakgatla-baga-Kgafela (2008), his eldest son and heir, Kgafela, was enthroned as *Kgosi* Kgafela II. He was at the time a well-known privately practising lawyer who had, amongst other things, proudly declared himself the attorney for 'Ditshwanelo – Botswana's Centre for Human Rights' in relation to this organization's protest against a death penalty judgement. After being enthroned, *Kgosi* Kgafela II soon manifested as a strong, outspoken *kgosi* who took an independent line in relation to the state, especially by applying violent means to instil discipline and respect for indigenous authorities.

Before I elaborate on this, let me explain that his father, *Kgosi* Linchwe II, represented a challenge to the state leadership already from the time of independence (see Parsons et al. 1995: 268, 278). Ostensibly, in an effort to get rid of his dissident voice during this critical period, he was sent as Botswana's ambassador to Washington in 1968. But upon his return in 1972 he continued to be outspoken against government agencies and policies, yet in ways that did not make it possible to accuse him of abusing power or otherwise misconduct of office. He had at an early stage aligned himself with the major opposition party (BNF), but he asserted to me in a conversation in 1977 that he operated 'beyond politics',[21] insisting on 'my right to express my views as the leader of my people'.

His challenging line was epitomized in 1975 by revitalizing the male initiation ritual of *bogwera* (Schapera 1978) – at once provoking President Khama[22] and reinforcing his already strong authority amongst the Bakgatla. The president attacked this venture as the renaissance of a wasteful, divisive ritual that 'smacks of seeds of disunity coming as it does at a time

---

21. Conversation with *Kgosi* Linchwe in his office, Mochudi, 10 January 1977.

22. President Seretse Khama and his modernist adherents had for many years counteracted cultural practices that smacked of 'tribalism', which thus came out clearly in the president's public attack of *Kgosi* Linchwe's revitalization of *bogwera* in 1975 (see Grant 1984: 8f.).

Illustration 4. The initiates arrive in the royal *kgotla* of the Bakgatla as the final stage of the *bogwera* in 1982. Courtesy of Sandy Grant.

when we thought we were winning the battle against tribalism'.[23] Seretse Khama's fear of a return to 'tribalism' and national disunity did, however, not come to pass, especially because no other *kgosi* took an interest in revitalizing a ritual practice that had been abandoned by the Tswana *dikgosi* for many decades (Chapter 2 above; Schapera 1984: 105). The Bakgatla alone did not amount to a threat to national unity, representing only a minor section of the population within a small territory. Together with the fact that there was probably no legal ground for intervention, this might be the reason why the state made no attempt to bring the *bogwera* to an end and there was hence no confrontation between the Bakgatla and the state on this matter. In fact the government was instrumental in accomplishing the first *bogwera* as the (Norwegian) regional medical officer executed the circumcision on state premises – the hospital in the Bakgatla royal town of Mochudi, in fact founded by the very same missionary society which required *Kgosi* Linchwe to abandon *bogwera*. Linchwe's immense authority amongst his people and the Bakgatla's enthusiastic participation in the *bogwera* emphasized the popular attraction of the symbolic wealth vested in the *bogosi*.

23. 'Towards Ten Years of Peace, Stability and Progress'. H.E. the President's Independence Day Message to the Nation, 30 September 1975. Government Printer. Quoted after Grant 1984: 8.

Let me recall at this point that several *dikgosi* abandoned the initiation ceremonies of *bogwera* (male) and *bojale* (female) at an early stage as required by evangelizing missionaries or stripped them of much of their ritual content (Schapera 1984: 71, 105–7).[24] *Kgosi* Linchwe took many people elsewhere in Botswana by surprise, and no other Tswana *dikgosi* or *merafe* followed suit, except in the very small *morafe* of Bamalete.[25] That there has been insignificant pressure from below amongst other peoples of Botswana to revive initiation ceremonies says much about the force by which they have been suppressed by the *dikgosi* since Christianity took hold. There prevailed, after all, considerable popular pressure for having them revived a long time after they had been abandoned (Chapter 2). Intriguingly, Linchwe let *bogwera* lapse after 1990 when he was co-opted by the state as the President of Customary Court of Appeal, seated in ministerial quarters of the capital. *Bogwera* as well as *bojale* were, however, soon revitalized by his son and heir, *Kgosi* Kgafela II, upon his enthronement in 2008. Some 1,500 'graduated' in the *bogwera* of 2009 – the largest number in Bakgatla history (see Illustration 5).

Bakgatla men participated enthusiastically from the beginning of Linchwe's revitalization of *bogwera*. With enthronement of Kgafela at a spectacular ceremony on 20 September 2008, where he arrived on horse-back in ritual attire in the presence of thousands of people and a large number dignitaries, he assured his subjects that they were about to get a *kgosi* who would be no less concerned with their cultural tradition than his late father. He called for a strengthening of the *bogosi* and reshaping of dwindling morality.[26] At the same time *Kgosi* Kgafela II asserted that he intended to work with the government to fulfill the people's aspirations. Actually, at this point he seemed to attach himself to state power as he let the state president Ian Khama – who is also the *kgosi* of the Bangwato

---

24. For example, everywhere they kept on forming *mephato*, however, only by summoning an age set of youngsters that were told that they had achieved the age of men and were to be identified as a *mophato* that was given a particular name (see Schapera 1984: 312 ff.; Livingston 2005: 96) After all, the *dikgosi* continued to mobilize the *mephato*, especially for access to communal labour. In the Bangwaketse, for example, members of a certain *mophato* proudly told me that they had built one of the primary schools in the royal town of Kanye in the 1950s (cf. Grant 1984: 7f.). The British clearly supported this practice. On the other hand, many men of the younger generation greatly appreciated the postcolonial state government's abandonment of *kgosi*'s power of calling the regiments for communal work.

25. At the level of local community, there are some very scattered cases which reportedly have kept *bogwera* and *bojale* alive (e.g. see Pnina Werbner (2009) on 'puberty rituals' amongst the Tswapong in the Central District).

26. See *The Botswana Gazette*, 23 September 2008.

– enthrone him as the *kgosi* of the Bakgatla by draping the leopard skin around his shoulders.

However, subsequently he starting complaining, like *Kgosi* Seepapitso, that less value is given 'to a *Kgosi* than to a council secretary or land board secretary', noting that their offices are 'posh as compared to the dilapidated structures occupied by chiefs.' Far more significantly, he expressed a deep concern about 'the government structures, which reduce chiefs [*dikgosi*] into servitude.' Wanting to be no less independent on the state than his father had attempted to be before he was co-opted, he declared, as the first *kgosi* in postcolonial times, that he would not be on the state payroll. He claimed that there was no such compulsion in Botswana's Constitution and legislation,[27] arguing that he was serving the state in many ways without being a civil servant: 'I have mobilized the tribe against crime and the continuing degeneration of social values. This is a massive contribution.'[28]

The state met this move only by excluding him from *Ntlo ya Dikgosi*, probably because he also refrained from taking on the presidency of the customary court; he left it with his younger brother. He has explained this arrangement by his larger commitments to ensure his subjects' welfare, instil discipline to beat crime and immoral behaviour and promote 'development' amongst the Bakgatla. Notably, it belongs to *Kgosi* Kgafela's wide-ranging plans 'to mobilize civil society to be politically active when it comes to interrogating burning issues',[29] the significance of which we shall see as we now proceed.

Kgosi Kgafela's ambitious approach is unparalleled amongst the *dikgosi* in postcolonial Botswana. As for development, he declared in a well-attended meeting in the royal *kgotla* – according to a national newspaper report which named him the 'Bakgatla sovereign' – that they are planning to build 'school, stadiums, shopping malls, residential homes' (including 'eco-homes') and initiating mining, dairy farming and a game reserve 'on the standards and magnitude of Madikwe and Pilansberg parks in South

---

27. On this score he was only partially right. It is true that the Constitution only mentions '*kgosi*' in respect of membership of the *Ntlo ya Dikgosi* (the House of Chiefs) and no legislation stipulates that the *kgosi* should be a civil servant and paid as such by the state. But it is evident from the Bogosi Act of 2008 (and the Chieftainship Act of 1966 which it replaced) that the *dikgosi* depend on state recognition in the sense that the state has full jurisdictional control over matters of appointment of a new *kgosi* and to suspend or remove her or him. What is more, every *kgosi* is required to 'to carry out any lawful instructions given to him or her by the Minister' (sec. 17(b)).

28. *See MmegiOnline*, 11 December 2009.

29. *MmegiOnline*, 11 December 2009.

Africa'.[30] The *kgosi* also wants 'to embark on a multi million Pula tourism project'. Such ventures are clearly inspired by the other, numerically major section of the Bakgatla located in the Transvaal beyond the South African border, which counts some 350,000 people and whose tribal administration, on an impressive website,[31] spells out their ambitious engagements and plans, especially in mining and tourism. These are 'tribal' endeavours of establishing commercial corporations that are also found elsewhere in South Africa (see Comaroff and Comaroff 2009). The website does, however, not explain that they are seriously troubled by factionalism – a problem which *Kgosi* Kgafela, claiming to be their symbolic apex, has declared he wants to bring to an end. The trouble is that apparently substantial sections of the South African Bakgatla do not recognize Kgafela as their supreme authority.

This situation reflects both historical conditions and contemporary circumstances. In brief, the Bakgatla-baga-Kgafela of Botswana, with Mochudi as the royal town, arrived in the present Botswana as late as the early 1870s, mainly as a consequence of Boer pressure. Before that time the Bakgatla had, for at least a century, gone through a complex process of dynastic rivalry, factionalism and division (see Schapera 1942b: 1ff.). When *Kgosi* Kgamanyane (r. 1853–70) brought a section with him to their present location in Botswana, a substantial proportion remained, yet at that time apparently recognizing Kgamanyane as their supreme authority. The person who presently claims the Bakgatla *bogosi* on the South African side, *Kgosi* Nyalala, has thus been installed by Kgosi Linchwe II. The significance of this hierarchical relationship is expressed in the most recent (South African) Bakgatla-baga-Kgafela Traditional Administration Annual Review[32] where *Kgosi* Kgafela feature prominently as *kgosi kgolo* ('great kgosi') above *Kgosi* Nyalala and the Traditional Council.

Kgosi Nyalala has been highly instrumental in accepting one of the largest platinum producers in the world – Anglo Platinum – to develop a mine of considerable size in the South African Bakgatla territory, with the *morafe* as a major shareholder. It was speculated on both sides of the border that while Nyalala's legitimacy depends on Kgafela, Kgafela might be handsomely supported financially. Kgafela's ambitious plans for 'development' – which he suggests involve the Bakgatla on both sides of the border – might be seen in this light.

But dependency on this financial source also helps to explain why Kgafela has not materialized his plans. The vast proceeds from the plati-

30. *MmegiOnline*, 29 March 2010.
31. http://www.bbkta.co.za.
32. See http://bbkta.co.za/userfiles/file/FINAL%20English%20BBK%20AR%202009-2010 .pdf (visited 15 September 2010).

num mining have brought *Kgosi* Nyalala under progressive challenge from different quarters. On the one hand, he has been facing a large number of charges for corruption, fraud and theft. On the other, his allegedly undue control over the proceeds from the platinum mining at the cost of 'the community' has given rise to attacks from at least one other royal dynasty, rejecting the seniority of Nyalala's descent and the superiority of *Kgosi* Kgafela. It is argued, for example, in an address to South Africa's Rural Development Portfolio Committee that 'we never had paramounts in the past… We are the descendants of the 11th house of Chief Pilane the First and we call ourselves Bakgatla ba Kautlwale. According to history and custom we should be equal to the Bakgafela [the dynasty of which *Kgosi* Kgafela II feature as the head]… [But] the apartheid government defined us to fall under the Bakgatla Bakgafela "paramount" and we have never been able to escape this mistake.'[33] *Kgosi* Nyalala is even seriously challenged within his own dynasty.[34] Although these challenges are made in the name of current community interests, they might well be motivated by personal greed for power and wealth, as in the case of many dynastic conflicts in the past. However, they are made in the complex political environment of the 21st Century that makes the outcome of the processes, still in progress, highly uncertain. This probably spills into the Botswana where *Kgosi* Kgafela has good reason to be worried about what his position is going to be in relation to the wealth generated amongst his 'subject' communities beyond the border.

In the meantime Kgafela has been seriously engaged in – and more and more troubled by – his campaigns ensuring that 'Kgatleng is going to be the leading territory of discipline.' Since the beginning of 2010 this agenda has increasingly manifested in his ambiguous relationship to the state. In the pursuit of restoring 'traditional values' and 'discipline' in support of the symbolic wealth vested in the *bogosi* and hence hierarchy of authority and control, he has intensified the practice of corporal punishment known as *kgwathiso* (flogging). For this purpose he has mobilized the age regiments (*mephato*). These harsh measures are, Kgafela has claimed, required to counter what are held to be major societal problems, including excessive use of alcohol – damaging to family life and often causing seri-

33. See 'Submission by Mrs. Mary Mokgaetsi Pilane and Mr. Mmothi Pilane of Bakgatla baKautlwale To Rural Development Portfolio Committee on The repeal of the Black Authorities Act Bill', see http://www.pmg.org.za/files/docs/100721bakgatla_0.pdf
34. The challenge is being fronted by *Kgosi* Nyalala's nephew (Thari Pilane), accusing Nyalala for 'plundering the tribe's wealth', see IOL/News for South Africa and the World, 14 December 2010, http://www.iol.co.za/business/business-news/bakgatla-bicker-over-royalties-1.1025121. See also *MmegiOnline*, 5 November 2010.

ous car accidents – increasing violence and other criminal offences. The problems have been growing over the past two decades in the wake of ever-larger numbers of unemployed people, especially among the younger generation, and also the escalating inequality of income and wealth (see Chapter 8). *Kgosi* Kgafela construes this trend as a matter of lack of discipline. He calls for the correction of current departures from customary values and principles of behaviour as expressed in the ostensible lack of respect for elderly people and authorities, even including the *kgosi*. In a press release by the Office of *Kgosi* Kgafela II and *Dikgosana* of Kgatleng District it is stated that '[w]e insist in inter-human respect within our society with emphasis on respect for hierarchy within the family up the structure to *Kgosi Kgolo*. Botswana was built on this Setswana culture of respect and shall recover from the present state of disintegration of respect. We shall not tolerate any compromise upon this fundamental social norm, especially respect for our dikgosi'.[35]

In this pursuit a group of drama students, for example, was accused of singing songs that are exclusively to be performed during initiation rituals (*bogwera*, *bojale*) and held to be a sensitive and secret part of the ceremony. They were brought to the *kgotla* and flogged. In response to reports and allegations of other flogging campaigns under police investigations, the attorney general issued a press statement about the ways in which corporal punishment should be administered under Botswana laws.[36] This was followed by a meeting between the minister of justice and *Kgosi* Kgafela which, according to a press release by the Office of the President,[37] was 'held in a cordial manner' and where the *kgosi* was requested to address the *morafe* and *mephato* in order to clarify the limits set by state law on flogging, violations of which are punishable as criminal offences of assault. The *kgosi* ostensibly consented to this request. But *Kgosi* Kgafela rejected the allegations that the *mephato* had taken the law in their own hands, pointing out that 'he had consulted with the Bakgatla and agreed on some measures that should be implemented to address *merafe*'s concern on indiscipline and general lawlessness in Kgatleng'.[38] The *mephato* were hence deployed to implement his decision. According to the mentioned press release, the *kgosi* assured the minister that the *mephato* operate 'in conformity with the law', whereas the minister expressed support and appreciation of the *mephato* in assisting the Botswana Police Service in the fight against crime.

---

35. *Sunday Standard Online*, 27 June 2010.
36. See *Daily News* (Gaborone), 25 January 2010.
37. See *Tautone Times*, no. 1 of 2010 (Electronic Press Circular of the Office of the President, 6 February).
38. These were, however, no substantiated characterizations of the situation.

Illustration 5. *Kgosi* Kgafela II, in ritual attire on horseback, leading the initiates of the 2009-bogwera back into the royal town of Mochudi. There were some 1500 graduates, the largest number in Bakgatla history.

However, prompted by the whipping of a 56 years old man which is illegal as the age limit is 40 years, the attorney general issued a statement in the government-controlled newspaper *Daily News* (25 January 2010) assuring people that they were living in a modern state of justice. Thus flogging or caning of people 'outside the foregoing legal framework is illegal and offenders can be charged with criminal offences for assault ... [The public] have the full protection of the law... and should not hesitate to report offenders or be intimidated from cooperating with the police and other legally sanctioned law enforcement agencies to ensure compliance with the rule of law.' In reaction to this statement *Kgosi* Kgafela called for a meeting in the royal *kgotla* (6 February 2010) where he, escorted by his younger brother, arrived dramatically on horseback in traditional garments, declaring 'to the ululations of his people that the Attorney General's regulations apply only to a Customary Court setting, and therefore would not govern regimental duties ... [Claiming that] "the constitution supports flogging, it allows parents and traditional leaders to discipline a person by flogging in the family, and at the *kgotla*. When we do so, we do not do so at a court of law, although we might be doing it at the *kgotla*.'"[39] He claimed that a High Court ruling did recognize flogging.

During the following months the activity of the *mephato* was stepped up as twenty horses were deployed by *Kgosi* Kgafela for patrolling the royal town of Mochudi on horseback. This endeavour reached one of its culmi-nations with the flogging of two pastors of the Family of God Church in Mochudi, whose congregation was accused of disturbing the public with noisy music and allegedly failing to comply with the *kgosi's* call to discuss the matter in the *kgotla*, while 'continuing with noise and break of peace ... over three successive nights'.[40] Complaints by the priest and others ostensibly flogged by members of different *mephato* lead to prosecution of the *kgosi*, his younger brother and thirteen other members of the *mephato* in the state courts. Despite this, flogging allegedly continued, one case re-portedly[41] being a pregnant women receiving public flogging by a *mophato* which is said to have caused her to suffer a miscarriage.

The state president, Ian Khama, said in a radio interview that the flogging was a matter of power abuse. It is an intriguing point, however, that Kgafela's concern with instilling discipline echoes one of the Khama government's major principles (Democracy, Development, Dignity, Disci-pline and Delivery). Rather than taking a confrontational line with the state government at this point in time, Kgafela responded by referring to encounters where he and the president expressed shared views as 'to rebuild the Botswana nation', encounters that ended up, he asserts, hap-pily and cordially.[42] Their common line was, above all, confirmed by the efforts to combat excessive consumption of alcohol by setting constraints on the sale of alcoholic drinks. Thus, Kgafela banned the cheap home-brewed *khadi*, sold from homes by mostly young, poor women, and de-clared that he was unleashing the *mephato* to flog people found drinking in morning hours, pointing out that the problem is so serious that 'in just one day 34 people were flogged'.[43]

At a later stage, Kgafela outlawed *shebeens* (unauthorized sale of alco-hol, mostly at residential places) in a popular meeting in the royal *kgotla*, stating that their customers are to be dealt with by the *mephato* and that he expected the minister of justice to instruct the police to also enforce this ban. Reportedly, it was unanimously agreed that *shebeens* were to be banned with immediate effect. The reporter related, however, that a *shebeen* owner dependent on the sale of beer for making a living, feared

39. Ibid., 8 February 2010.
40. 'A public statement by Bakgatla Ba Kgafela in respect of prosecution of *Kgosi* Kgafela and others' published in *Sunday Standard Online*, 27 June 2010.
41. The *Voice Online* (Gaborone), 15 October 2010.
42. See *MmegiOnline*, 8 February 2010.
43. Ibid.

to talk openly because of the danger of reprisals from *mephato*. A single mother of eight told him that she depended upon the income for sending her children to school, complaining that the *mephato* 'are going to kill us. They are brutal.'[44] This was obviously the reaction also amongst a very large number of other poor unmarried mothers depending on sale of beer, but muted from fear of severe punishment.

Fear and anxiety were, in other words, arising amongst the Bakgatla. The police received a number of complaints from victims of the flogging campaigns and in May 2010 Kgosi Kgafela, his younger brother and 13 members of *mephato* faced criminal charges for floggings.[45] This event initiated a turbulent judicial process – the case is still pending as this volume goes to press (November 2011). Kgafela has claimed immunity from prosecution, arguing that he, as the custodian of *bogosi*, prevails beyond the modern state. This claim was rejected by Botswana's High Court on 11 March 2011, ruling that 'dikgosi cannot act outside the constitution and laws prescribed by Parliament when all other functionaries of the state act within the statutory limitations; to do otherwise would clearly be unconstitutional.' His case was hence referred back to a magistrate court where the flogging is due to be judged according to state law.

The High Court established that no extra-state legal sphere exists under the authority of *dikgosi* since customary law has been absorbed by the modern state and made subject to the Constitution. Furthermore, it was stated that in precolonial time the *dikgosi* 'were kings. They were sovereigns… They held the power of the life and deaths of their subjects in their hands.' But customary law is dynamic and 'changes and develops over time.' By now, this court established, the *dikgosi* are subject to the state of justice.[46] The state prosecutor went further, claiming that Kgafela has just a ceremonial role because 'he opted not to take up functions of office of a Kgosi under the Bogosi Act and recommended that another member of his tribe be appointed as Motshwaralela Bogosi and thereby clothing him with the power to impose corporal punishment or go kgwathisa [to flog] after proper judicial process.'[47] This was, I recall, a part of Kgafela strategy in the pursuit of avoiding being incorporated in the state structure as a civil servant. And he fiercely rejected that flogging to instil discipline amongst his people is unlawful because it is a practice that, according to 'tradition', might be exercised beyond the sphere of the

---

44. Ibid., 28 June 2010.
45. At this point the High Court had already ordered Kgosi Kgafela to leave the Family of God Church alone after he had banned the church from worshiping in Kgatleng, the judgement being that was unlawful and unconstitutional.
46. See *MmegiOnline*, 14 March 2011, cf. *Sunday Standard Online*, 14 March 2011.
47. See *Sunday Standard Online*, 30 January 2011, cf. *MmegiOnline*, 26 January 2011.

customary court. That is, beyond the state jurisdiction; thus his claim of immunity.

Kgafela not only became increasingly challenging in relation to the judiciary. He has also become confrontational in relation to the state, attacking the Constitution for its lack of foundation in indigenous tradition. Asserting that he – as a *kgosi kgolo* – constitutes the link between his *morafe* and the royal ancestorhood (*badimo ba dikgosi*), he has argued that '[it] is my duty to tell you the true message from our ancestors. Our salvation lies in following their guidance and our culture.' Salvation is to break away from what he denotes a '"Tsotsi"[48] constitution' and a 'Tsotsi' Government [that are] masquerading as democratic institutions… As Batswana you need to be ruled by your Dikgosi. We have to go back to our original laws and norms.'[49] Hence he challenged the legitimacy of the Constitution.

In order to substantiate the claim that the Constitution is 'flawed and oppressive,' he demanded 'the file that contains talks, which gave rise to the Constitution of Botswana; Hansards of the Legislative Council[50] (transitional parliament from Bechuanaland to Botswana) between January 1965 and December 1966; and a file on consultation on constitutional drafting.'[51] The court and the prosecutor accepted this request and the case is about to be dealt with by the magistrate court. Moreover, complaining that efforts to enter a dialogue with the state leadership has failed, he has at this time turned in a sworn statement at the High Court in which he accuses President Ian Khama and others of using the Directorate of Intelligence Services to steal public funds. The person who draped him with the leopard skin has now become a major enemy.

Whether or not Kgafela's neo-traditional endeavour and attack on the state leadership will have lasting and wide ranging impact remains to be seen. At the moment, Kgafela's strategy and tactics in the pursuit of reforming the Bakgatla – and ultimately all Batswana – appear uncertain. It is true that Kgafela's challenge of the state government and call for return to ancient customs and for respecting *bogosi* appeal to many people. Kgafela's authority also remains strongly underpinned by his in-

---

48. 'Tsotsi' means thug or gangster, a notion that features as the title of a psychological thriller staged in the black township of Alexandra (Johannesburg), portraying an angry young man – named Tsotsi – living in a state of extreme urban deprivation, compelled to face his brutal nature and to enter a process of reform. This seems to be an obvious allusion to Kgafela's call for revision of Botswana's constitution and government.

49. See The *Voice Online*, 20 May 2011.

50. See Chapter 2.

51. See *MmegiOnline*, 7 June 2011, cf. Sunday Standard 9 June 2011.

dispensable role as the supreme figure in the conduct of *bogwera* which is joined by vast numbers of young men. Many people have supported Kgafela's objective of instilling discipline in the *morafe*, attracted by the *kgosi*'s rhetoric on the post-colonial state as corrupting 'our culture' with reference to the prevalence of excessive consummation of alcohol and broken homes leaving children without guardianship and guidance, the consequence being the generation of criminals. People have apparently also followed him for some time when arguing that the situation is so precarious that tough measures are required. Thus when Kgafela was jailed by a magistrate court[52] for a few days (November 2010) before the High Court released him,[53] the Bakgatla took to the streets in hundreds to express their protest.[54]

Nevertheless, over the last months it seems that popular support of *Kgosi* Kgafela has been on the decline. Also some notable *dikgosana* have apparently considerable reservations against his line. Such a development is not very surprising. Although the state relates officially to Kgafela through the judicial system, it is most likely that informal pressure is set on all the *dikgosana* who are on the state pay roll as officially recognized judges or arbitrators in customary courts at different levels. As civil servants, they are simply in danger of being sacked if siding with people breaking the law. What is more, they probably perceive Kgafela's line of claiming immunity unrealistic.

These *dikgosana* are people of authority in the various *dikgotla* around the *morafe* with considerable impact upon all the rank-and-files amongst whom many have not been comfortable with the perceived harsh and unpredictable flogging exercises. In particular, anxiety and fear have developed amongst the vast number of people who either sell or consume beer at the *shebeens*. Furthermore, these exercises are certainly not seen as measures adequate to remedy the everyday problems of the very large sections of the Bakgatle that are without jobs and poverty-ridden. It might be suggested that Kgafela's neo-traditional endeavour fails to address seriously the prevailing historical circumstances of class formation in this country (see Chapter 8), at least as long as all his promises of 'development' do not materialize.

Many of my interlocutors are also deeply concerned with the development of an extra-judicial field; not for the reason that it is beyond state jurisdiction, but because it is beyond the discursive field of the *kgotla*. In the second main part of this chapter we shall see the full significance of this as I shall explain people's deeply felt association with highly peaceful

---

52. *MmegiOnline*, 28 October 2010.
53. *SundayStandardOnline*, 7 November 2010.
54. Ibid., 5 November 2010.

procedures and practices to address all kinds of problems. They are governed, as we shall see, by a cultural orientation that contrasts sharply with Kgafela's autocratic, violent line. But they fear – some people say 'for my life' – to stand up in the *kgotla* in order to take Kgafela to task, by arguing, for example, that he is mistaken in claiming cultural authenticity as his way of instilling discipline. Also, all the fear people currently feel for 'telling the truth' in the *kgotla* is contrary to the central Tswana virtue of freedom of speech (*mmualebe o a be a bua la gagwe*), the significance of which I shall discuss in Chapter 6. There is thus a concern, especially amongst the younger generation, with what people see as Kgafela's authoritarian tendencies. What is more, his fashioning of indigenous authority as quite authoritarian has somehow been caught up in a popular discourse on 'democracy' vs. 'autocracy' on the national level that has recently propelled a considerable secession from the ruling party and the establishment of a new party – the Botswana Democratic Movement (initiated March 2010). This is a division that has been much nourished by the leadership style of President Ian Khama, perceived by many as 'autocratic' and 'dictatorial'. The two leaders' discipline rhetoric is not significantly different.

What makes *Kgosi* Kgafela's prospects still worse is that he has very little external support. As already indicated, the prospects seem meagre for substantial financial contributions from the South African Bakgatla. Moreover, in order to reform Botswana, i.e. by replacing the Constitution, he would need support from the other *merafe*, which he has not. My informants in other Tswana royal centres have no or little comprehension of Kgafela's neo-traditional endeavour and do not consent to his violent line as a genuine Tswana way of instilling discipline and restoring social order. Nor do they readily accept his claim of immunity and rejection of Botswana's Constitution. And without their support, he will not succeed since the Bakgatla of Botswana is quite small, both in terms of population and territory.

That said about the challenges and problems which Kgafela is currently facing, it needs to be added that he is a complex character, forceful and unpredictable. In short time he moved from being a notable lawyer who took on major human rights-cases, to combat social problems with violence. He has obviously considerable room for manoeuvre. For one thing, an increasing number of people see his call for a new constitution as unrealistic and are critical of the flogging campaigns. Another matter is that much of his rhetoric on restoring peace and order and living in accordance with ancestral advice and principles appeals widely, especially because many people are, I repeat, seriously concerned with all the unfortunate consequences of widespread and excessive consumption of alcohol.

If he finds less controversial and provoking strategies and tactics he might regain massive support by exploiting the symbolic wealth vested in the *bogosi*. Although Kgafela has been quite insubstantial so far in respect of 'development' that would help to improve the lives of all the poor sections of the Bakgatla, he has demonstrated that he is in a position to play the populist card in an effort to challenge the state government. During the lasting, at times violent strike amongst a vast number of low-paid government employees during April–July 2011 (see Chapter 8), he addressed his people and called for another reform of the Constitution. Reportedly he said that:

> Batswana should stop whimpering about a political and economic system that is failing them when they have the power to bring about constitutional changes that should ensure the establishment of a political and economic order that is supportive of economic and cultural justice and sustainability. Once the nation was both economically and politically empowered it would become the master and not the servant of the ruling class. "When you finally do that, you will not be striking for 16 percent. You will be in control of it," he said to thunderous applause. That, he said, would require a radical altering of the Constitution to make it conform to the cultural ideals and also satisfactorily address the economic situation in Batswana.[55]

Furthermore, prevailing as the supreme symbolic figure during *bogwera* Kgafela has recurrently a powerful platform to boost his authority and influence amongst more than one thousand young men when they spend weeks in the bush under his ritual leadership.[56] What is more, even though Kgafela has delegated the everyday administration of the customary court to his deputies, due to the pervasive character of these courts activities at all levels (see following main section of this chapter) they contribute immensely to reproduce the *kgosi*'s cosmological centrality and people's perceived existential dependency upon him as the incumbent of *bogosi*. Thus, even under the present circumstances Kgafela is, to be sure, vested with considerable authority. His consequent capacity of mobilizing people is certainly recognized by the state leadership which avoids confronting him directly with, for example, suspension as in the case of *Kgosi* Seepapitso IV, although Kgafela has been far more provoking. With all the intelligence service available to the state president, it has probably become evident that Kgafela should rather be left with the police and the judiciary.

---

55. *MmegiOnline*, 30 May 2011.
56. As he is prosecuted by the state and his case is about to be dealt with by the magistrate court (August 2011), he is announcing the dates for *bogwera* as well *bojale*.

The *Merafe*'s Challenges of the State

While this series of events centred on *Kgosi* Kgafela has not led to such direct confrontation between the *morafe* and the state political leadership as in the Bangwaketse case, the two cases are similar in two important respects. First, in both cases there is a demand for autonomy, challenging state sovereignty: in the Bangwaketse case, autonomy is claimed in relation to *bogosi*, especially when problems of incumbency arise, in the sense that forces surrounding it can only be dealt with by tribal elders to prevent major calamities. The *morafe* thus rejects the state's ultimate power in regard to central issues concerning succession to *bogosi*. In the case of the Bakgatla, there is a claim of exercising violence beyond the limits of state administration of justice (including customary courts), clearly rejecting the state's monopolization of violence – in the Weberian sense – no less than the defining characteristic of a modern, sovereign state.

Second, in both cases the demand for autonomy is justified with reference to 'our cultural tradition' – the cultural and symbolic wealth of the *bogosi* vested in the royal ancestorhood. This responsibility, it is argued, cannot be left with politicians that are coming and going and who might be of an origin with no tradition of *bogosi* and are even ignorant about it. It is entirely the responsibility of the *dikgosi* in the context of their respective *kgotla* and hence goes beyond what is stipulated in the modern state's constitution.

These cases represent the most serious challenges exercised by Tswana *merafe* in relation to the state in postcolonial times. They demonstrate the existence of significant forces embodied in the Tswana *merafe* and their prevailing potentials for political mobilization, even challenging the state. At the same time, they actualize important questions: why are these cases so rare? In other words, why has the relationship between the state and the *merafe* been predominantly peaceful – to the extent that the structures of the *merafe* have, as we shall see in the following main section and subsequent chapters, been highly instrumental to nation-state building?

Let me address these questions by briefly reviewing the two other officially recognized, major Tswana *merafe* with the potentials of representing a serious challenging force in view of their size. First, the Bakwena – being the most senior of the three major Tswana *merafe* in the country (see Chapter 1) – are caught up in a never-ending dynastic dispute on succession which goes back at least to the beginning of the twentieth century (see Chapter 2). Although party politics spills into the divide and the state is occasionally accused of keeping the divide alive in order to weaken the Bakwena, it has not led to direct confrontation with the state such as in the Bangwaketse-case. But there are strong sentiments amongst the Bakwena that the state should keep out of matters related to *bogosi*, which was strongly expressed as late as March 2010.[57] At any rate, the strong popular concern attached to issues of succession amongst the Bakwena some forty-five years after the curtailment of the executive powers of the *dikgosi* underscores how important matters related to *bogosi* still are.

Second, the by far largest *morafe* of the three major ones – the Bangwato – is that of the Khama dynasty and thus tightly aligned to the state. Initially through Seretse Khama, state president until his death in 1980, then through his son and heir, Ian Khama, *kgosi* of the Bangwato and commander of the Botswana Defence Force, Botswana's vice-president (1998–2008) and since 2008 the state president. The Bangwato of the royal town have thus constituted a major force in the ruling party since its inception by virtue of the mutually strong dependency between them and the Khamas. To mobilize the *morafe* against the state would hence be entirely against their own interests, although they have, as we shall see in the following chapter, occasionally taken its agents seriously to task. To the Bangwato the prevalence of the Khamas at the apex of the postcolonial state epitomizes the force of the Bangwato *bogosi*, anchored in the royal ancestorhood of Kgosi Khama III 'the Great'. Although the Bangwato were, as we saw in Chapter 2, caught up in a major crisis surrounding the royal house in the 1950s, they have not been riddled by succession disputes. After the *bogosi* had been occupied by low-profile regents for nearly thirty years, the Bangwato enthusiastically welcomed the enthronement of Ian Khama as their *kgosi* in 1979. Until his death the following year, Seretse Khama kept a *de facto* control over the *morafe* and was, for certain, highly instrumental in the smooth relationship between the *morafe* and the state. Ian Khama seems to have operated to the same effects after that time although he has never assumed office; the Bangwato *bogosi* remains occupied by a low profile regent.

The remaining officially recognized Tswana *merafe* are either very small (Batlokwa, Bamalete, Barolong) or contain vast groups of ethnic minorities that are, to a great extent, at odds with the dominant Tswana (Batawana). Recall, however, that there are a number of 'minority' communities within each of the *merafe* (Chapter 1). Since the mid 1990s they have started to represent a challenging force in order to obtain recognition within the state as autonomous entities independent of the Tswana *merafe* that are claiming superiority and 'owners' of territories where many

---

57. In March 2010, the state president appointed a task force to investigate the conflicts related to the dynastic dispute which has caused reactions amongst the Bakwena (see *Mmegi-Online*, 17 March 2010).

minority communities live. This challenge of the state will be dealt with extensively in the following chapter.

Returning, finally, to the Bakgatla and the Bangwaketse, while *Kgosi* Seepapitso was operating much as a lone wolf who rarely sought anchorage in the *morafe* for his criticism of politicians and civil servant, *Kgosi* Kgafela is currently attempting to engage the *morafe* in his ventures. Furthermore, Kgafela is far more principled and confrontational; he wants no less than a major revision of the state constitution which he sees rooted in colonialism and in disagreement with Tswana tradition. In his neo-traditional endeavours, Kgafela makes what he has named the 'Tsotsi' government responsible for the ugly social entailment of Western modernity. He calls for the rebuilding of the Botswana nation on authentic Tswana grounds.

As I have explained, it is highly uncertain whether Kgafela will succeed in his current endeavours. Nevertheless, the case is intriguing because it – like that of the Bangwaketse – clearly indicates the potentials of mobilization in support of *bogosi* and its custodian, the *kgosi*. Significantly, in both cases the sovereignty of the state has been under challenge, suggesting that we have at hand forces *external* to the state. This can, in Deleuze and Guattari's (1991: 361) conception be seen as a matter of rhizomes operating laterally across the spatially located state-controlled hierarchies of the *merafe* centred in *kgotla*. The mobilization of the Bangwaketse was obviously conducted beyond these limits, in the multitude of informal, nonlocalized networks, virtually spanning the entire *morafe*. And the Bakgatla's current activation of the customary practice of secretly debating delicate matters in relation to the state in a gathering in the veld of all initiated men of the *morafe*, known as *letsholo*, has also clearly rhizomic features since this institution has not been captured into the state structures of power. This institution is closely connected to that of *bogwera* which is secretly constitutive to the formation of the *mephato*, currently deployed by the *kgosi* beyond the limits of state jurisdiction. From the perspective of the state, this practice has obvious rhizomic features. Hence, as this case – and the Bangwaketse confrontation in the royal *kgotla* with the principal agents of the state – indicate, the *morafe* and the state are to be conceived as distinct assemblages of power.

And yet, as we shall see in the following section and subsequent chapters, the state has to a considerable extent managed to capture these assemblages' power into its structures. All this depends upon the fact that the symbolism, practices and institutions of authority vested in indigenous hierarchies are reproduced under post-colonial circumstance. One major engine of reproduction, continuously in operation, is that of customary courts, which are, at the same time, major instruments of social control, integral to the modern state's judiciary.

Reproduction of Indigenous Hierarchies of Authority

Popular subscription to what many people today speak of as 'our culture' and 'our tradition', finds one of its most important expressions in the customary settlement pattern: above all the royal towns of ten thousands of people, exceptional in the larger context of Africa (Gulbrandsen 2007). In the years immediately after independence, some people predicted, in the words of Kuper, that 'when the chief [*kgosi*] ceases to be the apex of the tribal government, then not only the ward, but the whole system of household clusters and alignments falls away' (Kuper 1975: 145; cf. Comaroff 1982: 157). Nevertheless, even at the present time, forty-five years after the time when patri-virilocal residence was practically compulsory, people choose voluntarily and in large numbers to comply with this customary practice. And if a man should be on bad terms with his agnates, he and his wife will either reside uxorilocally or, at any rate, in a dwelling (*lolwapa*) attached to one *kgotla* or another.

These features of close attachment to a *kgotla* and incorporation in the hierarchical order of indigenous authorities were especially pervasive during the early decades when the postcolonial state was established and consolidated (1966–1990), contributing greatly to its societal control and hence strength and stability. Although this period of time is the main concern in this volume, these structures have been of significance also thereafter because they continue to encompass substantial sections of Botswana's population as the royal towns and many villages have grown substantially since independence, especially for the following demographic reason. As pointed out in the Introduction, within this vast country the size of France and the Be-Ne-Lux countries combined, five out of the seven Tswana royal towns are located with a sufficiently short distance to the capital of Gaborone (which is by far the largest urban centre in Botswana) to allow commuting on a daily basis. With the high accommodation costs in urban centres, residence in rural areas is attractive. Even if people live and work most of the time in urban centres, they readily establish a residence in the 'tribal' ward (Gulbrandsen 2007).

This leaves us with the question: what is conditioning popular attachment to a *kgotla*? There is, of course, no single answer to this question, as people might have different reasons for their choice of settlement. Yet, I propose, there is one particular condition which seems ubiquitous: people's dependency on and even apprehension of the discursive field of the

kgotla. As in precolonial and colonial times, this discursive field is acti-
vated to a great extent for the administration of justice. What is known in
Botswana as 'customary court', is – as in the colonial past – an alternative,
state-controlled administration of justice to that of the magistrate court.
Although their procedures are, as we shall see, very different, both court
systems are required to judge cases on the basis of state 'common law' as
well as indigenous customs and laws (*mekgwa le melao*). The former law
system takes, as in colonial times, precedence when they diverge. In postcolonial times, the customary courts have continued to receive a very significant proportion of the number of cases brought forward for trial. This
is to some extent so because they are free of charge, but also because these
courts are strongly preferred by many people for reasons I shall elaborate in
this section. In any case, this choice creates a dependency between people
and a larger group of relatives and friends since they are in important respects the ones who deal with and pursue your case. Lawyers are not accepted within the customary court.

In this section I am therefore centrally concerned with the fact that a
significant part of the population are continuously engaged in these customary court proceedings – either as directly involved in a case or as relatives or friends. These proceedings are conducted in the discursive field of
the *kgotla* which, on all levels, involves a profound exercise of the symbolism of hierarchical relations of authority, anchored in ancestorhood and
hence indigenous cosmology.

The Value of Reconciliation and
the Attraction of the Discursive Field of the *Kgotla*

The customary courts are situated in the hierarchy of *dikgotla* that is
culminating in the royal *kgotla*. They were at Botswana's independence
recognized to the extent of being integral to the state administration of
justice which was, as already suggested, not common amongst other independent states in Africa. One reason is that such recognition was in
agreement with the broader efforts to capture the Tswana *merafe* into the
structures of the state; another was that by stripping the *dikgosi* and the
dikgosana of much of their executive power, they remained more distinctively judges, at least formally. That the indigenous judicial system was
captured into the state system for the organization of justice without apparent hesitation should, above all, be understood against the background
that the British found already at the establishment of the colonial state,
the existence of a highly sophisticated judicial system (Roberts 1972:
121). For reasons which should be evident from Chapters 1 and 2, this
was certainly no less so when the colonial state apparatus was absorbed by
the postcolonial state. Significantly, the courts of the *kgotla* by and large

complied ideally with – if not rational-legal principles in a strict Weberian sense – the principle of equality before the law. They could assert this by quoting two Tswana maxims: *molao sefofu, obile otle oje mong waone* ('the law is blind, it eats even its owner) and *malao tau oloma lemokgokgo* ('the law is a lion, it bites the great man too').

The exact extent to which indigenous virtues of equality before the law are complied with in postcolonial times is an issue in its own right; after all, even in such an egalitarian society as that of Norway with a judicial system founded upon legal-rational principles, the ideal of equality before the law has indeed been questioned, e.g. in relation to social class issues (see Aubert 1970: ch. 6). In Botswana I have very seldom registered complaints of this kind in relation to customary court verdicts, the reason possibly being that lower courts are connected to accessible appeal courts and, importantly, the court proceedings as well as the court councillors' talks are conducted in the presence of a large audience, especially in important cases and in instances of appeal.

Much in line with colonial state legislation, the postcolonial state has framed the Customary Courts Act (1966) and subsequently the Common Law and Customary Law Act (1987). The courts of the *kgotla* are officially named 'customary court', paralleling a structure of courts named 'common court' which is locally conducted by magistrates, from where

Illustration 6. The Bangwaketse royal *kgotla* with the old office of the *kgosi*. Courtesy of Sandy Grant.

Illustration 7. The new office of the *kgosi* and his tribal administration; the building also includes a courtroom – meaning that the proceedings might take place indoors, which is an entirely new practice. Courtesy of Sandy Grant.

cases can be appealed to the High Court and the High Court of Appeal. Particularly important cases are presented directly to the High Court, as we saw in the case of *Kgosi* Seepapitso IV vs. the State/Leema Gaseitsiwe. The integration of the customary courts into the state system of jurisprudence was profoundly asserted when the state established the Customary Court of Appeal in 1985 – with the former *Kgosi* Bathoen II as its first president, residing in the state ministerial quarters – presided over by the chief justice. Court cases presented to the customary court can, at any time, be shifted over to magistrate courts; cases from the Customary Court of Appeal can be appealed to Botswana's High Court. These court systems are in this sense tightly integrated. The significance of the customary courts within the context of the state administration of justice is illuminated by the physical upgrading of the customary court structures and the offices of the *dikgosi* as seen in the images of the Bangwaketse royal *kgotla* in Kanye (Illustrations 6 and 7).

The officially registered customary courts in the country number more than five hundred, and it has been stated officially that they handle some

80 per cent of all cases brought to court in Botswana.[58] Even though this might be an overestimation, the numbers are still very significant (cf. Molokomme 1994: 358ff.; Otlhogile 1993: 550). And note, in addition come the vast number of cases dealt with and resolved at lower levels – mostly by the courts conducted in a descent group's *kgotla* – which are not officially registered, and their cases are not recorded. Nevertheless, they are *de facto* integral to the hierarchy of customary courts as the heads of these courts are, of course, under the overall authority of the *kgosi* and hence the state.

There is one important practical reason for the considerable number of cases dealt with by the customary courts in the *kgotla*: these courts require, I reiterate, no pecuniary costs and they are easily available for anybody attached to a *kgotla*, even if they reside elsewhere for the time being. According to customary practice, other people attached to the *kgotla* voluntarily participate in the proceedings which typically go on for long hours and occasionally many days. Moreover, as I shall elaborate subsequently, the character of the proceedings – contrasting sharply with the magistrate's courtroom – constitutes indeed a major condition for the popular attraction of the customary courts. This means that the customary courts have significance well beyond any Western notion of administration of justice. As the title of this subsection suggests, reconciliation (*tetlanyo*) is here a catchword, and it is the meaningfulness of this practice, we shall see, that attracts people to present their cases to these courts in the discursive field of the *kgotla* and to engage in their proceedings. This cultural condition also contributes strongly to the fact that tensions and conflicts are translated into issues of communal concern and then readily brought to court. We have at hand a strong cultural inclination to conceive conflicts of any kind in judicial terms, including political conflicts, as we saw in the first part of this chapter.

In significant contrast to the discontinuity between people's everyday lives and the institutions dispensing law in Western societies (Conley and O'Barr 1990: 169; cf. Fuller 1994: 11), virtually all adults are entitled to participate in the resolution of each other's cases in these courts. It is crucial that conflicts and disputes are here not dealt with by the deployment of rules in the Western 'legal' sense but by a much more inclusive mode of litigation. The corpus of rules known as *mekgwa le melao* (see Chapter 1) includes an all-embracing range of rules and regulations that cover virtually every aspect of interpersonal relationships (Comaroff and Roberts 1981: 70ff). Although knowledge about this vast corpus varies

---

58. National Development Plan 9, 2003–2008, Para. 20.6, Government Printing Office, Gaborone, Botswana.

considerably, it is a normative repertoire with which people are basically familiar because it frames everyday life in many respects. Therefore, it 'belongs to the community in general and operates at every level of society' (Griffiths 1997: 144). In the discursive field of the *kgotla*, where the customary courts are situated, it gains a particular significance by virtue of the character of the proceedings with which one needs to come to terms in order to comprehend the attraction of these courts.

Let me remark here that Wilson (2001: 124–25) has attacked Comaroff and Roberts (1981) and me (Gulbrandsen 1996b) for applying an 'isolationistic perspective' in the study of 'Tswana law'. He calls for 'a thoroughgoing analysis of the transformation of customary law by successive states', but he fails to comprehend that a central issue is the nature of the proceedings in the particular discursive field of the *kgotla*. Regarding the question of 'transformation of customary law', it needs to be stressed that *mekgwa le melao* is not 'transformed' by state law but is possibly superseded by state legislation. One important, relevant question is thus rather how *mekgwa le melao* have been changed *under the circumstances of* successive states. As for precolonial and colonial circumstances, Schapera has provided the most extensive accounts probably ever compiled on the continent (espec. Schapera 1943b, 1947b, 1970; see also Roberts 1991; Gulbrandsen 1996b: 143ff.). I recall that the *dikgosi* were encouraged by the British to frame laws themselves and judge cases on the basis of *mekgwa le melao*, yet only to the extent that it did not conflict with laws and regulations made by the British (see Chapter 1). The postcolonial state has imposed the same regulation, which means that no case can be concluded in conflict with state legislation. Yet, as Roberts (1977: 3) states more generally for Africa, 'in practice litigants saw themselves free to make their own choice between the two systems, and to manipulate each system as best they could'. This still holds true in the present context, especially in relation to disputes handled at the lower-order court level of the descent group *kgotla* which is, I repeat, beyond the formal limits of the state (cf. Molokomme 1994: 357).

As I suggested in Chapter 2, the House of Chiefs in Parliament was intended to be an advisory body in respect of state legislation, especially on issues at the core of *mekgwa le melao*, like those of family relations, marriage, inheritance, and insult and minor assault cases. As far as I know, there exists no systematic study on the extent to which state legislation has replaced *mekgwa le melao* in these fields, central to the work of customary courts. But I have recorded some transformations of the *mekgwa le melao* made by a *kgosi* upon extensive consultation with the *merafe*. For example, one major issue amongst the Bangwaketse has been the division of inheritance (*boswa*), especially the family herd, upon the father's death. There has been a long tradition of leaving a major part of it with the eldest son (*moja boswa* – litt. the 'eater of the inheritance') under the pretext that responsibility for his mother, unmarried sisters and younger brothers remains with him. Under postcolonial circumstances, however, a long-term trend has been in progress with ever-increasing instances of the eldest son moving to urban areas or elsewhere, leaving younger siblings to take care of family and cattle, only to return at the father's death to claim his 'rightful' lion's share of the *boswa*. But, when brought to court, the *moja boswa* often remained without support and the court often pragmatically reasoned that the customary norms had to be suspended because the person had violated the conditions under which they were intended to apply. *Kgosi* Seepapitso stated to the Bangwaketse that under the circumstances of radical change, the norm could not be upheld and that the courts should, in each case, take proper account of which sons and daughters had actually cared for the parents and contributed to the maintenance and growth of the herd. It seems that this very significant transformation propelled by radically changing societal circumstance has been widely accepted. In other cases the *morafe* might be divided on the issue, with the result that the *kgosi* is unable to declare normative changes, as in respect of support to an abandoned girlfriend (*nyatsi*) which I have examined elsewhere (Gulbrandsen 1996a: 272ff.).

In any case, the customary courts operate in highly flexible ways, which follows from the situation whereby 'among the Tswana, where the social field is recognized to be fluid and negotiable, *mekgwa le melao* represents a symbolic grammar in terms of which reality is continuously constructed and managed' (Comaroff and Roberts 1981: 247). This means that judgement depends much on the merit of the case and, especially, the particular process to which it is subject under changing societal circumstances. More often than explicit declaration of normative changes by the *kgosi*, the multitude of such processes – in articulation with popular, everyday discourse – works to the effect of gradually and often tacitly transforming what, at any time, is conceived as *mekgwa le melao*. Such popular discursive practices certainly make people much more certain about the likely outcome of a dispute in the customary courts compared to the magistrate courts. But note, this also means that *mekgwa le melao* differs from one community to another, from one *morafe* to the other.

Since the character of the court proceedings follows from the fact that it is situated in the discursive field of the *kgotla*, let me explain that cases are typically initiated at the immediate local level, often within the domestic yard (*segotlo*). If unresolved, the case is brought into 'the open', i.e. the public domain of the descent-group court, from where it may be appealed through several court stages up to the royal court (*kgosing kgotla*) over which the *kgosi* or one of his deputies presides (cf. Schapera 1984: 98f.). In this way everybody is attached to courts which are situated in the midst of family compounds and at the same time integral to the hierarchical order of the *morafe*. We can hence speak of the Tswana as 'living their lives in court' (see Gulbrandsen 1996b). During court proceedings every adult male is in principle entitled to speak, to participate in cross-examination and to counsel the head of the court before the latter makes his ruling. Increasingly women have also been allowed to present their own cases, and today elderly women often participate in cross-examinations.

While the *kgotla* is popular in the sense of being the most prominent arena for all adult males, it is nevertheless intrinsically hierarchical. It is chaired by the genealogically most senior man, who is surrounded by a group of elders called *bagakolodi* (literally 'remembrancers', indicating their experience and their capacity as conveyors of customs) who serve as his councillors. Hierarchy is symbolized in various ways, most conspicuously in the spatial organization of the *kgotla,* with the elder next in rank to the headman located at his right hand, the next to his left, and the others in successive order according to their seniority. During the proceedings everybody is entitled to speak and participate in the cross-examinations, which might, I repeat, go on for many hours and even several days. Finally, the elders express their views in reverse order of rank, with the most senior elder speaking last, before the head of the *kgotla* concludes with his judgement. The judgement can be appealed from the descent-group court to the customary court of the ward *kgotla* and further to that of the royal *kgotla*, the Customary Court of Appeal and finally Botswana's High Court.

Although these proceedings might, with Western eyes, resemble mundane matters of dispute settlement, they are located in the discursive field of the *kgotla* whose cultural construction is important in order to comprehend the broader significance of this kind of court proceeding. Jean Comaroff has analysed the *kgotla* and its cosmological location by means of a structuralist approach, explaining how its hierarchical features are inscribed in space – in what we may label the *lolwapa-kgotla* complex – in terms of age and gender. She identifies the *segotlo*, the backyard of the *lolwapa* or domestic compound, as the creative focus of life, of procreation and thus of biological reproduction (Comaroff 1985: 54ff., cf. 1980). The social creation of male personhood is epitomized by transformations initiated at birth in the *segotlo*. From the *segotlo* the male person is brought out first towards the front yard of the *lolwapa* and later on, upon marriage, out of its confines, at which stage the male person is assigned a lower-order position in the *kgotla*. Male adulthood involves the gradual achievement of seniority, determined by genealogical position, age and personal capacity (ora-torical skills and an ability to accumulate knowledge). A male person's life cycle is concluded when he 'joins the ancestors (*badimo*)', a transformation customarily signified by his burial in the cattle kraal (*moraka*) adjacent to the council place of the *kgotla*. The burial place in turn reflects the close attachment of cattle to this symbolic core of Tswana cosmology.

Important indications of hierarchy are particularly apparent in the agency of the elders as mediators between the custodians of the moral order, namely the *badimo* (ancestors), and the people, who predominantly find their public expression in the context of the *kgotla*. While received ancestral wisdom and instructions are private matters, ostensibly often conveyed in dreams and very rarely explicated, they are frequently read as subtexts in people's conversation as evidence of good communication with their ancestors (Gulbrandsen 2001: 36f.). Many of my interlocutors asserted that the elders are empowered by spiritual forces vested in their ancestorhood by virtue of their tacit interactions with ancestors, through which wisdom (*kitso*) and knowledge (*botlhale*) are retrieved, capacitating elders to reconcile conflicting parties and hence establish social peace and order – *kagiso* (see below). The words of the elders and above all the decisions made by the head of the *kgotla* – at any level – are seen as ideally a matter of ancestral revelation.

From a Western point of view, this discursive practice readily appears to be distinctively 'secular' rather than 'religious'. To posit such a distinc-tion in the present context would, however, be highly misleading and would miss the crucial point. That is, the discursive field of the *kgotla* connects men, by virtue of the mediation of elders, to the spiritual agen-cies of supreme forces that are perceived as determining their existential concerns. This means that the apparently 'secular' field of *kgotla* discourse has, in people's imagination, remained closely connected with the *badimo* as the major custodians of moral order – as inscribed in *mekgwa le melao* – the source of social peace and harmony – *kagiso* – at all levels of the *morafe*. It was thus often suggested that 'in the *kgotla* we are with *badimo* and they are with us'.

This suggestion underscores the central point of this section: the dis-cursive field of the *kgotla* is vested with cosmologically anchored cultural and symbolic wealth of great existential importance that is essential to the exercise of authority in ways that ensure social peace and harmony. So why is *kagiso* of high existential importance and how does its significance help to explain popular attraction to the discursive field of the *kgotla*? To this we now turn.

In order to come further to terms with the popular attraction of the hierarchical order of the *merafe*, it is crucial to comprehend popular obsession with the state of *kagiso* and the centrality of practices of reconciliation. The *segotlo-moraka* axis embodies a hot-cold dimension, not particular to the Tswana, but ubiquitous throughout Southern Africa (Kuper 1982: 18ff.; cf. Schapera 1971b: 173). In Tswana thought, semen is perceived as a source of coolness and fertility par excellence, closely associated with the force of male ancestors (*badimo*) and spatially associated with the cattle kraal (*moraka*) adjacent to the *kgotla*. Diametrically opposite is the *segotlo*, the place of confinement for menstruating women. If the *segotlo* is thus hot, *kgotla* and the *moraka* are cool. The superiority of the male force in the act of procreation follows from the logic that 'cool' things heal and fertilize the 'hot', while the 'hot' endangers the 'cool' (Kuper 1982: 19–20, cf. Comaroff 1985: 174).[59]

The notion that 'cool' things are healing what is 'hot' underpins the male-centred hierarchies of authority, especially as exercised in the discursive field of the *kgotla*. The wide-ranging significance of this is particularly apparent if we invoke the virtues of *kagiso* – the state of harmony and peace. *Kagiso* is the socio-emotional state of 'coolness' and is widely perceived as being essential to human and animal fertility and health, as well as to abundant crops, prosperity and general welfare. As one proverb goes, *kagiso ke go bona mabele* ('peace gives plenty of corn').

This means that *kagiso* is not only the concern of parties directly engaged in a conflict. Conflicts are indeed always a collective concern because they give rise to destructive 'heat' (*mogote*) that is, in people's perception, threatening the community of family and descent group encompassing the conflicting parties. The extent of its impact is determined by the range of their authority. Precisely this threat was at the centre of the Bangwaketse's deep worry about the grave rift which the state created between *Kgosi* Seepapitso and his son Leema. A major conflict surrounding the *bogosi* is damaging to *kagiso* at the level of the *morafe* and hence threatens fertility, health and prosperity for everybody.

From my own observation that *kagiso* is a pervasive concern in *kgotla* discourses it follows that there is, as also Schapera (1971a: 244) has reported, always a major effort to reconcile conflicting parties, to create mutual understanding and to cool down heated atmospheres. All complaints and grievances must come to the surface. In this sense the process

---

59. The semantic associations of these concepts are indicated by the fact that 'the same word means "to heal" and "to cool" (*hola* in Tswana, *phola* in Zulu etc.) and one word may mean to be hot and unhealthy (e.g. *shisa* in Zulu) or heat and fever (e.g. *mogote* in Tswana)' (Kuper 1982: 20; see pp. 267–9 below).

is often a kind of catharsis – and was typically described to me in such terms as being a way of reducing the exhaustion of body and soul caused by social tensions. Moreover, such cases were often related to me as 'mis-understandings' (*go tlhoka kutlwano*, lit. to lack understanding) between the parties, not actually a conflict of interests and therefore not a dispute in the Western sense. Accordingly, much of the proceedings consist of resolving the conundrum of interpersonal intricacies in order to arrive at *kutlwano*, rather than establishing who is right in relation to the law.

The tremendous emphasis placed on keeping emotions at a low level and on behaving in polite, inoffensive ways is consistent with the explic-it aim of the proceedings, namely, reconciliation. In some rare instances where people expressed their anger or otherwise behaved in harsh and hostile ways in the *kgotla*, I witnessed how elders intervened in a warning tone '*o seka wa re tsenya boloi!*' ('Do not bewitch us!'). This is a notion that leads us to what is central here: that *kagiso* is very much a matter of finding social ways to master forces that are potentially creating destructive heat. Significantly, the Tswana verb *go hola* means both to cure and to cool down tensions and conflicts. According to this idealizing model, the collective project of 'cooling' – of overriding a state of 'heat' – should ideally be ob-tained by senior elders who are positioned within a hierarchical order and who execute the authority within the context of the *kgotla* in their efforts to reconcile conflicting parties. Among other peoples of Botswana, for ex-ample the Kalanga, such 'tempering' is attempted and achieved through a ritual process (see Werbner 1989: ch. 3). Similarly, Willoughby (1928: 196ff.) describes ritual practices through which peace is restored.

Of course, all the concern about *kagiso* does not imply that people perceive their society as particularly peaceful and their social environ-ment tensionless. On the contrary, many were quick to tell me that 'we are poor because we always fight'. Tension and conflicts in agnatic rela-tions also feature centrally in ethnographic accounts of the Tswana (e.g. Schapera 1963: 161, 169). In the case of the Southern Tswana (beyond the South African border), it has even been argued that 'agnation was associated with rivalry, intrigue and hostility ... agnates were assumed to have inimical interests and to engage constantly in efforts to "eat" each other'. (Comaroff 1982: 151; cf. Comaroff and Comaroff 1991: 131) For this reason, it is asserted, people had a preference for locating themselves and co-operating in productive activities according to matrilateral and affinal ties, to the extent of moving away from the agnatic context of town wards and even settling in cultivation areas. I have, as indicated, also found considerable preoccupations with conflicts and tension in the agnatic domain which have, in precolonial times when people were free to settle much more freely, entailed departure from the customary patri-virilocal principle, yet only very rarely beyond the village limit. People prefer to settle in another *kgotla*, for example with matrilaterals or in-laws or neolocally (with friends), and thus practically always in another *kgotla*. This underscores the crucial point: precisely because people always feel vulnerable to the 'heat' of conflicts, attachment to a *kgotla* is of existential importance or at least crucial for being anchored in a group of people in the case of being implicated in a conflict.

There is an important dimension of gender here. Not only the still prevailing dominance of patri-virilocal choice of residence but also the basically agnatic structuration of the discursive field of the *kgotla* and the highly patriarchal conception of authority – springing from an indeed masculine ancestorhood – underscore the pervasive character of male dominance. Yet, in postcolonial times women have gradually asserted their presence in the *kgotla*; presently I believe that nobody would re-act to their participation in cross-examination. In my experience, some women are well recognized as clever and powerful speakers, although male dominance is apparent in most cases.

The high value which many people – women as well as men – place upon the proceedings of the customary court as a way to 'cool' matters and avoid the destructive 'heat' associated with social conflicts is comprehensible in view of popular perception of the magistrate courts as operating in ways that easily escalate conflict and prevent people from participating in the proceed-ings to assist in reconciling the parties. This notion reflects some salient fea-tures of a Western courtroom where, as rendered by Roberts (1979: 20–21),

> [o]nce the issue is before the judge he is expected to decide the matter, rather than act as a mediator between the two disputants … Inherent in this method of adjudication is [often] the result that one party wins and the other loses … ; it is not an objective of the system that both parties should go away feeling that they have won, or even honours have been shared. … [O]nce the matter is in the hands of the legal specialists, the lawyers and the judge, they impose their own construction upon it in such a way that both the form and the course which the dispute takes are largely beyond the disputants' control. What is in dispute and how it is to be dealt with are determined by the reach of *legal rules*. (Italics added.)

Conversely, conflicts for which no legal rules apply are not judicable in the magistrate court, irrespective of any sense of grievance a disputant may feel. This is contrary to the court of the *kgotla* which draws upon the broad, undifferentiated body of norms (as *mekgwa le melao*) and takes its point of departure in the existence of a conflict that has to be resolved in the pursuit of *kagiso*.

Finally, because the proceedings of customary courts do not allow law-yers to pursue a case, but rely extensively upon popular participation in cross-examination and in helping to reach reconciliation, most people are from time to time engaged in the discursive field of the *kgotla*. Be-yond the importance of resolving a case, this is a highly meaningful en-gagement because the proceedings often invoke a wide range of central cultural ideas, themes and values of great moral significance. Above all, the proceedings are situated in a discursive field constituted by the cos-mologically anchored hierarchical order which they greatly contribute to reproduce.

Tswana Hierarchies at Large and Issues of Hegemony and Oppression

In postcolonial times, popular celebration of *bogosi* – and its incum-bent, the *kgosi* – is indeed expressed in enthronement ceremonies. The Bangwato, for example, were thrilled by the enthronement of the man they recognized as the rightful heir to the Bangwato throne (*bogosi*), Seretse Khama's son Ian Khama (cf. Chapter 2). Both here and more recently among the Barolong, Batwana, Bamalete and Bakgatla, the en-thronements were events of great festivity held in the presence of the state president, cabinet ministers and other high-ranking officials and thousands of other people. Most recently, Malope Geseitsiwe was cho-sen as the successor of *Kgosi* Seepapitso IV of the Bangwaketse after his death in March 2010. Although being the second son, he was selected in agreement with the royal family because his elder brother, Leema, is a cripple (see first main section of this chapter). Malope was received by the Bangwaketse with great and apparently unanimous enthusiasm and enthroned as *Kgosi* Malope II on 7 October 2011 by *Kgosi* Kgari Sechele III of the Bakwena, recognized by the Bangwaketse as the senior *morafe*. Assembled in the royal *kgotla* was the state president, the two living former presidents, cabinet ministers, a large number of other dignitaries and hundreds of people. Without being explicit about *Kgosi* Kgafela's challenge of the state, The Minister of Local Government took the op-portunity to underscore *Kgosi* Malope's subjection to the state and warn him against violent action against his people.

An intriguing case of popular enthusiasm about *bogosi* manifested itself in October 2001, when one of the minority Tswana communities – the Bakgatla-baga-Mmanaana, which is located within the territory claimed by the Bakwena – got their leader enthroned as a Tswana *kgosi* proper. While technically a senior chief's representative under the authority of the *kgosi* of the Bakwena, he was nevertheless – provokingly in relation to

178 • The State and the Social

the Bakwena – enthroned with a leopard skin,[60] a major Tswana symbol of sovereignty, as *Kgosi* Gobuamang Gobuamang II according to customary ceremonial practices (Schapera 1984: 59f.; cf. Gulbrandsen 1995: 424). An audience of some three thousand people, including state dignitaries, enthusiastically received him. For the Bakgatla-baga-Mmanaana this event was, to be sure, conceived as a tremendous victory, comprehensible in view of the long struggle against Bangwaketse and Bakwena supremacy.[61] As we shall see in my examination of minority struggles in the following chapter, it is precisely the recognition of their symbolic apex in line with the Tswana *dikgosi* which in many cases is of particular concern.

Intriguingly, the enthronement of *Kgosi* Kgafela II of the Bakgatla in 2008 was, I recall, performed by the state president, Ian Khama, underscoring that the enthronement ceremonies might feature quite as a state act. In these spectacular ceremonies the prominence of the *dikgosi* and their close association with state power are symbolized by the presence of the president or the vice-president of Botswana, in addition to cabinet ministers and members of Parliament. The *dikgosi*'s centrality in these proceedings demonstrates the subjection of the *merafe* to the state as well as expressing the state's dependence on these authority figures and the symbolic wealth vested in their respective *bogosi* (e.g. see Somolekae and Lekorwe 1998: 196).[62] This also means that where succession is under dispute (as it has recently been among the Bakwena and Bamalete), these conflicts receive considerable public and political attention on the national level.[63]

A number of political leaders, like the former state president Festus Mogae, are, as indicated earlier, ambivalent if not directly negative to

---

60. While *Kgosi* Seepapitso IV would certainly have seriously challenged this enthronement, the rather weak Bakwena response certainly reflects the lack of force of a royal house that for many decades has been riddled by dynastic rivalries.

61. It will be recalled from Chapter 1 that this section of the Bakgatla-baga-Mmanaana departed from the village of Moshupa in the Bangwaketse to Thamaga in Kweneng, under the leadership of the grandfather of Gobuamang Gobuamang II, Gobuamang I, who severely clashed with *Kgosi* Bathoen II.

62. The large turnout of high-ranking officials should thus be understood as their celebration of the *bogosi* – this despite the fact that they might have ambivalent and sometimes even conflicting relationships with particular *dikgosi*, especially in the context of the House of Chiefs (Vaughan 2003: 95ff.)

63. Let me note at this point that there are of course dissident opinions about the *bogosi* in postcolonial times – and also about particular *dikgosi*. For example, there are those so taken with Western modernity that they speak of the continued prominence of the *dikgosi* as a bizarre survival of the past. Such a view may have increased in the wake of the massive urbanization of the last two decades. Yet I still have the strong impression that most people hold the *bogosi* in high regard even when there is considerable ambivalence towards their incumbents – as always has been the case.

the *dikgosi*. This might be comprehensible in view of all the perceived trouble made by such a *kgosi* as Seepapitso IV or such a challenging *kgosi* as Kgafela II. Nevertheless, the state government has contributed immensely to the reproduction of *bogosi* – through the increasing support given to the customary courts, in terms of a substantial rise in the number of *dikgosana* on state-sponsored salary and numerous physical structures in *dikgotla* throughout the country. Moreover, a Cabinet Directive (no. 17/2001) even states:

> Dikgosi still have significant influence and authority at grassroots level on matters of culture and are therefore better placed to promote the protection and preservation of culture and national genealogical heritage ... Dikgosi shall therefore be responsible for a) Reviving those institutions and values that constitute "Botho" in our nation; b) Promoting law and order through effective judiciary, and mediatory roles in conflicts at family and local level; c) Promoting standardisation of mediatory processes and procedures in complex cultural matters such as inheritance and succession; and d) Maintaining the environment of peace and democracy through the promotion of participation and tolerance at grassroots by men, women and youth through the concept of Mmualebe ['free speech'] and preservation of Kgotla system.

Above all, government officials at all levels contribute, as we shall see in Chapter 6, immensely to activating the discursive field of the *kgotla* by requiring, with high frequency, *dikgosi* and *dikgosana* all over the country to call for *kgotla* meetings in order to conduct consultations with the people – of which President Masire's appearance in the royal *kgotla* of the Bangwaketse to engage people on issues of foreign reserves is but one example.

However ambivalent political leaders might be to the *dikgosi*, many people are, as we have seen, thrilled by having a vacant *bogosi* filled. I want to address this patent expression of popular adherence to the hierarchical order of the *merafe* in the pursuit of explaining the all-encompassing significance of practices and values exercised in the discursive field of the lower-ordered *kgotla*, as profoundly expressed in the Bangwaketse's concerns about the danger of large-scale damages caused by the perceived 'heat' surrounding the *bogosi*. At the level of the royal *kgotla*, the cultural paradigm of 'heat' and 'cool', in relation to *kagiso*, inscribed in the discursive field of the *kgotla*, thus encompasses the hierarchical order at large. This means that the potency of cooling matters of the authority vested in this discursive field is superior to all the subordinate *dikgotla*. Popular perception of the supremacy of this authority finds its expression in their readiness to appeal cases that they are unable to resolve at lower levels to the royal *kgotla*, where they expect the case to be dealt with by the most knowledgeable and experienced people in the *morafe* in proceedings headed by the *kgosi* or one of his deputies. If this is a proceeding that in popular imagination engages descent-group ancestorhood at the local level, at this level the *kgosi* acts as the custodian of the morality vested in the royal ancestorhood (*badimo ba dikgosi*). While these notions are – as I have explained – implicit in the discursive field of the *kgotla*, the *kgotla* proceedings are enacted in accordance with the semiotics of courtesy in relation to persons of authority. As indicated, these behavioural features are very apparent at the descent-group *kgotla* levels, and, of course, particularly so in the *kgosing kgotla*.

This amounts to a popular sense of being embedded in the larger, inclusive body of the *morafe*. If the people in their hierarchical configuration manage to keep the *morafe* cool, it is in a state of health, prosperity and fertility. According to this notion of cosmological order, the state of coolness depends greatly on the head of the body and the support it enjoys from the royal *badimo,* the ultimate source of power, morality and wisdom. This bodily metaphor is asserted by a central Tswana maxim, *tlhogo ke kgosi* ('the head is the *kgosi*'). At the same time the *kgosi* encompasses and embodies the essence of the nation, which is patently emphasized by the fact that he is addressed by the 'metonymic singular of the name of the ... [*morafe*], ... [e.g.] Mongwaketse,[64] the ruler of the Bangwaketse' (Comaroff and Comaroff 1997b: 130). This notion of the essence and source of the nation – Ngwaketse being the founding ruler – is also suggested by the practice that *kgosi* is addressed in the feminine – M*ma*. Moreover, the practice of naming the 'tribespeople' after the founding ancestor signifies – *pars pro toto* – the cosmological anchorage of the tribe in the ancestorhood of the dominant (royal) line of descendants from this first ruler. In line with what I explained in Chapter 1 about incorporation and assimilation of vast groups conquered or hosted, this is, to be sure, an important dimension of hegemony amongst the dominant Tswana *merafe*. Within the confines of each of these *merafe* there are, as we shall see in the following chapter, an ever-increasing number of communities that raise their voices against Tswana domination.

The resonance of these elements in people's everyday world is illustrated by the sense of excitement generated by participation in the royal *kgotla*. As one of my acquaintances stated, 'Kgosing kgotla gives you a particularly good feeling, because here, more than anywhere else, life is conducted in a very proper way'. He pointed in particular to the elaborate etiquette of behaviour by which respect is expressed, and also to

---

64. The prefix 'Ma' signifies singular, while 'Ba' signifies plural.

the beauty of the sophisticated rhetoric displayed by the most eloquent speakers of the *morafe*. These are speakers admired not only for aesthetic reasons but also for their ability 'to convey their strong views in ways that do not challenge anyone ... They are masters of *deep* Setswana'. Which means, in particular, that they have a solid command over a proverbial language in the form of which a range of Tswana maxims are phrased (see Schapera 1966; cf. Comaroff 1975). Such performance is an everyday event in the *kgosing kgotla*. Especially as this *kgotla* recurrently receives appeal cases by which, ideally at least, their highly appreciated experience, knowledge and wisdom manifest the cultural wealth of the *bogosi*, reconciling conflicting parties and counselling the head of the royal court before judgement. If people search the descent-group court in the pursuit of *kagiso*, they do so even more at the apex of *bogosi*. The consequent popular appreciation of the incumbent of *bogosi* – the principal custodian of ancestral morality – finds its most pronounced collective expression in the enthronement of a new *kgosi*.

In view of how people are thus ingrained in a hierarchical order – being very appreciative of the cultural and symbolic wealth of the *bogosi* – their deep concern with tension and conflicts surrounding the *bogosi* should be comprehensible. If the people are concerned about sustaining *kagiso* at the level of their immediate life context, this is, as we saw in the preceding section, no less so when *kagiso* is at the heart of *bogosi*. The forces at work within this context – challenging as well as protecting *bogosi* and its incumbent – will be addressed in Chapter 8. In that chapter I shall also be concerned with the implication of the clear-cut distinction which is made between office and incumbent – *bogosi* and *kgosi* – allowing that *bogosi*, with its hierarchical order, prevails even if a *kgosi* happens to be weak, unpopular or even wicked (see also Gulbrandsen 1995: 424). Presently my concern is with processes that contribute to sociocultural integration at the level of the *merafe*; hence I have focused on processes that connect the population at large to the royal centre.

The centrality of the *bogosi* and the *kgosi* is spatially symbolized by the location of *kgosing kgotla* in the midst of the royal town, often encompassed by nonroyal wards that represent no challenge to the incumbent of the *bogosi* (see Gulbrandsen 1996a: 58). As suggested in Chapter 1, relationships radiate from the royal town to major provincial villages, headed by prominent, often royal *dikgosana* from the royal centre, and beyond those are found minor villages with people of mostly alien origin. As I explain elsewhere (Gulbrandsen 2007: 67f, cf. Comaroff 1980: 642), a major distinction is made between, on the one hand, the civilized order of the royal town and villages and, on the other, the uncultivated wilderness of the encompassing bush, a major notion underpinning the concentration of the Tswana in large compact settlements, as epitomized by the royal towns that counted thousands – even tens of thousands of people already in the early nineteenth century (cf. Chapter 1 above). The discursive field of the *kgotla*, above all that of the royal *kgotla*, is strongly associated with civilization, which is a matter of ongoing discourse where ancestral morality – as expressed in the normative repertoire of *mekgwa le melao* – is continuously negotiated with the changing realities of life, both in relation to (as we have seen) court cases and to the state policies and programmes, which is a central issue in Chapter 6.

This means that the *bogosi* is not just a centre for the mundane exercise of authority. It is constitutive of values defining the hierarchical order; it sets the moral standards for civilized life. Yet, even if we add to this all the appreciation of the performative aspects of discursive practices in *kgosing kgotla*, we do not have at hand an 'exemplary centre' in the sense conceived by Geertz (1980) in his analysis of the ancient Negra of Bali. It is true that the massive discursive practices of the *kgotla* are, as in the case of the major state rituals of Negra, 'an argument, made over and over again … that worldly status has a cosmic base and that hierarchy is the governing principle of the universe' (Geertz 1980: 102). But the *kgotla* proceedings have a far more mundane, even everyday character, compared to the spectacular ceremonial events of Negra state rituals. Moreover the cultural construction of hierarchy differs of course very significantly. For example, while Negra is rendered as a 'theatre state' where the vast majority of people remain as distant spectators to the drama displayed in the state ceremonies, in the present context people are attracted by the dramaturgical qualities of *kgotla* proceedings to a great extent as participants. Not only that, the substance matter of the drama of the *kgotla* might well be people's own serious existential concerns and problems, springing from grave problems in relationship to conjugality and kinship. In the theatre of the *kgotla* during court proceedings, they are themselves actors in this very transparent, public scene.

The existential significance of the *kgosi* in people's lives as a major source of *kagiso* is reinforced by an important dimension of intimacy: *kgosi*'s engagement in any individual's small or large life crises, whether these involve marriage problems, disputes over inheritance, or accusations of insult (very common in this society where there is so much concern with respectful behaviour). Images of intimacy were also drawn for me by people who attributed to the *kgosi* (at least ideally) a deep personal concern for his subjects and an immense knowledge of the lives of virtually every family. *Kgosi* Bathoen II was often recalled – and highly esteemed – as a *kgosi* who readily visited people in their homes: 'He could even take up a small child and kiss it on its head – that was a blessing [*masego*] – the parents were immensely pleased, you know'. The force of hierarchical integration represented by such practices of intimacy was conditioned by the fact that the royal *kgotla* was never located far away from ordinary people but was found right at the centre of the densely populated royal towns (see Chapter 6).

All that said about the conditions for popular appreciation of the perceived cultural and symbolic wealth vested in the *bogosi* and people's adherence to the hierarchical order, I want to underline that all relations of authority are, as probably everywhere else, vested with ambivalence. A lot of people have experienced power abuse in such relationships. Furthermore, in the wake of the massive migration of people to urban areas during the last two decades and, above all, the ever-more-intense exposure to Western modernity, many have had a taste of personal freedom to an extent which has generated patterns of behaviour that are not readily compatible with the customary code of deference and submission to authority figures in the family and beyond. Thus combined with social deprivation and pervasive poverty that themselves foster the excessive consumption of alcohol, behavioural patterns that annoy and provoke many people are to be expected. Nevertheless, it is evident that – even in this late postcolonial era – substantial forces are at work in support of the hierarchical order of the *merafe*, notwithstanding that many people perceive it as deteriorating.

Another important question regarding the repressive forces inherent in the *merafe* concerns minority communities within their respective territories. This is a major issue in the following chapter. In the present context it is, however, relevant to point out that the minority communities are integrated into the hierarchy of customary courts, centred in the royal *kgotla* of each of the Tswana *merafe*. They have thus to bring their cases through this hierarchy before they can reach the Customary Court of Appeal on the national level. It is intriguing that minority protests against Tswana domination, in progress since the mid-1990s, have virtually never been concerned with this; their subjection to Tswana *dikgosi* as supreme judges seems still to be taken for granted. According to my information, members of previous subject communities such as the Birwa, Tswapong, Herero, Kaa, Kalanga and all the Kgalagadi groups located in territories claimed by the privileged Tswana *merafe* have made no protest against having to appeal their cases to a superior court that is presided over by one of the Tswana *dikgosi*.[65] It is indeed puzzling that even com-

---

65. The only exception of which I am aware is the Batswana's imposition of patrilineal inheritance rules on the Wayei, who have customarily adhered to principles of matrilineal descent (Lydia Nyati-Ramahobo, personal communication, November 2004).

munities located far beyond the confines of the Tswana *merafe* call upon the Bakwena or Bangwaketse *kgosi* for the establishment of a local appeals court.

This feature illuminates a point I shall elaborate in the following chapter: the various peoples incorporated in the sphere of the dominant Tswana *merafe* are (with only very few exceptions such as the San-speaking peoples) located within an overall cultural paradigm of so-called Bantu-speaking peoples of the region. Of course, there are normative variations (e.g. see Schapera 1965). But in their practices of jurisprudence – in sharp contrast to those of a Western court where what matters is who is right before the law – 'the successful contrivance of a relationship depends on the construal of as much of its history and contemporary character as possible in relation to the widest available set of normative referents … [V]eracity subsists … in the extent to which events and interactions are persuasively construed and coherently interpreted' (Comaroff and Roberts 1981: 237–38). Thus, when the *kgosi* of the Bakwena goes to the Kgalagadi village of Hukuntsi in Western Botswana in order to preside over an appeal case proceeding, he will, at least ideally, be concerned with the normative rules (*mekgwa*) to which this community subscribes. If the parties come from different communities – a practice that is more and more common as a consequence of increasing mobility – the court is presented with the challenge of reconciling different normative repertoires. This is a routine matter, especially in superior courts. The capacity to litigate beyond the limits of 'tribal' communities is confirmed above all by the establishment of the Customary Court of Appeal. When Bathoen Gaseitsiwe was appointed as its first president in 1985, nobody questioned his competence to deal with cases brought by people from other communities far beyond the reaches of the Bangwaketse. The court is composed of senior members of different communities in the country who are appointed by the state government. I have no information to suggest that they have had any major difficulties in working together. The convergence of cultural paradigms among peoples located within the domain of the Tswana *merafe* is patently illuminated by Werbner's (2004: 71) assertion that 'a central aspect of Tswana and Kalanga life is the living tradition of public argument in which both engage in their popular assemblies, the *kgotla* and *lubashe*, respectively … [with] many historically shared assumptions of public life order, civic virtue, constitutionality, and the rule of law'. He hence asserts the 'social and moral resemblances between Tswana and Kalanga'.

The unquestioned acceptance amongst minority communities of the subjection to the courts of the Tswana *dikgosi*, calls into question the extent to which coercive forces are at work. This was certainly the case in precolonial and colonial times. But I have no evidence indicating that submission has been enforced in more recent times, except when no other alternatives for appeal than the magistrate courts exist. In my view, this is rather a matter of successful exercise of Tswana hegemony, ensuring that the Tswana royal courts prevail unquestioned as superior. The taken-for-granted character of minorities' perception of the existing hierarchy of customary courts stands in intriguing contrast to minority leaders' protest against clauses in Botswana's Constitution that privilege Tswana *dikgosi* with *ex officio* membership in the House of Chiefs by virtue of a clause in the Constitution. Only quite recently some few minority communities have started to question their subjection to the jurisdiction of the dominant Tswana *dikgosi*.

Conclusion

The observation that the *dikgosi*, as presidents of their respective royal courts, tie in local courts beyond the confines of their realms underscores not only the force of Tswana domination. This observation epitomizes also the networks of power vested in the hierarchy of customary courts, captured by the postcolonial state and hence representing an extensive instrument of state control of the population. I find it helpful to try to understand this through Foucault's (1980: 122) conception of the state as superstructural in relation to a whole series of preexisting power networks (in the sense of having been generated during precolonial and colonial times), that is networks

> which embody relations of power which are not purely and simply a projection of the sovereign's great power over the individual … Between every point in the social body, between man and woman, between members of the family, between master and pupil, between everyone who knows and who does not, there exist relations of power which are not purely and simply a projection of the sovereign's great power over the individual; they are the concrete, changing soil in which the sovereign's power is grounded, the conditions that make it possible for it to function. (Foucault 1980: 187)

From this perspective it is intriguing how the postcolonial state in Botswana, at its inception, took immediate control over the structures of societal control vested in the pervasive networks of power radiating from the royal centres of the Tswana *merafe* down to all family heads. It is equally surprising perhaps that this 'capture' has been quite unique amongst postcolonial states in Africa, especially in the sense that these courts have been allowed to operate, to a great extent, on their own premises as far as principles and practices of the proceedings are concerned within the quite wide limits set by the state's Customary Court Act. The currently prevailing – and highly unique – case of *Kgosi* Kgafela illuminates that the state nevertheless is prepared to put its foot down when these limits are transgressed.

And this has been my central concern in the second main section of this chapter, where I have wanted to substantiate, first, the point that the customary courts – and the associated popular control of people's behaviour in everyday contexts – have been very useful to the postcolonial state by keeping the population in the societal fold. I have explained how the network of power has been centred in the hierarchies of customary courts that have proved highly instrumental to the state administration of justice, exercised predominantly on the basis of the indigenous normative repertoire of *mekgwa le melao* which is held in high esteem by everybody as cosmologically anchored ancestral morality, yet pragmatically adapted to changing societal circumstances in time and space. This has been so especially during the formative and consolidating decades of the post-colonial state, which is of central concern in this volume. Nonetheless, even under conditions of intensified modernity, the flexible and pragmatic character of the customary courts has been significant.

Second, all the concern with reconciliation and the participation of extended families, other relatives and friends in the proceedings endow the customary courts with the values associated with the discursive field of the *kgotla*. This means that the hierarchical order of the *merafe* is vested with a centripetal force – captured by the modern state – which might be contrasted with Foucault's reading of premodern European monarchies, in which the state is seen as 'a kind of "meta-power" which is structured essentially around a certain number of great prohibitive functions; but this meta-power with its prohibitions can only take hold and secure its footing where it is *rooted in* a whole series of multiple and indefinite power relations that supply the necessary basis for the great *negative forms of power*' (Foucault 1980: 122, italics added). This conception of a repressive state has arisen particularly in relation to these monarchies in which '[s]overeign, law and prohibition formed a system of representation of power' (Foucault 1980: 121). In view of the apparently premodern character of Tswana polities and hence jurisprudence, one might well expect the latter to be similarly characterized by 'negative forms of power'. It follows, however, from what has been explained in this chapter that people emphatically do not, on the whole, associate Tswana jurisprudence with the exercise of repressive forces. On the contrary, their ideas and practices of jurisprudence are grounded in a cosmology which makes the exercise of authority a major condition for social peace and order, that is *kagiso*, essential for fertility, health and welfare – in brief, *life*. By contrast, at least according to Foucault (1981: 134f.), the exercise of jurisprudence in Western societies is closely associated with the power of death (see Chapter 7).

This means that the modern state in Botswana features as superstructural to *existing* structures of exercising authority in a positive sense, structures that are predominantly generated from below and not imposed from above. Patently, we have here at hand processes and structures of sanctioning people's behaviour that reduce significantly the need for exercising negative state power, which is, as pointed out in the Introduction, an important condition for the strength of any state. In this particular case it is intriguing, moreover, that the focus of negative reactions from below towards what there are of repressive structures in the *merafe* – as in the case of minority communities captured within them – is directed towards people in the immediate context that operate as agencies of those structures.

In line with these features of 'positive power', we shall see, as we now proceed, how the modern state actively engages with the indigenous authority structures in appropriating their symbolic wealth and the discursive field of the *kgotla*. I shall do so on the basis of my present efforts to identify cultural and sociological conditions that give rise to the continued strong popular appreciation and support of the Tswana *bogosi*, as illustrated by the enthusiastic celebration of the enthronement of the *dikgosi* and substantiated by the mobilization of the Bangwaketse and the Bakgatla. These cases demonstrate that the popular appreciation and support of *bogosi* is still in force, despite many of the younger generation who have grown up in urban centres since the late 1980s and who have certainly escaped the *kgotla* and other 'tribal' contexts where values and virtues of the indigenous hierarchies are still of significance. At any rate, these cases assert that strong orientations of this kind were pervasive during the formative and consolidating period of the postcolonial state which is, I reiterate, my major concern in this volume.

The cases of mobilization are important, moreover, because they assert the potentials vested in the *merafe* of major challenges of the state, bringing me to ask why this has so rarely happened. One major answer is that the *dikgosi* have been effectively co-opted by the state and thus find it very hard to set an agenda for the *morafe*. This is, particularly so, in a country where the state leadership, on the one hand, officially celebrates the indigenous virtue of *mmualebe o bua la gagwe* ('free speech'), but, on the other, is quick to crack down on minority groups' public mobilization as unlawfully 'political' unless restricted to folklorist activity. As I pointed out, it shall be most interesting to see what the Bakgatla endeavour will trigger of state reaction and responses amongst other communities in Botswana. I am particularly concerned with the rhizomic potentialities in the

Tswana *merafe* and, indeed, also beyond Tswana confines – amongst all the minorities whose reactions to subjection to Tswana domination are, as we shall see in the following chapter, in progress.

Nevertheless, for nearly forty-five years, state and *morafe* – two obviously distinct assemblages of power – have co-existed in ways that have strengthened the former and reproduced the other notwithstanding the curtailment of much of the executive powers of the *dikgosi*. With this background the following chapters aim to come further to terms with how the postcolonial state has developed with such strength that the Tswana *merafe* and other indigenous structures of authority have, so far, been instrumental not only in ensuring social control and keeping at bay potential rhizomic forces but also in furnishing the state with symbolic power and arenas for state intervention in the population in the pursuit of making it integral to the formation of a modern state in Botswana.

Let me at this point reemphasize that my central concern in this volume is with the formative and consolidating decades of the postcolonial state. In view of the problem of establishing a strong state elsewhere in Africa, this was a highly critical period, especially because the modern state governments everywhere had to rely much on indigenous structures for keeping control over the population. The following chapters elaborate further how the Botswana state government succeeded in this effort when many other governments failed. The fast expansion of the state government after independence meant that an ever-increasing number of governmental employees – especially in the emerging urban and district centres – were brought into direct dependency on the state and, by extension, indirectly all their family members. In particular, since state employees are barred by law from engaging in politics, the state has ensured that these categories of often well-informed people are kept under control.

If we move beyond the formative and consolidating decades when migration to urban centres took off in the late 1980s, people have increasingly been brought into the dependency of the state in its very significant capacity as landlord – thus in major control of housing accommodations. From this point in time, the private sector of the economy in urban areas – always integral to the indeed state-centred political economy (see preceding chapter) – grew very rapidly, creating new structures of controlling all the people that moved beyond the everyday controls of indigenous authorities. As I suggest in Chapter 6, not only their dependency on private employers that have interest in sustaining the state leadership but also the state's far-reaching control of trade unions involve major conditions by which the flow of people to urban centres has been captured into a social order that underpins the strength of the state.

That the postcolonial state in Botswana prevailed after massive migration was initiated and the private sector of the economy started to expand, is mainly attributable to the capacities of the state that had already been established. To explain how these capacities became instrumental to develop such new structures of state control of the population as just suggested requires, to be sure, another volume. The following chapters are instead following the line indicated in the introduction to the present chapter: to examine, from different angles, further development of the postcolonial state in relation to the symbolism, practices and structures vested in indigenous authority structures.

Finally, despite major social transformations in the wake of urbanization during the last twenty years, indigenous authority structures have not lost their significance as underpinnings of the postcolonial state. It is an important demographic condition for this, meaning that the highly dominant urban centre of Botswana – the capital of Gaborone – is, within short reach, surrounded by four of the six Tswana royal towns and a number of major villages that are still, to a significant extent, organized according to customary principles of indigenous authority structures. This feature allows many people attached to the capital to keep in close touch with these contexts, especially because the relatively short distance allows people to live in these towns and villages while being employed in the capital.

Chapter 5

TSWANA DOMINATION, MINORITY PROTESTS AND THE DISCOURSE OF DEVELOPMENT

While 'African socialism', in various versions, had considerable appeal elsewhere on the continent in the years following Botswana's independence (1966), President Seretse Khama rejected it as a 'guiding ideology'. The occasion was an address at the Dag Hammarskjøld Centre in Uppsala (Sweden) in 1970, where he asserted that '[w]e in Botswana have chosen to develop our own guiding principles and describe them in terms readily comprehensible to our people … rooted in our culture and tradition' (Carter and Morgan 1980: 102). That is, 'our culture and tradition' in the singular – which might be taken to mean the dominant Tswana culture, indicating no sense of building a nation on cultural diversity. At the same time, Khama declared a strong front against tribalism as well as racism. In contrast to apartheid South Africa, Botswana featured successfully across the world as an exemplary island of humanism, peace and tolerance, epitomized by Khama's personal example of marriage (see Chapter 2).

The critical importance of the cohesion of the dominant Tswana elite to the establishment of a ruling group (see Chapter 3) made it not only unproblematic but natural to speak of 'our culture and tradition' in the singular in relation to major centres of power at the time of Botswana's independence. Despite the existence of non-Tswana 'minority' communities that possibly added up to a numerical majority, the naming of the independent state *Botswana* with Setswana as the national language was established without significant public protest, except from some complaining Kalanga voices (see Chapter 3). Thus stated Parsons (1985: 28) some twenty years after independence: 'What is remarkable about Botswana is how much … the legitimacy of Tswana-dom has been accepted and even supported by non-Tswana groups'. The answer might be the success in establishing what Werbner (2004: 38) calls 'the One-Nation Consensus' through assimilation and the favouring of homogeneity, leaving 'virtually no space in the public sphere for the country's many non-Tswana cultures, unless recast in a Tswana image'.

This notion suggests a dimension of coercion in the exercise of Tswana domination which, as we have seen, developed during precolonial, and especially, colonial times. In order to pursue this issue in the postcolonial context, it is important to be clear about the different ways Tswana domination had been exercised. In particular, I am concerned in this chapter with a major distinction between, on the one hand, the hierarchical order of the Tswana *merafe* which did not, as we saw in the preceding chapter, disappear by the establishment of the modern state in Botswana and, on the other hand, the vast minority communities within their realm of domination. This meant that Tswana repressive structures – with all their subtle, tacit practices of discrimination – continued to work also under the circumstances of the modern state and are actually still in considerable force. Their significance is patently reflected in the fact that it should take some thirty years after independence before the Tswana-dominated state leadership was publicly challenged by other minorities than the Kalanga (see Chapter 3). That is at the time when people of other 'minority' backgrounds had achieved higher education, made successful careers and gained sufficient confidence to stand up for their respective communities.

It is, as I shall explain in this chapter, at the same time highly significant that the Tswana-dominated state leadership made, from the outset, considerable efforts to present itself through ethnically neutral policies, to the extent of often making cultural diversity irrelevant (except for language). Important conditions for the state government's success in avoiding prevailing ethnic animosities and tensions surfacing are, I shall argue, to be found in the rise of a moral and political leadership grounded in indigenous, not only Tswana, virtues of progress and prosperity and which, at the same time, gave massive promises of 'development' and the acceleration of access to other attractions of Western modernity. This involved what I shall call a 'discourse of development' by which the state leadership attempted, quite successfully, to establish broad-based legitimacy.

I am thus concerned with how the Tswana-dominated ruling group managed to win hegemony by capturing the population – with no significant coercion – into a nation building discourse of universal progress.

Although the ruling group was clearly Tswana staffed, Seretse Khama and his political companions had a different and much larger agenda than perpetuating Tswana practices of assimilating minorities in the pursuit of bringing everybody into the Tswana cultural fold. Many of them – including Khama – were, after all, so strongly taken by Western virtues of modernity that they disregarded Tswana traditional clothing, dances, not to say ritual practices such as *bogwera* and *bojale* which might have been highly instrumental to demonstrate Tswana prominence. Their ambition was, on the contrary, to win hegemony and establish legitimacy as the moral and political leadership of a nation-state that was overwhelmingly oriented towards Western modernity, national unity and antitribalism – not only in relation to the dominant class (cf. Chapter 3), but in relation to the population at large. As we shall see in this and the two following chapters, while indigenous coercive structures, intrinsic in the Tswana *merafe* and other indigenous authority structures, kept the vast majority of the population in the societal fold during the formative and consolidating decades (1966–1990), the state featured in most respects as, in the Foucauldian (1980: 121) sense, a 'positive power' oriented towards consensus building through a gradualist strategy of capturing the population into the process of state formation. That is, a state of right, principled on liberal virtues of equity, freedom and democracy.

The wave of 'democratization' in Africa in the 1990s was not always conducive to national unity. On the contrary, as Berman et al. (2004: 9) maintain, multiparty politics has involved '[t]he fragmentation of broad, urban-based opposition movements into parties with core ethnic constituencies and the consequent regionalization of political competition'. The destabilizing potential of this situation has recently been evidenced in the once-celebrated democracy of Kenya. Why Botswana, a multiparty democracy since 1966, has maintained its stability is, I argued in Chapter 3, to a great extent due to a unification of major elites with a common interest in a strong, stable state government. This coalescence of elite interests has worked in support of nation-state integration by incorporating the Tswana *merafe* and other 'traditional' authority structures as instruments of government in the Foucauldian sense (cf. previous chapter). The following two chapters will examine how these structures have facilitated state intervention in the population. In the present chapter, I want to explain that despite the postcolonial state's massive modernization programmes, the discourse of development was not entirely sourced externally – that is, it entailed more than simply imposing Western modernity. This discourse, I shall argue, has drawn heavily on the symbolic wealth centred in the indigenous cosmology and authority structures.

In the first major section of this chapter I shall focus upon the formative and consolidating decades (1966–1990) of the postcolonial state. It is initiated by an account of how the symbolic wealth vested in indigenous structures of authority (see preceding chapter) was captured by the state leadership in the efforts of construing a legitimating imagery of the modern state. Since this symbolism is expressed in Setswana, I ask why minorities have not attacked it as a matter of 'Tswanification' of the state. The answer to this question forms a point of departure for examining the ways in which indigenous symbolic order has been blended with Western modernity. By extension I pursue an overarching issue in this volume – the transformative capacity of political leadership in different historical contexts. Here I consider Seretse Khama's agency of transformation in the light of how Tswana rulers have spearheaded radical changes at different historical stages by virtue of the cultural construction of their authority. This leads me to conclude the first main section of this chapter by discussing two potentially contradictory dimensions inherent in the discourse of development. That is, between, on the one hand, the collective value of the common good and, on the other, virtues of liberal individualism and commercial entrepreneurship.

In the second major section of this chapter I am going beyond 1990 because it was only at this time, as suggested, that minorities felt strong and confident enough to stand up in the public sphere against the perceived Tswana domination. I am here centrally concerned with the relationship between, on the one hand, the efforts of establishing an ethnically neutral discourse of development and, on the other, the state's declaration of social equality and liberal individualism. While the Tswana-dominated state government in important respects managed to establish the ruling group as legitimate by virtue of popular consent (*dumela*) to their moral and political leadership through the exercise of the discourse of development, Tswana domination continued in local contexts, as suggested, coercing minorities into Tswana hierarchical orders, especially by stigmatizing minority cultural practices. I shall examine this conflict, especially minorities' reactions towards perceived Tswana discrimination and their protest against being treated as second-class citizens.

Tswana Domination and the Discourse of Development

The postcolonial state leadership's most visible attempt to root the nation's guiding principles 'in our culture and tradition' can be found in the introductions to every National Development Plan, which assert that all the government's policies are founded on four national principles. These are:

Puso ya botho ka batho	Democracy
Ditiro tsa ditlhabololo	Development
Boipelego	Self-reliance
Popagano ya sechaba	Unity[1]

Together these principles, when applied in practice, are designed to achieve *kagisano* – social harmony'.[2] The overarching status of *kagisano* is apparent in the last two lines of the national anthem:

Ka kutlwano le kagisano	Through our unity and harmony
E bopagantshe mmogo	We stand in peace as one

The invocation of the powerful symbolism of *kagisano* – living peacefully together – and the major 'principles' that promote *kagiso*[3] constitute an attempt to ground the nation as a whole in virtues located at the core of people's existential concerns within family and community (see Chapter 4). This seems to have some correspondence with Kapferer's notion of, in the case of the Singhalese, the 'constitutive and determining force of nationalist culture at the level of personal inner being' (1988: 99). Yet it is clearly not an attempt to construct a national ideology 'that defines who belong and who do not' (Herzfeld 1992: 65); an ideology with great potentialities of tremendous violence, in such cases as that of the Singhalese (Kapferer 1988: 99ff.).[4] On the contrary, with its emphasis upon peace and unity, the postcolonial ruling group has attempted to construe a notion of the state as an inclusive and all-encompassing force. Although there are occasional idealistic allusions to 'our forefathers', these do not specifically refer to Tswana ancestors (although minorities might well make such an inference when the speaker is identified as Tswana). Moreover, there are no traces in this rhetoric of blood, descent and kin-

---

1. The full meaning is 'unity of nation', which denotes a 'tribe' in the sense of a culturally distinct entity.

2. National Development Plan 1976–81 (Government Printer, Gaborone, n.d.), 15.

3. *Kagiso* means 'peace' and 'harmony', while the meaning of *kagisano* is 'staying together in peace'.

4. It should be noted at this point that Botswana gained its independence at a time when it was surrounded by racist, violent states. Significantly, the country established its sovereignty in a highly peaceful manner and retained it, during the first twelve years, without even having a military force under the command of the state.

ship. Instead there is, as already suggested, a strong emphasis upon the postcolonial state as nonracist, antitribal, liberal and thus highly inclusive, also encompassing all white citizens.

Construing a Modern State: Images of Peace and Harmony

The significance of *kagisano* or *kagiso* is often emphasized in the rhetoric of political leaders. For example, President Seretse Khama, in a major speech[5] during the celebration of the tenth anniversary of Botswana's independence (1976), portrayed the state as the custodian of social peace and harmony:

> Botswana is a democratic country founded upon the ideal of *Kagisano* – harmony. This ideal is neither foreign nor new. It is rooted in our past – in our culture and traditions. On the whole, the past generations of Batswana always lived in peace and harmony. The sense of community and the spirit of mutual belonging, which continue to pervade our generation, are some of the most cherished legacies of our past. Today as we gather here to celebrate the end of a decade of development, peace and stability, let us rededicate ourselves to the consolidation of our democratic ideals because time and experience have shown that these ideals are on fertile ground in our country from which they continue to flourish if we continue to live together in peace and harmony in the spirit of *kagisano*.

The invocation of *kagisano* is not limited to such grand occasions. As I shall explain in the following chapter, the relationship between the state and the people in Botswana is largely manifested in the small-scale context of the local *kgotla* where this rhetoric prevails. And it is noteworthy that any attempts to present the postcolonial state capital, Gaborone, as the spatial apex of the nation have been scarce. Instead of adopting the usual symbolism of broad avenues radiating from monumental buildings, the capital is centred on a small pedestrian street with a modestly constructed parliament house at one end. The street is referred to as 'the Mall', a telling allusion to Western modernity lacking the symbolic force capable of uniting a nation. The impression of the capital city as focused on commercialism and consumerism – and hence on individualism rather than on the virtues of the common good – is corroborated by its expansion into new sections that are always centred on a mall. This pattern goes with another contrast to the rise of classic Western nation-states: it has not been spearheaded by anything like an urban bourgeoisie. During the formative decades of the postcolonial state, the ruling group

---

5. Reproduced in Carter and Morgan 1980: 324.

was much part of a cattle-obsessed, rurally anchored elite who retained a close association with their respective natal *kgotla* (since then there has been a gradual development of a more urban-focused elite network amongst people also engaged in off-farm economic venture, see Chapter 3).

Rather than engaging in spectacular ceremonies at the state centre, political leaders continuously travel across the country to engage in the discursive field of the *kgotla*, even in the smallest and most remote settlements. It is significant that they invoke the virtues of *kagisano* exactly where these are at their most meaningful to people. The *kgotla*, as I explained in Chapter 4, is perceived by people as particularly conducive to *kagisano*: it is in this discursive field that the notion of *kagisano* is at its most potent and thus most instrumental in infusing their political leadership with a spiritual dimension. The significance of this was, of course, most profound during the formative decades of the postcolonial state; yet, as I have argued, public spheres are also constructed in urban areas according to the discursive ideals of the *kgotla*.

The attempt to establish a close association between *kagisano* and democracy reflects the relationship between the postcolonial state maxim *Puso ya botho ka batho* (government of the people for the people) and the traditional Tswana saying *Kgosi ke kgosi ka batho/morafe* (The *kgosi* is *kgosi* by virtue of the people/tribe). The former maxim mirrors the various attempts to situate the postcolonial state in the symbolic wealth of the *merafe* while at the same time disempowering the *dikgosi*. It implies the existence of a popular check on people in positions of power which stems from the important distinction which the Tswana always make between person and position, incumbent and office. It conveys the idea of transparency in political life, which is most evidently expressed in the highly inclusive context of the *kgotla*. The efforts made by politicians to engage with people in this context by means of the celebrated virtue of 'consultation' thus constitute an important legitimation of power.

And the supreme power of the state is profoundly expressed by the title given to its head, *Tautona* ('The Big Lion'), resonant with all the force of the ruler as the major living custodian of *kagiso* and the common good. The significance of this force has been confirmed throughout the postcolonial era, which has overwhelmingly been characterized by order, peace and prosperity. Although the state adheres closely to the Weberian ideal of monopolizing the exercise of violence, it has relied to a very limited extent on the exercise of coercive power. Instead the state, with all its welfare programs, has always presented itself as benevolent, in close agreement with the Tswana virtues of the ruler as *motswanadintle*, meaning 'the one from whom good things are coming' (cf. Chapter 1).

One might well ask how postcolonial attempts to tap the symbolic wealth of the *merafe* could be pursued at the same time as disempowering the supreme custodians of the *merafe*'s orders – the *dikgosi*. This radical move was often justified as a means of reestablishing authentic Tswana principles of rule. According to this rhetoric, the nation-state government was to be distinguished from the supposedly repressive rule of the 'autocratic' *dikgosi* (see Chapter 2). Such criticism gained support from the lifting of many of the unpopular restrictions imposed by the *dikgosi*, including regulations concerning the production and consumption of alcohol. The *dikgosi* also lost their power to mobilize the age regiments as a labour force, which they had allegedly exploited for private gain. Freedom of religion was declared and the *dikgosi*'s ban on independent churches was suspended: a highly popular decision, as can be seen from the tremendous mushrooming of congregations beyond the controls of missionary churches. The custodianship of the tribal lands was transferred to the Tribal Land Boards, so that all people, especially those wishing to develop large farms, might be granted access to land. As the then vice-president Quett Masire put it, the goal was to end 'the arbitrary decisions of the chiefs' (quoted in Werbner 1980: 137).

Yet this was not entirely a hard-line strategy in relation to the *dikgosi*. It had to be balanced and, in agreement with Tswana pragmatic political practice, nonconfrontational. The *dikgosi* were after all still the heads of the *merafe* and, as I explained in Chapter 4, remained in position vis-à-vis their respective people with *de facto* authority far in excess of what was framed in the Chieftainship Act. The sincere concern to ground the state in the existing cultural and societal order that also included these authority figures was particularly apparent in an important speech delivered by Botswana's founding president, Seretse Khama, in the royal *kgotla* of the Bangwaketse a few years after independence:

> I and my Government have often been accused of conducting campaigns against the chiefs [*dikgosi*]. Nothing could be further from the truth. We are anxious to *build on the foundations of our traditional institutions*. We are concerned to maintain what is good and constructive in our traditional values. Traditional authority remains important both as channels of communication between government and people and as a stable element in the time of rapid change. But *let us be sure that it is really our traditional values that certain chiefs are defending and not their own privileged position*. Too often this privileged position rests not on genuinely traditional practice, but on the powers given to chiefs by the British, who strengthened the position of the chiefs in order to rule Botswana on the cheap. (Italics added.)

This statement concisely advances a distinction between 'certain chiefs' and 'genuinely traditional practice'. It is again alleged that the *dikgosi*'s

198 • The State and the Social

powers became overinflated during the colonial era, involving a departure from the authentic principles vested in the foundations of 'our traditional institutions'. That is the principle, Khama asserts, upon which 'we are anxious to build'.

However, the significance of the customary order to the state is well recognized by the *dikgosi* themselves, as expressed by one of the most significant figures amongst them, *Kgosi* Linchwe of Bakgatla (see Chapters 4 and 8). One and a half decades after the *dikgosi* had lost many of their executive powers, he asserted that they

> will continue to play a positive role in the affairs of the nation. We are the symbol of our people's glorious past. We provide a sense of belonging and our people have something to fall back on when they get disillusioned with the new way of life. *We create stability and encourage our people to respect their leaders. Batswana's respect for national government emanates from their traditional respect for authority.* (Italics added.)

This declaration of support from one of the most important *dikgosi* indicates their approval of the postcolonial state, notwithstanding their actual ambivalence towards (and at times harsh critique of) the political leadership. However, it is one thing to gain the support of Tswana royalty, but it is quite another to bring all the minority communities into the national fold given the ethnic contradictions inherent in the *merafe* outlined above. As I explained in Chapter 4, vast sections of those peoples who were ambivalent or antagonistic towards Tswana overlords have nevertheless been assimilated into the discursive field of the *kgotla*. Many of these communities have done so because this discursive field is constructed within a cultural paradigm that encompasses much of the larger region of Southern Bantu-speaking peoples.

Although a community of people might be sociopolitically alien to the hosting *morafe*, much of what is included in the *mekgwa le melao ya Setswana* ('Tswana custom and law') would not be at all unfamiliar to them.[6] The central virtues associated with hierarchy and order are quite pervasive across 'tribal' communities in the larger region (e.g. Sansom 1974), including the appreciation of a benevolent ruler (Schapera 1956: 108–9). In particular the wide-ranging significance of *kagisano* is reflected in the importance of reconciliation, which is reported from such diverse ethnographic contexts as that of the Tsonga (see Junod 1927: 210), the Zulu (Krige 1950: 59) and the Lovedu (Krige and Krige 1980: 192). The current importance of reconciliation and 'to live together in peace' in the larger region of Southern Africa is underscored by the centrality of these

---

6. For example, Werbner (2004: 71) stresses the similarities between Tswana and Kalanga.

virtues – expressed by the notion of *ubuntu* – in the efforts of legitimizing a post-apartheid state in South Africa. *Ubuntu* has been spearheaded by Nelson Mandela and Desmond Tutu, the latter stressing that 'you must do what you can to maintain this great harmony, which is perpetually undermined by resentment, anger, desire and vengeance. That is why African jurisprudence is restorative rather than retributive' (quoted after Wilson 2001: 9).

Although the situation at Botswana's independence was radically different from that of South Africa with the fall of the apartheid regime, Khama spearheaded the effort to ground the nation in harmony and unity, transcending ethnic divides. Despite his background as the heir to the throne of the largest Tswana *morafe*, Khama repeatedly attacked tribalism and racism, always arguing that 'tribalism' is 'the greatest enemy of independent Africa' (1980: 303). He insisted that a 'Motswana' (i.e. a citizen of Botswana) was any person 'who fully accepts and himself applies our ideals of non-racialism and democracy … [Moreover], this is independent Botswana, not Tswanastan … Our nation is defined by its common ideals and not by narrow ethnic criteria' (quoted in Parsons et al. 1995: 280). According to available records, Khama often condemned 'tribalism' (along with racism). There are, however, extremely few statements where – as here – he actually addressed the Tswana issue.[7] Remaining seemingly silent about the fact that Botswana was actually a multiethnic country, Khama and his companions created a legitimating discourse, as I shall now explain, which aimed at fulfilling the national virtue of 'unity' by means of the new virtue of 'development'. These qualities were either ethnically neutral or, as we have now seen, referred to central cultural values shared by most peoples within Botswana.

The Discourse of Development as Instrumental to Win Hegemony

I suggested above that nation-state building in Botswana was not characterized by the construction of grand national symbols in the capital city. Rather, efforts of creating national unity were made in the encounters between political leaders and the people in the context of their local *kgotla* in the villages throughout the country. In the following chapter I shall elaborate the discursive practices developed by the political leadership in the wake of the country's independence. At this point I want to explain that these practices were not characterized by complex ideological mes-

---

7. Parsons (1993: 75) notes 'Botswana's [attempt] to be a "non-racial" rather than "multiracial" state. The idea of non-racialism was expounded by Kenneth Kaunda in the 1960s, as a counter to the multi-racialism bruited about in the Central Africa Federation of the 1950s'.

sages, but concerned down-to-earth matters such as the practicalities of 'development'.

In relation to the population at large great emphasis was placed on welfare (see Tsie 1996). When I first went to Botswana in 1975, the benefits of self-government and independence were already strongly evident in providing water to most communities throughout the rural areas. The significance of this cannot be underestimated, not only because this is a critical resource for everyone in an environment characterized by very low and erratic rainfall. It also came as a blessing as there had been years of serious drought immediately before the year of independence. And in the course of the 1970s, the drilling of boreholes ensured a water supply irrespective of rainfall throughout the country. Water not only constituted a critical material resource. It was endowed with symbolic significance: as such, it was perceived as a manifestation of the benign power of *goromente* (government). At more or less the same rate, the state began a massive program of construction in village communities – schools, clinics and other public structures shot up all over the country. All these buildings were most apparent symbols of a new era, always painted white and therefore, whether intentionally or not, matching Tswana colour symbolism, in which white signifies fertility and prosperity. The state's command of technology and other resources was also expressed in a major road-building program, connecting even the most remote communities to a nationwide network of communication.

These welfare programs were launched as unquestionable improvements of the lives of all the nation's citizens. Although financially and technically the government was the driving force behind all these programs, from an early stage they often had a component of self-help. People were encouraged to establish village development committees all over the country whereby villagers contributed, mainly with labour, to the construction of classrooms, clinics and so on. They were thus engaged – to use government rhetoric – in the task of 'making our nation prosper'. The distinctive character of these programs found its most profound expression in what I shall henceforth refer to as the ruling elite's *hegemonic discourse of development*. As I shall elaborate in the following two chapters, this was exercised extensively in the context of all the *dikgotla* throughout the country.

Welfare was one major component in this discourse; the other was what I will refer to as 'empowerment'. The engagement of the population in the construction of a social infrastructure was clearly seen as a matter of making people aware of their own capacity for contributing to 'the improvement of our lives'. This rhetoric was perhaps even more apparent in relation to the extensive programs aimed at promoting productive activities in the fields of agriculture and animal husbandry. In Chapter 3 I explained how animal husbandry programs tremendously enhanced the potentials of herd growth amongst large-scale livestock owners. However, these programs were made available to everybody, rich and poor, and were extensively promoted by a vast network of so-called extension workers employed by the Ministry of Agriculture who stationed their supervising officers throughout the country. These were, as I shall elaborate in Chapter 7, typical programs of 'empowerment': the discourse of development included the rhetoric of *boipelego* (self-reliance), which is one of the four national principles underpinning the overall blessings of *kagisano*.

The rhetoric of *boipelego* refers to the level of the household as well as that of the community and the whole nation. It means that everyone was encouraged to 'improve [their] lives' by taking advantage of government support to enhance productivity – regardless of their productive assets at the outset. In this discursive practice, the poor as well as the rich were to take all opportunities available to them in order to engage more intensively in productive activities – for their own benefit as well as that of the nation. These agricultural and livestock programs were supplemented in the mid-1980s by another major state 'development' program known as the Financial Assistance Policy (cf. Chapter 3), which similarly aimed to empower people to engage in commercial enterprises at all levels. This program was also launched in the spirit of *boipelego* – and thus, as I have explained, *kagiso*.

Khama's Agency of Transformation and Unification

It might be said that the ruling group attempted to construct an image of the state as an agency of major transformation – that of 'development'. It would be wrong, however, to conceive this as a simplistic matter of leaving 'traditionalism' behind in favour of Western modernity. It is true that the first two decades of independence were characterized by a radical break with the colonial past in certain very obvious respects. Yet, as I have shown in Chapters 1 and 2, the peoples of this country had been exposed recurrently to the impact of an ever-changing larger world. We should remember, for instance, that *Kgosi* Khama III and other *dikgosi* complied with the evangelizing missionaries' request to abandon or entirely reform indigenous ritual and social practices, thus adapting Tswana cosmology to Christianity, and that they had a crucial role in the establishment of the Bechuanaland Protectorate.

It is not surprising, then, to find that Seretse Khama was also responsible for radical reform, establishing the authority as head of the nation and securing the legitimacy of government. He was after all the heir to the throne of the largest Tswana *morafe*. He had also proved himself as a strong leader. Hence, much of Khama's success in this was premised on the fact that 'ordinary people always found it difficult to distinguish Seretse's role in nationalist politics from his hereditary status as a kgosi' (Parsons et al. 1995: 199). Given this dual identity, Khama's authority transcended the confines of his own *morafe* and even those of the 'Tswana' in general. In due course he acquired the attributes of the sovereign – the *Tautona*. At an early stage, 'Masire decided to exploit Seretse Khama as the party's greatest asset – the *kgosi* who had become a commoner but still retained the authority of *bogosi* and for some people the charisma of martyrdom' (Parsons et al. 1995: 217; see Chapter 2).

This endeavour was apparently so successful that people projected their concept of authority onto Seretse's state leadership: after he had been elected president of Botswana for the first time in 1966, the turnout at subsequent elections declined substantially. When I questioned people about this in the mid-1970s, I was usually told, 'We have already got our leader'. Seretse Khama was thus successfully established as the supreme *national* authority, who by 'Tswana and non-Tswana alike [was] seen to be beyond the tribe in his efforts at nation building … [establishing] a broad working consensus that was tied to gradualism, compromise and much co-opting of political enemies' (Werbner 2002a: 677). This appreciation of him as a national leader – far beyond the confines of the Ngwato *morafe* of which he was the symbolic head – started to develop many years before independence. I suggest that this can be dated to his arrival from England to defend his marriage in 1948. At that time he was reportedly received with great enthusiasm by the Bangwato as well as the Kalanga (see Chapter 2).

In order to understand the political power inherent in the combined authority of the premodern *morafe* and the postcolonial state, we have to recognize the cultural premises for the transformations effected by Khama. These premises patently connect the order of the *merafe* and that of the republic. One curious but highly significant indication of the success of this connection was brought home to me in the mid-1970s when I encountered many people in various parts of the country who were almost unanimously appreciative of Seretse Khama. They said that 'as soon as he came to power, it started to rain', which was in fact true. During the first half of the 1960s Botswana was stricken by severe drought, and more than half of the country's cattle perished. However, the first decade following independence was generally characterized by generous rainfall and tremendous herd growth. Ironically, perhaps, after Khama died in 1980 and Quett Masire became president of Botswana, the country returned to years of serious drought. Given the nationwide scepticism towards Masire, a man of humble origins who had, as we saw in the preceding chapter, poor support even among his own people (see Gulbrandsen forthc.), the correspondence between leadership change and drought was widely noted. Seretse Khama was not only the heir to the Ngwato throne and the senior descendant of *Kgosi* Khama III ('the great'), with all that this implied in the popular imagination concerning the alleged link between the *kgosi* and the supreme ancestral powers (see Chapter 4), but had also, during his long struggle against Tshekedi and sections of the Ngwato aristocracy, demonstrated his personal force and integrity (see Chapter 1).

Seretse Khama's charisma (*seriti*) and his reputation of serving the common good were personal qualities that resonated profoundly with Tswana views on leadership and the ascription of authority. But I do not wish to reduce this issue solely to a question of Khama's descent and character. His agency was unique insofar as it was premised on his dual identity of *kgosi* and head of the postcolonial state, personifying both the cultural construction of authority and the socio-material conditions under which the postcolonial state evolved. In order to act as a major agent of transformation, he had no need to downplay his identity as a *kgosi*. On the contrary, as already suggested, Tswana *dikgosi* have often operated as agents of change, especially in mediating between external and internal forces and in their practice of legislation. For however concerned they may be with *kagiso* and hence with the virtues of hierarchical order and discipline, the Tswana do not dogmatically insist on ostensibly prescribed rules. As I have shown in Chapter 1, Tswana rulers always acted highly pragmatically within ever-changing historical contexts, even to the extent of making laws that entirely changed central ritual and social practices. This pragmatism is asserted in Tswana maxims such as *Gae lome ka le bolela laengwe* ('One bee does not use another's sting'), meaning that 'a *kgosi* should rule according to his own ideas, and not those of his predecessors' (Schapera 1970: 19). Moreover, as was observed many years ago, '[t]he tribe believes that the "chief's law" is an application of ancestral law to a new condition, just as our legislators believe that their statutes are in accord with Common Law' (Willoughby 1923: 99). Under colonial conditions, some of the *dikgosi* reacted to changing historical circumstances to such an extent that they have been portrayed as 'tribal innovators' (Schapera 1970).

As early as the 1950s Seretse Khama gained the reputation of an 'innovator' who was strongly committed to the common good and welfare of the people. For example, also during colonial times he repeatedly expressed his concern that ordinary people should have access to healthcare and that schools needed to be improved. Since cattle, however unequally distributed, represented an essential asset to all families' subsistence, he called for 'a cattle-owning democracy', asserting that 'the democratic way to spread wealth to virtually every family in the country was through the intensification and spread of commercial cattle production for export' (Parsons et al. 1995: 204). This idea of a major, highly radical reform would, though, never materialize.

Conflict of Class and the Discourse of Development

And yet, despite the successful transformations wrought by Seretse Khama and the efficacy of 'development' discourse, a major conflict of class was simmering, although it was many years after Botswana's independence before this conflict surfaced in serious societal tension (see Chapter 8). Here I want to explain how this conflict was, from the outset of the postcolonial era, actually inherent in the discursive practices of 'development', notwithstanding all efforts to resolve it.

While development discourse emphasizes 'the common good', i.e. the enhancement of national wealth and prosperity for all citizens, it also includes a strong entrepreneurial dimension – that of liberal individualism. In Chapter 3 I stressed the importance of this dimension to elite cohesion. In that chapter I explained, moreover, how the flow of resources from the state treasury (particularly from development aid and diamond revenues) gave a tremendous impetus to the large herd owners' accumulation of cattle. While the national principle of *boipelego* (self-reliance) was embedded in this discursive practice to draw attention to everyone's contribution to national 'development', the inherent inequity of many 'development' programs and projects was either vastly underplayed or justified by rejecting any critique of the privileged people whose prospering enterprises ostensibly contributed so much to the wealth of the nation.

The entrepreneurial dimension of development discourse finds a specific Tswana expression in the mentioned 'national principle' of *boipelego*, which idealizes economic – and political – independence. At this point let me recall the Tswana maxim, 'A man who has got cattle is a man who can talk' and the ambiguity inherent in accumulating cattle (see Gulbrandsen 1996a: 182ff.). I shall address this ambiguity first by considering the accumulation of cattle as a means of bringing oneself out of the dependent position of a *mokopi* ('the one who begs'). With cattle, a family exploits common land resources to ensure its subsistence. This in turn depends on good animal husbandry and a well-managed household, in addition (naturally) to family harmony (*kagiso* – 'Where there are quarrels, there is poverty'). All the government's appeals to 'improve one's life' by increasing the productivity of animals and fields find considerable resonance among most people. This is especially so when they are accompanied by supportive government programs rather than taxation.

Although it is true that wealthier families are in a better position to take advantage of these programs, I want to stress that the 'development discourse' does not confine itself to political rhetoric. The state has set up a wide-ranging network of agricultural extension workers who travel on their bicycles from smallholder to smallholder in order to offer advice on increasing yields. The government has also spent substantial resources on an agricultural research station. This has not only been directed at wealthy cattle owners and large-scale crop producers; efforts have been made to design smallholding 'packages' including some financial support, albeit the actual impact on smallholders has been very limited (see Chapter 7; cf. Gulbrandsen 1996a: Ch.10).

We can see that in these instances the development discourse has been carried out in a purely practical way. The state's commitment to the population is evident to everyone who avails herself or himself of its support. Nor is this discourse restricted to bridging the gap between poor and rich: the state development programs conscientiously avoid favouring particular ethnic groups. On the contrary, because most programmes have been from the outset rural and agricultural in their orientation (although, increasingly, urban-located elites have taken much benefit from them), the state has made every effort to appear as a countrywide inclusive force, propagating the unquestioned overall aim of development in the pursuit of national unity and hence peace and prosperity.

While Khama anticipated these development ideals by making the case for a 'cattle-owning democracy', it has become ever more apparent that state 'development' policies in relation to cattle have resulted in anything but socioeconomic equity. Let me at this point address the other side of cattle accumulation, the side which is associated with selfishness and greed. As already indicated, the divide has increased between the privileged minority who have been able to reap vast benefits from the state 'development' programs and the unprivileged majority, a major section of whom have remained below the official poverty line.[8] Since the political significance of this issue will be examined more comprehensively in Chapter 8, I shall limit myself here to a brief survey of how the contradictions generated by governmental 'development' programs are reflected in political rhetoric.

Seretse Khama advocated 'fair income distribution' among the people of the country, without which, he maintained, '*kagisano* at the national level will not succeed'.[9] Already from the beginning of the diamond-mining era, Khama stressed that the income from mining should be avail-

---

8. See Gulbrandsen 1996a; Nteta et al. 1997; Siphambe 2005.
9. See Carter and Morgan 1980: 311.

able for the development of the 'nation as a whole'.[10] In the same vein, he instituted a major land reform that involved the fencing off of vast tracts of communal land to counteract overgrazing and the deterioration of pastures (see Gulbrandsen 1996a: 337ff.). Khama condemned increasing land erosion as 'totally against our national principle of social justice'. Yet, at the same time, he headed a government whose officials always asserted that entrepreneurial success is not detrimental to the development of the nation as a whole. On the contrary, it was maintained, in the spirit of Western liberalism, that individual wealth will in due course 'trickle down' and benefit the rank-and-file population (see Gulbrandsen 1996a: 361ff.). In an effort to conceal and thus deny its inherent contradictions, it is claimed that the accumulation of wealth – premised on the honourable work of an industrious person – in the end serves the nation and hence everybody.

The National Policy of the Tribal Grazing Lands, which paved the way for this land reform, epitomizes the contradiction between the rhetoric of state policies and their actual impact. In brief, while allowing huge areas to be fenced off as large private ranches owned by a small number of extremely rich cattle entrepreneurs, it has left the majority of the rural population with ever-more-crowded and unregulated commons. These contradictions find their most obvious expression in the mounting inequality of income during the postcolonial era, a damning indictment of the discrepancy between the rhetoric of development and the actual effects of government programs allegedly aimed at combating poverty. What was launched as a *national* policy has proved no force for national unification. On the contrary, it epitomizes postcolonial contradictions: between the common good and individual accumulation of wealth; between those who had the initial assets required to take full advantage of state programs and projects and those who did not.

Quite contrary to Khama's wishful thinking of the state as instrumental to develop a highly inclusive 'cattle-owning democracy', that ensures everybody prosperity, cattle has – especially when combined with diamonds (see Chapter 3) – been a major vehicle in generating a minority of wealthy people and vast numbers of people persistently located below the official poverty datum line. In this perspective, the 'discourse of national development', of which Khama himself was a major author, masks the contradictions of 'African socialism' (that he condemns), for example in Nyerere's version. As Ferguson (2006: 75) reminds us, he was concerned

---

10. Quoted in ibid., 294. At the opening of the First Session of the Third Parliament (18 November 1974) he asserted, 'We regard Botswana's mineral resources as a national asset which we sell to get money with which to improve the life of people and succeeding generations' (Carter and Morgan 1980: 319).

with 'conflicting moral obligations: selfishness versus sharing, exploitation versus solidarity, individual acquisitiveness versus communal mutuality'.

The successive political leaderships' efforts to underplay the significance of such conflicts by rhetoric of the national importance of individual's economic success and of common benefit of the extensive state distribution of social services did not suffice to counteract rank-and-file reactions to the progressive state sponsoring of a privileged minority with an ever-wider spectrum of opportunities for accumulation of wealth (see Chapter 3) in a situation where a substantial section of the population remained below the official poverty datum line. These reactions towards people who rose to wealth as revenues from diamond mining started to accumulate in the state treasury, go, however, beyond the scope of this volume which has been restricted to the formative and consolidating decades (1966–1990). In Chapters 6 and 7 we shall see how the hegemonic discourse of development has manifested itself in practice, partly legitimating state policies by capturing the population into its overall modernity project, partly creating new cultural orientations in the population, heightening consciousness of class within the context of the political economy of the state. In Chapter 8 I shall bring the different issues of class together especially in identifying subaltern discourses which, in certain respects, can be seen as counterhegemonic.

Efforts for National Unity and Issues of Second-Class Citizens

In this second main part I am chiefly concerned with the contradiction between, on the one hand, the state leadership's efforts to win hegemony by establishing national principles of equal citizen rights, an ethnic blind 'discourse of development' substantiated by wide-ranging welfare programmes and, on the other hand, minorities' perception of being treated as secondary citizens, subject to dominant Tswana's everyday, local practices of discrimination and made invisible in the symbolism of the nation-state.

Let me stress at this point that although the state leadership continued to be Tswana dominated (as it still is in the sense of numerical majority of people speaking Setswana as their first language), this leadership has never tried to capture the population into a nation-state order in terms of a distinctively 'Tswana' symbolism. That would, of course, have been very counterproductive in relation to their efforts of winning hegemony in relation to the population at large; as being accepted as the legitimate moral and political leadership by a national electorate that, as we shall see briefly, is highly composite ethnically. Another matter is the progressive recruitment of people whose first language is different from Setswana to the state leadership and high offices in government. As I explained in

Chapter 3, this started shortly after independence with the incorporation of well-educated Kalanga occupying senior offices at an early stage. They were, in due course, followed by other non-Tswana, and people of a wide ethnic spectrum are found in high positions at present. It is true, as I explained in Chapter 3, that the Kalanga-Tswana elite relationship has been riddled by ambiguities and tensions. But with the development of mutual dependencies, especially as the private sector of the economy developed, there has, as argues Werbner (2004: 85), been in progress a 'build-up of interethnic trust, partnership and alliances'.

Such a pluralist development amongst people of different ethnic origin who are, nevertheless, to a significant extent class-positioned equally in the state-centred political economy (see Chapter 3), is, in my view, nothing but what should be expected in the present context. Nevertheless, Tswana domination continues to prevail in a multitude of local contexts throughout the country. For example, Tswana political leaders might well engage a prominent Kalanga lawyer in relation to their business affairs and tour the country on political campaigns to capture people into the ethnically blind discourse of development. But as soon as they arrive at their cattle post with herds of hundreds of livestock, they readily shift to a radically different register when relating to their Bakgalagadi herders and the community to which they belong.

In the present part of this chapter I am going beyond 1990 because it was, as suggested in the introduction, not until the 1990s that minority protests against Tswana domination and stigmatization became a public issue proper. I shall first make a brief overview of 'minorities' and address issues of stigmatization and pressure to assimilate. I then explain the rise of ethnic pride and claims of recognition amongst minorities in the 1990s. This leads up to an examination of the state leadership reactions towards minorities' protest against perceived unjust favouring of dominant Tswana in Botswana's Constitution by establishing a presidential commission. I shall explain how their recommendations triggered severe Tswana reactions illuminating the continued force and political impact of elites at Tswana royal centres. This leads me to discuss the current conditions for the politics of recognition that are in progress.

Some Demographic Features of Minorities in Botswana

As I have already illuminated in Chapter 1, 'minorities' is a composite category in the present context. One crude division can be made between Tswana- and non-Tswana-speaking communities. Amongst the former there are, however, communities that are fully assimilated and incorporated sociopolitically in one of the Tswana *merafe* recognized officially by the British and then by the postcolonial state. There are, moreover, communities that will claim they are no less 'Tswana' than the former and retain their distinct Tswana identity, but live in a village separate from the royal town, as for example Bakaa in Kgatleng, the Bakgatla-ba-ga-Mmanaana in Kweneng and the Bangwaketse or the small community of Bahurutshe living in the northeastern corner of the Bangwaketse. Although they have submitted to the Tswana maxim of 'When an elephant crosses the river, it becomes a small elephant' under the conditions of the postcolonial state politically weakened *dikgosi*, there is a drive for autonomy as patently expressed by the enthronement of the head of the Bakgatla-baga-Mmanaana at Thamaga (see preceding chapter). Amongst these peoples, it has no meaning to attack dominant Tswana for being stigmatized, but to protest against not being treated with due respect. Since the major issue in the politics of recognition which I shall examine below concerns the privileged status of the *dikgosi* of the officially recognized Tswana *merafe* in Botswana's Constitution, these communities along with many non-Setswana-speaking communities attack this concession as discriminatory.

It is hard to assess the number of people belonging to the different language communities, because there is an inclination to underreporting minority language identification which follows from what I say about stigmatization in the following subsection. With this reservation, the following figures published in 2005 by the Department of History, University of Botswana, are sufficiently indicative for the present purpose notwithstanding the fact that figures of this kind always being somehow controversial:[11]

- The eight officially recognized Tswana merafe: 50%.
- Other Tswana merafe: Bahurutshe, Bakhurutshe: 6%
- Other Sotho-Tswana:
  - BaBirwa: 4%
  - Batswapong: 7%
  - BaKgalagadi: 7%
  - Total: 18%
- Kalanga: 15%
- Hambukushu: 2%
- WaYei: 2%
- Basarwa: 2%
- Other: 4%

These figures suggest a total of 56 per cent Tswana, with 50 per cent of the officially recognized *merafe*. However, since only the Bahurutshe/Bakhurutshe are distinguished as 'other Tswana', such Tswana communi-

---

11. Compiled by M.H. Lekorwe, M.G. Molomo, W.B. Molefe, D. Sebudubudu, L.L. Mokgatlhe and K.K. Moseki, see http://www.thuto.org/ubh/bw/society/afrob.1.htm.

ties as the Bakaa and Bakgatla-baga-Mmanaana are included among 'the eight officially recognized'. To the extent they claim distinctiveness as 'other Tswana', the number of Tswana belonging to the dominant *merafe*, shrinks to less than 50 per cent.

This figure is, furthermore, challengeable in view of the fact that 'Bakgalagadi' comprise, besides a number of groups living in Western Botswana, numerous communities found scattered in vast areas within the domains of the dominant Tswana *merafe*, with all that involves of exposure to stigmatization and hence underreporting of primary language with the desire of being identified as Tswana 'proper' (see Chapter 1 and below). It is highly unlikely therefore that they do not comprise more than the 7 per cent indicated above.

As for location, with the massive drain of people to urban centres since the late 1980s, a substantial number is no longer found where they or their parents once were living. With reference to the categories listed above, let me briefly suggest that Hambuskushu and WaYei are located in huge areas in the North West District where the Batawana claims supremacy. Here are, in addition, many Basarwa groups that are also found in other parts of Botswana, including the Central District where thousands of impoverished herders are under the domination of the Bangwato. The Batswapong living in the eastern part of the Central District and the Babirwa are living in the same district under Bangwato domination. So are the Kalanga who are to a great extent found in the North East District.

Let me stress that such figures have, of course, considerable political significance; they are therefore controversial and might well be contested. Nevertheless, they bring out a few major points which are not easy to reject: there are a large number of communities in the country that do not identify themselves as Tswana. Amongst those who do so, there is a considerable number of people who fall out-side the dominant Tswana communities. This means that 'minority' communities in Botswana add up to a population that compares favourably in numbers with the dominant Tswana. Demographically, moreover, minority communities have in common political integration of a much smaller scale and that they live, to a great extent, dispersed throughout vast territories assigned to the dominant Tswana by the British (see Chapter 1), often far from the Tswana royal towns, where many of them were not allowed to settle in pre-independence times. At the same time, they differ significantly in their being positioned highly differently in respect to dominant Tswana hierarchical classification.[12]

---

12. These general points find support in the comprehensive figures present in Schapera's (1952) *Ethnic Composition of Tswana Tribes* which also reveals all the groups that have been

Stigma and Pressure to Assimilate

The character of these repressive practices to which many minorities are subject can be conceived in terms of Eidheim's notion of 'when ethnic identity is a social stigma' (1969). In his contribution to Barth's (1969) celebrated anthology on ethnicity – 'Ethnic Groups and Boundaries' – Eidheim (1969: 41ff.) relates his initial fieldwork experience in a coastal community in northern Norway. Knowing that he was on the edge of the Lappish areas, all he heard and saw nevertheless indicated that he was in the midst of a Norwegian fjord community. But, in due course, he was gradually brought beyond 'the public sphere' and to 'ethnically closed stages', only to find that the community was in fact deeply divided. In particular, the public sphere only allowed 'the presentation of self' as 'Norwegian', while all cultural traits associated with 'Lappishness' constituted an image that amounted, in the Goffmanian sense, to a stigma (Eidheim 1969: 47–48; cf. Goffman 1963). With great caution, the stigmatized Lappish identity was cultivated and displayed in strictly secluded spheres of interaction.

In eastern Botswana, a somewhat similar kind of stigmatization is evident along the border zone between those who identify themselves as Tswana 'proper' and the vast number of minority communities, particularly those located within the larger *merafe* (Bakwena, Bangwaketse, Bangwato and Batawana). As I indicated in Chapter 1, during my fieldwork in a large outlying village within the *morafe* of the Bangwaketse, I had quite a similar experience to Eidheim's. At first I perceived the village 'community' as uniform, with everybody saying that 'we are all Bangwaketse here'. Only as I gained people's confidence was I explained by a minority that they were the 'true' Bangwaketse (Tswana), while the rest were actually a separate, inferior 'tribe'. The Bangwaketse village kgosana told me that 'we try to them teach "proper customs"', that they were 'actually Makgalagadi' from a particular group named 'X'. I was warned, however, never to use this name – 'Then they will kill you!' In due course, as I worked myself into this community, I got ample evidence of their cultural distinctiveness – and of how this distinctiveness was cultivated within secluded spheres of interaction. I was also related all their humiliating experiences in relation to those who identified themselves as 'true' Bangwaketse, including not being allowed to share meals with them and the rejection of any request for marriage between young men and women from the two different communities who had fallen in love with each other. Nevertheless, they had a strong desire to identify themselves as 'Tswana' and rejected any notion of 'Kgalagadi'. The leader of this

assimilated into the dominant Tswana communities (cf. Chapter 1 above).

group explained at length to me that their totem was *phala* (i.e. impala) and that they originated from a group which is recognized as Bangwato – hence Tswana. This case perfectly illuminates how the complex interface between 'Kgalagadi' and 'Tswana' opens for manipulations. According to Schapera's records (1952: 72) the Phaleng is of 'Kwatleng' stock and thus classifiable as Kgalagadi amongst the Bangwato.[13] He relates that they were conquered and made subjects to the Bangwato under the reign of *Kgosi* Mathiba (r. 1780–1795); while a number of them scattered in different directions, one group remained and became closely attached to the *kgosi* as *motlhanka*, being fully assimilated and achieving the recognition as Bangwato. It was to these people the leader of the community in the Bangwaketse construed their origin to ascertain that they were Tswana proper.

Similarly, Solway (1994: 257) reports from her fieldwork in a Western Kweneng community that in the late 1970s, 'the ethnic identity of local people was a very sensitive issue'. They presented themselves in most contexts as Tswana (in this case Bakwena). Only after a period of time did they reluctantly identify themselves as distinctively different from the Bakwena, which 'can be understood as a response to the stigma carried by that identity, by the term's lack of political salience, and by the weakness of "Kgalagadi" as an identity' (Solway 1994: 258). In another Kweneng village with a substantial community identified by Tswana as 'Kgalagadi', Helle-Valle (1996: 82–83) found this community 'powerless, exploited and stigmatized ... [without] the socio-cultural power to define their own identity'. He stresses the 'vague, but polysemous meaning' of the label 'Kgalagadi', which in Tswana usage has a particularly persuasive, derogatory potency (83). Over the years I have made numerous observations in other communities classified as 'Kgalagadi' within the domain of the officially recognized *merafe*, which amply confirm wide-ranging stigmatization and discriminatory practices. In one village, for instance, the Tswana *kgosana*'s sons would order children identified as Kgalagadi to bring them water when thirsty and to render other personal services. In all these

---

13. A further indication of the fluidity of the category of 'Kgalagadi' is the fact that while the Bakwatleng are classified as 'Kgalagadi' amongst the Bangwato as well as the Bakwena, they are amongst the Bangwaketse fully assimilated and integrated in the *morafe*. Once I presented to a Kwatleng *kgosana*, Gaboletswe Ketsitlile, Schapera's accounts of the 'ethnic composition of the Tswana Tribes' (1952: 43) indicating that he was 'actually' a Mokgalagadi. He responded with a loud and lasting laugh – 'Yes, yes, – it is true, I am a Mokgalagadi – and I am very proud if it! Very, very proud of it!' He was one of *Kgosi* Seepapitso's closest deputies as the senior chief representative in the royal *kgotla* and is now the right hand man of *Kgosi* Malope enthroned in October 2011. While Mr. Ketsitlile's was identified as a Mokwatleng, his mother was of royal origin – the cousin of *Kgosi* Bathoen II. 'But that means nothing' he always told me, 'only the male line counts among our people.'

contexts, there has been a heavy pressure not only to speak Setswana in public but even to hide the practicing of their own language. I highlight these eastern Botswana situations because discrimination is not as apparent here as elsewhere in the country, especially in relation to all the San-speaking groups that have been severely marginalized or squeezed out of their hunting-gathering territories.[14] Nevertheless, discrimination is pervasive in eastern Botswana where vast numbers of minority groups are located in the hierarchical structures of the Tswana *merafe*.[15] In these areas, Tswana domination of all the small minority communities has gained momentum in postcolonial times as a consequence of the accelerating commercial livestock production, which involved a pervasive expansion into their habitats and serious ecological marginalization.[16]

However, in Botswana the pressure to assimilate is a distinctively different matter from that found in the Lapp–Norwegian relationship. While assimilation in the latter context involved integration in an egalitarian community of fisher-peasants, in Botswana it has meant a muted acceptance of being located in a very inferior stratum in the hierarchical order of the Tswana *merafe*. More recently it has become apparent that the (often tacit) humiliations to which they have been subjected have been highly counterproductive to the creation of a sense, among the Kgalagadi and other Tswana-dominated communities, of being recognized members of the nation. The massive pressure to perform on Tswana terms in public, and hence all the embarrassment involved in breaking this code, helps to explain why it has taken more than thirty years after Botswana's independence for the perceived Tswana domination to be seriously challenged.

Rise of Ethnic Pride and Claims of Recognition within the Nation-State

At the same time this helps to explain the strength of the minorities' demand, emerging in the late 1990s, to be recognized and respected as

14. See Wilmsen (1989: ch.3) for a comprehensive, historical account of this process (cf. Silberbauer 1965; Guenther 1976; Gulbrandsen et al. 1986; Solway and Lee 1990; Motzafi-Haller 1995, 2002; Saugestad 1998; Hitchcock 1978, 2002; Mazonde 2002). This issue has even attracted considerable international attention in connection with all the protests against the state's attempt to move San-speaking communities out of the Central Kalahari Game Reserve (see Good 1999b, 2008; Solway 2009).

15. The same also pertains to the Tswana (Tawana) dominated northwestern region (see Nyati-Ramahobo (2001, 2002 and below in this chapter).

16. This process was propelled by all the state's momentous support of livestock industry (see Chapter 3), epitomized by a major land reform by which the government opened (1976) for privatization and enclosure enormous tracts of tribal grazing lands, known as the National Policy of the Tribal Grazing Land (see Hitchcock 1978; Wily 1979, 1981; Gulbrandsen 1985, 1987, 1992; Solway 1986; Werbner 1993; Peters 1994).

culturally distinct communities, equal to those of the Tswana within the context of the nation. Moreover, it helps us to understand the Tswana reluctance to give up their privileges when challenged (see below). However, it does not explain why minorities have come out in force over the past decade or so. Why are the Kgalagadi and other minorities no longer ashamed of their ethnic identity? Why do they speak their language freely in public and in the presence of the dominant Tswana?

In order to answer such questions, we need to consider a different set of state processes. These processes are anchored in what I have identified in this chapter as the 'hegemonic discourse' of development, a discourse comprising a blend of Western modernity and pan-Bantu values. As we shall see in further detail in the two following chapters, this discourse has facilitated political leaders in their extensive (and intimate) interactions with communities all over the country and in the implementation of large-scale, national and universal policies and programmes, universal in the sense of being available to everybody irrespective of ethnic affiliation. These initiatives have certainly contributed to tempering the animosity generated in the relationship between dominant Tswana and minorities. However, in order to explain the recent mobilization of the minorities, I want to argue that the state leadership's emphasis on equal rights has exacerbated the contradiction between the principles of a republican democracy and the official recognition of the eight Tswana *merafe*.

This contradiction has become ever more manifest under conditions generated by the government's attempts at liberalism and modernization. First, within the context of the *merafe* the various government 'development' programmes have helped to alleviate some of the stigmatization of non-Tswana communities in terms of their lack of such markers of civilization as Western-style housing, cars, education, more sophisticated attire and so on. With the growth in cattle ownership and with high education and good jobs for some of their people, the ground was prepared for what Solway (1994: 261) has identified as an awakening ethnic pride. From the mid-1980s she recorded, amongst a Kgalagadi community in Western Kweneng, an increasing concern with the distinct language of Sekgalagadi, which was more and more used in the presence of outsiders.

Second, this is only one example among many of the rise of ethnic consciousness, which was reinforced by the recruitment of young people from non-Tswana communities into urban careers. The urban context has proved 'emancipating' in the sense that people from minority groups feel less inhibited about identifying their origins. As one of my Bangwaketse friends related to me with a flavour of astonishment, 'Here in town some of them say right away that they are Bakgalagadi – they are even proud of it, can you imagine?' Similarly Solway (1994: 133) reports from her interviews with many members of different minority groups that 'they prefer to speak their own language or English rather than Setswana, which they define as "the language of oppression"'. Third, these popular trends have given rise to an intellectual elite employed in high governmental offices, yet still with close attachments to their respective ethnic communities in rural areas.

Challenging the Constitutional Privilege of the Tswana *Merafe*

The progressive resistance to Tswana domination has expressed itself in two distinct initiatives that subsequently coalesced. First, in 1995 a motion was tabled in Parliament that requested the government to render Sections 77, 78 and 79 of the Constitution 'tribally neutral' (Government of Botswana 2000: 1–2). The motion was adopted, but the government found the matter so 'sensitive' that it had to be handled 'with utmost care and without undue pressure' (7). Then in the same year a university professor from a minority was highly instrumental in forming a movement among her people – the Wayeyi within the Tswana *morafe* of Batawana. The movement was called the Kamanakao Association. *Kamanakao*, meaning 'their remnants', indicates the purpose of maintaining and developing 'the remnants of Shiyeyi language and culture', reflecting their perceived massive Tswana domination. The professor, Lydia Nyati-Ramahobo (2002: 691), reported how people 'grieved about the present chiefship and passionately expressed their strong feeling that they were not free, as long as they were under the rule of a Motawana chief imposed by government'. This experience inspired the activists to go beyond the initial purpose of the association (the promotion of 'language and culture'), declaring in 1998 that 'the Wayeyi people would like to have a paramount chief' and thus separation from the Tswana. In April 1999 the Wayeyi installed their paramount chief, despite being told by the minister of local government and lands that this would be in disagreement with Botswana's legislation. From this followed a series of events culminating in a rejection by the agents of the state of all their claims of establishing a separate chieftainship on the grounds that it was incompatible with the Chieftainship Act, the Tribal Land Territory Act and Sections 77–79 of Botswana's Constitution.

At this point the Wayeyi hired a lawyer and brought the case to the High Court where 'in a strongly worded judgement the Chief Justice struck down a key section in the chieftainship law; it was discriminatory, denying citizens their constitutional rights' (Werbner 2004: 60). This was an important victory, yet only a half one as the Chief Justice established that it was beyond the High Court's competence to declare any part of the Constitution unconstitutional; he referred this matter to Parliament, indicating 'that there was an urgent requirement for the government to deal with the issues lest the general good of the country suffer' (Werbner 2004: 61).

At this time, this work was already in progress. In March 2000 the Kamanakao Association wrote to the United Nations Secretary-General who made an inquiry about the matter, which incited the president (Mogae) to appoint a twenty-one-member commission known as the Presidential Commission of Inquiry into Section 77, 78 and 79 of the Constitution of Botswana (also referred to as the Balopi Commission after its chairman). As indicated above, the issue had been raised in Parliament in 1995 but treated as a 'hot potato' and not dealt with seriously until this time. The commission was required 'to seek a construction that would eliminate any interpretation that renders the sections [77, 78 and 79 in the Constitution] discriminatory'. Those who had feared that bringing this issue into public debate would amount to opening a Pandora's box should not have been surprised. The process which was sparked off exposed numerous conflicts between the dominant Tswana and their previous subject communities – not least because of the former's continuing control of the state.

In brief, the commission conducted nearly fifty public meetings (mostly in the *dikgotla*) all over the country in the typical Botswana fashion of 'consulting with the people' (see the following chapter). Reportedly, many people were of the opinion that '[w]ithin a democratic republican political order, there is no place for institutions that exclude some on the basis of their ethnic identity or social origin' (Government of Botswana 2000: 45). The commission asserted that '[t]here is a widely held view that either all tribes or none should be listed in the Constitution' (95), and that there was 'strong support for the retention of the House of Chiefs as long as all citizens feel represented because many continue to regard Chiefs as an embodiment of the nation's cultural identity' (96). Accordingly the commission recommended that the Constitution should be changed in order to 'ensure that every citizen is represented in the House [of Chiefs]', a title which, tellingly, was now to be given in Setswana: '*Ntlo ya Dikgosi*'.

As Werbner (2004: 45) has pointed out, the 'Commission opened a space in the public sphere for long silenced voices, for dissent and resentment, which had been simmering increasingly for decades'. It was a measure of the issue's tremendous political significance that the state president, Festus Mogae, presented his government's conclusions (which had been issued in a Draft White Paper) on the matter in person in a number of *kgotla* meetings around the country. These included encounters with many minority communities, who greatly appreciated his acceptance of the major recommendation made by the Balopi Commission. For example, on a visit to the minority community of Tswapong of the Central District (under Bangwato domination), it was reported that '[s]peaker after speaker congratulated Mogae for his efforts ... [and] praised him for his fearlessness in bringing about the reforms even when he was faced with daunting adversity. – "*Tautona o pelokgale*" [the big lion is fearless]'.[17]

However, in the royal centres of the larger Tswana *merafe*, the president was not welcomed as a 'fearless lion'. On the contrary, the constitutional changes proposed were entirely rejected, as was the proposal of division of the country into geographical zones, from which each member of the *Ntlo ya Dikgosi* was to be elected. This was a measure to detribalize recruitment to the *Ntlo*, which also meant that the *dikgosi* not only had to be elected but would then represent only a restricted portion of the territory over which they still claimed superior authority – their *morafe*. For example, when appearing in the royal *kgotla* of the Bangwato, the president was fiercely attacked: '[T]he Bangwato made it very clear that they would not entertain changes that would place their paramount chief Ian Khama on the same level as chiefs from inferior tribes', a change which readily followed from the proposed geographical zoning of the country and which they adamantly rejected. The speakers in the Ngwato royal *kgotla* claimed 'ownership' of the whole territory constituting the present Central District and hence superiority over all leaders of 'alien' tribal communities which they had ostensibly hosted and accommodated within their territory (cf. Chapter 1).[18] If the 'subject' communities claimed autonomy, it was stated, they would have to settle elsewhere. This was the prevailing view confronting the president in all Tswana royal centres. [19]

---

17. *Mmegi*, 10–16 May 2002.

18. As in the words of one of them who 'traced his origins to Thaba Nchu in South Africa. He said his elders fought with Bangwato, were defeated and surrendered to them. "Therefore everybody who feels discriminated against must pack and go." ... He said that people who said they were being discriminated against were an ungrateful lot, who had been given succour by benevolent tribes when they were fleeing wars' (*Mmegi*, 5–11 April 2002). In the Bakwena capital the attacks on the president became more severe and extended to serious personal accusations, which now made the issue one of apologising for the insult (*Mmegi*, 19–22 April 2002).

19. When I came to the Bangwaketse shortly after these proposals had been published, they were on high alert, seeing the proposed changes as another attempt from 'certain quarters' in the government 'to kill the *merafe*'. These quarters were identified as controlled by 'Makalaka' (degrading Tswana term for Kalanga). They were especially furious about the proposed division of each of the *merafe* into geographical sections, and that their *kgosi* was therefore 'being divorced from considerable sections of his subjects'. A 'group of concerned' (as they named themselves) among the Bangwaketse found their counterparts in the centres of the various other *merafe* as well. These were not only people of wealth or high rank. Many of them were also retired senior civil servants with extensive networks in the centres of power. With their strong local influence, wealth and considerable spare time, they had the capacity to exert tremendous pressure on the state leadership. Such pressure groups developing among elites at the centre of

The opposition was well co-ordinated – it was strengthened by the activation of the Tswana movement known as *Pitso ya Batswana*[20] – and it even attacked the proposal from within the BDP itself. The Bangwato elite constituted a major power base for this party (cf. Chapter 2). Moreover, their *kgosi*, Lt. General Ian Khama, was also Botswana's vice-president, which gave them another route into the centre of power. The president and his supporters were compelled to give in (cf. Nyamnjoh 2004: 44). The status quo was assured. The eight *dikgosi* retained their position as *ex officio* members by virtue of the incumbency of their respective *bogosi*.

The critical aspect of this constitutional change was that while the eight *dikgosi* became members by virtue of being the supreme authority of the eight Tswana *merafe* – in other words because of their ethnic distinction – the remaining members were to be elected from geographically zoned areas, virtually all of which were ethnically mixed. Furthermore, the Chieftainship Act was sustained, which legislates that there exist eight 'tribes' in the country, in each of which there shall be 'an office of Chief'.[21] Sustained was also the Tribal Territories Act, which identifies the 'chiefs' (i.e. the Tswana *dikgosi*) and tribes with their respective 'tribal territories', namely, the Bamangwato, Batawana, Bakgatla, Bakwena, Bangwaketse, Bamalete and Batlokwa Tribal Territories.[22] Hence, the Tswana and their *dikgosi* continued to feature prominently as *ex officio* members of the *Ntlo ya Dikgosi* by virtue of their ethnic distinction and as the apex of 'tribes' that occupied 'tribal territories' in their own name; territories actually including a vast array of ethnic minorities. However, as described above, since the remaining members of the *Ntlo ya Dikgosi* were to be recruited on the basis of ethnically mixed zones, there was *no way in which these members of this chamber in the Parliament could signify the existence of any particular ethnic group.*

---

the *merafe* were co-ordinated by the pan-*merafe* movement of *Pitso ya Batswana* (Forum of the Tswana). This had been formed in response to the establishment of SPIL – the Kalanga Society for the Promotion of the Ikalanga Language (see Chapter 3).

20. See preceding footnote.

21. Some years later (2008) the Chieftainship Act was replaced by the Bogosi Act, yet with minor changes only (see preceding chapter).

22. The small area in the extreme southeastern corner of Botswana inhabited by the Barolong community known as Tshidi, with their royal centre beyond the South African border (in Mafeking, see Comaroff 1977), were officially recognized by their *kgosi* and their area defined in the Botswana Boundaries Act as 'Barolong Farms'.

Contradictions of Equal Citizen's Rights and Tswana Dominance

This arrangement therefore served to reinforce the Tswana's symbolic prominence within the context of the national assembly. The minorities remained as invisible and insignificant as they had always been. Minority leaders condemned the revised version, claiming that it was even worse than the disputed sections in the existing Constitution.[23] At this time, the Wayeyi had been joined by a number of other minority groups who had been energized by the government consultation exercises; they had been instrumental in the forming of a national coalition of minority communities with the telling name Reteng – 'We are here'.[24] It had become possible to speak about the unspeakable in public (cf. Solway and Nyati-Ramahobo 2004). For many people the experience of discrimination and disregard for their language and other cultural traits constitutive of their self-identity now found its expression in public discourse and organized activities.

The question today, then, is what impact the growing minority mobilization is likely to have on 'national unity'. This question is particularly pertinent in view of the remarkable Tswana insistence – contradicting the principles of equity to which the ruling party subscribes as fundamental to a liberal society and a republican democracy – on a privileged position within the national assembly and hence within the nation. While this contradiction is nourished tacitly in everyday encounters throughout the country between members of the dominant Tswana communities and those of minority communities, it has found its most apparent manifesta-

---

23. They rejected the bill in its entirety, viewing it as a mockery to democracy and a waste of time. The proposed representation to the House of Chiefs was objected to on the following grounds: 1) 'Chiefs from Tswana speaking areas [are] designated in accordance with their custom of permanency … The names of their areas reflect their ethnicity hence recognized as tribes'; 2) The majority of the other members of this House should be recruited on a territorial basis which 'in all cases will be multi-ethnic', making tribal representation impossible from groups other than the Tswana and 'all non-Tswana speaking tribes will continue to be unrecognized and un-represented'. Thus despite the government's proposal to expand the House of Chiefs substantially in ways that would most likely increase representation de facto of 'non-Tswana speaking tribes', the proposal was considered even more unacceptable than the existing legislation, because the bill 'transferred … Acts of Parliament into the Constitution in their discriminatory nature'. (Comments addressed to the Government of Botswana on Bill No. 2003, by *Reteng*: The Multicultural Coalition of Botswana, December 2003.)

24. Its full official name is RETENG: The Multicultural Coalition of Botswana (http://www.geocities.com/reteng_we_are_here/index_files/Page400.htm) and it serves as an umbrella organization for minorities. Its major aims include promoting the linguistic and cultural diversity of Botswana; cultivating an appreciation, knowledge and understanding of unity in diversity and a tolerance for multiculturalism; promoting legal reform in order to create an enabling environment for the recognition and promotion of multiculturalism in Botswana; and instilling and cultivating a sense of self-esteem and national pride among all ethnic groups of Botswana.

tion in a highly public space where it prevails with great symbolic significance: the National Assembly.

The symbolic value at stake here is epitomized by the fact that the minorities make small claims relating to the major conflict of interest in the country, namely, the mounting inequality of wealth distribution. Nor is this a struggle for political power, since the *Ntlo ya Dikgosi* is only an advisory body with very limited impact on government decisions. Yet we have at hand a struggle for minority empowerment: that is, a fight for equal rights – for official recognition of their languages and cultural traditions and for the right to be respected in public as equal to the Tswana majority. Although this is largely an everyday matter of abandoning Tswana discriminatory practices, the very visible representation in the *Ntlo ya Dikgosi* has become a major focus of minorities' identity struggle.

Although opposition parties have attempted to benefit from this struggle, especially in local election campaigns (cf. Solway 2004: 140f.), the important point is that the contradiction underpinning this struggle has struck the ruling party at its heart. As described above, even the president himself had to backtrack after what Werbner (2004: 53) has appropriately named Tswana neoconservatives mobilized against the recommended constitutional changes. All the way back to pre-independence discussions within the BDP, there were members who wanted to get rid of the *dikgosi* by establishing a republican state. As I explained in the latter part of Chapter 2, when Khama and his followers wanted to incorporate the eight Tswana *dikgosi* in the House of Chiefs, it was a measure to prevent them from 'going off on their own to find allies who might destroy the national unity' (Masire 2006: 76).[25] It says a lot about the significance of these authority figures and their respective elites that more than forty years after independence they continue to represent a potential problem for national unity.

The contradiction centred in the ruling party can be spelled out as follows. On the one hand, the party is deeply committed to republican democracy and equal rights. On the other hand, it has constructed a state government which has relied heavily on the orders of the Tswana *merafe* as instruments of government, one major implication being the reproduction of the symbolic wealth of their cosmology and hierarchies (cf. the preceding chapter). These are hard-core beliefs, still prevalent among significant sections of dominant Tswana, who without hesitation reject any proposed equality between their *kgosi* and leaders of former subject communities. By extension, they reject the notion that members of these

---

25. Recently Masire (2006: 74) has regretted that 'the issue of chieftainship has not disappeared with time as Seretse and I had hoped'.

communities deserve to be treated with the respect that they themselves enjoy.

One critical question, then, is how persistent the 'hard-core' Tswana neoconservative camp actually is. Let me make the following sugges-tions. Under present conditions in Botswana, I expect a comprehensive marginalization of the neoconservative camp as a vast urban-born age cohort which now embarks on urban-focused careers. The information I have recently gathered in urban areas indicates that ethnic origin is of limited significance in terms of discrimination. In these areas people are significantly more judged on the basis of socioeconomic standards, which only to some extent match minority–majority relations. At the same time, minority organizations now developing under the umbrella of Reteng are increasingly bringing minority cultures and languages into the public space. These are unchallenging initiatives, merely demanding the recognition of a multicultural Botswana. They even accept Setswana as a national language as long as their own languages are destigmatized and the cultivation of their own traditions is acknowledged as contributory to the nation as a whole.[26]

The modernist section of the ruling party clearly supports such a trend of multiculturalism. President Mogae asserted to me[27] that whenever he was asked by minority groups to open a conference: 'I am coming!' He confirmed Werbner's (2004: 58) account that the state president has wel-comed the 'cultural organisations' as a contribution to *nation building* and the enrichment of *national culture*', at the same time as he has warned mi-nority organizations against becoming 'para-political with a hidden politi-cal agenda' (see Werbner 2004: 58). It should be added here that the state closely monitor all nongovernment organizations, which can operate only on the condition that they have been given a permit and registered in accordance with the Societies Act (of 1972). They are required to com-ply with its regulations which, most importantly, bar these organizations against any form of 'political' activity. They are required to submit regular reports on their activities to the Registrar of Societies (cf. van Binsbergen 1993: 33ff.).

---

26. For example, Werbner (2004: 71, 2002b: 735–36) relates that in the context of Zimba-bwe (with substantial Kalanga communities beyond the Batswana border) 'I found, as van Bins-bergen did, that the first allegiance of Botswana Kalanga communities "was to the Botswana state and not an international Kalanga ethnic identity" (van Binsbergen 1994: 167)'. With more general reference to the study of relationships between ethnic communities in Botswana, Werbner (2002a: 678) warns against focusing only on competition, exclusion and conflict and calls attention to studies that highlight processes of transcendence of difference, co-operation, inclusion, coalition building and trust.

27. Conversation, 17 January 2008.

It appears, then, that there is no immediate danger of any political mobilization working as a destabilizing force. That minority leaders tend to support the nation-state is confirmed by Solway, who relates that the various 'cultural organisations' are mostly led by people who are 'young, educated, urban-based, and hold valued formal sector employment' (Solway 2004: 138). In contrast with many ethnically based organizations in other countries, it is significant that none of these leaders has shown any political ambition; rather, as Solway (2004: 139) states, '[f]or the most it is a moral commitment, not a road to personal gain'. In other words, these are people who fall well within the hegemonic discourse of development and are hence closely attached to mainstream political life in Botswana. The state in Botswana, therefore, is currently not threatened by 'tribal' mobilization. This trend corresponds to Englund's (2004: 3) assertion that '[d]emands for recognition of minorities in postcolonial Africa ... do not necessarily defend an autonomous sphere of civic activism but, on the contrary, represent an effort to become a part of, and therefore to transform, the state'.

Nevertheless, the *Ntlo ya Dikgosi* continues to feature as a persistent symbol of Tswana domination, underscoring minorities' perceived status as second-class citizens. Paradoxically, while Seretse Khama saw 'tribalism' as the major threat to national unity, the Constitution that he fathered includes significant opportunities for non-Tswana communities to claim recognition as distinct 'tribes' and also representation, as such, in the national assembly. This claim continues to be relevant given that, some forty years after the establishment of a republican state in Botswana, the country has not really replaced adherence to hierarchical notions of differential respect ('honour') with what Taylor (1992: 27) has conceived as 'the modern notion of dignity ... in a universalist and egalitarian sense ... [which is] the only one compatible with a democratic society'. This involves what he calls 'a politics of recognition' that rejects the existence of 'first-class' and 'second-class' citizens and assures the equalization of rights. It is true that such rights are inscribed in Botswana's Constitution. Yet the Constitution is inherently contradictory as long as it also contains provisions that serve to reproduce hierarchical notions of respect. This is a thorny matter because it perpetuates conflicts of differential respect versus equitable dignity in informal encounters throughout the country. The existence of such contradictions seems to correspond with Herzfeld's (1997: 83) assertion, with reference to Kapferer's (1988) analysis of Australia, that '[d]emocracy (or, better, "democratization") is not necessarily equivalent to greater tolerance'. Herzfeld argues that the 'logic of tolerance' – in other words, 'multiculturalism' – might actually heighten the sense of otherness and hence increase ethnic tension. It is still too early to tell if this will happen in Botswana.

Conclusion

Kapferer (1988: 136) has argued – with particular reference to Australia – that '[w]ar and death in war are common themes of modern nationalism'. In the present case, I propose, the cosmological dimensions of death and destructive forces are also central to the construction of a national ideology, yet in a radically different manner. As we have seen, in the present case there is a strong – cosmologically grounded – emphasis on life-promoting consensus, harmony and peace (*kagiso*). The nonchallenging character of this ideology seems to have been conducive to the Tswana-dominated postcolonial state leadership in their efforts to establish hegemony by appealing to this notion in efforts to capture the whole population into a national discourse of development that profoundly undercommunicates ethnic differences. Focusing in the first major part of this chapter on the formative and consolidating decades of the postcolonial state, I explained Seretse Khama's successful agency of introducing a Western-fashioned nation-state in the context of massive premodern structures by, amongst others, creating a nationally unifying symbolism drawing upon the existential significance of *kagiso*, intrinsic to people's everyday lives. Hence, the notion needed no impressive rhetoric; it is, as I elaborated in Chapter 4, readily evident – across the ethnic spectrum – as an omnipotent spiritual force imperative to well-being. In this sense one might speak of political leaders' invocation of *kagisano* in 'practical' development discourses, especially in the context of the *kgotla*, as a 'sacralisation of the political in nationalism' (Kapferer 1988). Moreover, the cosmologically anchored imaginary of the modern state in Botswana as the major warden of peace and harmony was, during the first decades of independence, strongly nourished by its sovereignty over a vast territory that everywhere bordered on those of wicked, racist regimes. In other words, the postcolonial state government proved as capable as the British (see Chapter 1) to prevent annexation to these states of violent authoritarianism.

Strikingly, while efforts in the West to develop an imagery of national unity and state sovereignty found its most apparent expression in all the symbolism of pomp and power at the centre of the state, the capital of Gaborone remained for decades without any such manifestations. On the contrary, the capital was to a great extent populated by American and European experts and volunteers who dominated the Western-styled ministerial quarters and had great visibility on the shopping street, known as the White Mall, and most other public spaces. As the Batswana gradually started to migrate to the city for jobs in the 1970s as lower civil serv-ants, shop employees, house maids and garden boys (for the *Sekgoa* and the few indigenous, high-ranking officials), there developed an African Mall, marking indeed that the nation-state capital was a highly ambigu-ous place. It took about forty years after independence before a national monument of a Western kind (see the front cover), that of the Three *Dik-gosi*, was in place – a monument that was also surrounded by considerable ambiguity as it was contested by minorities as an outraged expression of Tswana domination. This was, I recall, a matter of rejecting the signifi-cance of Tswana moral and political leadership – i.e. its hegemonic role – at critical historical stages (see introduction to Chapter 1).

The ruling group, however Tswana dominated, has, with the exception of this monument and privileging dominant Tswana in the Constitution and Setswana as a national language, not made much in the way of con-struing officially a national symbolism in a Tswana idiom. As I have ex-plained in this chapter, the ruling group's effort of winning hegemony as the moral and political leadership of the nation is most apparent in what I have identified as the 'discourse of development'. This is a discourse by which, as we shall see in the following two chapters, the state leader-ship has manifested the significance of the modern state in the midst of people's life locally, much more than in power symbolism at the apex of the state. The attempts to create and reproduce an attractive imagery of the postcolonial state have to a great extent involved political leaders' extensive engagement in the discursive field of the *kgotla* throughout the country, where, as we shall see in the following chapter, the 'discourse of development' gains much of its hegemonic power by being fused with the symbolic wealth and spiritual forces embodied in this discursive field.

In this chapter I have described how the agents of the state have at-tempted to create an imaginary of the postcolonial state in Botswana in terms of cultural values with which most peoples of the country strong-ly identify. These are virtues of a benevolent ruler, the custodian of the common good, which encompass indigenous as well as Western efforts to bring prosperity and welfare to every citizen. Through this quite suc-cessful merging of indigenous and Western values the population has – as we now proceed – been gradually made familiar with the language of a modern government.

And yet, however much this hegemonic discourse of development and all the welfare programmes brought the attention of the rank and file away from the massive state support of private entrepreneurship and individual accumulation of wealth during the formative and consolidating decades of the postcolonial state (cf. Chapter 3), the ever-more-pronounced realities of poverty amongst the vast majority has given rise to progressive tensions of class relations. In Chapter 7 I shall elaborate on how state interventions accelerated this development. Chapter 8 moves beyond the formative and consolidating decades examining how the state-centred class formation found its expression in popular reactions towards political leaders from the mid-1990s and onwards.

Nevertheless, Tswana domination prevails in minorities' perception. In the second part of this chapter I pursued this issue by going beyond 1990 because it was only after this time that minorities voiced in public their sincere dismay. Intriguingly, this was the time when there was, claims Werbner (2004: 84), in progress a development between Kalanga and Tswana elites characterized by 'interethnic trust'. Since this development was ostensibly nourished by interethnic entrepreneurship amongst people of power and wealth, it might gain broader significance as elites of other ethnic groups join in. On the other hand, this is obviously not a matter of doing away with ethnic affiliation and identification, which means that the *potentialities* of ethnic conflict prevail even in these quarters.

This point is epitomized by the fact that Tswana elites are divided – and also the ruling party – in their orientation. That is, between, on the one hand, people like the state president who were, as we have seen, prepared to give considerable concessions to minorities and, on the other hand, people attached to Tswana royal centres protecting the privileged position of dominant Tswana as illuminated by the tremendous symbolic significance of their claimed territorial overlordship.

It is in the light of these orientations that minorities' perception of Tswana domination and oppression should be understood. While public protest against being treated as secondary citizens focused on Botswana's Constitution and legislation, minorities' perception is predominantly nourished through pervasive, everyday – often subtle and tacit – discrimination. This is, to be sure, an intrinsic aspect of Tswana hierarchical order which is, as I indicated in the preceding chapter and shall substantiate further in the chapter that follows, profoundly reproduced by virtue of its significance to the postcolonial state.

However, urbanization seems to involve processes that counteract ethnic divides at the elite level and also makes rank-and-file minorities less prone to Tswana discriminatory practices (see Solway 2004: 132). During my most recent fieldwork amongst the Bangwaketse (2008), I recognized how this development spills back into rural contexts where people more readily identify themselves as, in the urban context, Bakgalagadi. This was, of course, a venture of recognition in a context of intense Tswana domination, a late instance of shift 'from shame to pride' (Solway 1994).

But ages of stigmatization are not forgotten. Generally, there has over the past two decades been an ethnic consciousness which is also nourished by the formation of cultural associations which are, revealingly, kept under state surveillance.

Again, as this underscores, the development in progress is not a case of national unification with ethnic differences being a matter of the past. On the contrary, all the efforts of 'recognition' amongst minorities – linked up with a wider international movement for 'multiculturalism – represents a major process of ethnic mobilization in this country. Thus, corresponding to my argument in the preceding chapter about the potentialities of mobilization amongst the Tswana *merafe* in relation to the state, it can be suggested that processes working in support of minorities' perceived position as secondary citizens, placing them potentially exterior to the state, might create breeding grounds for rhizomic forces or, in the language of Deleuze and Guattari (see Introduction) 'war-machines'. While the postcolonial state leadership has succeeded, to a great extent, in creating an imagery of Botswana as ethnically quite homogenous, the reality is that the 'minorities' might add up to numbers that outweigh the dominant Tswana. In the meantime, the state in Botswana remains under the control of a Tswana-centred dominant class. This was, as we have seen in this chapter, patently manifested by their confrontations with the state president in the Tswana royal *kgotla* when the president attempted to make some concessions to minority communities.

Chapter 6

ANTIPOLITICS AND QUESTIONS OF DEMOCRACY AND DOMINATION

The postcolonial state leadership in Botswana has always taken pride in the country's international reputation as one of Africa's most successful democracies. They are quick to explain that the sustainability of parliamentary democracy in Botswana reflects the 'fact' that 'democracy is deeply rooted in our culture'. One of Botswana's previous vice-presidents stated once that '[w]e haven't learned democracy from America or England. It is inborn ... grew from a system developed by our forefathers'.[1] This has often enough been re-asserted by other modern political leaders. Such a notion of 'democracy' obviously reflects an attempt to create an imagination of the postcolonial present in terms of an idealized past, representing another major case of appropriating the symbolic wealth vested in indigenous institutions of authorities. This effort of bridging the past with the present, the known with the unknown, finds its most apparent expression in one of the 'national principles': *puso ya batho ka batho* ('government by the people for the people') which paraphrases the highly esteemed Tswana maxim *'Kgosi ke kgosi ka batho/morafe'* ('The king is the king by virtue of the people/tribe', see Gulbrandsen 1995; cf. previous chapter).

This might sound like a successful 'customisation of democracy to African conditions' which has been called for by Ake (2000: 174) and oth-

---

1. Peter Mmusi quoted in Wylie (1990: 211); this notion is asserted enthusiastically by one of the most forceful and out-spoken *dikgosi* in postcolonial Botswana, see Chief [*Kgosi*] Linchwe II 1989: 99.

ers after Africa came under Western pressure of 'democratization' in the 1990s. Quite a number of scholars envisaged how 'traditional authorities' might become instrumental to meet such a request. For example, Skalnik spoke of 'traditional institutions' as 'elements of direct democracy complementing representative democracy' (1996: 119, see also 2004) and Owusu (1997: 143) stresses 'the enduring and positive strand in Africa's political traditions – the democratic values of many traditional politics'.[2] Karlstrøm (1996: 491), moreover, argued forcefully that '"the relative success" of the Government of Uganda in implementing innovative democratic reforms and policies ... suggests that whereas much academic analysis pins its hopes of democratization in Africa to the emergence of Western-style institutions of civil society and attendant Western-style democratic culture, equal attention at the very least should be paid to the compatibility of democratic reforms with existing political cultures'. However, after the millennial turn, scholars have started to wonder, as in the words of Kyed and Buur (2007: 10), if one can generally 'take it for granted that traditional leaders genuinely act in accordance with the interests of their constituencies and that the recognition of the chiefs supports the increased inclusion of local populations?' They quote several cases exemplifying how 'traditional leaders' might challenge elected politicians to the extent of undermining their authority. In other cases, traditional leaders have voluntarily or by force been involved 'in mobilising the rural electorate', or they have 'used party politics to their own advantage' (14–15).

Botswana is, as we shall see in this chapter, a case in point to show how indigenous authority figures might be brought under the control of elected political leaders and exploited by the ruling party without being bluntly engaged in political mobilization or taking advantage of party political endeavours themselves. I shall pursue this issue here with the point of departure in the fact that they are, by law, barred from political activity by virtue of being co-opted into the state structure as civil servants (cf. Chapter 4) and not, as I stressed in the Introduction, as political clients.

It is true that the Tswana *dikgosi* and other senior, 'traditional' authorities constitute an advisory chamber of the Parliament (the House of Chiefs) and are included, as *ex officio* members, in district councils and

---

2. He argues that '[t]he major problem of contemporary African democracy is ... the discovery and the establishment of workable institutional structures ... suited to contemporary African circumstances *that embody pre-existent democratic values, ideals, and principles* ... [The] vibrant strand in African political traditions directly relevant to democratization [is] ... the set of "leadership norms" often enshrined in oaths, song and drum texts, maxims and proverbs, prayers and ceremonies' (Owusu 1997: 143–44, italics added; see also Owusu 1986; Kunz 1991; Kimble 1953: 11).

land boards (cf. Chapter 4). Although the House of Chiefs occasionally gives them a chance to level critiques against the government which are given some public attention through newspapers, the general pattern is that they operate only in their own capacity and have little impact either on government or on the public.[3] In the district councils and land boards, they might make some impact by virtue of their authority. However, even the most forceful *dikgosi* have – to their own frustrations (Chapter 4) – become less and less active in these contexts where party politics, from which they are excluded, prevail.[4]

In order to come to terms with the political significance of 'traditional authorities' in Botswana, I shall go beyond the relationship between these figures and the state. In this chapter I am especially concerned with the highly esteemed discursive field 'owned' by these authority figures – that of the *kgotla* – and how state control over the indigenous authority figures has given leaders of the ruling party a most privileged access to a public sphere of intimate, frequent articulation with the population all over the country. These endeavours might, as suggested by the introductory remarks, appear as a successful mediation of electoral democracy and 'African' virtues of democracy. Most apparently, political leaders engage intensively with people in these contexts in terms of the indigenous discursive of 'consulting with the people'.

There is, however, a significant twist to this practice that is of major concern in this chapter: By manipulating the discursive principles of the *kgotla*, the ruling party leaders have been able to monopolize this discursive field and thus marginalise the political opposition.[5] I shall explain, moreover, how the *kgotla* serve to exercise the hegemonic discourse of development in ways that readily depoliticize potentially controversial issues. In the view of the political processes which I am examining in this chapter, the assertions quoted at the beginning hence turn out as ideological rhetoric rather than statements grounded in reality.

---

3. In this House, they have, on the whole, shown very limited capacity to engage critically in debates about major policy issues and the government's extensive 'development' programmes. Much of their attack on cabinet ministers, whom they can call upon for examination in this chamber, reflects their persistent dismay about having lost most of their executive powers. In this pursuit they have represented few others than themselves; they have not appeared as spokespersons for all their impoverished subjects nor have they acted as spearheads for the up-coming class of entrepreneurs (see Vaughan 2003: 97ff, 2005).

4. Their consequent marginalized position in this context is further underscored by the fact that the major line of conflict during the first independence decades often went between this political body and what was called the District Development Committee, composed of 'development' planners and other bureaucrats with close links to the central government (see Picard 1987: 177ff.)

5. See Picard (1987: 271) who speaks of a 'one party state' (cf. Holm 1988; Good 1996, 1999a, 2002, 2008; Maundeni 2001; Taylor 2003; Good and Taylor 2005).

On the other hand, as I shall show in this chapter, all the efforts by political leaders to achieve popular support through close, frequent interaction with people all over the country in the context of the *kgotla* makes Botswana less of an 'elite democracy' or 'nominal democracy' than many Western countries. Although the political system in Botswana shares, of course, many of the problems common amongst modern, electoral democracies, political leaders in Botswana make considerably greater efforts to cultivate the electorate than in many other countries with a democratic constitution. Yet it is quite ironic that the tremendous concern with popular support drives, as we shall see in this chapter, the ruling party to such an obviously undemocratic practice as that of virtually monopolizing the most important public sphere for articulation with the population – the *kgotla*.[6]

Let me re-emphasize that I am presently predominantly concerned with the formative two and a half decades of the postcolonial state. During these years, I recall, the large majority of the population was still living in their natal 'tribal' locations, in the setting of the *kgotla* as described in Chapter 4. During the latter part of the 1980s movement to new urban areas – above all to the capital, Gaborone – accelerated. Yet the villages were by no means deserted, for two reasons which I have elaborated elsewhere (Gulbrandsen 2007).[7] Also in view of the fact that the vast majority of the constituencies for elections to Parliament were in the rural areas (also after 1990), the discursive field of the *kgotla* has remained politically very significant.

Conflicting Scholarly Notions of 'Tswana Democracy'

The question of democracy in Botswana has sparked off a debate about how democratic the country's political heritage actually is. Some scholarly accounts have represented Tswana polities as 'paternalistic' to the

---

6. Although Good (2008) points out a number of important constitutional, legislative and other formal aspects of Botswana's political system, especially those that give the president particular powers, which appear undemocratic, his accounts need to be complimented with an examination of political 'games' within the context of the state and political parties in order to determine the extent to which they manifest in undemocratic practices. It is also of significance in this context how indigenous ideas, practices and institutions of power play into 'modern' political processes.

7. In brief, people were still attracted to their village *kgotla* for reasons explained in Chapter 4, meaning that many of those who were working elsewhere established a residence there according to patri-virilocal principles. Moreover, the demography of Botswana is such that a major proportion of the people are concentrated in the east. In fact five of the Tswana royal towns are located within less than one and a half hours' driving distance from Gaborone. Even after 1990, therefore, many people still have a close attachment to a *kgotla*.

extent of being 'highly authoritarian' (Holm 1988). Parson asserts that 'the powers of the *kgotla* were advisory', and he limits its significance to a 'forum' which 'the king [*kgosi*] and his officials could use ... to generate a consensus before taking action and to sense opposition to particular proposals' (Parson 1984: 16; cf. Good 1992: 70). Molutsi and Holm (1990: 326) maintain that '[o]pposition was bound to be cautious, if there was any at all'; moreover, '[o]rdinary citizens were left largely outside the struggles determining policies'. Wylie, in her portrayal of Tshekedi Khama and his reign over the Bangwato, goes further and conveys the image of an autocratic 'patriarch' under whose rule the role of the *kgotla* was gradually diminished (1990: 209; cf. Chapter 2).

Jean and John Comaroff, however, hold that such characterizations of Tswana politics do not bear scrutiny and maintain that 'the *kgotla* was always a site of active political contestation in which, far from merely being exercised, sovereign authority had to be negotiated' (1997b: 136).[8] Ngcongco, on the basis of interviews with elders in Kgatleng, Ngwaketse and Kweneng, concludes that with the exception of peoples considered to be inferior (such as the Bakgalagadi and Basarwa) and women, 'the Tswana *kgotla* as a public assembly operated in a fairly *democratic fashion* ... the system operated in such a way that it checked and restrained the powers of the leaders' (1989: 46, italics added). Similarly, Mgadla and Campbell argue that '[a] *kgosi* who acted according to custom and in the interest of the group as a whole retained allegiance and respect. He allowed the *kgotla* to become a mechanism of popular control' (1989: 49, italics added). Odell even speaks of the *kgotla* as 'a remarkably democratic institution' (1985: 65). Roberts, while pointing out that 'the ruler's capacity to achieve a decision he wanted depended upon his standing', asserts that 'even the position of an apparently strong and popular incumbent could be eroded if he attempted repeatedly to push through measures for which there was no support' (1985: 77). Schapera – the only scholar who has written a first-hand account of the *kgotla* at a time when the executive powers of the *kgosi* had not yet been curtailed by the postcolonial state – had this to say in 1938:

> In theory great freedom of speech [*mmualebe o a be a bua la gagwe*] is permitted at these meetings. In practice the fear of subsequent reprisals by the Chief [*kgosi*] often acts as a deterrent. But if feeling is running high, the Chief and his advisors may be openly criticised and reprimanded, often in very strong terms. Should most of the speakers express views different

---

8. John Comaroff, referring to the Tshidi of South Africa, asserts that 'although freedom of speech is, in theory, permitted to all orators, the extent to which this freedom was exercised varied widely' (1975: 142).

from those favoured by the Chief and his advisors, the latter will try to argue them round. Normally, however, the voices of the headmen, if they support the Chief, will carry sufficient weight with the general body for the decision secretly arrived at to be approved, and thus enable the Chief to carry his policy into effect. If it appears from the course of the debate that opinions are sharply divided, the Chief may order men to divide into groups, according to their opinions. The relative strength of the two parties is then clearly seen. If the Chief feels that he has sufficient support, he will regard the decision as favourable, and go ahead with his policy. But if his own supporters are in the minority, he must accept defeat as graciously he can. *The Chief is in strict theory able to override the wishes of his people, but in practice he can rarely venture to do so.* Their co-operation is essential for the successful government of the tribe; should any Chief act contrary to the public opinion as here expressed the result would be disaster. (Schapera 1984: 83, italics added)

These observations clearly support the view that despite the degree of deference towards hierarchical positions shown by his followers, the *kgosi* was heavily dependent on popular support (including all recognized male heads of families who were representing women, young men and people classified as servants or otherwise not full citizens). In a very general sense, therefore, the people had a significant impact on the decision-making process. Yet the *kgosi* was expected to make the final decision – that was his privilege and also his responsibility. Ideally, any major decision would not be made without extensive consultations, culminating with a *lebatla* or *pitso*, a popular meeting in the royal *kgotla*.[9] Since this procedure was backed by the colonial state, there was some room to disregard opposition and apply tough measures.

Nevertheless, what this actually meant in terms of popular approval varied considerably according to the individual ruler. Cases in point are the two major figures during the last decades of the colonial era, Tshekedi Khama of the Bangwato and Bathoen II of the Bangwaketse (Illustration 3). They are both portrayed as extremely forceful, yet they exercised power in quite different ways. Thus Tshekedi, having managed to turn the majority of the Bangwato against him, ended up being humiliated, with severe damage to his reputation (see Chapter 2). Bathoen, by contrast, came into conflict with an emerging entrepreneurial elite. But although his regime might have seemed autocratic by Western democratic standards, he enjoyed tremendous support from vast sections of his subjects: having abdicated in 1969, he joined party politics and defeated the vice-president, Quett Masire, by a large majority.

---

9. *Lebatla* (pl. *mabatla*) is used by the southern Tswana *merafe*, while *pitso* (pl. *dipitso*) is more common amongst the northern *merafe*.

Precisely because Bathoen moved from his position as *kgosi* of the Bangwaketse to become a member of Parliament and leader of the major opposition party – the Botswana National Front (BNF) – without having to declare any fundamental change in constitutional orientation or political attitudes, his story helps us to view the *dikgosi's* exercise of authority in the context of the *kgotla* less ethnocentrically than those scholars who dismiss them as autocrats located in an oligarchy would have us believe.

The Art of Indigenous Government: On Virtues of Consultation, Consent and Truth

In exploring this topic, I shall refer to various accounts of the regime of *Kgosi* Bathoen II before he – like the other *dikgosi* – was stripped of much of his executive power at Botswana's independence. These accounts fall neatly into two opposing categories – corresponding largely with conflicting scholarly notions of indigenous regimes as explained above. The following narrative, which depicts Bathoen's conduct of *lebatla* in the royal *kgotla* as highly autocratic, exemplifies the negative view:

> Before any issue was presented to the *kgotla*, the *kgosi* had discussed the matter carefully with his confidential advisers, including his paternal uncles, important headmen and those others he selected as particularly supportive and knowledgeable.[10] More than that: in important matters he used a network of people which he developed to tacitly move around and pick up popular opinion. When it came to the *lebatla*, the *kgosi* had more or less formed his opinion. The word was put freely, but if it was an important matter, people were always careful. And when one of a certain category of people had spoken, people thought that 'now we have heard the words of the *kgosi*'. And after such a 'mouth-piece' had spoken, all those who followed expressed views in line with him – so as to please the *kgosi*. Oh, no, nobody dared to take a different line after that! In the end the *kgosi* spoke and concluded the matter. And after people went home, people were afraid to talk critically about the event, even in private. Because Bathoen had spies [*batlhodi*, sing. *motlhodi*] all over the place. There were a few people who could say to Bathoen, 'No, I think that this is wrong, – I think that you should do so and so'. The Reverend Andrew Kgasa was amongst these people, but they had to do it privately. They could not just stand up in the *kgotla* and say things like that. People were very afraid to talk critically about him in those days, because they never knew what might happen to

---

10. It will be recalled that *Kgosi* Bathoen abandoned a number of councillors attached to his predecessor. Paternal uncles of the *kgosi* are constitutionally closely attached to the royal office, situated at his right-hand side in the *kgotla* according to rank. However, with the other councillors it is more a matter of selection. Bathoen, not uncontroversial at the time, replaced Ntabogang's councillors with educated men more or less of his own age.

them. If a person dared to oppose Bathoen, he would be punished as soon as he got a case presented to the *kgosing kgotla*. You see the whole system was entirely undemocratic; there was no way in which popular opinion found its proper expression! On the surface it appeared that the *kgosi* consulted the people, but it was all managed and manipulated.

Statements of this kind were typically pronounced by the kind of people who had been at odds with him during the latter part of the colonial era – the up-and-coming entrepreneurial elite of 'new men' (see Chapter 2). Since then the new men had joined the BDP, while Bathoen had become leader of the opposition. This certainly motivated their largely negative, at times even hostile, portrayal of his style of government (see Masire 2006: 24ff.). In addition, there were others who in certain contexts aired critical views of Bathoen's exercise of power. But on the whole, like most of the Bangwaketse, they praised Bathoen as a powerful *kgosi* who had the interests of his people at heart. It is important to recall at this point the appreciation of a *kgosi* such as Bathoen for his determination to 'kill' (*bolaea*) any challenging factions. When he was enthroned in 1928, the Bangwaketse had been troubled for more than a decade by conflict of power at the royal centre following the assassination of his father, *Kgosi* Seepapitso III (r. 1910-16) in 1916. Bathoen's ability to restore the *kgosi's* authority, bring these rivalries to an end and thus promote *kagiso* was duly acknowledged even during my fieldwork some fifty years later.

This appreciation of a *kgosi* who carries out his office with wisdom as well as strength goes together with a relatively high tolerance of what the preceding quotation describes as 'manipulation'. The large majority of the Bangwaketse assigned much more importance to their perceived image of Bathoen as a ruler who treated everyone justly, regardless of rank. He was spoken of by most people as a *kgosi* who adhered to the ideals of free speech – *mmualebe o bua la gagwe* – in the *kgotla*. Many also credited him with being 'the kind of man who – no matter the kind of question asked – he would answer it. And he would not say that so and so is bad because he asked a particular question. What he did was to try to answer it'. These engagements with the people in the *kgotla* at a personal level – i.e. this responsiveness to popular concerns and problems – are of course a major attribute of the idealized ruler as a *motswadintle*.[11]

While these accounts give various reasons for the popular support enjoyed by Bathoen, they do not fully explain how the *kgosi's* exercise of

11. In order to explain Bathoen's allegedly fine character (*botho*), people emphasized how good he was to women: 'He wanted to give full justice to women. He was called *monna yo moshweu wa mosadi* ['the white man of the women' – white being the colour associated with blessing]' (see Chapter 4).

authority in the discursive field of the *kgotla* can be idealized as 'democratic'. In other words, what does the Tswana maxim *kgosi ke kgosi ka morafe* actually involve? The main point is that in contrast to a Western-style democracy, in which the centrality of competing and conflicting interests and the consequent political stratagems and confrontations are taken for granted, there is no notion here of a political field in which such interests can be resolved – even temporarily, if necessary – by a majority vote. Western systems are based on the assumption that politics is a matter of reaching a collective decision in a situation of conflict, and often in a highly individuated societal context. The political system of the *kgotla* is based on the opposite assumption: *that there exists one particular solution to any issue, the one that benefits the common good and not any particular group representing a majority interest.* My informants unanimously stressed that it was not acceptable for speakers to represent particular individual interests or interest groups. That would be tantamount to factionalism: in other words, the kind of conflict that creates heat in the *kgotla*, detrimental to *kagiso* and thus threatening the *morafe* as a whole (see Chapter 4).

Thus, when an issue is presented to the *kgotla*, the ideal is to find a solution to the problem at hand that benefits the *morafe* as a whole – or at least one that people can live with; the ideal objective is always to find a solution that serves the common good. I was often told that the *kgosi* encouraged 'everybody' to speak so that he could draw on all the experience, knowledge and wisdom of the *morafe*.

Since a good decision depends on experience, knowledge and wisdom, and since the basic popular premise is that such cultural resources are unequally distributed, in principle it is not problematic to acknowledge that the utterances of a senior person carry more weight than those of someone of lesser rank. This premise is firmly inculcated in everybody – within the context of the family and descent group *kgotla* – from early childhood (Chapter 4). Popular participation in the decision-making process has thus 'always' been predominantly perceived as a matter of consultation (*therisanyo*). Ideally, consultation should contribute to the store of knowledge and information required by the *kgosi* for his ultimate decision.

I should emphasize once more that this process is not about balancing conflicting interests; rather, it attempts to arrive at the 'true' solution to a problem. Bathoen's authority – and that of similar *dikgosi* – arose from the fact that he was widely esteemed as the supreme source of 'the truth' (*boamarure*). As one experienced elder put it,

> *Kgosi* Bathoen was so immensely respected because people always experienced that the decisions he reached were good for the people. That is, in the end he resolved an issue so that consensus was achieved. I remember

that at *lebatla* one particular man used to praise him, saying: '*Kgosi*, you are our eyes. When you have seen, we have seen. You are our bible with the word of God; you are given to us by God. Whatever you say is what God says'.

This statement echoes what I have recorded elsewhere as a widespread appreciation of Bathoen's regime. He enhanced his authority by introducing numerous initiatives that placed him among those *dikgosi* whom Schapera has identified as 'tribal innovators' (Schapera 1971).

The notion of 'truth' is patently conceived as a matter of *dumela*, i.e. consent (with connotations of acceptance and agreement). Arriving at the 'truth' means making decisions for the common good which are perceived as sensible and hence mainly beneficial.[12] As I explained in the preceding section, these decisions may well involve radical changes provided they are backed by popular consent and believed to be evidence of good communication between the *kgosi* and his ancestors.

My interlocutors explained how Bathoen 'always' concluded court and *lebatla* proceedings by *carefully explaining his reasoning and conclusion*: 'He was very clear in his talk – he wanted everybody to understand his reasoning and final decision properly. There shouldn't be any confusion in the *morafe*; everyone should understand the importance of complying with his decision'.[13] This point was often made along with comments about his allegedly generous acceptance of 'any question in the *kgotla*, even from persons of very low rank'. He is recalled by the vast majority of my interlocutors as the *kgosi* who always responded at length in order to ascertain that people really understood his points.

That these practices were much valued reflects the great importance which people attach to knowledge and wisdom. In Chapter 4 I explained how these virtues are grounded in the everyday life of lower-level *lekgotla*. Since the *dikgosi* constitute the apex of the hierarchy of courts, their court proceedings involve them in more frequent encounters with their subjects than in the *lebatla*. In the *dikgosi*'s court proceedings it is common for their subjects to encounter them as the ultimate source of wisdom and knowledge and the supreme living custodians of morality. These qualities are demonstrated in cross-examinations and particularly in the *kgosi*'s extensive concluding statement in support of his judgement. Similarly, the

---

12. *Kgosi* Bathoen, by contrast to Bakwena rulers, is commonly praised for 'all the development he brought to the tribe'. He is remembered as the *kgosi* who, for example, organized the construction of schools and advocated the enrolment of girls as well as boys, supported the improvement of agricultural methods and prepared for the first agricultural show in the protectorate, to be held in Kanye.

13. Therefore, as he once explained to me, he attached great importance to attendance at the *lebatla* (conversation at his home in Kanye, December 1986).

Comaroffs (1997b: 133) have observed among the Southern Tswana how *kgosi* authority depends on '[w]ords, spoken in the *kgotla* ... assumed to have great pragmatic power to affect the world'. As I explained in Chapter 4, oratorical skills are held in high esteem; a speaker who demonstrates verbal sophistication is described as a person 'who knows "deep" Setswana'.

In short, these idealized descriptions of *Kgosi* Bathoen's regime suggest that the discursive field of the *kgotla* is premised upon the ideal of the *kgosi*'s consultation (*therisanyo*) with his people and with his ancestors. In this way, it was believed, the *kgosi* based his decisions on wisdom and knowledge and enforced them with strength and authority. This is, I reiterate, a regime where decision making is not a matter of compromising conflicting interests, but one in which the ruler's final word is a matter of establishing the true collective answer to a problem or challenge that faces the whole *morafe*. In other words, his decisions were legitimized as the voice of a collective, with unified interests in achieving the common good. The true answer/decision connotes *dumela* and reconciliation (*tetlanyo*) – and thus all the constructive forces of *kagiso*.

The concept of 'truth' can clearly be seen as integral to the exercise of hegemonic leadership: the surrounding discourse reveals a pervasive awareness that wisdom and knowledge are distributed in a highly unequal manner. The fact that these qualities are believed to be cosmologically anchored justifies the unequal weight given to people of different rank in the hierarchical order of the *morafe* (Chapter 4). However, as the emphasis placed by informants on Bathoen's performative capacities demonstrates, the establishment and exercise of authority in the *kgotla* depends not only on oratorical skills but also on the knowledge and judgement relevant to the often litigious issue at hand. With 'innovatory chiefs' (see Schapera 1970) such as Bathoen, practical and technical knowledge of the increasingly encroaching modern world was an important source of authority. It seems that Bathoen's authority was boosted in particular by his ability to clothe radical changes in culturally familiar garments that generated comprehension and consent (*dumela*).

While consultation with the people is important in order to gather all the available information before reaching a decision guided by knowledge and wisdom, the exercise of authority in the *kgotla* is also a matter of 'enlightening' the people. Bathoen's comprehensive public explanations of the reasoning that informed his decisions, coupled with carefully formulated instructions about how these decisions should be implemented, illuminate perfectly how people's idealization of the *kgotla* was conducive to hegemonic domination. In other words, the way in which Bathoen exercised his authority confirmed his subjects' belief that he was indeed the rightful *kgosi*.

When operating effectively, this system reinforced people's appreciation of their ruler by virtue of his ostensible capacity to reach the 'true' conclusion by means of extensive consultations. Yet this was not a 'democratic' system in the Western, egalitarian sense. As I have explained, the Tswana and other peoples of Botswana recognize that knowledge and wisdom are unequally distributed and that some speakers carry more weight than others. According to indigenous perceptions, elderly men in particular possess these cosmologically anchored qualities. As I first explained in Chapter 2, the young 'new men' appearing in the 1950s thus constituted a force which could justifiably be suppressed, as readily happened when they challenged the establishment. This is a dimension of the *kgotla* which should not be underrated and which, as we shall see subsequently, continues to exert an influence on postcolonial consultations with the people.

The Political Significance of the *Kgotla* in Postcolonial Times

The ruling group's efforts to establish the image of the postcolonial state as benevolent and friendly met with significant success, partly because they were perceived as having a vision beyond Gaborone, the state capital. In accordance with my previous examination of Tswana discursive practices in relation to the exercise of authority (as customarily centred in the *kgotla*), such ventures involve a considerable degree of intimate interaction between ruler and subjects, such as we have seen in the relationship between *dikgosi* and their people.

When I lived in a Bangwaketse village during the 1970s and 1980s, one of the most salient aspects of political life was the recurrent arrival of cabinet ministers, members of Parliament, district councillors, and government bureaucrats at different levels to deliver addresses in the village *kgotla*. If very high-ranking officials – such as cabinet ministers or even the president himself – were due to arrive, the visit was announced at length on the radio and a government vehicle with loudspeakers on the roof toured the village. My Western acquaintances employed as senior officers in central government, who had experience of other African countries, were astonished by the extent to which cabinet ministers and members of Parliament frequently travelled from village *kgotla* to village *kgotla* in an attempt to explain the principles of development to people in the most direct way.

This is an intriguing practice in view of the fact that since independence almost every village has had an arena – known as a 'freedom square' – specifically designated for political meetings and rallies. Yet the *kgotla* continues to be the favoured place for officials to address the people. As the state president, Festus Mogae, has put it, 'The kgotla has remained an essential non-partisan forum for national consultation [*therisanyo*] and a fountain of wisdom on development and policy initiatives'.[14] Nevertheless, this does not mean that the *kgotla* is without political significance, as the minister of foreign affairs, Lt. Gen. Mompati Merafhe, clearly has indicated: 'I consult my people in the *kgotla* and that is the reason why they continue to elect me in thousands. *Kgotla* provides an excellent forum'.[15] Another reason for the postcolonial *kgotla*'s significance is its presence in urban as well as rural areas. On the basis of observations in an urban quarter in Francistown (Botswana's second largest city), Van Binsbergen asserts that the *kgotla* 'provides a welcome instrument in the hands of the Botswana state elite seeking to legitimate and perpetuate its position of power' (1995: 24).[16] However, there are conflicting views on how the 'Botswana state elite' take advantage of the *kgotla*: according to the Comaroffs, '[I]t seems injudicious to conclude, as van Binsbergen (1995: 25–8) does, that the appeal to "the *kgotla* system" – dubbed a "neotraditional façade" – is merely a cynical effort by an authoritarian "state elite" to subjugate, appropriate, and manipulate local institutions' (Comaroff and Comaroff 1997b: 139).

These conflicting views reflect the ambiguous nature of the postcolonial state in Botswana: strong and determined, yet friendly and accommodating, with a very limited use of physical violence. In what follows, I shall pursue the argument developed in the preceding chapter: that the hegemonic domination of the ruling elite depends significantly upon the cultural and symbolic wealth vested in the discursive field of the *kgotla*.

---

14. *Botswana Daily News*, 30 January 2001. As I am writing these lines, President Mogae is about to stand down (in April 2008) after being in office for ten years, which according to the Constitution is the limit of service. Presently he is making his farewells to the nation by visiting the people in the *dikgotla* throughout the country.

15. Speech in Botswana Tribal Administration Service Association's (BOTASA) Eighth Conference, in which he stressed the significance of the *kgotla* (*Mmegi*, 10 December 2003).

16. The last British resident commissioner of the protectorate, Peter Fawcus, has stated in retrospect that 'the kgotla eased the transition from colonial government to parliamentary democracy by offering a forum for traditional legitimacy to ministers, MPs and civil servants to explain their policies and test public opinion on new proposals. Extensive use was made of this forum by national leaders' (Fawcus 2000: 170). Similarly, a political scientist observed at an early stage that the *kgotla* 'acts as the means of offering traditional authority to the introduction of new ideas, ways of doing things, and regulations issued by new elites at the central and district level' (Vengroff 1972: 128).

On the other hand, the extent of this domination should not be exaggerated; within the confines of hegemonic development discourse there is, as I shall explain subsequently, some scope for criticism of political leaders.

Monopolizing the *Kgotla*

I shall take as my point of departure President Mogae's emphasis on the *kgotla* as a 'non-partisan forum'. The banishment of party politics from the *kgotla* has had a significant impact on the development of democracy: *it means that the opposition parties are effectively excluded from the* kgotla, *while the ruling party monopolizes this immensely important field of articulation with the population*. One may well argue that the postcolonial *kgotla* has counteracted the development of a parliamentary democracy based upon a multiparty system.

I shall address this issue by asking how the ruling party (BDP) – which is after all a *political* party – has been able to take advantage of the *kgotla*. Why do the ruling elite find it so much more attractive than the 'freedom square'? And why has the population not only accepted their monopolization of the *kgotla*, but also shown a strong preference for the *kgotla* themselves?

Let me begin answering these questions by explaining that politicians of the ruling party visit a *kgotla* in their capacity of agents of the government; they are almost always accompanied by civil servants, ranging from permanent secretaries to local agricultural extension workers. This organized group of officials is typically introduced by the owner of the *kgotla* – the *kgosi* or a *kgosana* – as representatives of *goromente* 'who want to consult with us'. The situation is thus defined in the customary idiom of the discursive field of the *kgotla* (cf. Chapter 4).

From observing a vast number of such meetings, it is clear to me that 'consultation' involves two somewhat different kinds of exchange between government officials and the people. For example, following the announcement of a new programme or a reform (such as a change in the land tenure system) the officials might seek people's opinion on policy issues. One important purpose here is to gauge popular opinion during the preparation of a particular 'development' programme. On the other hand, and much more commonly, programmes and reforms that have already been decided might be presented, the idea being 'to consult with the people' in the sense of explaining how such programmes and reforms might actually affect them and to respond to any questions raised. This kind of exchange is not so much a consultation as a propaganda exercise concerning state 'development' programmes in agriculture, education and health. All such presentations are delivered in an apolitical manner, in the sense that virtually all the programmes and policies in question are 'universal' – they serve the common good and are available to everyone. There is apparently no conflict of interest involved, nor is there any need to attack other political parties: the ruling elite collectively appear as a *motswadintle*. Moreover, with their capacity to inform and to answer questions raised in the *kgotla*, the elite also conform to the notion of authority as the custodian of 'truth'. And when a round of questions and answers comes to an end, the 'true answer' will ideally be clear to everyone; the exchange can then be concluded in an atmosphere of understanding (*kutlwano*) and consent (*dumela*), fully in line with indigenous views on how *therisanyo* should be conducted.

Given this definition of the situation, any attempt to invoke party political affiliations is immediately condemned. The political opposition parties are thus entirely excluded: in other words, the ruling party has monopolized the most significant space for public discourse. Thanks to its control over the government apparatus, it can readily engage with the people in the *kgotla* by *finding the best solution for the common good*. In this way, cabinet ministers, members of Parliament and the state president, supported by a technical staff of bureaucrats and extension workers, are perceived to possess the knowledge required to resolve issues in the 'true way'.

The success enjoyed by political leaders as authority figures in the *kgotla* is closely linked to their participation in this discursive field as pri-

Illustration 8. Villagers encounter state officials in a village *kgotla*. Photo by Ørnulf Gulbrandsen.

vate persons. I have already referred to the performative aspect of *kgotla* discourse and the great importance attributed to oratory. The poise and eloquence demonstrated by high officials in particular is an intriguing feature of these encounters; many of them were acknowledged by the people I lived with as masters of 'deep Setswana'. Such performative qualities are crucial in communicating the wisdom and knowledge that will convince the people of the *kgotla* and win their respect. Beyond words, respect can be reinforced by a particular personal capacity known as *seriti* (i.e. the capacity to convince people – 'charisma'). A person with *seriti* is assigned authority as a natural and indisputable matter.

Another important point in the state officials' favour is that virtually all of them are themselves farmers, have grown up in a village, and in fact still have much in common with the communities they encounter in the *kgotla*. Their intimate experience of all aspects of life in these communities enables them to talk about projects and plans in an idiomatic language that communicates their awareness of the existential struggle of the underprivileged.

This means that these *kgotla* discourses are fertile ground for the domestication of Western theories and practices in such fields of knowledge as agriculture and medicine. Authority figures are allowed – even expected – to be pragmatic enough to adapt Tswana ways and practices to the larger world. As suggested by the account of *Kgosi* Bathoen's performance as an 'innovatory chief', this complex discursive practice was initiated long ago and depended on certain cultural premises. Let me suggest that it had its somewhat sudden birth more than a century ago in the first Christian *dikgosi's* attempts to justify their abandonment of various central ritual and social practices (see Chapter 1). The transformations in question here are not simply a matter of 'modernization' or 'Westernization' in a unilinear sense. It is as much a process of adapting alien values and practices to Tswana cosmology, as can be seen from the way in which the *kgotla* continues to operate as a discursive field anchored by a belief in the potency of ancestors, a belief that enjoys a pragmatic coexistence with Christianity (Gulbrandsen 2001). Postcolonial rulers have the advantage of being able to place themselves at the Tswana epicentre of such cultural transformations.

These postcolonial *kgotla* encounters have had a further important consequence: the two forms of authority – the head of the *kgotla* and the agents of the state – mutually reinforce each other. On the one hand, high-ranking state officials boost the authority of the head of the *kgotla* by subjecting themselves to it, showing the customary signs of respect. On the other hand, these state officials are incorporated into the most senior positions of the *kgotla* and are given seating adjacent to the head.

As chairman of the meeting, the head frames the discourse in a way that attributes authority to – in fact authorizes – the regime of truth on which the government agents' message is based. For example, the *kgosana* or *kgosi* often closes the meeting by acclaiming the public officials' statements. These endorsements take on particular significance owing to the position from which authority is exercised: the head of the *kgotla* has a close association with the senior ancestors, to whom the people addressed ultimately belong (see Chapter 4).[17]

The continuing significance of the *kgotla* is confirmed by the fact that various aspects of its discursive practices are spilling over into other political encounters, as the following account shows:

> [At] the election meetings held by the BDP … local people expected the president or a 'close advisor' (i.e. a cabinet minister) to present themselves; constituency politicians … were not good enough. After all, and this is the point, these meetings were knowingly *modelled on the kgotla*, that space of intersection between state and civil society … Their objective was not just to discuss matters of social concern, to play populist, consultative democracy. It was also to evaluate the performance of the president and his party. And to hold him accountable for the extent to which the BDP met the demands of good government. (Comaroff and Comaroff 1997b: 138, italics added; cf. Molutsi and Holm 1990: 334)

In Chapter 8 we shall see how a cabinet minister – in a major political confrontation in Parliament – took opposition politicians to task for trying to exaggerate societal tension and conflict. More generally, Colclough and McCarthy have observed that

> [t]he daily business of the National Assembly is conducted in a manner closer to the best of the African one-party states than to the Westminster model. The model is not so much the government benches against the opposition as Ministers against the backbenchers. Sometimes, indeed, opposition members are seen to support the government when its own backbenchers are critical. Thus the role of the National Assembly, like that of

---

17. It is significant that the encounter remains entirely dependent on management by the head – or the owner – of the *kgotla*, the custodian of all its cultural and symbolic wealth as anchored in his *badimo* (ancestorhood, see Chapter 4). In former times the head was seated in front of the fireplace at the centre, a patently symbolic position. Today he still sits at the centre, flanked on both sides by state officials in order of rank. He assumes this supreme position even in the presence of the state president – or the vice-president, as in the present case. From this position he carefully monitors and sanctions departures from the discursive principles. And, it should be noted, these are principles that favour precisely the kind of 'regime of truth', in the sense of reaching a solution that serves the common good and steers clear of conflicting political interests.

the traditional Kgotla, is to audit proposals made by those in authority: to approve them and occasionally reject them. (1980: 46, quoted in Comaroff and Comaroff 1997b: 140)

Against this background, it is easy to understand why a political leader such as cabinet minister Merafhe, quoted above, attributes his huge electoral support to engagement with the people in the *kgotla*. As we have now seen, political leaders try to gain popular support by establishing authority in much the same way as the *kgosi* or *kgosana* have always done in the discursive field of the *kgotla*. And in this pursuit the ruling group has been extremely fortunate in commanding vast state resources that have enabled them to deliver the promised benefits – to appear as a true *motswadintle* (the one from whom good things are coming). As we shall see in the following chapter, they have been able to substantiate their promises by distributing resources in close interaction with the people.

Finally, it should be noted that the postcolonial leadership gains strength from the *kgotla*, which gives government officials an opportunity to articulate their capacities both as agents of the state and as respected 'tribesmen': as mentioned above, they often have considerable standing in the context of the *kgotla* because of their capacity to address the people with skilled oratory and to reveal 'deep' knowledge. The ruling group can be said to exercise its hegemonic domination on the 'two superstructural "levels"' identified by Gramsci: 'civil society' and 'the State' (Gramsci 1991: 12). This dual domination has served the discourse of development effectively, because the encounter between agents of 'civil society' and of 'the State' occurs in a discursive field that – as I explained in the previous chapter – is highly conducive to create a hegemonic discourse which blends indigenous and Western notions and virtues. Moreover, within this context rural-located elites and urban-based political leaders and state bureaucrats encounter the hegemonic domination in relation to all the rank and file sections of the population: the shared character of their basic interests and orientations are confirmed and their cohesion as a ruling or dominant class is recurrently reproduced and transformed. This point links up with the argument which I developed in Chapter 3 in relation to the mutually reinforcing dynamics in the relationship between an evolving ruling class and the state.

Hegemony and Challenging Authority

The accomplishment shown by political leaders in the *kgotla* also casts light on the status of freedom squares. Inquiring why people flocked to the *kgotla* while showing very little interest in the political rallies held in the freedom squares, I often received answers such as, 'In the *kgotla* we go for the truth; in the freedom squares, people are told lies'. It is preferable to encounter agents of the state in the context of the *kgotla*; many people are frightened of the heated atmosphere of the political skirmishes in the 'freedom squares' and the perceived disrespect with which people address each other (cf. Helle-Valle 2002: 190). As might be expected, this preference stems from the importance attached to reconciling conflicting parties, reaching consent (*dumela*) about the best solution and thus promoting *kagiso*.

It is tempting, therefore, to propose that the ruling party is exploiting the symbolic wealth centred in the notion of *kagiso* for all it is worth, both to establish a national hegemonic discourse of development and to monopolize the discursive field of the *kgotla*. Let me at this point invoke what Laura Nader terms 'harmony ideology' as a measure that 'may be used to suppress peoples by socialising them toward conformity' (1990: 291). She argues that 'examples from Africa indicate the double impact of Christian mission and colonial courts on African law and the consequent ubiquitousness of harmony ideology' (1990: 296; cf. Chanock 1985). In this view, 'harmony' is an imported or invented notion, consciously deployed by people in power to exercise their domination. This is not the case in the present context, however. It would be a mistake to suggest that the hegemonic domination characterizing all *kgotla* engagements is a conscious tactic or a well-designed plot. Culturally as well as socially, the political leadership is as integral to the discursive practices associated with the *kgotla* as is the general population.

Although the notion of *kagiso* is embedded in political discourse, the postcolonial leadership has not attempted to embrace up-to-date 'harmony ideology'. Notions of peace and harmony are no less powerful for this fact. On the contrary, they are given a particular force within the workings of *kagiso*. The notion of *kagiso* is as it were bodily incarnated in the sense that it retains great existential significance in people's everyday lives (Chapter 4). The virtues of peace and harmony are thus instinctively perceived as residing beyond critical reflection and dispute. And this of course makes them much more powerful as a means of exercising hegemonic domination than virtues imported from outside.

Nevertheless, the concern to reach consent and to maintain *kagiso* does not mean that people cannot voice objections or otherwise take issue with government officials. First, people are invited to ask all kinds of questions about government programmes and projects, and these may indeed be critical as long as they are delivered in a respectful manner. This follows from one of the *kgotla*'s chief virtues: that of letting all views be put forward in order to find the best solution to a problem. Hence, at certain stages government officials might even encourage extensive debate, as happened at the time the National Policy on Tribal Grazing was developed. At the same time, this case is a good example of how the government set the frame of the debate. There is no space here to question the tremendous *de facto* privatization of common land by wealthy cattle owners who appropriated vast pastures by drilling their own boreholes (see Peters 1994: 197ff.; Gulbrandsen 1996a: 332). Nevertheless, when a cabinet minister was touring the village *dikgotla* in his constituencies, he had to tolerate criticism from large-scale cattle owners who were dissatisfied with the prices offered by the Lobatse abattoir for their livestock or the Ministry of Agriculture's ability to furnish them with heifers. Government projects might even be rejected or an alternative course of action proposed. Rather than prioritizing projects in relation to the needs and interests of different sections of the population, therefore, '[i]n almost all cases the discussion deals with implementation issues in a given village' (Molutsi and Holm 1990: 34).

Within this discursive frame, even rank-and-file people may complain, for example about services and support promised by government officials on a previous occasion. Typically there are complaints about poor water services, medical staff who do not work to people's satisfaction, co-operatives which do not trade their cattle in the approved manner or schools that are overcrowded and in need of more classrooms. Such complaints are even made to the state president when visiting a remote village.

However, if anybody questions major policy directions which favour those who are already wealthy and privileged, they are, as I have observed on a few occasions, effectively silenced. They are readily regarded as disguised opposition politicians who dare to bring 'politics' – and hence heat – into the *kgotla*. The wealthy – and hence dominant – members of the *kgotla* will argue forcefully, together with the government officials, that all the policies in question will benefit the nation. Even if some 'industrious' people gain particular benefits from them, that too will help poor people, albeit indirectly.

Moreover, if anyone voices his criticism aggressively, in an overt attack on a visiting politician, he is immediately taken to task by the head of the *kgotla*, who will be quick to dismiss him for transgressing the code of *kgotla* conduct, ensuring *kagiso* (cf. Chapter 4). Reactions to aggressive speakers were particularly negative if he (always a man in my experience) was of a younger generation (which means below forty in this context), because he was alleged to bring shame on his parents.

According to my observations, there were two interesting exceptions to the protection enjoyed by visiting state officials. At the time of my first fieldwork in the mid-1970s, *Kgosi* Seepapitso IV of the Bangwaketse (the son and heir of *Kgosi* Bathoen II, as already indicated) had recently been reinstalled after a year-long suspension for alleged misconduct in office (cf. Chapter 4). When cabinet ministers and MPs – always of the ruling party, it need hardly be said – came to address the Bangwaketse in the royal *kgotla* in Kanye, *Kgosi* Seepapitso chaired the meeting in an unusually relaxed way, leaving people considerable space to level attacks on the visiting officials. When I questioned the *kgosi* about this practice, he merely referred to the principle of freedom of speech asserted by Botswana's Constitution. A similar kind of reaction to state officials was evident in the case of *Kgosi* Linchwe II of the Bakgatla. Apparently, these two were the only 'traditional' authority figures who dared to leave state officials without the expected protection against people wanting to push them to the wall. But even in these instances they were not challenged on major policy issues such as the directions responsible for the increasingly skewed distribution of cattle, or government support of the *de facto* privatization of the commons. Rather, at this level – that of the royal *kgotla* – people of wealth and commercial ambitions were present in large numbers and, as already indicated, complained about government inefficiency and insufficient support for their entrepreneurial efforts. This should not be surprising in view of what I have explained about the cohesion of elites in Chapter 3. Nor, in view of the inequality of wealth distribution inherent in the hierarchical order of the *merafe,* is it any surprise that there was virtually nobody who took the small man's point of view. Although they too were present in large numbers, they kept quiet. As a result they were drawn into discursive processes in which government policy remained unquestioned and taken for granted. In fact the aggressive nature of wealthy people's attacks only asserted that in this respect the wealthy and powerful were strongly united. Hence, the hegemonic discourse of development prevailed.

Evasion

On the other hand, in certain respects ordinary villagers' complaints might well have an effect. This came home to me once when I first witnessed people from the village where I was living at that time complaining to the vice-president in the *kgotla* about the roof of the clinic, which had blown off. They were impatiently waiting for the district council to get the roof back in place. The following day I was visiting a friend, the district council secretary, when he received a phone call. 'It's Quett', he whispered as they chatted extensively before the vice-president came to the matter in hand: he expected the district council to have the roof repaired in due course.

In this and many other cases, people see that the government delivers the goods. Hence, many people see a point in attending all encounters in the *kgotla* initiated by visiting political leaders in the guise of government officials. But there are exceptions.

One reaction is that of evasion. While adult males were compelled to attend the *kgotla* during precolonial and colonial times when the *kgosi* or a *kgosana* called for a meeting (*lebatla, pitso*), there is no requirement to do so in postcolonial times. In consequence, there are people who keep away from the *kgotla*. According to my records, the vast majority of these people comprised men of the younger generations (under the age of forty), who were engaged in labour migration and would spend some months in their home village between work contracts (Gulbrandsen 1996a: 195ff.). Their daily occupation consisted largely of drinking parties, which often started early in the day. Evasion can be seen as a kind of resistance to the discursive field of the *kgotla* and the hegemonic discourse of development. Helle-Valle (1996: 251ff.) has given an illuminating account of beer parties that reveals how core values of the *kgotla* – hierarchical order, subjection to authority figures and respectful behaviour – are contradicted by these parties' egalitarian and fluid nature. Their anarchic quality, he argues, is a matter of negating officialdom (1996: 277). Furthermore, as I have explained elsewhere, the values associated with beer parties – the pleasures of leisure – are diametrically opposed to those of 'development' as propagated by agents of the government (Gulbrandsen 1996a: 182ff.). Again Helle-Valle (1996) provides extensive examination of the discursive practices of beer parties: highly meaningful to the participants, negative towards officialdom though without openly challenging it. Nevertheless, however politically uninformed the devotees of beer parties may be, they engage in a discourse which takes place every day throughout the country and which, under particular conditions, has certainly considerable rhizomic potentiality (see Chapter 8).

A One-Party State?

A ruling party which has stayed in power ever since independence and which has always dominated interactions between politicians and citizens would appear to indicate that Botswana is actually a one-party state rather than a republican democracy. However, to describe it as either a one-party state or as a 'paternalistic democracy' fails to explain the complexity of the relationship between postcolonial rulers and the people of the country during the formative decades of independence. On the basis of my present analysis of how the ruling party has engaged intimately and intensively with the discursive field of the *kgotla* throughout Botswana, I shall close this chapter by explaining how the opposition parties became as it were marginalized by the ruling party's depoliticizing measures.

One point is that the ruling party excluded all political opposition from the *kgotla* by defining it as a nonpolitical arena – relegating political rallies to the so-called freedom squares. This measure was easily justified in indigenous political discourse, in which virtues of nonconfrontation, consent and 'truth' prevail. As I have explained, this is a practice founded on the premise that there is one good ('true') solution, favourable to the community as a whole, and it chimes perfectly with what I have called the hegemonic discourse of development. Both of these invited people, on a disinterested basis, to find the best technical way to implement particular 'development' policies whose importance was beyond question. It is critically important, of course, that that this hegemony went beyond words. As I shall explain in the following chapter, it was substantiated by extensive government intervention.

As a result, the ruling party and the government it dominated exercised its hegemony so forcefully until the late 1980s that it was no simple matter for the opposition to establish a convincing political alternative. During the first two independence decades it is difficult to see how they could have attacked a government that provided new schools, clinics, water supplies, roads and so on, even in remote villages, or one that was quick to implement nationwide feeding programmes as soon as there was a shortage of rain. All the opposition could do – being thus captured within the hegemonic discourse – was to criticize the ruling party for not providing these services fast and widely enough.

Only when the ruling party and its government came under fire in the beginning of the 1990s in the wake of serious corruption scandals, some of which even involved the vice-president and cabinet ministers (see Good 1994), could the opposition parties seize the offensive for some years; and they did fairly well in the 1994 election. During this later postcolonial stage – with a substantial number of people now living in towns where they increasingly faced problems of unemployment, poverty, and discrepancies between aspirations and reality – the ground was prepared for rallying people against the ruling party on fundamental issues of government policies. These policies could be seriously attacked for generating escalating socioeconomic inequalities and causing massive poverty. In Chapter 8 I shall address the question of why the opposition parties have failed to exploit this situation in order to develop a radical political alternative to that of the ruling party.

Here it should be emphasized that if the opposition had represented no significant threat whatsoever, the ruling party would hardly have made such an effort to cultivate its relationship with the population within the context of the *kgotla* and to launch a number of popular programmes in advance of election. Hence, the notion of a 'one-party state' is misleading, as is above all testified by the ruling party's heightened alertness after being seriously challenged by the opposition in the 1994 election, when the BNF increased their seats in the Parliament from three to thirteen, while the BDP's seats were reduced from thirty-one to twenty-three.[18] From the point of view of the ruling party, it is particularly worrying that the opposition has taken a strong hold upon the ever increasing urban centres whose growth accelerated in the late 1980s.

Conclusion

I shall conclude this chapter with the point of departure in the observation that there are limits to the kind of criticism people can level against political leaders in the context of the *kgotla*. In view of political leaders' often dominant position within this context, it may be asked to what extent the discursive field of the *kgotla* qualifies for being a 'public sphere' at least in Habermas' sense. In his conception, a 'public sphere' comes into being 'when private individuals assemble to form a public body which can *operate independently, unrestrictedly and critically in relation to state authority*' (1974: 49 italics added, cf. 1992: 27ff.; Taylor 1990: 98). This issue links up with the broader notion of Botswana as a strong state within a weak civil society (Molutsi and Holm 1990). In this context it is highly relevant that the postcolonial government has, as I explained in the previous chapter, framed a law (the Societies Act of 1972) which requires all voluntary organizations in the country to comply with the regulations of the Registrar of Societies, including the regular submission of written reports on their activities. At times, agents of the government also bring these activities under direct surveillance. Such surveillance might even extend to political rallies in freedom squares, which according to

---

18. For the 1994 parliamentary election, the total number of seats was increased from thirty-four to thirty-six owing to the establishment of two new constituencies in the rapidly growing urban areas. It was particularly alarming for the BDP that the proportion of votes declined from 65 per cent at the 1989 election to 54 per cent at that of 1994, while the percentages for the BNF were 27 and 47 respectively. If there had been an election of members of Parliament according to proportional representation rather than that of one-member constituencies, the BNF would have been represented by an even larger number of members in Parliament. The fact that the BDP had gained 75 per cent in 1979 while the BNF was supported by only 19 per cent of the electorate is further evidence of this trend. However slow this trend is, it is a *trend* which is much attributable to urbanization since the opposition is much more dominant in urban areas (see Wiseman 1998). Nevertheless, the BDP prevails as the ruling party, mainly because the major opposition party, the BNF, was divided before the 1999 election. With a divided opposition the ruling party had the great advantage in the one-member constituency representation. Hence in both the 1999 and the 2004 elections the BDP gained barely more than half of the votes yet still captured the vast majority of the seats (see Mogalakwe 2006: 15).

van Binsbergen's observations in northeastern Botswana were 'attended by uniformed police who taped the proceedings' (1995: 23). It is true that since the 1980s Botswana has developed independent newspapers,[19] yet they are increasingly 'in the firing-line of government intolerance intransigence' (Good 2008: 61).

Furthermore, Maundeni (2004: 33) argues that the state has brought nongovernmental organizations under centralized control by compelling them to join the umbrella organization known as the Botswana Council of Non-Governmental Organizations (BOCONGO)[20] in ways which militate against 'autonomous operation'. He asserts that '[t]hese joint councils have enormously expanded the power of the state by silencing the public voice of non-cooperating NGOs' (Maundeni 2004: 74). Thus, while there has, as observed by Carroll and Carroll (2004), been a substantial increase in the number of NGOs since the early 1990s, these authors fail to recognize the extent to which these organizations have been captured into the state structures of control and surveillance.

The trade unions, for example, have been put under pressure by the state to form a federation – the Botswana Federation of Trade Unions (BFTU) – in order to develop structures within which the state can intervene more efficiently (Mogalakwe 1997: 71–72). It has been stipulated that trade unions have to be properly registered and issued with a certificate of registration by the government Registrar of Trade Unions in order to operate as legal organizations. The Ministry of Labour and Home Affairs is empowered to send a representative to attend every meeting in this body, including the federation's executive committee meetings. Moreover, the Registrar of Trade Unions can authorize people to inspect books containing the minutes of various bodies, including the executive committees of individually registered trade unions (Mogalakwe 1997: 89). Furthermore, the 'trade unions are made deliberately weak by being forced to negotiate at plant or enterprise level' (Mogalakwe 1997: 106–7, cf. Holm et al.: 1996: 52).

The frustration caused by state intervention is epitomized by union leaders who have accused the state of keeping them under surveillance by the Special Branch, as, for example, on one occasion it was alleged that 'the police masqueraded as union members' (see *Mmegi*, 15 December 2005). However, it says much about the efficiency and strengths of repressive state forces that the state was seriously challenged by major waves of strikes for the first time as late as April 2011 – forty-five years after

---

19. Before this time, there was only one newspaper in the country published by the government and hence, as the radio, was under tight state control.

20. See http://www.whiteband.org/PressCenter/Coverage/gcapinmedia.

the birth of the democratic republic. At this time, public sector unions organized vast sections of governmental employees in strikes that escalated into serious, long-lasting confrontations with the state leadership, at times entailing violent conflicts (see Chapter 8). It remains to be seen if people's experience of the series of heated events has contributed to empower trade unions organizing the unprivileged rank and file sections of the public service.[21]

Durham (1999: 196) has countered the notion of weak civil society in Botswana, arguing that there is as a strong scholarly tendency to measure 'civil society' in purely Eurocentric terms. She points out that 'ever since the mid-nineteenth century, Tswana chiefdoms have witnessed the growth of other public spheres alongside the royal court – voluntary associations, commercial projects, and especially the church'.[22] The increasing number of such organizations has clearly expanded 'civil society' in a broad sense. In view of this point and the extensive character of the encounters between the political leaders and the population in the context of the *kgotla*, it appears that Botswana does *not* have an unquestionably weak civil society. This point is apparently supported by more recent trends, as suggested by Richard Werbner (2004: 194): 'The tide is turning … toward higher visibility and more open-lobbying by politicised pressure groups'.

   This conundrum can be resolved by invoking the dimension of class. It seems that the major impact of 'civil society' in Botswana, is, as always has been the case, predominantly anchored in the dominant class. In postcolonial times, this includes such people as Kalanga high officials and successful businessmen, who Werbner (2004) has examined, as well as such elites as that of the major Tswana *merafe* who has the capacity to place considerable pressure on the state leadership. This was abundantly illus-

---

21. Pnina Werber (2010a) has, however, recently identified *divisive* forces in operation within one of the major unions, the Manual Workers Union (historically far the largest union in Botswana) that might have the opposite effect. In addition to examining factional politics in this union under the condition of party political infiltration, she highlights interestingly the very ambiguous relationship between trade unions and political parties in this country.

22. This is important because these organizations, including local Red Cross and YWCA (of the World Young Women's Christian Association), have for many decades indeed organized vast numbers of women in villages across the country. Botswana Teachers Union and Botswana Civil Society Union were both founded before World War II. This feature remains unrecognized by Carroll and Carroll (2004: 341) who instead speak of 'the rapid expansion of civil society in Botswana' as a very recent matter, asserting that 'the nid-1980s … saw the start of the women's movement in Botswana'. They claim 'that there was very little consultation between the state and this rudimentary civil society until the mid 1990s' (ibid.: 339),showing no comprehension of the widespread significance of the *kgotla* where also women engage extensively in encounters with governmental officials.

trated by the ways in which even the president was challenged in several royal *kgotla* during the debates of the Balopi Commission's recommendations (see Chapter 5). That is, as I have explained in this chapter, by the same groups who work strongly in support of the state leadership by virtue of their exercise of hegemonic domination in the context of the *kgotla*. These and other sections of the dominant class are, to be sure, equally prepared to support the state's repressive treatment of trade unions and even endorse legislations that open for state control and surveillance of NGOs. At the same time, the very extensive practices of 'consulting with people' in the context of the *kgotla* around the country impacts certainly upon governmental officials in many ways as it represents an unusual channel – in the larger African context – of direct communication, also for unprivileged sections of the population. It might, of course, be argued that these encounters are somehow dominated by the officials who are left with few commitments (Noppen 1982) and whose massive interventions in local communities prevent civil society developing in more organized ways. Nevertheless, in many cases they offer citizens a possibility to make their concerns and problems utterly clear to people in a position to do something with them.

In this chapter I have been centrally concerned with the ways in which the agents of the state attempted to exploit the *kgotla* in order to incorporate the population in the process of state formation. In this context, the *kgotla* certainly is serving as a public space to people of authority and wealth as they could more freely than the rank-and-file express their views and even attack government agencies for their shortcomings in relation to their promises in particular fields of 'development', especially those related to their own entrepreneurial interests. But this represented no challenge to the hegemonic discourse of development. Quite the contrary, which also means, as I have argued, that the population was placed under a 'double domination' in the Gramscian sense.

The extensive practice of this hegemonic discourse – centred on all the technicalities of development – justified the ruling party's monopolization of the *kgotla* which prevented the population from being exposed to conflicting issues and orientations of political significance. This antipolitical venture was, however, not met by significant popular reactions and demand for more 'democratic' practices. On the contrary, the ruling party could take advantage of people's deep dislike of the freedom squares with all their political confrontations, while appreciating the highly pragmatic, technical – and peaceful – discourse of 'development' in the *kgotla*. The agents of the state hence benefited from the prevailing non-competitive virtues of truth seeking and the assurance of *kagiso* inherent in the discursive field of the *kgotla*. Within the discursive limits thus set by agents of the state and the 'owners' of the *kgotla* – which most people took for granted – one might speak of this as a public sphere, although not fully satisfying Habermas's requirements. For within these discursive limits, people were rather compelled to engage in issues of 'development' and to come forward with their queries in terms of discursive requirements set by the agents of the state. It is important to bear in mind also that the agents of the state were appearing to people as custodians of immense wealth, very much more than any *kgosi* could dispose to the benefit of his subjects, with which they allegedly wanted to 'improve people's lives'. It is hence comprehensible why people easily made themselves subjects to the discursive requirements of 'constructive consultations'.

Thus, during the formative decades of the postcolonial state (1966–1990) with which I am mainly concerned in this volume, the agents of the state managed to involve vast sections of the population, intimately and continuously, in ways that merged progressively their own orientations, desires and virtues with that of the modern state. Conversely, their frequent engagements with people in the *kgotla* all over the country represented a major impetus to the reproduction of the *merafe* and other hierarchies of authority which were incorporated in the postcolonial state as instruments of government.

All this underscores how indigenous political institutions and practices have been captured into the overall process of state formation which is, however, not unambiguously democratic. For by appropriating the discursive field of the *kgotla*, not only party political rivalry has been prevented from being exposed to the public: Since the owners of the *dikgotla* – the *dikgosi* and *dikgosana* around the country – are incorporated into the state as civil servants, the *dikgotla* are, to be sure, not easily available for local, popular mobilization in ways agents of the state identify as 'political'.

Chapter 7

GOVERNMENTALIZATION OF THE STATE
On State Interventions
in the Population

Ranked amongst the twenty-five poorest countries on earth at its independence and widely viewed as a highly peaceful, democratic island in
the midst of authoritarian regimes of racism and violence, Botswana became a favourite target of Western aid agencies. From its early beginnings
the post-colonial state received vast financial and technical foreign support for 'development' purposes – which was *not* discontinued when the
flow of revenues from diamond mining into the state treasury started to
accelerate in the late 1970s (see Harvey and Lewis 1990: 198ff.). Foreign
aid has, with very few exceptions, been channelled through the state to
government-conducted 'development' projects and programmes. NGOs
have hence played a limited role in postcolonial Botswana, and their engagements have at any rate been under very close state control. In this
chapter I want to explain how the strength and sustainability of the postcolonial state in Botswana can be related to the state's expansion into
society, much in terms of what Scott (1998: 187) has identified as the
progressive 'creation of state spaces where the government can reconfig-
ure the society and economy of those who are to be "developed"'.

  Botswana's quite exceptional 'underdevelopment' at the time of decolonization – as seen in a larger African context – reflects the British
disinterest in the protectorate's resources (see Chapter 2) as epitomized
by their location of the colonial state administration outside the country

– in the South African township of Mafeking. Immediately after independence, however, the British took a leading role in developing a modern state bureaucracy in the capital of Gaborone and at district centres. Another significant indication of 'underdevelopment' was the exceptionally low level of education. The consequent shortage of competent indigenous people to staff the rapidly expanding civil service was compensated by the arrival of large numbers of Western 'experts' and 'volunteers'.

They were, to be sure, well versed in Western principles of bureaucratic administration and very instrumental to the institutionalization of the modern state government and the socialization of the Batswana into the bureaucratic order of civil service. Also, the massive presence of these expatriates during the two first independence decades was important for keeping the state quite clean of corruption scandals until the late 1980s. Moreover, as the evolving civil service adhered quite closely to principles of universalism, people's dependency on patronage was gradually reduced (Solway 1994: 266). These practices of the postcolonial state were, as we shall see in this chapter, highly conducive for the efforts, explained in the previous chapters, of creating an imagery of a benevolent state of social justice – and to conceal the fact that a restricted number of well-positioned people with initial resources reaped a lion's share of state resources (cf. Chapter 3).

In the present chapter, I want to examine the impacts of the state 'development' programmes and projects by focusing upon the extensive ways in which the 'development' agencies of the state involved directly with the population. Significantly, beyond the state bureaucracy located in the capital and district centres, an array of state agencies expanded throughout the rural areas, including large numbers of agricultural and veterinary extension officers, teachers, health workers, water-supply mechanics and so on, engaging intensively and persistently with individuals and communities throughout the country. I have found it particularly helpful to analyse the massive implementation of state projects and programmes in terms of the Foucauldian notion of 'the art of modern government'.

Echoing Gramsci's (1991: 268) notion of the individual's 'self-government' as the 'normal continuation' and 'organic complement of state', Foucault (1990: 82) speaks of the 'art of modern government' as a matter of a distinct rationality: 'to develop those elements constitutive of individuals' lives in such a way that their development also fosters that of the strength of the state'. Foucault (1978) has elaborated this notion of 'state rationality' in the theoretization of 'the governmentalization of the state' to which I now proceed in order to clarify the approach by which I want to examine major state 'development' interventions, mainly during the formative and consolidating period (1966–1990). This leads me to discuss the establishment of vast state apparatuses – i.e. the creation of a 'govern-mentalized' state – by which the postcolonial state in Botswana started to intervene in the population from shortly after independence.

This is, though, not a matter of 'state-initiated social engineering' which concerns Scott (1998: 4–5), enforced by 'an authoritarian state that is willing and able to use the full weight of its coercive power to bring... high-modernist designs into being.' Rather, we have at hand a case of state-craft demonstrating subtle and tacit practices by which the state works on people's subjectivities in an effort to feature as a positive force in the popu-lar imagination. But, note, however soft and friendly, the governmental interventions with which I am presently concerned are, the process is not to be conceived as a democratic one in any reasonable sense of that word. Rather, it is a process of *inculcating* individualizing dispositions conducive to making the government of society a matter of individuals' 'self-govern-ment'. Moreover, beyond Foucault, I finally propose that these dispositions are giving rise to subjectivities that, in a progressively market-ridden kind of society like the present one, readily generate major conflicts (of class) which I shall address in the following chapter.

On Governmentalization of the State

Concerned with the development of the modern Western European state, Foucault (1978: 20) suggests that since the eighteenth century these states have increasingly intervened into the population in ways characterized by care for and concern about the subjects. From these interventions have, he argues, henceforth emerged state-society relationships distinctly differ-ent from the dominant forms that preceded them historically: 'the State of Justice' and 'the Administrative State', that is 'sovereignty' to which people submitted by obedience to the law. Since sovereignty did not cease to play a role (Foucault 1978: 18–19), this was not a matter of abrupt discontinuity from one form to the other but a gradual 'governmental-ization of the state' which, crucially, involved a major shift away from a state whose domination primarily depended upon prohibitions and pun-ishment. That is, states which relied on the 'negative power' of law, creat-ing subjects who submitted primarily from anxiety and fear. In due course 'governmentality' became the dominant form and, asserts Foucault, at the present time 'we live in the era of governmentality'. This involved a pas-sage from a state order of 'sovereignty' in the meaning of a single point of command to the modern era (cf. Hardt and Negri 2000: 88) in which, according to Foucault (1980: 122) 'the State' should be conceived as operating as 'super-structural' in relation to 'a whole series of existing power networks' located beyond the state itself.

This era is characterized by power relations within society that 'have become more and more under state control ... power relations have become progressively governmentalised, that is to say, elaborated, rationalised, and centralised ... under the auspices of the state' (Foucault 1982: 224). This notion relates closely to what was suggested above: the strength of the state is a matter of developing particular elements constitutive of individuals' lives. The governmentalization of the state in the Foucauldian sense is hence a *positive* task as 'population comes to appear above all else as the ultimate end of government, that is the welfare of the population since this end consists not in the act of governing as such but in the improvement of the condition of the population, the increase of its wealth, longevity, health, etc'. (Foucault 1978: 17). The transition to a state of benevolence found strong expression in its attention to the processes of life. While the 'old power of death ... symbolised sovereign power', the 'highest function [of the modern state] was no longer to kill, but invest life through and through' (1998: 139). The population thus becomes 'the object in the hands of the government, aware, vis-à-vis the government, of its wants, but ignorant of what is being done to it'. The governmentalization of the state, Foucault (1978: 17–19) argues, involves a particular rationality which depends upon acquiring highly complex, extensive knowledge of the processes related to population, especially because the means of generating popular welfare are all 'immanent in the population'. The state thus intervenes in the population by means of a range of 'absolutely new tactics and techniques',working on people's subjectivities and hence managing 'the population in its depths and its details'.

The governmentalization of the state was, in this conception, a long-term historical transformation of Western states, in progress well before the decolonization of Africa. That is, by the time Western states became heavily engaged in the establishment of modern, independent states on this continent. The profound impact of Western hegemony in this matter is most apparent in the taken-for-granted adaptation of principles of democratic rule and modern bureaucratic government. More tacitly, but no less taken for granted, were precisely such practices of government which Foucault has identified as 'governmentality'. Just as there was no need for reinventing parliamentarian democracy and modern bureaucracy, practices of governmentality were received as major elements of a state apparatus that should unquestionably be directed towards 'development'. That is, the improvement of the life of each and everybody within the state realm.

The imitation of Western state practices and structures was extremely apparent in Botswana. Not only because the decolonization was very peaceful and the Constitution of the independent state was created in close co-operation between the outgoing British resident representatives and the incoming Batswana political leaders. It was also because, I recall, the level of education was very low and the governmental institutions were predominantly staffed by Western 'experts' and 'volunteers'. The strong presence of Western 'experts' and 'volunteers' was essential not only to the development of a modern state bureaucracy and to socialize Batswana civil servants into 'rational', universal principles of decision making. They also represented driving forces in creating ministries which were instrumental in translating vast foreign aid into 'development' projects and programmes which have always been implemented in the name of the state, i.e. by civil servants attached to a governmental ministry or department.

The strong 'development' orientations of the postcolonial state were soon reflected in the national 'development' plans. All its objectives of 'improving the lives' of everybody correspond well to the Foucauldian notion of the population as the ultimate end of the state. This is particularly apparent in what I have identified as a hegemonic discourse of 'development' wherein the *raison d'être* of the state was much a matter of caring for the population – its longevity, welfare and prosperity. In the previous chapter we saw how high state officials started at an early stage after independence to address the population, with high frequency, in the local context of the *kgotla* all over the country about the state's plans, projects and programmes of 'development'. In the present chapter I want to illuminate how the state created a wide ranging network of governmental 'extension' workers designated to work closely and continuously with local communities and families all over the country for opening up for state intervention.

Such modern state practices of 'development' – which are found throughout the postcolonial world – can, of course, be examined from many perspectives, as reflected in scholarly literature. As indicated in the introductory remarks, my present concern is mainly to examine major, welfare-oriented state interventions in the population in the pursuit of the overall objective of this volume – to come to terms with the formation of a strong and sustainable state in Botswana. I am hence centrally concerned with the extent to which these interventions serve state efforts of legitimation and, importantly, capture the population into networks of state power. Yet, although I argue that these evolving features of the postcolonial state in Botswana became progressively more dominant, it is important to bear in mind Foucault's assertion that the negative powers of 'sovereignty' never ceased to play a role – as I underscored towards the end of the previous chapter and as we shall see more extensively in the chapter that follows. For now, however, the focus is on the exercise of power in which Foucault took a particular interest, denoted 'technical and positive' (cf. 1980: 121).

State Agency of Western Medicine

Foucault's strong concern with 'positive power' finds, as already indicated, one of its expressions in his point that the 'old power' of the sovereign – symbolized above all by the power of death – was 'carefully supplanted by the administration of bodies and the calculated management of life' (Foucault 1981: 140). This transformation involved the development of an 'era of biopower', as he named it, which can be traced in many fields. In this and the following two sections I am concerned with this notion of the modern state as the supreme power of life, intervening in the population by means of governmental 'techniques and tactics' that are directed towards human bodies in the pursuit of enhancing the population's longevity.

State exercise of bio-power is particularly evident in the field of health. While Foucault describes the development of bio-power as a long-term historical process within the context of Western states, this development had, of course, reached an advanced stage at the time of Botswana's independence. This kind of power was embedded in the knowledge and practices brought along by all Western 'experts' and 'volunteers' that populated and dominated the civil service, at least during the two first postcolonial decades.

Under the heavy impact of Western medical doctors, health workers[1] operated from the outset on the basis of the conception of indigenous healing practices as conflicting and incompatible with the kind of 'rational' knowledge upon which 'modern' health practices are founded. Although this view was slightly modified after President Khama's visit

---

1. Shortly after independence, international aid agencies were ready to develop full-fledged medical services. Yet it was always in the name of the state; all the expatriate health workers were distinctively civil servants – nongovernmental health agencies never represented any significant part of the landslide spread of health services. Nongovernmental health services were predominantly provided by missionary hospitals, mainly in the Tswana royal towns where they had been established during colonial times, decades before independence. Curiously, the first medical doctor in the country – David Livingstone – arrived as early as 1842 (see Livingstone 1857).

to China in the mid-1970s, Western biomedicine has, to be sure, prevailed as the dominant knowledge base. Still, 'universal', biomedical knowledge, like agronomy (see below), was to be adapted to local contexts by the development of more specific knowledge of health conditions in the population, always with the aim – in typical governmental style – of intervening with appropriate techniques and tactics. It was thus established that '[t]he main diseases in Botswana … are roughly the same as those known in the countries of northern Europe around the middle of last [i.e. the nineteenth] century … The most common communicable diseases are tuberculosis, measles and sexually transmitted diseases' (Staugård 1985: 38). Epidemiological investigations laid the ground for extensive vaccination campaigns all over the country. True, such surveys only accelerated when the HIV/AIDS epidemic started to take off in the late 1980s (see following section).

Furthermore, the state's recurrent National Development Plans asserted that the prevailing health problems 'have their roots in the poverty and the climate of the country. Respiratory, intestinal and skin infections owe their prevalence to insufficient and poor *nutrition*, insufficient and unclean *water supplies*, lack of proper *sanitation*, poor *housing* and *lack of knowledge* about nutrition and personal hygiene, about the collection, storage and use of water, and about the disposal of human waste and refuse' (Government of Botswana n.d.: 259, italics added). The state's identification of people's health problems was thus emphatically conceived as a matter of poverty and cognitive limitation. Although not stated in official texts, words like 'traditionalism' or 'backwardness' would readily be added by state medical agents to describe local reliance on the 'traditional medicine' provided by indigenous doctors/diviners (*dingaka*, ngaka) and other indigenous healers. Major interventions were hence directed towards people's bodily practices; to inculcate such self-governing practices that enabled 'communities and individuals to take responsibility for improving health'.[2]

For the purpose of thus intervening 'in depth and detail', there was established a cadre of health workers with the intriguing title of Family Welfare Educators (FWE) – suggesting how the family has become 'the privileged instrument for the government of the population' (Foucault 1978: 17). FWEs were recruited from among the communities in which they were supposed to work, under the assumption that they would operate comfortably in intimate situations. The knowledge they were supposed to disseminate was gained through an eleven-week course conducted by

2. See National Development Plan VI, 309.

the Ministry of Health. Their identification with the various government health policies was recurrently reproduced through the supervision of nurses. Like the agricultural demonstrators (see below), the FWEs were designated to operate in a particularly interventionist way. Their task was to approach people in their homes and to address all the everyday domestic habits that had been identified by the state as detrimental to nourishment and health. This involved a vast number of practices related to the preparation of food, the cleaning of houses and other issues of basic hygiene, including drinking water, latrines and garbage. In considerable detail the FWEs instructed people how drinking water should be boiled, latrines should be constructed and garbage properly disposed of. They tried to convince people to change bodily practices such as spitting and using the bush around the villages as a toilet, always hammering home the dangers of contagion and infection. In order to improve nutrition, the FWEs promoted the virtues of vegetables, explaining how people of simple means could grow vegetables themselves. Such campaigns, directed towards the intimate domains of people's lives, more or less followed existing blueprints of early Western health campaigns, also often aiming at reducing the prevalence of tuberculosis.

Obviously, with such state interventions in a sociocultural context where numerous agents of other knowledge systems are actually operating in competing ways with those of Western biomedicine, it is hard to know the extent to which the latter has an impact upon people's consciousness. I shall illuminate the intricacy of this issue in the subsequent section where I address state intervention in relation to the HIV/AIDS epidemics. Yet the fact that the frequency of tuberculosis in Botswana has dropped significantly during the period of time such state campaigns have been in operation suggests their significance. One important point here is that indigenous healers of various kinds often conceive state health workers – as well as each other – as competitors in the same market. This means that people are accustomed to shop around in order to obtain preventive as well as curative measures that work. Although detailed investigations of people's hygiene and nutrition are lacking, the fall in such a major disease as tuberculosis indicates the impact of all the efforts by WFEs to inculcate new bodily practices. To the extent that this is the case, one may well speak of the formation of new subjectivities in the sense of people's changing comprehension of how they relate to each other in intimate relationships and of the transformation of such a central family practice as that of eating.

At any rate, free of any charge the FWEs have made the benevolent state present in the domestic sphere around the country. Although they might at times have been perceived as imposing, in all my experience most people were sympathetic to their efforts of 'improving our lives'. Their often intimate relationships with the population also mean that people were from an early stage linked closely up with the other local health workers – midwives and nurses. Medical doctors toured their respective districts for treatment of patients identified by the local health workers. Medical doctors, in turn, transferred those who required specialist treatment to hospital. In the course of less than a decade after independence, the state had established a pervasive network of agencies which represented an ever-stronger supplement to all the indigenous practitioners who continued, nevertheless, to be the dominant curative source.

Pregnant women represented from the outset a particularly important target group. They are offered not only maternity control, but also information about practices of hygiene and nutritious food. In addition, in a number of villages there have been established maternity wards for expectedly difficult births. Already in the mid-1970s I could observe how pregnant women were attracted to these services in large numbers. The perceived value of these state agencies was certainly reinforced by the distribution of nutritious food to expecting mothers so generously that it represents a contribution also to their respective family's consumption. The generosity of the state is underscored by the fact that not only these food supplies but medical treatment in general is provided free of charge or at a very low fee.

Moreover, the landslide development of this network by which vast sections of the population were linked up permanently with the state, involved the establishment of important instruments of government for running various health related campaigns. During the first Independence decades smallpox and measles especially caused numerous child deaths. The efficiency of Western medicine was demonstrated by the various vaccination campaigns which in short time reduced the death numbers substantially. Campaigns in the malaria infected areas (mainly north-west) had a similar impact. The multistranded capacity of the progressively institutionalized health network is patently illuminated by how conducive it was to link the population up in a further dependency on state benevolence: the distribution of food to all the needy people in the country during times of drought and crop failure.

With the background of these accounts, it seems evident that the kind of benevolent, caretaking interventions in the population which Foucault sees as a defining characteristic of 'governmentalization of the state' pertains to the implementation of health policies, programmes and projects in the state 'health sector'. Thus, in a short time after independence, the state was able to legitimize its existence as a major source of longevity and welfare – as a true *motswadintle*. Through its use of 'tactics and techniques' – rather than exercising power in an overt sense – agents of the state soon started to engage intimately with an ever-increasing section of the population, subjecting it to a perceived role of dependency in matters of existential importance. This meant, at the same time, that the state manifested itself through a major section of its governmental apparatus not in the form of a perceived repressive, controlling force, but as unmistakably caretaking and constructive.

Furthermore, this development can be related to that element of the governmentalization of the state which Foucault (1978: 21, 1990: 60ff.) has denoted 'pastoral power'. This involves a particular individuating force which is apparent in the ways in which Western medicine subjects the individual body to their regimes of cure and care. The actual individuating impact of this force is, however, somehow tempered by a central aspect of indigenous medical practices that direct attention towards the social context of a sick person, involving a range of concerns related to jealousy and breaking moral rules. In order to establish adequate remedies in the instance where sickness is diagnosed by a diviner as, for example, a matter of *dikgaba* (making a senior person 'sorry in the heart'), *boloi* (sorcery) and other occult practices or ancestral punishment, at least the extended family is mobilized and heavily engaged in the matter.

While indigenous healers conceive agents of Western medicine – and each other – as competing in the same 'market' and hence often antagonistically related, these collective concerns do not necessarily imply any resistance towards agents of Western medicine. Precisely the notion of 'market' is suggestive for the situation: just as people have 'always' moved from one indigenous healer to another, Western medicine has to a great extent become one option amongst several others. This means that there has not been any significant resistance towards state interventions in this field. But there is one exception to this – that of the HIV/AIDS epidemics. All the popular resistance to interventions in this respect, to which we now turn, is intriguing in relation to the question of the governmentalization of the state because it demonstrates perfectly how agents of the state were faced with the problem of subjecting people to the regimes of health care by working on their subjectivities – and how they have gradually managed to reduce the resistance.

Governmental Interventions in the Times of AIDS

Interventions in the population by state health agents all over the country gained tremendous momentum in the wake of the explosive development of the HIV/AIDS epidemic in Botswana. Since the first person infected by the virus was identified in 1985, the numbers have been steadily on the increase to the extent that Botswana featured, in the late 1990s, as the country with 'the highest recorded prevalence of HIV in the world' (Heald 2002: 1). Since then it has risen further. Obviously, in view of the delicacy of this matter (see below), statistical records on this matter are uncertain. It is well established, however, that the number of persons with HIV/AIDS has been continuously on the increase. According to one report, in 2004 no less than 24.3 per cent of the population (total c. 1.8 million) aged 15–64 were infected (Carter et al. 2007: 822). Three years later, about the same percentage (24) of infected population was found in the 15–49 age bracket.[3] Although some figures suggest that there has been a slight decline amongst certain categories – especially pregnant women attending antenatal clinics – there are good reasons to assume that the gross figures are still rising.[4] It has recently been reported[5] that 'fifty people in Botswana get infected daily', which amounts to some 18,250 a year.

In view of these alarming trends, it is not surprising that the state president declared (in 2003) that 'the fight against HIV/AIDS remains the greatest single challenge we face as a Nation'.[6] This challenge is more than a matter of caring for suffering individuals. At stake here are vast human resources of critical importance to the overall political economy of the country. The president took a leading role in fighting HIV/AIDS, including setting a personal example by making public the result of a blood test (negative), challenging the other political leaders to do the same. Drawing upon substantial international support in terms of finances and

3. UNAIDS and World Health Organisation 2008: 6.
4. Ibid.
5. See *Mmegi,* 6 February 2009; reporting from a recent BOTUSA-workshop. BOTUSA is, according to their website, 'a partnership of the Government of Botswana and the [US] Centres for Disease Control and Prevention that provides technical assistance, consultation, funding, and conducts research with the Botswana government and other local and international partners for prevention, treatment, care and support, and surveillance of HIV/AIDS, tuberculosis, and related conditions'.
6. 'State of the Nation Address' by His Excellency Mr. Festus Mogae, President of the Republic of Botswana, to the First Meeting of the Fifth Session of the Eighth Parliament, Gaborone, 10 November 2003.

expertise, the state has expanded the health services – and bureaucracy – tremendously.

The first instance of HIV was identified in 1985. Already in 1988 the state government 'acted speedily in an attempt to avert the coming epidemic and launched its first massive awareness campaign in 1988' (Heald 2006: 1). The infrastructure for state interventions was, as explained, established with a well-staffed countrywide network of clinics and health posts. Nevertheless, despite an ever-expanding state apparatus for intervening in the population by campaigns and 'development' programmes and projects, the prevalence of HIV has, I reiterate, been more and more acute.

One major campaign centres on the message that HIV is transmitted above all through sexual intercourse, as reflected in the motto of the government campaign – that of 'ABC' – by means of which great efforts are made to inculcate three major principles of individual sexual discipline: 'Abstain', 'Be faithful' and 'Condomise'. This campaign rests on the assumption that the population's prevailing sexual practices are indeed responsible for the extraordinarily high rates and rapid spread of HIV/AIDS in Botswana (e.g. Carter et al. 2007: 829; cf. Halperin and Epstein 2004). There is hence a significant moral dimension in the ABC code, and the deadly danger of this sexually transmittable virus is repeatedly hammered home by the health agents of the state, calling for, in the Foucauldian sense, self-government as well as self-surveillance.

However, to judge from the ever-increasing figures indicated above, this campaign has had limited impact. There is not enough space here to address this issue comprehensibly. Yet, in order to try to illuminate the intricate interface between governmental interventions of this kind and important existential concerns amongst the people, let me suggest why the ABC propaganda has become a thorny issue and met with widespread resistance if not total rejection (see Heald 2002; cf. Ingstad 1990). According to my own and others' research, the ideal of sticking to one partner is not much in line with current sexual practices (see Gulbrandsen 1986b, 1996a: ch. 11; Helle-Valle 1999, 2003; Pitso and Carmichael 2003). The information I have gathered over the past thirty years suggests that frequent changes of sexual partner prevail indiscriminately up and down the social ladder, in the rural heartlands of the *merafe* as well as in the fashionable urban areas, and among the married as well as the unmarried.[7] In popular discourse the resistance towards the state's bio-political

---

7. It has recently been reported (Carter et al. 2007: 828) that '[n]early one of four Batswana in this survey who had sex the last 12 months reported having had concurrent sexual relation-

ABC campaign has often been thematized as a matter of taking away, as expressed by one of my male acquaintances, 'the last pleasure which poor people like us are left with'. Or as Helle-Valle (1999: 391) recorded: 'Do you know what AIDS really means? It means American Ideology for Discouraging Sex'. Thus, any recommendation of 'abstention' – and to stick to one partner ('be faithful') – fell readily on barren ground. As for the use of condoms, men typically spoke of this practice as a matter of eating chocolate with paper on. Many women with whom I talked about this matter rejected condoms on the ground that 'I do not want to be treated as a prostitute'. In this atmosphere of resisting state intervention in the most private and highly esteemed parts of their lives, such rumours like 'condoms spread AIDS' travelled fast. During the late 1990s there was hence a strong resistance building up against the ABC campaign.

There are also some deeper reasons why many people have so strongly rejected state interventions in this field. When health workers present HIV/AIDS as a sexually transmittable disease through blood exchange, they invoke an idiom of great existential concern amongst most Batswana. As Schapera (1971 [1940]: 173ff.) has explained in considerable detail, sexual intercourse is associated strongly with the idea of blood exchange. Pursuing this issue during my own field work, it has not been difficult to receive confirmation of such conceptions as, 'during intercourse the woman's vaginal secretion, which is identified with her 'blood', enters the man's body through the urethra and 'summons' his semen (also termed 'blood')' (Schapera (1971 [1940]: 174). This links up with the pervasive significance of the hot-cool distinction in the thought of Tswana and other peoples of Botswana[8] that is well anchored in indigenous cosmol-

---

ship over the course of their relationship with their current partner. Forty percent suspected that one of their recent partners had other partners at the same time, and a third disagreed that most people they care about are faithful'. It is hence concluded that 'concurrency in Botswana is common'. The long-term and culturally persistent character of this sexual practice is testified not only by my own records since the mid-1970s (Gulbrandsen 1986b): forty years prior, Schapera (1933: 68–69) reported that '[f]ew of the BaKxatla, whether men or women, are still virgin at marriage. The *maxwane* (boys who are incorporated in the next *maphato* [age regiment]) are notoriously addicted to sexual licence ... Often two maxwane will copulate in succession with the same girl'. In his 'Married Life in an African Tribe' – once highly controversial for reason of being highly explicit on Tswana sexuality – Schapera (1971b: 187) related that 'adultery in the part of women seems to have increased considerably as a result of labour migration'. As for men, the Bakgatla told him that 'a man is naturally inclined to be promiscuous. "A man, like a bull cannot be confined to one kraal,"' says their proverb which one 'enthusiastic informant confirmed by stating: "They are the bulls of the tribe"' (182–83).

8. As noted (Chapter 4), Kuper (1982: 18ff) substantiates the existential importance of the 'hot'/'cool' opposition in the lives of Southern Bantu-speaking peoples in general. For the Tswana, this has been thoroughly documented by Schapera (see especially 1971b; cf. Comaroff 1985: 102–3, 174; Chapter 4 above; for the Kalanga see Werbner 1989: 311).

ogy (e.g. Comaroff 1985: 68). The existential significance of the notion of 'hot' versus 'cool' is reflected in a number of important taboos (*meila, singl moila*) related to personal conduct in relation to sexuality.[9]

The Batswana have, in other words, strong ideas of contagion through sexual relations (cf. Ingstad 1990: 34). In this sense one may well say that they are culturally overdetermined to comprehend the significance of blood exchange in relation to transmission of the HIV virus. Taking into account, furthermore, how readily most people talk about sex[10] and how often they change partners and involve themselves with more than one sexual partner at the same time, their strong resistance towards blood testing in order to determine whether they are HIV-positive presents us with a conundrum.

This conundrum can be resolved, I propose, if we consider what it would mean to a person to be identified as HIV positive in this context, taking into account that most people do not trust health workers' assurance of keeping test results secret. The health workers teach everyone who wants to listen that the HIV virus is not only transmittable by sexual intercourse. It is indeed deadly if not treated, and it cannot be removed by any cure. In other words, a person who considers being HIV positive might not only be told that he or she is in danger of being deadly sick. The person runs the risk of being identified as a person with whom nobody will engage sexually. That would be a disaster for men as well as women. Schapera (1971b: 162 ff., see also 1933) has related in a rarely detailed ethnography of sexual relations based upon his field work amongst the Bakgatla in the 1930s, that sexuality is highly esteemed – amongst men as well as women – for reasons that go far beyond procreation. As monogamy had, at that time, been generally enforced, the pleasure of sex was, Schapera reported, cultivated extensively in pre- and extramarital sexual relations. Reading these pages to friends of mine on different occasions, the common response was: 'He is telling the truth', asserting, in addition, that sexual intercourse is not only a matter of immediate pleasure;

---

9. A person can become 'hot' for a wide range of reasons, like being in a period of mourning after the death of a spouse, having visited a newly confined mother, being in a menstrual period, having had sex recently etc. A 'hot' person can inflict harm in a number of ways. In the particular case of sexual intercourse, Schapera (1971b: 174) explains that if a woman's '"blood" is "hot," it is too "strong" or "heavy" for the man; it thickens inside his body, and cannot be ejaculated, but settles on his lips and loins'. In consequence, if not properly 'doctored' he might become seriously ill from a range of different diseases and even die. Furthermore, '[s]imilarly, if a man with "hot blood" sleeps with a woman, his "blood", instead of mixing with hers in her womb to make her conceive, flows over into her lips, where it remains to trouble her'.

10. Schapera (1971b: 161) reports that he experienced this kind of openness already in the 1930s: 'I was continually struck by the open importance they attached to sexual aspects. They have little prudery in matters of this kind'.

it is essential to bodily strength, health and vitality. The prevailing values, conceptions and practices of sexuality are, in the case of men, epitomized by the proverbial notion of 'A man, like a bull, cannot be confined
to one kraal' (see footnote 7, cf. Gulbrandsen 1986b). For women sexual
relations entail pregnancy and motherhood, involving crucial values of
caring, central to the construction of womanhood.

The risk of being identified as HIV positive and known as such in the
larger social context is tantamount to risk being excommunicated from
one of the most attractive and esteemed spheres of life. Added to this
existentially crucial concern is that the state's ABC campaign underscores that 'AIDS is a sexually transmitted disease infecting the blood
... [strengthening] its popular association with dirtiness, heat, and promiscuity' (Klaits 2010: 47). The notion of 'promiscuity' in the Botswana
context (*bobolete* or *boaka*), explains Helle-Valle (1999: 388ff), contrasts
sharply with the common Western notion as it does not necessarily involve condemnation of women that make material gains from plural sexual relations. The women who are stigmatized are in addition perceived
as egoistic and antisocial, spending the resources they gain on themselves
– typically being addicted to alcohol – and thus leading a life that involves grave neglect of their children.

This notion links up with a long-standing conception of other diseases
as sexually transmitted in the sense of being sourced by women who irre-
sponsibly have engaged, as suggested above, in sexual relations in a state
of being 'hot', e.g. having recently had a miscarriage, being in the menstrual period or newly bereaved (see Schapera 1971b: 173ff.; cf. Livingston 2005: 172f.). This conception spills into current popular discourse on
HIV/AIDS in ways that readily condemn HIV-positives as promiscuous
in the sense of being careless, irresponsible and destructive (see Klaits
2010: 46ff.). This conception affects thus above all women; however,
people have for long also condemned a man if he has slept with women
identified as 'hot' (see Schapera 1971b: 177). These features of stigmatization and consequent shame are patently expressed in all the cases where
patients in their terminal phase are hidden. The significance of the shame
connected with HIV/AIDS as a 'sexual disease' is particularly apparent
during funerals at which time nobody would dare to suggest openly that
the deceased has been infected by the HIV virus (see Klaits 2005).

Does all this mean that the massive state interventions to combat the
spread of the virus for more than two decades have been counterproductive in the sense of intensifying popular negative discourse on HIV/
AIDS? There have been some indications of a lower rate of increase in
the number of HIV-positives over the past years, the most important one

being a decrease in HIV infection levels among pregnant women attending antenatal clinics from 36 per cent in 2001 to 32 per cent in 2005 (see UNAIDS and World Health Organisation 2008: 6). If this is actually a trend, it probably reflects that these women comprise a section of the population which is most intensively under the influence of state health workers (cf. preceding section). But this is still a weak trend, which underscores how hard it has been for state bio-politics to influence people's subjectivities in the pursuit of changing their sexual practices. Nevertheless, this is a trend which corresponds well with the following response from many of my male acquaintances, especially amongst the younger generation, when I ask if they are not worried about having multiple partners: 'Now I condomise, and then it is no problem'. For reasons already indicated, abstention and to be faithful are not in question, while the C in the ABC campaigns seems gradually and reluctantly to be accepted. To the extent this is true, the state interventions in the population have changed their regime of sexual behaviour and hence, in the present context, a significant aspect of their subjectivities.

There is, moreover, a recent trend for an increasing number of people to go for blood testing, which appears contradictory to what I explained above about fears of being stigmatized as HIV positive. In my analysis this trend is comprehensible in light of the availability of antiretroviral therapy (ARV) since 2000. While this option was earlier met with considerable scepticism in the population, people's experience of an ever-increasing number of their young relatives and friends being seriously ill and dying 'like flies' and, also, testimonies of people who have actually benefited from this therapy have raised the receptivity of the medication. Actually, it has increased very substantially over the last years and is now (March 2009) approaching 150,000 patients who are on this government- and foreign aid–sponsored, extremely expensive ARV medication.

All the resources spent by government and aid agencies on campaigns – and especially medication – illuminate state practices that represent the defining characteristics of a modern, governmentalized state – the state that provides life, rather than threatens its subjects with death. That is, a state whose end is the longevity and welfare of the population and which, in the pursuit of reaching this end, intervenes in the population, even in the most intimate spheres of people's lives. The conception of the wealth of the state as, in a Foucauldian sense, vested in the population, is expressed in the state leaderships' tremendous concern about the high death rates caused by the epidemics. Not surprisingly, the fear is that the prevalence of HIV/AIDS amongst the younger generation, in particular, is going to reduce seriously the effect of all the resources which the state has invested in the population – in the pursuit of improving everybody's lives as well as increasing the wealth of the nation.

This development has tremendously intensified the interface between the state and the population – and ultimately brought an ever-increasing number of people to a life-critical dependency on the state by their acceptance of ARV medication. Thousands and thousands of people are subjected to the state health regime for the rest of their life. On a daily basis their medication reminds them about their fundamental dependency upon a benevolent, caring state. In this sense they are captured into the state-centred web of power. People's adoption of these medical practices thus involves, as suggested in the introductory remarks with reference to Foucault, the development of those elements constitutive to individuals which at the same time give strength to the state.

In my view, this is a very important connection because the perceived, existentially critical dependencies on the state do not only pertain to all the people actually on medication, but also to their close relatives. Moreover, its political significance is underscored by the fact that a vast section of the people on medications includes precisely those people who represent a potential challenge to the sustainability of the state: young, poor men between twenty and forty years living in urban centres (cf. the following chapter).

Yet, however important, this trend involves a critical ambiguity: the irony is that ARV does not limit the spread of the virus. On the contrary, it keeps HIV-positive people fit to be sexually active. And so they can be without other constraints that they might set on themselves. For, as it is often complained of these days: 'Now we cannot judge by people's appearance if they are positive or not'. This conception underscores the individuating force of this state regime which offers individuals secret blood tests and subsequently equally secret medication, keeping the person free from any symptoms of HIV/AIDS with which the population have, in due course, become very familiar.

The expansion of such state health regimes in relation to the mounting numbers of HIV-positives means, I re-emphasize, that an ever-larger portion of the population is brought into permanent dependency upon existentially critical state health care. Obviously, this is a kind of subjection to the state which adds to its strength. Moreover, momentum is given to the expansion of the state bureaucracy which engages internationally with donor agents and research centres and, above all, strengthens the network of state health institutions all over the country. This expansion of a governmentalized state is, however, extremely costly. Not only the human resources and physical infrastructure to cope with such large numbers of patients but also the medication itself represents a tremendous financial challenge. Even if the state has some success in all the efforts to obtain foreign support, it will always be left with an ever-increasing bill unless its health agencies succeed in radically reforming people's sexual practices. It all very much depends upon the diamonds.

State Efforts to Enhance the Wealth of the Nation

The enhancement of popular productivity – to ensure the welfare of each and every one and hence the wealth of the nation – is an ingrained dimension of any Western governmental state. Western agents of 'development' readily perceived ample space for improving crop and animal husbandry practices. At the time of Botswana's independence, the country was heavily dependent upon import of food yet, at the same time, characterized by gross underuse of labour and land (Gulbrandsen 1996a: ch. 8) A number of Western agricultural experts, in addition to those few left over from the colonial state, worked in two complementary directions. On the one hand, the existing very modest agricultural extension service was expanded tremendously and had reached most of Eastern Botswana (where the vast majority of agriculturalists live) at the time of my first arrival in 1975. On the other hand, substantial resources were devoted to establishing crop and animal research centres in order to adapt Western agronomic and veterinary knowledge to the specific conditions for crop and animal husbandry in Botswana. This also involved conducting extensive statistical surveys of farming practices, generating knowledge that formed a baseline from which to design various improved farming regimes (see Gulbrandsen 1996a: 135 ff.). In turn, this kind of knowledge was fed into Botswana's Agricultural College, which produced a large number of agricultural extension workers, known as agricultural demonstrators (ADs).

During my early days in Botswana, I followed some of the ADs on bicycle or horseback over long distances – from farm to farm – and observed their enthusiastic promotion of so-called improved husbandry techniques. In many instances farmers would already have heard about these new techniques from the authoritative presentations given by visiting high-ranking officials in their local (see the preceding chapter) *kgotla*. In these local contexts I could observe how the ADs meticulously attempted to explain the effects of the new techniques. They followed up the farmers' progress by revisiting them frequently in order to assure them about the applicability, cost-effectiveness and productivity of various new methods. They shared the farmers' happiness when they succeeded and encouraged them to try again when they failed. Occasionally these ADs would request government trucks to bring larger groups to see the impressive growth of maize and sorghum in the fields of these successful pioneer farmers. Among these official efforts to deal persistently with farmers in 'depth and detail' in their everyday lives, one, in particular, stood out: a group of British agricultural specialists who set up a resource centre, far from any village, amidst a farming community where they lived with their own families and engaged with the surrounding farmers on a daily basis.

All the ADs were incorporated in the state bureaucracy, linking them up with a hierarchy that expanded the ministerial headquarters in the capital through a nationwide network to the regional and district offices. This hierarchy monitored the work on the ground and continuously passed on information to the ADs, who would then attempt to convince those farmers who had reached a certain level of competence to go on brief, intensive courses. Their identity as *farmers* was further sustained if they succeeded in gaining a diploma. These were a significant asset for farmers who wanted to apply for financial support from the government, since they expressed the farmers' commitment to the agricultural values propagated by the government. These state campaigns and interventions were subsequently systematized in composite packages, including donkey draught-power, by which numerous smallholders received some state subsidies, although by no means to the extent which cattle owners who operated on a commercial level gained from state livestock programmes (cf. Chapter 3).

No campaigns were required in relation to these cattle owners: the tremendous economic benefit of all the state-sponsored livestock schemes was quickly realized, bringing many of them into a tremendous spiral of economic growth. Still, these private enterprises have always been highly integral to a governmentalized state being heavily dependent upon all its projects and programmes (cf. Chapter 3).

Commercial cattle raising has developed a spirit of accumulation that flourishes a long way down the social ladder, involving a number of younger people of middle-range social background. During the first two decades following independence in particular, these were ambitious people, often educated with a handsome salary as government employees. This meant they were at once caught up in the structures of governmental intervention in agriculture and subjected to the state structure as civil servants, and this involves another structuration of subjectivity in resonance with state domination.

While the middle-range and large farmers and cattle owners have benefited very substantially from the financial and technical support, state projects and programmes have not contributed significantly to raise the productivity amongst smallholders for reasons which I explain extensively elsewhere (Gulbrandsen 1996a, esp. ch. 6). Until the beginning of the 1980s, the typical rural household amongst these sections was economically based mainly upon labour migration to South Africa, with animal husbandry and agriculture as supplementary sources to varying degrees. They were only partially and often temporarily able to adapt to 'improved' production practices, and they have hence been under limited impact of state agricultural development programmes.[11]

In the 1980s the conditions became even worse because the possibility for labour migration declined substantially, while opportunities for unskilled labour increased very significantly with the rapid expansion of the urban centres, especially the capital of Gaborone. This means that while young men – always on temporary contracts with mining companies in South Africa – used to return for ploughing, they were now on permanent contracts and progressively oriented towards an urban adaptation. In addition to this came a progressive decline in crop prices which resulted in the economic significance of arable farming falling correspondingly.

This trend was accelerated with successive years of drought which prompted the state to intervene with a new programme. Known as ARAP,[12] this programme subsidized smallholders heavily by covering their cost of hiring a tractor for ploughing their fields. The programme, increasingly combined with substantial handouts of food, placed an ever-increasing section of the rural population on a quite permanent dependency on the state for obtaining basic subsistence goods. However, while the previous agricultural programmes had been campaigned with reference to one of the 'national principles' – that of *boipelego* (self-reliance), which applies to the individual family as well as to society at large (cf. Chapter 5) – the vast sections of impoverished people more and more relied on the state. I have observed how agents of the state during their campaigns have increasingly expressed concern that people will continue to be passive recipients of public support. 'Development', it was insisted, 'is a matter of helping people to be self-reliant'. The government should assist, but people themselves must actively engage in improving their lives, promoting their communities and contributing to nation building (cf. Durham 2002: 152). Hence, however welfare oriented, the government programmes and policies, as elsewhere, have the idea of empowerment as an important component (cf. Gupta and Sharma 2006: 285f.).

And yet, even if the state has failed to empower all the poor rural families to produce at least what is sufficient for their own subsistence, one may argue that they have nevertheless been captured into networks of

---

11. The temporality of engaging in agricultural programmes reflects the fact that there was usually a short span of time between when a male family head finished labour migration and one or more of the sons started supplying the family with cash from this source (Gulbrandsen 1996a: 177ff.).

12. Accelerated Rainfed Arable Programme.

state power because of their strong dependency on the state for survival. This point is testified by the fact that this section of the population has always represented a substantial electoral support of the ruling party. Their support has been rewarded and cultivated, especially prior to elections, by generous 'rural development' programmes.

The Spread of Western Education

The governmentalized state's tactics and techniques of intervention – in depth and detail – are particularly apparent in the field of education. The fact that the levels of education at independence were very low, even by African standards, reflects the extent to which the British kept the population 'underdeveloped' rather than any rejection of Western knowledge. I have explained how the virtues of knowledge and wisdom form the core of the discursive field of the *kgotla*, being told more than once that 'a little knowledge is dangerous'. With the increasing significance of 'modern' issues also in the context of the *kgotla*, formal education in schools was hence widely appreciated. I often enough registered how people who spent most of their time in the bush (at the cattle post) were regarded as uncivilized and ignorant about matters that counted. These matters were naturally concerned with 'traditional knowledge', including familiarity with the vast normative system of *mekgwa le melao* and a command of 'deep Setswana' with all its metaphorical complexities. However, there is no indication of a fundamental distrust of, or a ban against, 'Western' knowledge. In line with the pragmatic Tswana approach to external forces, epitomized by their early fascination with evangelizing missionaries, they saw the utility of appropriating such cultural resources and rarely perceived them as threatening. As issues of modernity became more and more important in the context of the *kgotla*, where knowledge-based reasoning is not only required but highly esteemed (see Chapter 4), education was increasingly considered as crucial. Indeed in due course it became an asset of considerable political significance, as manifested by the up-and-coming 'new men' (see Chapter 2).

This appreciation of knowledge meant that the massive postcolonial state intervention in education was nothing more than most people had been led to expect. During the first decade following independence, primary schools were constructed all over the country. This development accelerated in the 1980s with an almost equally widely dispersed expansion of secondary schools. In due course higher education was developed, with the capacity to train and educate vast numbers of undergraduate and graduate students.

While it would be wrong to make a sharp distinction between 'traditional' and 'Western' knowledge, discursive practices for disseminating knowledge in modern educational institutions differ radically from those of the *merafe*. In the latter case, knowledge and wisdom are markers of rank. Within Tswana cosmology senior people – ultimately the royal ancestors – are the recognized custodians of collective cultural and symbolic wealth, including knowledge and wisdom. Junior people are not supposed to acquire knowledge actively in the sense of making inquiries and 'asking too many questions'; they are to be informed when it is appropriate and timely. The extent to which this practice is inculcated in children often came home to me in the form of teachers' complaints about the ostensible timidity of their pupils. I was told, for example, that

> they are simply afraid to ask questions; we have a great job to make them confident to engage actively in acquiring knowledge. I have to tell them all the time to ask questions; when I teach them to take issue with me and express disagreement ... to object against what we as their seniors are saying, they get confused ... it might take several years to get them to feel free to perform in such ways. Sooner or later they recognize that only in such ways they can make good achievements and prosper.

In other words, through educational institutions the state intervenes persistently on a broad front in relation to the population, working on young people's consciousness to create subjectivities that are instilled with aspirations to acquire knowledge in order to prosper in the pursuit of social mobility, on a highly individualized basis. With vast numbers of expatriates in the civil service, the state was always ready during the first independence decades to absorb most of those who received at least secondary education. Within this context, they were further socialized into a state apparatus where many of them actually became themselves part of the apparatus of governmentality – as health workers, agricultural demonstrators, veterinary assistants, teachers etc.

This means that the large majority of young, educated sections of the populations were caught into a web of state power they could not easily escape as long as there were very few career options. This involved, in particular, that they were all barred from engaging in politics and committed to be loyal to the authorities within the structures in which they were employed. In view of how integral the private sector – which expanded from the late 1980s onwards – is to the state-centred political economy in Botswana, this web of power also encompassed the increasing numbers employed here.

Conclusion

In view of the massive state interventions in the population 'to increase of its wealth, longevity, health, longevity, wealth' (Foucault 1978: 17), there can hardly be any doubt that the postcolonial state in Botswana appears – in marked contrast to the preceding colonial state – as a state where governmentality has been in strong progress. In this respect, the postcolonial state represents a radical break with the preceding precolonial and colonial states. But, note, the governmentalization of the postcolonial state has depended much upon 'positive power' – in the Foucauldian sense – vested in indigenous authority structures (see Chapter 5). Recall also how indigenous administration justice all over the country has become integral to the modern state at the same time as it has remained an existentially positive force in people's lives (see Chapter 4).

As I indicated in the preceding chapter and as I shall elaborate in the chapter that follows, this does not mean that the state embodies no repressive and violent structures. It means that the state, in highly apparent ways, has expanded very extensive networks of agencies that articulate constantly and directly with people all over the country in their respective communities. As we have seen, they even appear frequently at people's doorsteps to provide state support. Although people are not always attracted by what these agencies have to offer, especially in the field of health, or are able to exploit state services, as in agriculture, the agent's of state nevertheless try to appear as gentle and supportive. Consequently such interventions as I have reviewed in this chapter convey, at least, an image of the postcolonial state as a *positive power*. Patently, these state interventions seem to support the legitimacy of the state as they to a great extent satisfy all the expectations that are continuously raised in the population by, as I explained in the preceding chapter, state officials who encounter people recurrently around the country in the context of the *kgotla*.

There is a further significance to this that follows from the high degree of correspondence between, on the one hand, what I have identified as the hegemonic discourse of development exercised by these officials in the *kgotla* context (Chapter 6), and, on the other hand, the discursive practices – for example, in the fields of agriculture and health 'development' – into which people are drawn constantly by all the state 'foot soldiers'. That is, these state agencies have continuously attempted to inculcate such ideas and practices in the population which are conducive to develop a popular imaginary of the state as benevolent and hence inhibit celebrated qualities of indigenous authorities (cf. Chapter 5).

In a sense, these are hegemonic practices to which most of the peoples of this country and beyond have been subject since the evangelizing missionaries arrived in the early nineteenth century (see Comaroff and Comaroff 1991). There is, however, a tremendous difference in scale, intensity and resources distributed. In addition comes, importantly, the all-embracing penetration of market forces which, in a short time after independence, generated ever-more-extensive features of consumerism. These processes, combined with state exercise of the hegemonic discourse of development, have certainly worked upon people's subjectivities in ways highly conducive to the development of a capitalist, 'developmental' state. The significance of these processes is most apparent in the massive formation of 'modern' subjectivities through Western education and the progressive employment of Batswana by state and private enterprises. Education is obviously the field in which the 'governmentalized' state has most successfully worked upon subjects in 'depth and detail', inculcating such dispositions that attune the rapidly growing younger section of the population to live and work in urban centres, radically different from that of descent-group, 'tribal' contexts in the rural areas.

While education certainly is a matter of developing individuals in ways conducive to the strength of the state (Foucault 1990: 82), state interventions in the fields of agriculture and health are, in this respect, a more dubious matter. In agriculture, I have explained, state interventions did not succeed on a broad scale, partly because the vast majority lacked the initial assets to take advantage of them and partly because the state has intervened amongst these sections of the population with such forms of subsidies that they were brought into a permanent dependency on state support for their basic subsistence. This is obviously a matter of state care for the population, ensuring its longevity etc. But these interventions do, to be sure, not make the state strong by enhancing the nation's productivity. On the contrary, they are tapping the state treasury. Nevertheless, the ever-increasing popular dependency on the state has contributed to continuous popular support of the ruling party and has hence been important for the strength and sustainability of the state.

A similar argument can be made in relation to health. On the one hand, it is, as we have seen, questionable how much state interventions in this field have impacted on popular bodily practices 'in depth and detail'. Most apparently, all the shortcomings of the ABC campaigns have had disastrous consequences for thousands and thousands of individuals and families as well as for the entire nation with the tremendous loss of valuable human resources. On the other hand, some state campaigns have succeeded, like those which have increased the acceptance of blood testing and medication that counteract the consequences of the HIV/AIDS epidemics to a certain extent. This trend has progressively reduced all the suffering amongst the very large number of people who are HIV positive. Furthermore, the medication has constrained the loss of young, well-educated persons. This trend works obviously in support of the 'developmental' state. Moreover, the fact that a very substantial and rapidly increasing section of the younger generation are critically dependent on state-sponsored medication for the rest of their lives is certainly a matter of bringing vast numbers of potentially rebellious people under tight state control. The other side of the coin, however, is that the medication is, at least at the present time, extremely expensive. Only a diamond-driven state economy can possibly manage to 'care' for the population to this extent.

All the state campaigns and other interventions in the wake of the HIV/AIDS epidemics illustrate perfectly the progressive character of governmentalization of the state: As we have seen, at the time this epidemic took off, extensive governmental practices and structures for intervening in the population in relation to 'health' were already in place. With this epidemic, these practices and structures expanded tremendously. A similar point can by made in relation to food distribution. Furthermore, in the field of agriculture initial practices and structures of 'extension services' facilitated the intervention in the population by ever-new 'development' programmes which resulted in a progressive expansion of these practices and structures themselves.

In summary, although it is hard to known exactly how these interventions have been working upon people's subjectivities, it seems reasonable to maintain that the state's massive, widespread and persistent intervention in the population has contributed to the fact that the population, in various ways, has been caught up in the processes of state formation. First, I have identified a range of indigenous power relations of in the domains of agriculture, education and health in the process of being governmentalized, 'that is to say, elaborated, rationalized, and centralized ... under the auspices of state institutions' (Foucault 1982: 224). Patently, in the course of only a couple of decades upon the Independence, vast numbers of young people have been caught up in disciplinary institutions of primary and secondary schools and higher education that have been instilling radically new cultural orientation and social aspirations. That is, disposition critically important for subjecting people – without question – to new structures of power radiating from the centre of the modern state. I have made a similar argument for the all the state health campaigns. The impacts of these and a number of other state interventions in the populations are reflected in the rapid and smooth character of Botswana's wide-ranging post-colonial transformations.

Second, a governmentalized state like the present one depends on the employment of a very large number of people as civil servants who are, for obvious reasons, captured into the state process in very committing

ways. Third, a 'governmentalized' state embodies a tremendous apparatus
– in the form of personnel and physical structures – distributed permanently and widely throughout the country in ways that express powerfully
the existence of the state. Moreover, the transformative potentialities of
these apparatuses make the state always able to intervene in the population in new ways.

All that said about the development of practices and structures of 'governmentality' which might be seen as operating as 'State apparatus of capture' in the sense of Deleuze and Guattari (1991: 424ff.), I shall finally
emphasize that a govermentalized state might, apparently paradoxically,
generate forces counteracting hierarchy, order and hence the strength of
the state. That is, forces with rhizomic potentialities. These closing words
are intended as a prelude to the following chapter which pursues this issue by addressing the question of postcolonial class formation. I shall, in
particular, be concerned with societal conflicts in progress, springing from
what I shall identify as a contradiction between the common good and
individual accumulation of power and wealth.

Foucault's (1978: 21) conception of 'governmentality' includes, as suggested above, a major element of what he calls 'the pastoral'. Foucault derives his notion of 'pastoral power' from the Christian notion of 'the shep-
herd-sheep relationship as one of individual and complete dependence'.
He asserts that this notion had for more than a millennium been linked
to a defined religious institution when it 'suddenly spread to the whole
social body' which, in combination with 'political power', gave rise to 'an
individualising "tactic" which characterised a series of powers' (Foucault
1982: 215, cf. 1990). Apparently, this notion of 'pastoral' power has some
resonance with the Tswana maxim *Kgosi ke modisa ya morafe* ('The *kgosi* is
the shepherd of the *morafe*'). However, this is a notion of authority that
operates in support of the 'common good' – above all *kagiso* – by keeping
subjects obedient to the law which, Foucault (1978: 12) stresses, predates
'governmentality'. It is a matter of collective 'submission to sovereignty' while he is concerned with governmental practices that lead 'to an
end which is "convenient" for *each* of the things that are to be governed'
(1978: 13, italics added). Hence, the state's exercise of 'pastorship' represents a major 'individualising power' (Foucault 1990: 60).

This contrast is apparent in all fields examined in the present case:
animal and crop husbandry practices were 'customarily' conducted within
the larger context of the extended family where, significantly, productivity was promoted by indigenous practices of 'medication' under the
overall conduct of an extended family figure. By 'governmental' interventions, however, state agencies relate to the individual 'farmer' by making

productivity – and profitability – a matter of individual husbandry skills and economic management. Furthermore, in contrast to the highly individualized, even confidential, approach of state health workers, people's health problems are indeed a family, even community, matter in most indigenous contexts of diagnosing and treatment. Above all, the modern system of education brings children into contexts where their individual capacities are continuously in focus, being stimulated constantly to *achieve* knowledge and actively progress as self-governed individuals in ways that contrast, as I have explained, radically with the regime of knowledge within family and community contexts.

Consequently, together with commodity and labour market forces, these state interventions have certainly contributed very substantially to the generation of *individual* aspirations amongst an ever-larger section of the population. This is, of course, most apparent amongst those who successfully are entering modern careers bringing them to power and wealth. But, as we shall see as we now turn to the next chapter, this also applies to large numbers of people who do not succeed and amongst whom there are consequently significant discrepancies between aspirations and achievement.

This development is closely related to the issue of class formation, which I shall, finally, comment briefly upon with reference to Foucault's (1978: 17) assertion that the *population* is 'above all else the ultimate end of government' within the 'governmentalized' state: however helpful I have found the conception of 'governmentality' for coming to terms with processes which have obviously contributed to make the population gradually integral to state processes in the present context, this quotation leaves the impression of a state governed by altruistic interests vested in the state itself, beyond the population. Above all, it is a conception of the state as unaffected by the interests of any dominant section of the population. In order to remedy this limitation we need to compliment the present examination of state processes from the perspective of 'governmentality' by taking into account such processes and structures as I analysed in Chapter 3. The following chapter hence centres on social and political repercussions arising from state interventions that have, in important respects, served the interests of the people of power and wealth, yet kept vast numbers in poverty and left an ever-increasing number of young people in a state of disillusion.

Chapter 8

ESCALATING INEQUALITY
Popular Reactions to Political Leaders

The strength of the postcolonial state and the sustainability of the ruling group are clearly conditioned by its successful capture of the different
parts of the population into the processes of nation-state building. This
development involves, however, transformations that work upon the relationship between the different categories of people. In Chapter 5 I explained how the state's subscription to liberalism and social equity spills
into the prevailing relationships between dominant Tswana and minorities. I indicated how state policies and programmes have progressively
divided the population into social classes – a multitude of social classes in
the sense of Hardt and Negri (2005: 104ff.) which have evolved within
a highly state-centred political economy. In my comprehension they fall
into two major categories: on the one hand, the privileged few who have
been advantaged by the generous state programmes supporting, financially and technically, commercial enterprises and rise to power and wealth;
on the other hand, the large majority who have been drawn into state dependency through the various welfare programmes, vast sections of which
are persistently stuck in poverty. Hence I am centrally concerned with a
major division of class that is driven by the political leadership's management of the diamond-sourced wealth of the state treasury.

   These transformations are, of course, not particular to the modern
state development in this country. But they have some distinctive repercussions which I shall examine in this chapter, to a great extent following

from the fact that they are strongly propelled by a state-centred political economy. Most apparently, political leaders-cum-successful business-
people have come under attack in a pervasive popular discourse which
identifies such people as abusers of power and occult practitioners. This
discourse is conceived in terms of indigenous notions of power and power
abuse, with great significance for popular surveillance of rulers' exercise
of authority and people's critique of authorities' power abuse. We shall
see how people, armed with such notions, are constructing highly damaging narratives, resembling Scott's (1990: 4) 'hidden transcripts'. The discourse – centred on imaginaries of ritual murder – focuses critically on the
problematic of the hidden exercise of power amongst people of power and
wealth and has, I shall argue, gained a strong existential significance amid
many people because of the ambiguous constructive/destructive dynamic
of 'magic', giving rise to deep moral concern and causing widespread anxiety and fear (cf. Evans-Pritchard 1984: 51ff.). In the present context, I see
the development of this discourse as another aspect of how the symbolic
wealth vested in indigenous structures plays into modern state formation.

As this suggests, this is a discursive practice that traces rhizomic forces
at the centre of the state, which means that it captures a spectrum of people that goes beyond all the unprivileged sections of the population. Yet,
the driving force in this subaltern discourse is a progressive polarization
between the few who have, in popular perception, risen rapidly to power
and wealth and the large majority of people amongst whom a substantial
part falls below the official poverty datum line.[1] This situation of 'poverty in the midst of plenty' (Gulbrandsen 1996a) has become increasingly
critical for the legitimacy of political leaders. They have spearheaded an
economic 'development' which has made the country amongst the most
inequitable on earth (see Good 2008: 67; Samatar 1999: 189). This is the
implication of not only the generous financial and technical support of

---

1. In 1975 the government conducted a 'rural income distribution survey' which concluded
that 45 per cent of the population was living below the official poverty datum line, amongst
whom a significant section were living significantly below official poverty datum line which
means *extreme poverty* (see Gulbrandsen 1996a). About 40 per cent of the population had an
income not significantly above the poverty datum line, while only some 10 per cent were distinctly well off in terms of income (Government of Botswana 1976: 76–77). Ten years later
the number of households below the poverty datum line had *increased* to 59 per cent. In the
wake of massive movements to the urban centres of Botswana from the mid-1980s, regional
differences emerged, with more than 70 per cent under this threshold amongst the population
of the western part of the country, while the percentage was significantly lower in urban areas,
which is natural because the majority of those that were able to reside there also had income
(see Siphambe 2005: 203). On the whole, during the period of time with which I am mainly
concerned (1966–1990) wealth discrepancies accelerated and a substantial proportion of the
population were left in poverty, even in extreme poverty. This gross picture has been perpetuated to the present.

a privileged minority, but also of the state's salary scale that ranges, on a monthly basis, from less than 1,000 to 30,000 pula² and more (cf. P. Werbner 2010b: 698f.). The consequent progressive polarization of the dominant class and those classes positioned disadvantageously in relation to the state and its treasury, patently reflects that the poorest 40 per cent of the population 'experienced a fall in their income from 11.6 per cent in 1993/94 to only 5.8 per cent, while the share of the richest 20 per cent rose from 59.3 per cent at the start of the period to 70.9 per cent in 2002/03' (Good 2008: 68).

In order to background the issue of this chapter, let me briefly review some aspects of inequality and class formation evolving during postcolonial times. Although there seem to be egalitarian tendencies everywhere (Parry 1974), none of the communities I know in Botswana subscribes to egalitarianism in a radical sense, the San-speaking peoples being an obvious exception (Gulbrandsen 1991). Their appreciation of hierarchy finds its expression, as Burchell (1824: 347) observed amongst the Tswana nearly two hundred years ago, in a perception of authority and wealth as two sides of the same coin. This notion reflects how people have 'always' seen wealth – especially in the form of cattle – as a critically important condition for exercising authority in the pursuit of social order and hence *kagiso*; that is, I recall, the life-giving common good upon which everyone depends (Chapter 4 above). We have seen how this perception underpinned the cattle-driven political economy of the Tswana rulers and thus the expansion in scale and strength of their polities. In other words, the hierarchical order of these polities presupposed a close connection between authority and wealth; culturally perceived as not simply 'natural' but, indeed, existentially critical to everyone (see Chapter 1 above; Gulbrandsen 1996a: ch. 3).

This compares well with Taylor's (2004: 11) suggestion that in Western, premodern social imaginaries, 'hierarchical differentiation itself is seen as the proper order of things'. With the individualizing forces of modernity, these imaginaries come under challenge, as we shall see in the present case. Although the political leadership has tried to draw upon the symbolic wealth of indigenous, premodern structures of authority, it has at the same time made the case for its antithesis – individual achievement – which is, as we shall see, associated indigenously with the dangerous personal characteristics of greed and selfishness. Virtues of individual achievement have been, as we saw in the preceding chapter, promoted forcefully

---

2. One dollar gives approximately 6.7 pula (August 2011).

by the state itself, from the beginning of the independence era, through governmental interventions in the population in the effort of reforming people's subjectivities in accordance with the orientations of the modern state. Combined with massive expansion of commodity markets, people's attraction to individual consumerism has been strongly stimulated.

Added to this comes that while wealthy people, i.e. owners of large cattle herds, used to be very careful with displaying their wealth, post-colonial developments mean that rich people now do not worry about driving around in luxury cars, appearing in expensive clothing and living in large, attractive houses in fashionable quarters. Hence, the conditions for poor people to perceive their poverty as a matter of personal misery is far stronger than it was before this development took off in the mid-1980s. One critical aspect of state intervention has accelerated this de-velopment: undermining small-holding agriculture and directing young people into secondary schools and higher education which, combined with urbanization and consumerism, have generated strong aspirations for well-paid jobs. These are, however, aspirations that less and less can be met by the labour market, *leaving many young, educated people with an acute discrepancy between aspirations and achievements*.

These are, to be sure, developments that can be traced in many places throughout the world. What makes the present case particular is, first, the pace of the transformations, second, the rather extreme features of massive poverty in the midst of plenty and, third, a cultural context that enables people to create narratives of political leaders' perceived power abuse, feeding into pervasive subaltern discourses.

I want thus to explain the development and the exercise of a popular discourse on occult practices that involves the formation of a particu-lar kind of class consciousness amongst the poor and unprivileged that focuses on the state leadership because it is, to a great extent, people's positioning in relation to the state treasury – sourced by the diamond industry – which determines their destiny. With the point of departure in a series of events which was perceived as a matter of dreadful occult prac-tices, I shall demonstrate how notions of power and power abuse rooted in indigenous cosmologies have been given a particular meaning in the postcolonial context of representational democracy, bureaucracy and the market economy. In the final part of this chapter I ask what the implica-tions are of the emerging class consciousness in relation to political pro-cesses and party politics. Since I am here concerned with transformations that gained momentum only after the late 1980s, the ethnography of this chapter will predominantly be from the time after 1990.

The Tragic Death of Segametsi and Its Aftermath: 'People in Botswana Disappear These Days!'

On 6 November 1994, the body of Segametsi Mogomotsi – a fourteen-year-old schoolgirl – was found killed with her genitals taken away outside a school fence in Mochudi, the royal town of the Bakgatla (cf. Chapter 4). This village is less than an hour's drive from the capital of Gaborone and is closely integrated with it. Although I was not in the field when the murder occurred, the repercussions of this and other similar cases were evident later in 1994, when I returned to the field, and during all my subsequent fieldwork. During my last visit (in 2008) the concern with Segametsi was still evident, emphasizing the continued significance of this case in the popular imagination.[3]

The murder, which recalled a case when two Gaborone girls were killed in similar fashion, was often discussed among my friends and acquaintances, and everyone was prepared to offer an opinion. 'We were all terribly shocked', one woman told me. 'She had been killed in the most brutal manner ... the murderers had taken away her private parts'. This act, repeatedly alluded to by my informants, is usually identified as the distinctive characteristic of a ritual murder. Beyond the tremendous anxiety caused by the murder of a young girl in the midst of the village, many people were horrified by its exceptional brutality: 'Do you know what these cruel people do? People say that they cut off the private parts while the person is still alive! They believe that it becomes even more powerful in that way. It is terrible! Terrible! People are so scared'.

It is generally agreed that the genitalia of a young girl are extremely potent 'medicine', known as *muti*.[4] I heard numerous similar accounts of babies and especially young girls who had vanished. In the words of one man:

> The problem is that the police never find the bodies. People are terrified by what is going on; they are so afraid of leaving their children alone. Children, in particular, are disappearing in Botswana these days, I am telling you! Therefore, people have become very, very upset by this case, because this is not the only one. There are many, many! And do you know what? They are always increasing when an election is approaching. Why? That is the time when the big politicians feel a need of strengthening themselves.

---

3. Within the limits of the present work, I pursue the issue of 'ritual murder' predominantly with reference to the case of Segametsi; I intend to deal with other cases in future writings.

4. *Muti* is a widely used word for 'medicine'. It is perhaps significant in this case that it is spoken of as a Zulu loan word. The sorcerous actions of *muti* are the power of the outside.

They make themselves invulnerable and lucky in attracting electoral support – and they can make other politicians flat and useless.

Everyone I spoke to was very clear that 'all of the disappearances' – especially of children[5] – which had allegedly increased very substantially in frequency and number since independence,[6] were connected to 'all those people who now go for riches, fame and power'. As one informant put it, 'We have no other way to explain how some people become very rich overnight'.

Certainly no one was surprised that shortly after Segametsi's body had been found, the police arrested two prosperous businessmen who were also politicians. Rumours that these particular individuals were involved in occult practices had already been circulating. However, when the police were unable to establish sufficient evidence to keep them in custody, the men were released shortly afterwards. This was followed by the arrest of four other men, three of whom were prosperous businessmen involved in politics. The fourth was in fact Segametsi's father, who was kept in custody because he had supposedly confessed to being involved in the killing of his daughter. But the three businessmen-cum-politicians were also released owing to lack of evidence. They then allegedly held a celebration at which *Kgosi* Linchwe II of the Bakgatla, who I have already introduced in another context (see Chapter 4), was believed to be a participant. We shall see the significance of this in due course. The community was enormously provoked by the release of the suspects, as one newspaper reported:

> Enraged schoolchildren take to the streets, vowing to find the murderers of their schoolmate, Segametsi. The students[7] are met by the police who try to disperse them, a few kilometres from the school. Hell breaks loose and a serious clash ensues. The students win the first round of the battle and proceed to Sekobye's (one of the suspected murderers [who was released]) and set his home alight. They also burn Kgetsi's home (another suspect [also released]) and as in Sekobye's house, nothing is retrieved from the house. Boulders, bushes, stumps and rubbish bins are used to block the roads. Soon the Molefhi Secondary School students join the fray, and the students fight the police, who have since been joined by the paramilitary riot squad.[8]

5. Since the mid-1990s I have recorded numerous complaints of this kind; occasionally they also features in the press (e.g. see *MmegiOnline*, 24 February 2004).

6. Since this time, anxiety and fear connected with disappearances of people who are never found have become more and more widespread, which is comprehensible in view of the increasing number of people being reported missing. For example, in October 2007 no less that 483 people had gone missing since the beginning of the year (*MmegiOline*, 12 October 2007).

7. 'Students' here are synonymous with 'schoolchildren'.

8. *Mmegi*, 24 February–2 March 1995.

During the confrontations with the police, several youths were seriously wounded and one was killed. Although the schoolchildren were the activists here (cf. Burke 2000: 210; Durham 2004: 599), many of the adults in the village were at pains to stress that the parents had encouraged the schoolchildren. The release of the suspects had inflamed more general sentiments relating to the widespread fear of ritual murder, implicating those 'who become rich overnight' as the perpetrators of such crimes. A newspaper interview with one of the released suspects reported that he was arrested 'because of rumours doing the rounds in Mochudi that he uses human parts to enhance his business. He said that the problem started after he had bought himself a Land Cruiser'. Defending himself, the suspect 'challenged the Bakgatla to follow their custom by going to the grave of Segametsi and applying traditional medicine to determine the real culprit'.[9] It is significant that all those detained by the police and attacked on their release were, I recall, successful businessmen and politicians.

The political tension became such that one of the district councillors sued another on the grounds that the latter had interrupted his speech during a political rally, shouting 'Segametsi o kae? Segametsi o kae?' ('Where is Segametsi?') He also complained that during another rally the defendant had stated, allegedly referring to him: 'You are hereby warned to be on guard, because there is a lion on the loose in the village. The lion today masquerades as a sheep but when it reveals its true colours, it is capable of destroying you'.[10]

The force of anger among the general population was directed towards prosperous business people and was further expressed in subsequent riots (16–17 February 1995) by university and secondary-school students in the streets of Gaborone, in which windows were broken and numerous stores damaged. Stories about occult practices amongst people who were becoming wealthy 'in ways we cannot otherwise explain' seem to have intensified during this period. They found confirmation some months later when a twenty-five-year-old man from the Bangwaketse capital of Kanye was brought before the High Court and prosecuted for having murdered and dismembered a six-year-old child. The police discovered the child's forearms behind the accused man's sofa. In his confession, he reportedly stated that he had 'killed the child so that he could strengthen his liquor-selling businesses.[11] About the same time, fears of ritual murder spread in Maun,[12] where a three-year-old girl went missing. In this case, 'the police

9. *Botswana Guardian*, 10 February 1995.
10. Ibid., 13 December 1996.
11. Ibid., 16 June 1995.
12. The capital village of the Batawana in the North-East District.

together with tribal authorities called a *kgotla* meeting at the Maun *kgotla* to hear a group of traditional doctors throw bones and speak to the ancestors to determine what could have happened to the girl … The doctor [said] she is not alive'.[13]

More than a year after Segametsi's murder, the *Botswana Guardian* informed an official in the district administration of an alleged confession made by Segametsi's father a few days after the murder. Apparently the father, a relatively impoverished man, stated that he had been pestered by a businessman in Mochudi who promised him a great deal of money to find a child for *muti*, the purpose being to 'strengthen' the bottle store which he was about to open. They agreed that one of the businessman's employees should lure Segametsi away, and on the following night the father should appear at a prearranged place to receive the money. There, '[I] found five people in the vehicle with the child. She was then bound … When we got to the ponds, three of the men got off the vehicle and took a canvas material and Segametsi with them … I could hear my child grunting pitifully in an attempt to scream'.[14] This disclosure did, however, not close the case; Segametsi's father was in fact judged insane and released from custody. Nonetheless, the news only reinforced the Bakgatla's suspicions not only of the father but also of the businessmen who had been arrested and then released.

The general anxiety about ritual murder in Botswana aroused by the Segametsi case was fleshed out in countless other stories describing the mysterious occult quality of such murders.[15] A particular feature of the murders is that in almost all instances, the body is never found. The body is so well hidden, people say, 'that even the flies cannot find it', meaning that the murder normally takes place far out in the bush and the body is buried deep in the Kalahari sand. The exceptional thing about the Segametsi case was that the body was actually found.

That the rioting students and schoolchildren acted as spearheads of a much broader popular movement against people of power and wealth is evident from the events that followed. The Bakgatla gathered in the royal *kgotla* in a major meeting, chaired by *Kgosi* Linchwe. They had come to meet with high government officials including the attorney general and two cabinet ministers, who arrived under heavy police protection. These

---

13. *Botswana Guardian*, 16 June 1995.
14. Ibid., 1 March 1996.
15. Let me add here that since then there has been an ever-increasing concern about this trend in rural as well as urban areas, more recently expressed by the fact that 'according to police reports at least 500 people have been reported missing since the beginning of 2010', many of whom will never be found or be found dead, with suggestions that they have been killed for ritual purposes (*MmegiOnline*, 5 August 2010).

officials made every effort to reassure the gathering that everything was being done to identify the murderers. No one was convinced; moreover, *Kgosi* Linchwe was subjected to intense criticism and accused of having influenced the police in their decision to release the detainees. This was substantiated, so the critics said, by his participation in a celebration held by the businessmen following their release: 'After all, he was known to be their close friend'. The situation became uncontrollable, and the government officials and the *kgosi* needed police protection in order to escape the crowd. As they drove away, their cars were pelted with stones.

During this meeting, the attorney general had declared that the government would call in Scotland Yard detectives to investigate the murder of Segametsi. A few days later, *Kgosi* Linchwe called for a *kgotla* meeting in order to select a group of tribesmen to help the detectives with their enquiries. But the debate again centred on the role of *Kgosi* Linchwe. One of my informants, who had been present, related that 'the *kgosi* was so heavily attacked in the *kgotla* that he was weeping! We have never seen anything like that. His uncles declared, "We do not trust you any more."' The press reported that co-operation with Scotland Yard was rejected on the grounds that the people 'did not have any confidence in them as they were being called in by Government, and therefore open to manipulation. The meeting then reportedly ended in a stalemate'.[16] After the meeting, the people went on to destroy the property belonging to those allegedly implicated in the murder. Another riot ensued, culminating in a confrontation with the police and heavily armed security forces.

These events triggered the mobilization of university students in the capital, Gaborone. Joined by a number of other people from less wealthy sections of the city, they marched towards the parliament building, where they forced their way into the members' chambers and ended up in a major battle with the police. The president's bodyguards were seriously injured, upon which soldiers entered the university campus and beat up the students. This precipitated another street riot the following day, leading to another confrontation with the police and soldiers. A number of students were seriously injured.

The government was now under sustained attack in the press and elsewhere for the heavy-handed way in which it had imposed social control. In Mochudi this had even involved the killing of a young man, which contributed further to the polarization of the relationship between state and public. All this was exacerbated by the lack of progress with the Segametsi case. Segametsi's father, as we have seen, had been judged insane and released from custody; and to date the Scotland Yard report has not

---

16. *Botswana Guardian*, 17 February 1995.

been released by the government. The whole situation encouraged rumours, travelling well beyond Mochudi village, which alleged that the actual recipients of the *muti* derived from Segametsi's private parts were people in high-ranking official positions.

The dramatic riots in the wake of Segametsi's murder were at that time unique in the postcolonial history of Botswana. Nothing of the kind had happened within living memory, and the people themselves were taken aback – indeed, in a state of shock. The supposedly peaceful and harmonious order of political life in Botswana – an idealization no doubt, but true to some extent – seemed to them to have been completely shattered. The tragic story of Segametsi continued to engage people as a topic of conversation, often giving rise to a number of other stories about vanished children whose disappearance was attributed to the occult practices of the rich and powerful. Since then there have been other occasions on which popular reaction has spiralled out of control, as in the royal town of the Bakwena, Molepolole, in 2004, when it was once again countered by the prompt action of heavily armed police.[17]

Occult Practices and the Ambivalence of Political Power

During my early years in Botswana (in the mid-1970s), I was only very occasionally given accounts of the kind of occult practice – that of 'ritual murder' – with which I am concerned here. For example, it was related that a headman in a named remote village conducted such a practice in his efforts to empower himself and others. More curiously, perhaps, I was told that some people were engaged in such practices in their effort to protect the farm where President Seretse Khama – seriously ill – spent his last days. Intriguingly, in commenting upon the case of Segametsi, many of my elderly friends and acquaintances were quick to suggest that 'ritual murder is nothing new to us'. Referring to what now might be conceived as a mythic past, I was told that the *bogwera* (male initiation ritual) began with one of the initiates being taken away and killed; the flesh of the sacrifice was then used to fortify the chosen location for the conduct of *bogwera* (in the bush) and to protect and strengthen the key persons in ritual proceeding: the *kgosi* and his deputies.[18] This notion of 'ritual murder'

17. *Botswana Gazette*, 13 and 27 October 2004; *Midweek Sun*, 27 October 2004.

18. I was told, moreover, when the new *mopatho*, on the return, marched through the royal town and passed the compound of the young man sacrificed, they pushed a stone, rolling toward its gate: "Then everybody knew who had been killed this time – the parents could say nothing, they just went into their hut in sorrow." Some of my interlocutors suggested that this was one of the practices that conditioned the missionaries' rejection of *bogwera*.

hence involved a practice perceived as essential to the conduct of one of the most important rituals in the *merafe* – the creation of a new *mopatho*. By contrast, in postcolonial times 'ritual murder' is given a radically different significance. As the case of Segametsi suggests, this practice is entirely condemned; not only because of the cruel murder, but also because the practice is connected to people perceived as being driven by greed and selfishness, who abuse their high offices, operating in ways damaging to the common good, keeping the vast majority of people in poverty.

In order to explain the role played by indigenous notions of occult practices in the postcolonial discourse on power abuse, I shall briefly recapitulate a few relevant aspects of the cultural construction of authority among the Tswana and most other peoples of Botswana.[19] The supreme authority of the Tswana *kgosi* is, as I explained in Chapter 4, acknowledged in such sayings as 'The king is the shepherd of the *morafe*'. The *kgosi* should therefore not only be rich but also generous, the source of wealth for all – he is the *motswadintle*. As I explained in Chapter 4, in Tswana thought, the *kgosi* is hence *ideally* the principal custodian of the common good. As I suggested in the introduction to this chapter, the consequent coalescence of power and wealth is a most natural and self-evident sign of authority: a *kgosi* without sufficient material resources would not possess the force to preserve societal peace and order. These are the major conditions for *kagiso* – the source of fertility, health, and welfare for everybody. Such an ideal is, as I have explained, maintained through unselfish exercise of authority and pursued through the *kgosi's* authoritative conduct of the proceedings in the *kgotla*. Here the *kgosi's* authority is grounded, I recall, in his availability and openness to his subjects which forms the celebrated context for establishment of consent, reconciliation and thus *kagiso*.

Their concern with *kagiso* is mirrored in the widespread horror of occult attacks, indigenously known as *boloi* (sorcery). Even the *kgosi* cannot easily escape them; on the contrary, he is believed to be a main target of powerful magic[20] which aims to make him soft (*nolohala*) or, even worse, 'flat' (*papetla*): that is, politically impotent and thus unable to exercise authority and preserve *kagiso*. In order to fortify the royal office (*bogosi*) and his own person, the *kgosi* is ideally entrusted with the most powerful magicians (*dingaka*) of the entire *morafe*, who are supposed to provide the strongest

---

19. These features of authority are broadly shared by most Sotho-speaking peoples and hence Bantu-speaking peoples in Botswana beyond the limits of Tswana (see Schapera 1956).

20. There is copious historical evidence indicating the extent to which accusations of *boloi* have been a significant aspect of dynastic disputes. See, for example, Burchell (1824: 439, 457, 551–52); Campbell (1822: 166), Livingstone (1857: 118, 137–38) and Mackenzie (1971: 389–90, 404–6, 421–22).

productive and protective 'medicine' (*ditlhare*). Ideally, the royal centre extends its protective and productive medicine down through the hierarchy of headmen, heads of descent groups and family heads who mix it with their own *ditlhare* for the purpose of fortification.

In this sense the *bogosi* constitutes a major source of 'magic' empowerment of the entire *morafe* which is perceived inherent in all relations of authority. These idealized, magical features of authority relations, which echo those of Weberian patriarchy, have in important respects been ideologically carried forward into the republican state of Botswana by virtue of all the efforts of capturing the symbolic wealth of the *bogosi* into the process of state formation (cf. Chapter 5). Such magically based authority differs substantially from that of Western states (see Coronil 1997; Taussig 1997). The 'magicality' of contemporary Botswana is grounded in cosmological meanings and practices which, as I explained in Chapter 4, are integral to everyday life in the 'traditional' but no less contemporary setting of the *merafe*.

Yet in order to come to terms with how this 'magicality' now manifests itself in popular imagination of occult practices, detrimental to the common good, it is important to comprehend all the ambiguities and uncertainties springing from two important conditions. First, the *dingaka* are not only providers of promotive and protective 'medicine'. They are also the source of 'black magic' and thus of the exercise of sorcery (*boloi*). Secondly, all engagements with the *dingaka* are necessarily secret in order to prevent occult attacks that make efforts of protection and promotion futile. This applies not only to *kgosi* but also to all persons of authority. The consequent ambiguity surrounding authority figures at all levels is reflected in two distinctively different kinds of fear amongst subjects. On the one hand, there is a positive notion of fear – *tshaba* – connoting natural respect (*tshisimogo*) for authorities who rightfully discipline their subjects for the sake of social order and hence *kagiso*. On the other hand, there is the notion of 'fear' known as *boifa* that is radically different: it is connected with the secretive exercise of power, epitomized by the damaging practice of *boloi*. Authority figures that create *boifa* are, to be sure, those associated with power abuse, above all dangerous occult practices. Those operating in such ways in high offices – whether in the context of *morafe* or the modern state – are damaging to *kagiso* on a large scale and therefore represent a serious threat to everybody.

As I explained in Chapter 4 the *dikgosi* are, by virtue of being installed in the *bogosi*, the sole link with the royal ancestorhood – hence, the cosmological centrality of the *kgosi* as the major custodian of morality and hence social peace and *kagiso*. Yet, in indigenous cosmological thought there is a sharp distinction between office and incumbency, meaning that even the *kgosi* might *actually* be an agent of dangerous occult forces, driven by such abhorrent motivations as greed, selfishness and jealousy. Therefore the *kgosi* is closely monitored by his subjects, always concerned with this potentiality of power abuse. Their concern can, in particular, be connected to the fact that the *kgosi* is perceived as necessarily engaged in the secretive dealings with, as suggested above, the most powerful agents of 'magic' – the *dingaka ya kgosi* (the king's doctors). People's consequent ambivalent relationship to a *kgosi* – springing from the ambiguities surrounding the *dingaka* – is clear in the proverb 'A king is like a knife; he might cut his sharpener', the sharpener (those who give him power) being his subjects.

This notion suggests, in fact, that the *kgosi* himself is a *potential* sorcerer. Although being the incumbent of the *bogosi* and hence cosmologically situated as the custodian of ancestral morality, the distinction made between office and incumbency allows for perceiving the *kgosi* as a human being with his personal inclinations. In popular view he might well be recognized as a ruler who works vigorously for the welfare of his subjects and, above all, ensures peace and harmony – *kagiso* – through his overall administration of justice (cf. Chapter 4). Yet, in Tswana experience there are characters amongst the *dikgosi* with a kind of greed for power and wealth that might motivate for occult practices, damaging to the common good (see Gulbrandsen 1995: 432ff.). Popular alertness follows from the fact that the ambivalence attached to persons in position of authority is pervasive. This ambivalence is not restricted to the most senior persons of the *morafe*; popular alertness towards authority figures as potential sorcerers pertains to all levels of the *morafe*. Thus this alertness is continuously reproduced in everyday life.

In the light of these ambiguities and contradictions I came to realize why people so often told me that 'it always depends upon the nature of the person', and why they engaged so intensely in discussions about the character of their authorities, at all levels. These concerns are reflected in the centrality of the popular discursive field of the *kgotla* in Tswana life and specifically in their idealization of life in the public space – where leaders on all levels are committed to communicate with their people and are kept under surveillance on a daily basis. Under such conditions people can ideally be sure that a leader is governed by the morality of 'the common good' and not by greed and selfishness. In Chapter 6 I explained how contemporary political leaders travel from village *kgotla* to village *kgotla* all over the country, intimately engaging with the people. This extensive practice clearly indicates the present significance of the ideals of exposing authorities to the population.

Nevertheless, as I shall elaborate subsequently, these efforts do certainly not suffice to counteract the growing popular concern about power abuse within all the hidden political and bureaucratic arenas that have evolved with the formation of the modern, postcolonial state. Popular imaginary of hidden exercise of power – nourished, as I have just explained, by the notions of authorities as potential sorcerers – is, under postcolonial conditions, strongly stimulated by people who suddenly rise to power and wealth 'in ways we cannot understand'. In the present chapter I am therefore centrally concerned with how the discourse of ritual murder, which has evolved under these circumstances, captures effectively and critically the perceived trends of personal greed and selfishness amongst the postcolonial state leadership.

The Discourse of Ritual Murder and Development of Class Consciousness

In view of its pervasive critique of political leaders as epitomes of the dominant class's appropriation of the common wealth vested in the state treasury, the discourse of ritual murder can be conceived as a major expression of a growing class consciousness. This development corresponds to some major transformations of which the state was, as we have seen in the preceding chapters, the driving force. When I first arrived in Botswana in the mid-1970s, most people were still resident in their natal villages and predominantly depended on both labour migration to South Africa and a degree of subsistence farming. During the first two decades of independence (i.e. until about the mid-1980s), Botswana was characterized by high levels of optimism. Wealthy people became wealthier, essentially because the state heavily subsidized their livestock production. Access to well-paid jobs in government and private industry was facilitated by government-supported higher education. The development of a modern state infrastructure and state social services, as well as programmes of urban development, cushioned the population against the economic downturn occasioned by the reduction of South Africa's longstanding recruitment of migrant labourers (a factor that had been highly important to Botswana's economy) (Gulbrandsen 1996a).

As we have seen in Chapters 5, 6 and 7, the benefits of modernity were promulgated by political rhetoric, which in turn was buttressed by increased state resources due to foreign aid and the expansion of the diamond industry. Nevertheless, from the early 1980s onwards, I witnessed a growing undercurrent of dissatisfaction, especially among the underprivileged. They started to speak of government officials as 'fat stomachs', often wondering how relatively young people could afford their attractive cars and appear in such nice suits. Dissatisfaction was particularly apparent in urban areas, which started to expand substantially at this time.[21]

The criticism of the new rich as people who had manipulated social connections with the government for their own interests was brought to the forefront of public consciousness in the late 1980s. In a major corruption scandal, senior government officials were accused of illegally appropriating large tracts of extremely valuable residential land in the vicinity of the capital. As suggested in Chapter 6, during the succeeding years there were a number of similar scandals, in which high-ranking officials such as the state vice-president were involved (see Good 1994, 2008: 50ff.). These incidents nourished all kinds of rumours of government-based corruption relating to the securing of government loans, access to otherwise unobtainable grazing and water rights and so on. It is impossible to say how well founded these rumours were. Nonetheless, throughout the 1990s the word 'corruption' was on most people's lips (cf. Chapter 3). This coincided with an economic recession: not only was there a steep rise in unemployment among educated youth, opportunities for migrant labour in South Africa dried up and the urban construction industry at home suffered substantial job losses. The consequent gulf between the expectations encouraged by the hegemonic discourse of development and the ever more harsh economic realities widened as young people with secondary-school education increasingly faced joblessness.

The discrepancy between expectations and reality is a situation in which an occult discourse might gain significance. But such discourse is not a mere expression of political and economic circumstances in the 'surface/depth' sense that still prevails in much anthropological analysis. The occult discourse is integral to social and political processes, as much a part of the core as it is of the surface. It is more than a cognitive frame for the interpretation of experience: politically and socially it is instrumental both in creating dimensions to the contexts of which it speaks, and in orienting people in Botswana towards a particular emotional state in which they may achieve some means of changing their circumstances. Here the occult discourse itself comes to have effect.

---

21. The rise of corruption in the late 1980s coincides with the rapid expansion of the off-farm economy and the commercialization of vast land property in the vicinity of the capital of Gaborone. The low rate of corruption before that time is sometimes attributed to the moral standing of Seretse Khama. While it is hard to assess the significance of this, I have, in brief, argued elsewhere (Gulbrandsen 2006) that as long as the various elites were predominantly engaged in commercial agriculture and livestock production, they ensured themselves – through 'legal' political and administrative decisions – a lion's share of the state wealth through generous governmental programmes and projects (see Chapter 3).

I have already explained that concerns about occult forces are intrinsic to the lived-in world, at least in the rural context of the *morafe*. There is also a sense that magical powers have to some extent broken free from the control of the *morafe* and from integration within hierarchical social orders. They are not subordinate to the authority structures of the *merafe* in the same way as they once were. People comment that the *dingaka* often now operate independently of the authorities of the *morafe*, the *kgotla* and extended kin, and serve individual interests that stand in opposition to the social order as a whole. Momentum is added to this trend by a discourse of urban/rural contrasts, one relationship whereby people grasp the magical nature of current reality. Many allegedly dangerous *dingaka* are now believed to be settled in urban neighbourhoods composed of strangers. Ambiguous enough as internal forces, they have intensified their danger by becoming reconstituted as malevolent powers of the exterior with considerable rhizomic potentialities.

Here I should note that a discourse of rural/urban contrasts (viewed as analytic constructs of everyday social realities) that centres on the role of *dingaka* might also be grasped as a reality: one that refers to a process whereby power, in its magical aspect, is perceived as having separated itself from the social body (the body of the people) and as now acting in opposition to the social body or the social order. More broadly, this is a discourse in which state leaders are no longer in a constitutive relationship to society; rather, it is oriented destructively against it.

This notion of greed and selfishness was – in more general terms – nourished under the condition of massive movement of people to urban centres, beginning in the late 1980s. Disembodied from the dense social relationships of wards with their hierarchical order of authority and ideals of harmony, people from the same natal origin were spatially scattered and absorbed into individuated occupations which brought some few people to wealth and power while the majority remained poor. These features of a perceived dangerously individualized and competitive environment shaped the popular view of the town as representing the negative inversion of harmonious village life, much along the lines of an earlier functionalist anthropology that conceived urban life as the dysfunctional alter of rural existence. Such imagery is driven by political and economic forces underpinning an ever-more-apparent class division, manifesting itself particularly in urban areas, yet spilling back into rural contexts as shown by popular reactions to the murder of Segametsi in the royal town of Mochudi. Although processes of individuation and disembodiment from the indigenous hierarchical order centred in the discursive field of the *kgotla* have accelerated in the urban context and are also most evident there, it is important to bear in mind that processes of individuated wealth accumulation – focused on cattle – have been as much rural as urban linked. After all, people who have risen to power and wealth and are mostly located in urban centres often keep in close contact with the *kgotla* of their respective natal groups (cf. Chapter 4).

Power, Wealth and Notions of Occult Practices

The events surrounding the death of Segametsi gain much of their significance as part of a general discourse concerning occult forces. This discourse treats these events as a dimension of recent negative political and economic developments. Vital to this discourse is a critique of the state leadership, which is measured against indigenous cosmologies of the state as these relate to Tswana kingship. The destructive magical aspect of power becomes dominant when such power separates from its social integument, from its embeddedness in social relations. This occurs when power withdraws from contexts in which it is subject to moral and social surveillance. If, as Foucault suggests, the power of European states lies in their capacity for social surveillance (rather than being the object of surveillance), the Tswana state (as imagined and idealized) is a state whose capacity for the surveillance of its agents is controlled and limited by its subjects (see Gulbrandsen 1995). As such, it is a polity that has some resonance with the idea developed by Pierre Clastres (1987) in his celebrated attempt to distinguish the nature of non-Western political orders from the ideas (in political science and in political anthropology) to which they were conventionally subordinated.

My argument here is that the Segametsi case and the related occult discourse highlight the magical negativity of the modern state, using the idealized Tswana state as a measuring rod. Furthermore, this idealization, this imagery, is a consequence of the fact that in contemporary Botswana, forms of social and political relations relevant to ways of idealizing the precolonial state have continued into the era of modernity and independence. This imagery has constituted a conscious paradigm for the formation of the postcolonial state. Moreover, while social and economic inequalities underpin the general anger that surrounded Segametsi's death, this anger has increased its effect through a discourse of the occult that directs the feelings of outrage towards the perceived violation of indigenous political and moral values which the modern state has paradoxically commandeered for its own legitimation (cf. Chapter 5).

To ensure the local legitimacy of the republic, government officials engaged the village *kgotla* in the establishment of the new order (see Chapter 6). The public was encouraged to present its needs in the forums of the *kgotla,* at which government policy was also presented. During the formative period of the postcolonial state, government agencies largely succeeded in establishing the state by building on the sociopolitical order of indigenous authority structures. As I explained in Chapter 2, Seretse Khama, the founding president of Botswana and heir to one of the major Tswana kingdoms, exemplified this trajectory. He successfully appropriated much of the symbolic wealth vested in these kingdoms. The postcolonial state manifested itself as a *motswadintle* according to indigenous ideals of exercising authority (Gulbrandsen 1995).

Under the rule of President Khama, which continued until his death in 1980, the state established its legitimacy as the supreme agency of welfare and prosperity – and thus of *kagiso.* The nation-state appropriated the same moral space for the exercise of power that had previously been restricted to the *merafe.* As I explained in Chapters 5–7, it was on this foundation that the state leadership attempted to establish its hegemony by, quite successfully, presenting itself as champion of national development and custodian of the common good.

But of course the modern nation-state and its bureaucratic order constitute a sociopolitical construction by which they are ideologically appropriated and encompassed. The manner of encompassment, however, has exposed the agents of the modern state to a critical discourse on power and power abuse that was once suited to the problematic of authority in the circumstances of Tswana kingship. The discourse was now more intense because progressive tensions of class played increasingly into it. The organization of power in modern states – and Botswana is no exception – is bureaucratically hidden from the public. In terms of the ideology of the *kgotla,* which the instruments of the state had appropriated, such secrecy was indicative of the abuse of power and, further, of the involvement of state agents and their associates in malevolent sorcery. Such a contradiction was generated and exacerbated in the very contemporary scheme of things. Thus, the more officials used the *kgotla* as a mechanism of public consultancy (as they did even in the events surrounding Segametsi), the more they became subject to the critical discourse of the occult which perceived them as involved in dangerous, antisocial and secretive practices.

State bureaucracy, idealized in Western discourse as a depersonalized decision-making system which treats all citizens on an equal basis, appears from the point of view of many people as the epitome of the secretive exercise of power; they regard the arena of state activities as removed from popular inspection and control. As such it is the very antithesis of the idealized public space of decision making, namely, the *kgotla,* where the personal character (*botho*) of authority figures is monitored on a daily basis. By contrast, in a bureaucratized polity people see few or no possibilities of gaining information about the character of the people to whom they are subjected.

The hidden and therefore dangerous potential of the bureaucratic order of the modern state is also seen to be a dimension of the increasing individualization of everyday life. In urban areas, people of power and wealth live more and more apart from society. True, they remain within kinship networks that often include poor people, and they frequently visit their natal village where they encounter the underprivileged. However, in their everyday lives they mostly inhabit separate residential areas, moving around in luxury cars and following a way of life that contrasts radically with the idealized traditional elite who used to feature centrally in public life and who took pride in being approachable and available to everyone. Hiding behind solid walls in gardens protected by vicious watchdogs, these people increasingly give out signals of distance, superiority and indeed exclusiveness. The warning signs on their gates – *tshaba ntswa* (beware of the dog) – have gained considerable symbolic significance in popular parlance. This feature coincides with personal extravagance and the development of a culture of conspicuous consumption – behaviour that epitomizes selfishness and greed. Such people are readily perceived as witches and sorcerers in the discourse of the occult. In their individualized success they transcend the moral bounds of an ideology founded on the ideals of the indigenous order, an order that ensures peace and harmony and all the blessings of *kagiso* (see Chapter 4).

The speed with which such people have risen to prominence provides one explanation for the anger and anxiety they inspire. It follows logically from notions of a hierarchy of forces and their agencies that such a degree of rapid success and prosperity is evidence of access to particularly powerful *muti*–'medicine' extracted from the bodies of human beings. This is reflected in various stories going round, such as 'When election approaches, more and more children are disappearing'. The plots contained in these narratives express, in my interpretation, a fundamental anxiety about being subject to a state that is increasingly in the hands of people governed by hidden agendas and involved in secret wars from which they gain tremendous benefit but which are highly destructive to society as a whole. Most people share this anxiety and anger because for many years they have enthusiastically supported the establishment of the postcolonial state and in many respects have placed their destiny in the hands of this all-encompassing polity.

Overall, there is a sense that political leaders have betrayed the public. The state and its agents have seemingly broken their compact with the people to the extent that moral questions about the use of power have become increasingly acute, especially for the underprivileged people who see the well-to-do as driven by greed and selfishness, rapidly accumulating wealth and assuming positions of power. This is a trend that contributes markedly to the perception that the state has failed as the source of well-being and as the producer of beneficence. Even worse, these are political leaders that 'eat our children', that fight the people and create destructive 'heat' – negating the cool harmony that is essential to the promotion of *kagiso* (cf. Chapter 4).

This aspect of Tswana political thought, anchored in the indigenous cosmology, is exemplified by the public attack on the once beloved *Kgosi* Linchwe in the aftermath of Segametsi's murder. The anger directed towards *Kgosi* Linchwe had much to do with the fact that he had been the highly respected and much-praised custodian of the moral order as the incumbent of the *bogosi* of the Bakgatla. As I recall, he was a brave and eloquent challenger of senior government officials when they came to address his people. He had been recognized as a true protector of *kagiso*. For this reason in particular, people were annoyed by his decision to leave royal office and accept the state president's offer to chair the Customary Court of Appeal, a position firmly located in central government. In the wake of *Kgosi* Linchwe's appointment, all kinds of suspicions developed about his having been co-opted and corrupted by powerful government officials. His association with the alleged murderers only confirmed the view that he had lost his integrity. And it was rumoured that he was the one who secretly conveyed to 'people in high places' the *muti* derived from Segametsi's private parts. This allegation was of course grounded in the government's heavy-handed response to the students' protests, in the rumour that *Kgosi* Linchwe had persuaded the police to release the suspects, and in the police force's apparent ineffectiveness in identifying and apprehending Segametsi's murderers. All this, and the potential malignancy of continuing government secrecy, was compounded by the government's refusal to disclose the findings of the Scotland Yard investigation.[22]

These various aspects relating to *Kgosi* Linchwe's involvement in the Segametsi affair constitute what can be referred to as the 'hidden transcript' underlying the events. That is to say, the contradictions within the hybridized structure and practices of state leadership were brought to the fore. *Kgosi* Linchwe became a focus of these countervailing forces: his association with members of a new class and the evidently secret actions

---

22. As of 2008, the report has still not been released, allegedly because identifying the murderer(s) would be detrimental to national security. The withholding of the report continues to nourish popular subaltern discourse on ritual murder as a critique of the political leadership. At his death in August 2007, *Kgosi* Linchwe had not been cleared of popular suspicion concerning his involvement in the murder of Segametsi.

of state bureaucracy exposed him to the criticism that he was abusing the power appropriate to the Tswana kingship, namely, openness and availability to public scrutiny. Integrated into the bureaucracy of the modern state, the ideals of the *merafe* are no less integral to contemporary Botswana. And it is from this that a discourse of the occult gains its strength: by identifying agents of the state as the magical consumers of its symbols of beneficence – its children – and as being engaged in the sorcerous destruction of a social order that they should ideally be generating.

Political Elite Domination and Questions of Popular Mobilization

In view of the extent to which the subaltern discourse of ritual murder thematizes major features of social inequality and injustice, the question is how it played into politics. At the time Segametsi was brutally killed, the ruling Botswana Democratic Party (BDP) had been troubled by internal conflicts and by cases of corruption among some of its most senior people, including cabinet ministers (see Good 1994). The leaders felt vulnerable in relation to the opposition. This had been evident for quite some time in the urban centres where the largest opposition party, the Botswana National Front (BNF), enjoyed more support. In this context, the ruling BDP now also seemed to be in danger of losing several of its rural strongholds.

The aftermath of the murder of Segametsi provided ideal conditions for political mobilization by the opposition parties. In particular they could have challenged the continued delay in releasing the Scotland Yard report which would certainly have appealed to the people immensely. But relatively quickly the opposition stopped putting pressure on the ruling party to release the findings. Why they did so reveals much about the conditions for launching such protests in Botswana, and the difficulty faced by those demanding such radical changes that would benefit the majority, namely, the underprivileged.

According to my records, in popular view the BNF would not have taken the risk of being blamed for encouraging further riots and societal unrest: 'You know, we Batswana love peace, we hate fighting. And the BNF would lose support if they could rightfully be blamed for stirring up people to fight in the streets'. This point was strongly confirmed on a particular occasion, when one BNF member of Parliament asked, with reference to a 'threatening letter' sent by the university students to the president (see the first section above), what the government was intending to do about the very real possibility of an explosive situation arising again. In response, the minister of presidential affairs alleged that 'the Honourable Member's question is intended to prepare the ground for riots ... I am further aware that demonstrations have been planned for some time and the Honourable Member seems to be playing his usual facilitative role'. The MP fiercely denied any such connection, while the minister appealed strongly 'to all responsible citizens and residents to exercise restraint for the treasure of peace, stability and security'.[23] In a similar yet much more explicit vein, the youth section of the BDP accused the BNF of being directly involved in the riots of Gaborone and Mochudi.[24]

The BNF thus found it politically necessary to respond very vigorously to such allegations, denying any past, present or planned involvement in any popular uprising against the government. The BDP issued a similar statement, evidently fearing that any invocation of this case, which remained a political hot potato, would link the party to a popular movement that might threaten 'societal peace and order'. Yet the BDP repeatedly stressed that any threat to the stability of the country came from the major opposition party (BNF), alleging that the latter was using the case 'as a fertile ground for revolution under the pretence of being sympathetic to the bereaved'.[25] Hence, whatever potentials there might have been for exploiting popular reactions to political leaders as the basis for radical political mobilization, politicians strove mightily to avoid the danger of being identified as a potential source of social instability. As I have stressed in several contexts of this volume, conflict and tension are, in indigenous thought, ipso facto fundamentally damaging to *kagiso* and therefore opposed to prosperity, health and welfare for everybody.

There is a further twist to the party-political aspects of the Segametsi case: those suspected, arrested and then released by the police, and persistently accused by the people of having committed the horrible crime, were prosperous businessmen as well as prominent politicians of the major opposition party (BNF). The ruling BDP seems to have exploited this connection for all it was worth in an attempt to connect the BNF to the ritual murder. Of course, the BNF fiercely repudiated any connection with the case, and took steps to suspend this party member, even though he had not been prosecuted. This was done entirely on the basis of him having been judged and convicted by public opinion. In other words, political leaders of the opposition are equally vulnerable to popular accusation of power abuse. In popular view they are part and parcel of 'goromente' – the state government.

This means that the tragic case was translated into a party political game about placing guilt for the horrible death of Segametsi. In popular

23. *Botswana Gazette*, 1 February 1995.
24. *Botswana Guardian*, 24 February 1995.
25. *Botswana Daily News*, 14 December 1995.

perception, members of the opposition party were as much as those of the ruling party potential suspects because they were equally a part of the rivalry and competition for political power which was seen as the chief driving force behind ritual murders. Recall how people angrily expressed that 'when election is approaching, our children are disappearing'. The distaste for party politics links up with what I explained in Chapter 6 about the contrasts between the highly positively valued discursive field of the *kgotla* and the condemnation of the freedom squares. Not only the hidden, secretive character of modern bureaucracy (see preceding section), but also the confrontational and fighting nature of electoral democracy is nourishing the popular discourse of ritual murder.

Under such conditions it is quite obvious that the opposition parties had no possibilities for taking advantage of the popular discourse on ritual murder. Hence no attempt was made to use this discourse politically in order to ideologize the growing class consciousness amongst all the poor and unprivileged sections of the population. The danger for opposition politicians of themselves being accused of the exercise of ritual murder reflects the existence of a fundamental structural condition – that of class division – deterring the opposition from exploiting such cases in order to mobilize people for radical political action. It is significant that those who prevailed in popular discourse as suspects of grounding their political strength and economic success in occult practices were well represented among the prominent members of both the BNF and the BDP. Thus, in spite of asserting 'We are going continuously to fight for the release of the report. We don't care who is implicated in it, be it a BNF member or whoever, as our policies do not condone murder',[26] it was in due course recognized that to encourage public concern about a case of this kind might backfire. The BNF therefore fell silent about the matter and did not challenge the president on keeping the Scotland Yard report secret.[27]

The opinion of many people that BNF political leaders were equally likely to commit such a horrible crime for power and wealth as those of the BDP is intriguing in view of the fact that the BNF was established by a group of self-proclaimed socialists returning from higher education in

---

26. Stated by District Councillor Philip Lebotse in a Kgatleng District Council meeting (see *Botswana Gazette*, 19 July 1995).

27. In the wake of other murders of children classified as 'ritual murders', the Botswana Congress Party which split off from the BNF (1998) considered a protest march aimed at heightening the awareness on unresolved ritual murders and expressing complaints that, in the words of their spokesperson, 'people who go missing under dubious and mysterious circumstances' are never found. Yet they eventually decided against 'demonstrating now because we feel it would be irresponsible as emotions are still running high'. They were in other words alarmed by the prospects of being accused of stirring up violent action (see *Mmegi*, 30 January–5 February 2001).

Eastern Europe and the Soviet Union. Despite this identification, they have never made any serious effort to challenge the liberal developmental discourse which formed the ideological base of the postcolonial ruling group (cf. Chapter 5). On the contrary, many central BNF activists have taken extensive advantage of the various government policies and programmes in the pursuit of their own – often successful – economic entrepreneurship (cf. Makgala 2006: 149). Hence the BNF has never made any serious criticism of, for example, the highly unequal division of common tribal lands resulting from the allocation of borehole sites to individual farmers, simply because there are many important BNF members who have benefited from being allocated borehole sites. Similarly, any proposal concerning radical policies to counteract the very skewed distribution of cattle – the most significant force as well as expression of class division – would certainly have ended up falling on barren ground within the BNF. This feature is epitomized by Makgala's (2005: 320–21) indication of a close connection between, on the one hand, the BNF president of 1977–2001, the Eastern Europe–educated Dr Kenneth Koma, and, on the other hand, leading members of the ruling party. Ostensibly their relationship was of a commercial kind, meaning that Dr Koma was operating just as 'capitalistically' as leading figures of the ruling party, benefiting handsomely from the state's extensive 'development' programmes (cf. Chapter 3).[28] This self-proclaimed socialist's engagement with leading members of the ruling party in commercial pursuits exemplifies the considerable degree of integration of the entrepreneurial class across the political spectrum.

In other words, the 'entrepreneurial class' is very well represented across the party political spectrum: leading figures of all significant parties are equally taken by a commercial spirit, caught by the hegemonic discourse of development and oriented towards individual liberalism. Thus, as long as political parties are dominated by such class interests, they are not likely to develop a more radical political orientation. The persistence of this feature has most recently (March 2010) been confirmed by the succession of a significant faction of the BDP, entailing the establishment of a new party: Botswana Democratic Movement. This is largely a protest

---

28. According to Makgala (2005: 320–21), 'in the 1980s he lashed out at the BDP government's Financial Assistance Programme as useless to the people, although he benefited from it to build up his businesses'. In 1984 he was hence attacked by a cabinet minister (BDP) who claimed 'at a political rally that "about P40,000 has been granted to … Koma and [BNF vice-president] Bathoen Gaseitsiwe from the Financial Assistance Programme to be used in their Kgobati Construction Company and also to pay the workers of the company" [*Daily News*, 27 November 1984]'. Makgala (2005: 1) relates that '[i]n late 2001, Koma was reported to have engaged in a profitable business deal with Satar Dada, the multi-millionaire BDP Treasurer and the country's motor industry magnate'.

movement directed against the state president, Lt. General Ian Khama, for his allegedly antidemocratic practices and attitudes. Although this is a very important development in the sense that this is the first time the BDP has experienced a faction breaking away and forming a new political party, there is no sign of an agenda that represents a radical departure from the major political orientations of the present government. This obviously reflects that the people splitting from the BDP represent no distinctively different interests from those who have remained.

This means, finally, that the 'grand coalition' identified in Chapter 3 prevails across the political spectrum despite all the conflicts and rivalries amongst elites, underpinning a more or less tacit consensus about major governmental policies and political practices. That is, policies and practices which militate against the development of a radical political force, springing from subaltern discourses like that I have examined in this chapter amongst the unprivileged and impoverished section of Botswana's population. And note, this is also a matter of a cross-party consensus about monopolizing the public, political space which to a great extent implies agreement about curbing of the public sphere – to the extent that trade unions and other NGOs are kept under state surveillance. At least, there have been no strong opposition voices attacking this practice.

I discussed the state's tight controls of NGOs towards the end of Chapter 6 and argued that its impact is testified by the fact that only very recently (April 2011) – forty-five years after the independence – trade unions mounted a major, highly confrontational challenge of the state. In brief, some 90,000 public sector workers went on strike that lasted about two months. Within the present limits I can only relate briefly that the massive mobilization of, especially, all the low-paid governmental workers should be seen against the background of the tremendous salary gaps within the civil service I explained at the beginning of this chapter. The significance of this has, over the recent years, accelerated with substantial increase of essential consumer commodities. The massive reactions reflect the neo-liberal restructuring of the public sector, perceived as sustained attacks on employee's rights. Moreover, it might be that legal changes[29]

---

29. By virtue of the Public Service Act which came into force 1 May 2010, civil servants were allowed to strike, excluding military, police and prison services; health workers may strike under certain condition. This act was received with trade unions' general satisfaction, although it was complained that it had been seriously delayed as Botswana had committed it to legislate already in 1997 by ratifying three International Labour Organization (ILO) Conventions (e.g. cf. The Gazette 28 March 2010). However, in the wake of the 2011 strike, the government wants to include diamond sorting, cutting and selling services, teaching services and veterinary services, as essential services set under considerable constraints in respect of striking, ostensibly in the interest of the nation.

made in 2008 relaxing somewhat the state's tight control of trade unions have been of some significance. President Ian Khama's uncompromising, hard line and total unwillingness to engage in dialogues with trade union leaders – in obvious conflict with indigenous virtues of consultation – contributed strongly to harsh and long term confrontations. His perceived authoritarian style was testified by the deployment of armed forces and the secret service.

The claim was a 16% salary hike, especially with reference to the fact that civil servants' salaries had not been raised for the previous three years. The government rejected this claim in lasting, tough negotiations, maintaining that such an increase would undermine the economy of the state already hit by the slowdown in the global economy after 2008 that reduced revenues from diamond mining. As demonstrations escalated and spread from towns to villages,[30] not only the public service was paralyzed as, amongst others, hospitals and schools were closed. People took to the streets in large scale demonstrations that, at times, culminated in violent confrontation with the police.[31] The Batswana took themselves by surprise, as during the riots in the wake of the Segamentse murder. Never before had rank and file people engaged so extensively, seriously and violently in a confrontation with the state.

The scale and intensity of popular mobilization was probably largely due to the engagement of social media and other internet facilities, releasing forces far beyond trade unions' control – demonstrating, in my analysis, the extent to which all the unprivileged rank and file sections of the population have accumulated frustrations and antagonism against a political leadership perceived as vastly self-serving and greedy. That is, the kind of perception which has for a long time been spread throughout the social field by such subaltern discourse which I have examined in this chapter, now even more pervasively and with high intensity. Thus, while the trade union leaders might be captured into the orbit of state control by its enforcement of the Public Service Act, the series of events at hand patently indicate the opening up of spaces exterior to the state with considerable potentials of generating rhizomic forces.[32]

---

30. E.g. see *MmegiOnline*, 30 May 2011 and 10 June 2011; *SundayStandardOnline*, 28 April 2011.

31. The conflict was particularly heated in Botswana's second largest city, Francistown, as illuminated by the follow snub: http://www.youtube.com/watch?v=yYpwQGYY598

32. This is, to be sure, recognized by the state leadership that over the past two decades has expanded very significantly its various forms of secret service (e.g. Good 2008: 99ff.). In particular, after General Lt. Ian Khama became the state president in 2008, the military intelligence service has, in popular perception, been attached even closer to the political leadership of the state.

In view of this and the timing of the strike, it is no surprise that many of my interlocutors saw the very heated situation in Botswana in the light of the 2011–spring revolutions in the Middle East and North Africa. The capricious character of the massive mobilization of poor and unprivileged people was, significantly, quickly realized by the political opposition parties which apparently spotted new ways to, finally, combat the ruling party.[33] But because of all the unpredictable subaltern discourses on occultic practices nourished by major undercurrents of animosity to people of power and wealth, it is highly uncertain how this is going to work itself out.

Conclusion

While some of the general statements that have been expressed by anthropologists concerning occultic practices in Africa can be applied to my material, the Botswana data indicate some modification. Thus, Ciekawy and Geschiere state that witchcraft discourses have an 'amazing capacity … to link global changes directly with local realities [because of] their basic open-endedness. Witchcraft discourse forces an opening of the village and the closed network: after all, it is the *basic interest of the witch to betray his or her victims to outsiders*. The image of the witch flying off to meet fellow conspirators and offer them relatives is a central one in African societies' (1998: 5, italics added; cf. Geschiere 1998). This statement has some application to the material I have presented, but notions such as 'open-endedness' gloss too much and fail to consider sufficiently either the ideas that are embedded in sorcery or occult discourse, or their pro-

---

33. *The Time Live* reported (10 May 2011): 'The country's three largest opposition parties have moved to capitalise on the unrest by throwing their support behind unions, giving fiery speeches at workers' rallies and urging the ouster of President Ian Khama's government. Duma Boko, head of the opposition Botswana National Front, called on Botswana to replicate the revolutions in Egypt and Tunisia. "There are different ways to take over governance, and that includes by force," he said at a recent press conference in support of the strike held by the opposition parties. "If we can come together we can take our government as it happened in Egypt and Tunisia." For the Botswana Movement for Democracy, a breakaway party from the BDP, the strike undermines the ruling party's contention that Botswana is a model democracy. "This is clear from the government's refusal to accept workers' demands for a pay hike, under the pretext that the economy has not yet recovered from the recession," said its leader, Gomolemo Motswaledi. Political analyst Zibani Maundeni, a lecturer at the University of Botswana, said the strike has introduced a new element to domestic politics since opposition parties had not previously counted unions as a constituency. "Opposition parties are now openly involved in labour issues and the workers have also struck a relationship with the parties. But it remains to be seen how this relationship will work in future," he told AFP.' See also *MmegiOnline*, 13 May 2011 and *SundayStandardOnline*, 26 May 2011.

duction in social and political transformations. I have concentrated on the way notions of sorcery and other malevolent ritualistic practices are related to specific cosmologies of power. In the Botswana situation, sorcery is part of a critical discursive field relating to a context in which the order of a contemporary bureaucratic state aims, to a considerable extent, to legitimate its practices through appropriating ideas and understandings pertinent to the imaginary of that state/society constituted in the terms of Tswana kingship.[34]

These terms, I hasten to add, are not simply an invention of modernity or of the colonial era. The 'invention of tradition' arguments (Hobsbawm and Ranger 1983) miss the fact that in the Botswana situation ideas and practices relevant to Tswana kingship and the social relations of which it was the centre, have continued into contemporary contexts as a modernity alongside – and, to a degree, in complementary relation with – the formation of a rational bureaucratic state order of the Western kind. This is a point I believe that scholars such as Comaroff and Comaroff (1993) would recognise. What I have pursued here are the contradictions that such continuities open up in the contemporary order of the Botswana state, and especially in the circumstances of the political and economic crises attendant on global developments, leading to considerable discrepancies in wealth and life-chances.

These processes work into a social and political world in which certain cosmologies of power are in play. The discourse surrounding ritual murders and the anxieties and fears that such discourse propels in itself, while conditioned in global economic and political processes, are not mere expressions of those processes. Rather, the discourses I have discussed engage particular orientations to social and political realities which see in them a specific kind of personally and socially dangerous significance. This significance is one that in a way deflects attention away from the global forces that are operating and focuses attention on no less real forces of contradiction that lie at the heart of the historical and political formation that is the contemporary Botswana state.

---

34. Needless to stress, perhaps, I have not suggested in this volume that powerful and rich people are *actually* conducting occult practices like 'ritual murder' in order to empower themselves. I have no information of such a kind because this is a question clearly irrelevant in relation to my efforts of coming to terms with how occult practices feature in popular imagination and discourses. However, let me suggest that ambitious people have, over the last couple of decades, joined pentecostal churches in large numbers, ostensibly for obtaining spiritual support to gain power and wealth. This development has, as far as I know, no evident impact upon popular imagination and discource of 'ritual murder', most likely because people do not perceive adherence to such churches, on the one hand, and exercise of occult practices, on the other, as mutually excluding.

Undoubtedly, occult discourse in Botswana refracts individual uncertainties and vulnerabilities of an everyday nature that are often connected with unemployment and the many exigencies of urban life, as I have explained. But it is much more than this. It is motivated in the crisis of a modern state, a crisis that is as much moral as it is material. One central feature of such a moral crisis is the fact that the rational order of the bureaucratic state involves practices that must contravene continuing indigenous notions (which agents of the state encourage) that power must be open to the public surveillance of the *kgotla*. The critical discourse surrounding sorcery and ritual murders builds in this kind of contravention that lies impossibly at the heart of the modern state.

Occultic discourse is thus not an irrational expression of uncertainty. On the contrary, it is a response to the conflicting rationalities which are integral to the construction (and legitimation) of the modern state in Botswana yet at the same time generating spaces exterior to the social order it encompasses. That is, spaces with potentialities of generating rhizomic forces attacking this order. Further, the occultic discourse is directed explicitly to the problematics of power. Most particularly, it addresses the perceived abuse of power, such perceptions being driven by social inequalities and incompatibilities created by Botswana's integration within larger global processes.

CONCLUSION

I started out by examining the formation of the small Tswana states on the edge of the Kalahari – known as *merafe* – from the late eighteenth century because, as I have argued, they gave rise to sociopolitical practices, institutions of authority and structures of domination that were of a great significance, first, to the development of a colonial state and prevention of annexation to neighbouring racist regimes. Second, by virtue of their enhanced force and range of domination under the British wing, especially in relation to other communities, the Tswana *merafe* embodied cultural and social conditions that gave rise to a ruling group of the postcolonial period and to the formation of a dominant class in persistent support of it.

I have attempted to show that the modern state in Botswana can be seen as the successor to the premodern polities of the past in the sense of incorporating them successfully within the apparatus of the modern postcolonial state. The colonial mediation of indigenous sociopolitical institutions and practices, including major structures of domination, centred in Tswana kingship as vital dimensions of postcolonial Botswana, has been important to the development of a strong, modern state with a sustainable government.

There is a larger point to this understanding. The specific Botswana case underlines the point that what is marked as 'tradition' is a multiple rather than singular phenomenon. Tradition is full of potentiality in its carrying forward into modernity. It is not necessarily a deadening force. It has many possible trajectories which are not given to it in any essentialist sense, but which may be released in its very continuity and carrying forward into novel contexts and situations. In other words, the blaming of tradition for failure often derives from a limited orientation to tradition, however this may be defined, and an accentuation of its negativity without consideration of what could be its positivity.

At the same time, this antiessentialist position also allows for nuance in the notion of 'positivity' by explaining how Tswana domination of minorities has at once been instrumental to the establishment of a strong state *and* the perpetuation of repressive structures and practices. That is, structures and practices with long genealogies that tend to exteriorize to the state parts of the population with considerable rhizomic potentialities.

In order to come to terms with the development and consolidation of a strong modern state that has been capable of drawing upon potentialities of the indigenous symbolism and institutions of authority, I have attempted to transcend a government-centred approach. That is, I have rejected – as circular – the argument that the sustainable and progressive strength of the postcolonial state in Botswana follows from the force and efficiency of its bureaucracy, the sustainability of the government and the persistence of the parliamentarian democracy since these are major *characteristics* of a strong modern state – which are to be explained. I have also argued that Botswana's tremendous diamond wealth cannot explain in any straightforward way the extraordinary strength and sustainability of the state, because diamonds elsewhere in Africa have in many cases fuelled major political conflicts and violence. The same goes for Botswana's reception of massive financial and technical aid to develop its government, social services and economy: it is abundantly evident from a number of other 'developing' countries that such intervention represents no guarantee for the formation of a strong state.

Postcolonial state formation in this country is best comprehended by considering the whole range of encompassing social factors that might be of significance. In line with this approach, and with a particular focus upon the formative and consolidating period (1966–1990), I have shown that the development of the modern Botswana state should be understood as a matter of particular – if not exceptional – *conjuncture of conditions* in the historical context of the country's independence and the following two decades. This conjuncture was critical to the development of a grand coalition of elites that formed decisively a persistent support of the ruling group and made the state prevailing as superstructural to a highly inclusive social network of power throughout the country. This was a matter of conjuncture between: (1) the existence of a state leadership embryo emerging under the conditions of the colonial state and within the context of indigenous polities; (2) the presence of a number of powerful Tswana *merafe* that gained strength and scale within the colonial state, incorporating most of the population in hierarchical structures, including vast non-Tswana subject communities; (3) the existence of a stratum of dominant elites across the Tswana *merafe* with very strong, shared value orientations in respect of the politico-symbolic and commercial centrality of cattle; (4) immensely privileged access to global markets for the beef and subsequently diamond trade; and (5) the supply of massive foreign financial and technical aid.

Given the combination of these conditions, I have explained, the modern state soon gained momentum as an independent force which achieved supremacy by assuming control over a wide range of existing power networks, capturing not only the elites, but the population at large in the process of state formation. This involved, on the one hand, a dialectical relationship between the state and the most important Tswana elites, giving rise to major transformations of the political economy, which entailed a progressive diversification of an always state-dependent, dominant class. On the other hand, by virtue of incorporating the dominant elites into the process of state formation, the hierarchical structures of authority vested in the Tswana *merafe* as well as in the communities which they have always attempted to incorporate and control, were captured into the networks of power upon which the state increasingly prevailed as superstructural.

Under the impact of major global forces, the modern state evolved within preexisting structures of social relations, even though it reconstituted aspects of their meaning. That is, the modern state relied, on the one hand, upon capturing into its hierarchies indigenous structures of social control and domination and adapting them to its own order, thus contributing strongly to their reproduction. One important aspect of this has been the modern state's efforts to appropriate the cosmologically anchored symbolic wealth vested in indigenous institutions of authority, underscoring the significance of the larger social order to the development of the postcolonial state in Botswana.

On the other hand, these institutions have facilitated massive state interventions in the population and captured people into processes that have been working upon their subjectivities, gradually forming them – more or less – as subjects to the modern state. Taking also into account how the dominant elites were, from the outset, caught up in the postcolonial state and profoundly transformed, we may as well speak of Botswana as a society of the state as vice versa.

All this means that we have at hand a case of postcolonial transformations which, during the formative and consolidating decades (1966–1990), gave rise to a strong state by very limited use of violent, coercive measures. This is in itself a significant expression of how the strength of the state has been achieved by capturing, to a great extent, the larger social context integral to its order. Although it goes beyond the scope of the present volume, I have suggested that after the state was well consolidated by virtue of the centrality of its diamond-driven political economy in relation to the development of the private economic sector, its strength and domination have recurrently been reproduced. The recession in the wake of the international financial crisis immediately affected Botswana's economy and represented a clear warning about the country's vulnerability to fluctuating income from diamond mining as it was, in a few months, reduced by some 50 per cent. The market is now improving and at the time of writing, the state has asserted its potency by announcing that it will take on a leading role in developing Botswana as a global diamond centre.

Obviously, Botswana's diamond-driven political economy underpins, as I have argued in this volume, the state's strength, the force of the ruling group and the government's wide-ranging social control. At the same time, the single-sourced character of the political economy makes, of course, the state highly vulnerable to the diamond world market. In view of how critically important state income from diamond mining is, the question is what the prospects might be in the case of a radical and persistent drop in prices.

This is, to be sure, an issue riddled with uncertainties, and I shall briefly make some suggestions with the point of departure in Deleuze and Guattari's (1991: 361–62) notion of state sovereignty as a relative matter, depending upon what the state is able to capture into its domain. In accordance with this conception, 'the social' is always an ambiguous matter in relation to the state: it is partly captured into the order of state, the extent of which determines the strength of the state. Partially 'the social' is escaping the state, remaining exterior to it and potentially standing against the state as, in the conception of these authors, a 'war-machine'. That is, a diffuse and polymorphous kind of rhizomic force which is deterritorializing and operating in ever-new disguises (see the Introduction). Because of this feature of the war-machine – as an always-unpredictable potentiality – it might be difficult to conceptualize and examine it as a 'pure form of exteriority' to the state (Deleuze and Guattari 1991: 354).

Therefore, I have certainly not succeeded in identifying all such potentialities in the different social contexts of state formation from precolonial times and onwards. Still, this conception of exteriorities to the state has, for example, been useful to comprehend the significance of the efforts of the small states on the fringe of the Kalahari to capture into their structures the ever-increasing, small groups in flight into their territories in the wake of the recurrent turmoil further east in the region. It has helped, furthermore, to see how these small premodern states captured missionary churches into their structures, amongst other things, to counter the rhizomic potentials of 'independent' churches, operating nomadically in changing disguises with an antihierarchical orientation. Also, the highly ambivalent relationship between Tswana rulers and the colonial state is patently a matter of the latter conceiving the former as only partially integral to the order of the colonial state.

This is an ambivalence that has been carried into the postcolonial era. For example, we have seen cases of claim of autonomy that amount to challenging the sovereignty of the state. In particular, in respect of ultimate control over *bogosi* and instilling social order in support of *bogosi* by means of violence. These cases indicate, I have argued, the existence of exteriors in relation to the state with considerable potentials of rhizomic forces. In view of the prevailing popular consciousness of *bogosi* as vested with symbolic wealth of considerable existential significance, these potentials may, under other overall political conditions, manifest in ways that transform the institutions of the *merafe* from representing major structures of state social control to becoming breeding grounds for rebellious attack on the state. While the dominant Tswana elites comprise a major part of the 'grand coalition' underpinning the post-colonial state leadership, it is not given that they will cohere under the condition of a weakened state; their rhizomic potentiality is evident.

Moreover, a substantial part of the population with non-Tswana ethnic identification has remained muted within the repressive structures of the Tswana *merafe*. Despite the postcolonial state leadership's efforts to appear ethnically neutral by launching nondistinctively Tswana 'development' programmes and acknowledging everyone's formal citizen rights in the spirit of liberal individualism, various minorities have developed a sense of exteriority to the state, attacking the state leadership for treating them as secondary citizens. This sense of exteriority is nourished by their perceptions of the state being represented chiefly by dominant Tswana. That is, the same category of people who in a multitude of informal, local contexts readily express, in subtle and tacit ways, Tswana overlordship and even arrogance. Notwithstanding the efforts to capture non-Tswana into the process of nation-state building, the sense of exteriority to a Tswana-dominated state represents, as have I argued, a potentiality of rhizomic forces. This potentiality is evident as 'minorities' probably comprise about half of Botswana's population.

The development of Botswana's modern political economy presents another condition for the generation of exteriorities to the state and hence rhizomic forces. As I have explained, this postcolonial economy is to a great extent principled upon Western virtues of liberal individualism, involving a radical discontinuity with the indigenous order where, ideally, inequality of authority and wealth is combined with the overall adherence to values of the common good. This is, as we have seen, an important backdrop for rank and file people's reaction towards political leaders who they perceive as ridden by greed for power and wealth, appropriating a lion's share of the wealth of the nation-state. Their reaction finds one of their expressions in a subaltern discursive practice identifying such people as engaged in occultic fights at the centre of the state. That is, occulic practices located, in popular perception, exterior to the state in the sense of generating rhizomic forces destructive to social order – to *kagiso* – and thus dangerous to everybody. The progressive development of this kind of subaltern discourse reflects an expanding exteriority of the state – manifesting in political leaders' increasing hidden exercise of illegitimate power which, together with escalating discrepancy between rich and poor, expands and intensifies subaltern discourse. That is, discourses beyond the order of the state with the rhizomic potentialities which manifest, as we have seen, in occasional popular reactions that give rise to violent confrontations with state forces.

In the light of this development, it is not surprising that many of my interlocutors compared what they perceived as the development of dangerous social disorder and violence during the 2011-strikes, with the spring revolutions in the Middle East and North Africa, initiated a few months before. This case represents a major culmination of a long term trend, representing a gradual shift from the popular imaginary of the state as a friendly, non-violent do-gooder – a *motswadintle* – to a state in the hands of self-serving people, a state that might deploy violent means against its citizens. A state with a hugely expanded intelligence service that has, in popular perception, clearly rhizomic features: it is everywhere and nowhere, always in new disguises, generating uncertainty, anxiety and fear in spaces where people used to feel safe. Of course, the ruler's use of spies is, I recall, a practice with long genealogies in this country. But that does not mean that people are habituated to such practices and readily accept them. On the contrary, it means that people are very sensitive and critical of such operations. They are often spoken of as a matter of destructive power abuse because hidden exercise of power is always perceived as potentially dangerous. As the 2011-strike also indicates, this is a trend that gains momentum under the conditions of economic decline and is hence much connected to the global economy because of the highly diamond-driven character of Botswana's political economy.

I have discussed the conditions for radical political movements attacking the current state of affairs that vastly privilege people of power and wealth and argued that the 'grand coalition' prevails, unifying such people across the party political spectrum in a basic agreement about major state policies. This involves major constraints upon mobilizing all poor and unprivileged classes of the population in forceful political endeavours that properly pursue their interests and problems. Yet, the progressive development of an increasingly pervasive subaltern discourse, nourished by indigenous cosmological notions of destructive forces, involves the development of raising class consciousness. This is a matter of identifying 'the existing *conditions* for potential collective [class] struggle' (Hardt and Negri 2005: 104). The subaltern discursive practices in progress during postcolonial times involve the formation of a radically new kind of popular consciousness about difference and inequality that increasingly identifies people in high places not as cosmologically anchored custodians of the common good. On the contrary, indigenous cultural schemes of authority and power constitutive of these discursive practices generate narratives wherein such people feature more and more as persons driven by greed for wealth and power and operate in ways that are damaging to *kagiso* on a large scale and hence destructive to the entire nation.

Finally, this is a trend that has been in progress since early post-colonial days, however – like that of growing ethnic tension – it manifested itself significantly first after 1990. This patently underscores the dubious character of the post-colonial state in Botswana: on the one hand, vested with an immense capacity to capture the population into the process of state formation with very restricted exercise of violence. On the other hand, tacitly relying on subtle tactics, repressive practices and structures of domination. In retrospect, the significance of the latter is certainly perceived by many people as more and more critical.

BIBLIOGRAPHY

Abbink, Jon G. 2005. 'Local Leadership and State Governance in Southern Ethiopia. From Charisma to Bureaucracy'. In O. Vaughan (ed.), pp. 159–84.

Ake, Claude. 2000. *The Feasibility of Democracy in Africa*. Dakar: CODESIRA.

Asad, Talal. 2004. 'Where Are the Margins of the State?' In V. Das and D. Poole (eds.), pp. 279–88.

Aubert, Vilhelm. 1970. *The Sociology of Law*. Harmondsworth: Penguin.

Awasom, Nicodemus F. 2005. 'Traditional Rulers, Legitimacy and Shifting Loyalties: The Case of North West Chiefs in Cameroon'. In O. Vaughan (ed.), pp. 305–27.

Badiou, Alain. 2005. *Being and Event*. London: Continuum.

———. 2008. *The Meaning of Sarkozy*. London: Verso.

Barth, Fredrik. 1959. *Political Leadership among Swat Pathans*. London: The Athlone Press.

Bayart, Jean-Francios. 1986. 'Civil Society in Africa'. In Patrick Chabal (ed.), *Political Domination in Africa: Reflections on the Limits of Power*, pp. 109–125. Cambridge: Cambridge University Press.

———. 1993. *The State in Africa: The Politics of Belly*. London: Longman.

Bayart, Jean-Francois, Stephen Ellis and Beatrice Hibou. 1999. *The Criminalization of the State in Africa*. Oxford: James Currey.

Beaulier, Scott A. and J. Robert Subrick. 2006. 'The Political Foundation of Development: The Case of Botswana'. *Constitutional Political Economy* 17: 103–15.

Berman, Bruce J. 1998. 'Ethnicity, Patronage and the State: Politics of Uncivil Nationalism'. *African Affairs* 97: 305–41.

Berman, Bruce, Dickson Eyoh and Will Kymlicka. 2004. 'Introduction'. In B.J. Berman, E. Eyoh and W. Kymlicka (eds.), pp. 1–19.

Berman, Bruce, Dickson Eyoh and Will Kymlicka (eds.). 2004. *Ethnicity and Democracy in Africa*. Oxford: James Curry.

Bertelsen, Bjørn. 2003. '"The Traditional Lion is Dead." The Ambivalent Presence of Tradition and the Relationship Between Politics and Violence in Mozambique'. In C. Goirand (ed.), *Lusotope 2003. Violence et Controle de la Violence au Bresil, en Afrique et a Goa*, pp. 263–281. Paris: Editions Karthala.

———. 2007a. 'Ambivalence of Tradition and State. On the Anthropology of a Politics of Justice in Mozambique'. Paper presented at the session 'Reconstituting Political and

Legal Anthropology in Africa'. at the 106th Annual Meeting of the American Anthropological Association, Washington DC, 28 Nov.–2 Dec. 2007.

———. 2007b. 'Violence, Sovereignty and Tradition: Understanding Death Squads and Sorcery in Chimoio, Mozambique'. In A.M. Guedes and Maria J. Lopes (eds.), *State and Traditional Law in Angola and Mozambique*, pp. 201–61. Coimbra, Portugal: Almedina.

———. 2009. 'Multiple Sovereignties and Summary Justice in Mozambique. A Critique of Some Legal Anthropological Terms'. *Social Analysis* 53(3): 123–47.

Bhinda, Nils et al. 1999. *Private Capital Flows to Africa: Perception and Reality*. The Hague: Fondad.

Bienen, Henry S. 1970. *Tanzania: Party Transformation and Economic Development*. Princeton, NJ: Princeton University Press.

Binsbergen, Wim van. 1987. 'Chief and the State in Independent Zambia'. *Journal of Legal Pluralism and Unofficial Law* 25–26: 139–201.

———. 1993. 'African Independent Churches and the State in Botswana.' In M. Bax and A. Koster (eds.), *Power and Prayer: Anthropological Essays on Politics and Religion*, pp. 24–56. Amsterdam: VU University Press.

———. 1994. 'Minority Language, Ethnicity and the State in Botswana'. In Richard Fardon and Graham Furniss (eds.), *African Language, Development and the State*, pp. 142–88. London: Routledge.

———. 1995. 'Aspects of Democracy and Democratisation in Zambia and Botswana: Exploring African Political Culture at the Grassroots'. *Journal of Contemporary African Studies* 13(1): 3–33.

———. 1999. 'Nkoya Royal Chiefs and the Kazanga Cultural Association in Western Central Zambia To-Day—Resilience, Decline or Folklorization'. In E. Adrian B. van Rouveroy van Nieuwaal and Rijk van Dijk (eds.), pp. 97–134.

Bratton, Michael and Nicholas van de Walle. 1997. *Democratic Experiments in Africa: Regime Transitions in Comparative Perspectives*. Cambridge: Cambridge University Press.

Brown, J. Tom. 1921. 'Circumcision Rites of the Becwana Tribes'. *Journal of the Royal Anthropological Institute* 51: 419–27.

Burchell, William J. 1824. *Travels in the Interior of Southern Africa*, Vol. 2. London: Longman, Hurst, Rees, Orme, Brown & Green.

Burke, Charlanne. 2000. 'They Cut Segametsi into Parts: Ritual Murder, Youth, and the Politics of Knowledge in Botswana'. *Anthropological Quarterly* 73(4): 204–14.

Buur, Lars and Helen M. Kyed. 2007. 'Traditional Authority in Mozambique: The Legible Space between State and Community'. In L. Buur and H.M. Kyed (eds.), pp. 105–30.

Buur, Lars and Helen M. Kyed (eds). 2007. *State Recognition and Democratization in Sub-Saharan Africa: A New Dawn for Traditional Authorities?* New York: Palgrave Macmillan.

Campbell, John. 1822. *Travels in South Africa, Undertaken at the Request of the London Missionary Society*, 2 vols. London: Westley.

Carroll, Terrance and Barbara Wake Carroll. 2004. 'The Rapid Emergence of Civil Society in Botswana'. *Commonwealth and Comparative Politics* 42: 333–55.

Carter, Gwendolen M. and E. Philip Morgan. 1980. *From The Front Line. Speeches of Sir Seretse Khama*. London: Rex Collins.

Carter, Marion W. et al. 2007. '"A Bull Cannot be Contained in a Single Kraal": Concurrent Sexual Partnership in Botswana'. *AIDS Behaviour* 11: 822–30.

Chabal, Patrick and Jean-Pascal Daloz. 1999. *Disorder as Political Instrument*. Oxford: James Currey.

Chanock, Martin. 1985. *Law, Custom and Social Order: The Colonial Experience in Malawi and Zambia*. Portsmouth, NH: Heinemann.

Charlton, Roger. 1991. 'Bureaucrats and Politicians in Botswana's Policy-making Process: a Reinterpretation'. *Journal of Common Wealth Studies* 29 (3): 265–82.

Chief Linchwe II. 1989. 'The Role a Chief Can Play in Botswana's Democracy'. In J. Holm and P. Molutsi (eds.), pp. 99–102.

Chirenje, J. Mutero. 1978. *Chief Kgama and His Times, c.1835–1923*. London: Rex Collings.

Ciekawy, Diane and Peter Geschiere. 1988. 'Containing Witchcraft: Conflicting Scenarios in Postcolonial Africa.' *African Affairs* 41: 1–14.

Claessen, Henri J.M. and Peter Skalnik (eds.). 1978. *The Early State*. The Hague: Mouton.

Clastres, Pierre. 1987. *Society Against the State*. New York: Zone Books.

Cohen, Ronald D. 1985. 'Warfare and State Formation'. In H.J.M. Claessen et al. (eds.) *Development and Decline: The Evolution of Socio-political Organization*, pp. 278–289. South Hadley, MA: Bergin & Garvey.

Colclough, Christopher and Stephen McCarthy. 1980. *The Political Economy of Botswana. A Study of Growth and Distribution*. Oxford: Oxford Univ. Press.

Comaroff, Jean. 1980. 'Healing and the Cultural Order. The Case of the Barolong boo Ratshidi of Southern Africa'. *American Ethnologist* 7(4): 637–57.

———. 1985. *Body of Power—Spirit of Resistance. The Culture and History of a South African People*. Chicago: The University of Chicago Press.

Comaroff, John. L. 1975. 'Talking Politics: Oratory and Authority in a Tswana Chiefdom'. In Maurice Bloch (ed.), *Political Language and Oratory in Traditional Society*, pp. 141–61. London: Academic Press.

———. 1977. *The Structure of Agricultural Transformation in the Barolong*. Gaborone: Government Printer.

———. 1980. 'Class and Culture in a Peasant Economy: The Transformation of Land Tenure in Barolong'. *Journal of African Law* 24(1): 85–116.

———. 1982. 'Dialectical Systems, History and Anthropology: Units of Study and Questions of Theory'. *Journal of Southern African Studies* 8(2): 143–72.

———. 2002. 'Governmentality, Materiality, Legality, Modernity. On the Colonial State in Africa'. In J.-G. Deutsch, P. Probst and H. Schmidt (eds.), *African Modernities*, pp. 107–34. Oxford: James Currey.

Comaroff, Jean and John Comaroff. 1986. 'Christianity and Colonialism in South Africa'. *American Ethnologist* 13: 1–20.

———. 1991. *Of Revelation and Revolution: Christianity, Colonialism, and Consciousness in South Africa*. Chicago: University of Chicago Press.

———. 1992. *Ethnography and the Historical Imagination*. Oxford: Westview Press.

———. 1993. 'Introduction'. In J. Comaroff and J.L. Comaroff. (eds.), *Modernity and Its Malcontents: Ritual and Power in Postcolonial Africa*, pp. xi–xxxvii. Chicago: University of Chicago Press.

———. 1997a. *Of Revelation and Revolution: The Dialectics of Modernity on a South African Frontier*. Chicago: University of Chicago Press.

———. 1997b. 'Postcolonial Politics and Discourses of Democracy in Southern Africa: An Anthropological Reflection on African Modernities'. *Journal of Anthropological Research* 53(2): 123–46.

Comaroff, John L. and Jean Comaroff. 1981. 'The Management of Marriage in a Tswana Chiefdom'. In E.J. Krige and J.L. Comaroff (eds.), *Essays on African Marriage in Southern Africa*, pp. 29–49. Johannesburg: Juta.

———. 1993. *Modernity and its Malcontents: Ritual and Power in Postcolonial Africa*. Chicago: Chicago University Press.

———. 2009. *Ethnicity, Inc*. Chicago: University of Chicago Press.

Comaroff, John L. and Jean Comaroff (eds.). 1999. *Civil Society and the Political Imagination in Africa*. Chicago: University of Chicago Press.

Comaroff, John L. and Simon A. Roberts. 1981. *Rules and Process: The Cultural Logic of Dispute in an African Context*. Chicago: University of Chicago Press.

Conley, John M. and William M. O'Barr. 1990. *Rules versus Relationships: Ethnography of Legal Discourse*. Chicago: University of Chicago Press.

Coronil, Fernando. 1997. *The Magical State: Nature, Money and Modernity in Venezuela*. Chicago: University of Chicago Press.

Crehan, Kate. 2002. *Gramsci, Culture and Anthropology*. Berkeley: University of California Press.

Crowder, Michael. 1987. 'The Statesman: Tshekedi Khama'. In Fred Morton and Jeff Ramsay (eds.), pp. 45–64.

Dachs, Anthrony J. 1972. 'Missionary Imperialism – The Case of Bechuanaland.' *Journal of African History* 13 (4): 647–58.

Das, Veena and Deborah Poole. 2004. 'State and Its Margins'. In V. Das and D. Poole (eds.), pp. 3–33.

Das, Veena and Deborah Poole (eds.). 2004. *Anthropology in the Margins of the State*. Oxford: James Curry.

Deleuze, Gilles and Felix Guattari. 1984. *Anti-Oedipus*. London: Continuum.

———. 1991. *The Thousand Plateaus*. London: Continuum.

De Boeck, Filip. 1996. 'Postcolonialism, Power and Identity: Local and Global Perspectives from Zaire'. In R. Werbner and T. Ranger (eds.), *Postcolonial Identities in Africa*, pp. 75–106. London: Zed Books.

de Heusch, Luc. 1982. *The Drunken King, or, The Origin of the State*. Bloomington: Indiana University Press.

Dijk, Rijk van and E. Adrian van Rouveroy van Nieuwaal. 1999. 'Introduction: The Domestication of Chieftaincy: From Imposed to the Imagined'. In E.A. van Rouveroy van Nieuwaal and R. van Dijk (eds.), pp. 1–20.

Du Toit, Pierre. 1995. *State-Building Democracy in Southern Africa. A Comparative Study of Botswana, South Africa and Zimbabwe*. Pretoria: HSRC Publishers.

Dumont, Louis. 1986. *Essays on Individualism*. Chicago: Chicago University Press.

Durham, Deborah. 1993. 'Images of Culture: Being Herero in a Liberal Democracy'. Ph.D. diss., University of Chicago.

———. 1999. 'Civil Lives: Leadership and Accomplishment in Botswana'. In John L. Comaroff and Jean Comaroff (eds.), pp. 192–218.

———. 2002. 'Uncertain Citizens: Herero and the New Intercalary Subjects in Postcolonial Botswana'. In R. Werbner (ed.), *Postcolonial Subjectivities in Africa*, pp. 139–70, London: Zed Books.

———. 2004. 'Disappearing Youth: Youth as a Social Shifter in Botswana'. *American Ethnologist* 31(4): 589–605.

Dutfield, Michael. 1990. *A Marriage of Inconvenience: The Prosecution of Ruth and Seretse*. London: Robert Hale.

Eagleton, Terry. 1991. *Ideology*. London: Verso.

Edge, Wayne A. 1998. 'Botswana: A Development State'. In W.A. Edge and M.H. Lekorwe (eds.), pp. 333–51.

Edge, Wayne A. and Mogopodi H. Lekorwe (eds.). 1998. *Botswana. Politics and Society*. Pretoria: Van Schaik Publishers.

Eidheim, Harald. 1969. 'When Ethnic Identity is a Social Stigma'. In F. Barth (ed.), *Ethnic Groups and Boundaries*, pp. 39–57, Oslo: Universitetsforlaget.

Englebert, Pierre. 2002. *State Legitimacy and Development in Africa*. Boulder, CO: Lynne Rienner.

———. 2005. 'Back to the Future? Resurgent Indigenous Structures and the Reconfiguration of Power in Africa'. In O. Vaughan (ed.), pp. 33–60.

Englund, Harri. 2004. 'Introduction: Recognizing Identities, Imagining Alternatives'. In H. Englund and F.B. Nyamnjoh (eds.), pp. 1–32.

Englund, Harri and Francis B. Nyamnjoh (eds.). 2004. *Rights and the Politics of Recognition in Africa*. London: Zed Books.

Ergas, Zaki. 1987. 'Introduction'. In Zaki Ergas (ed.), *The African State in Transition*, pp. 1–22. London: Macmillan.

Evans-Pritchard, E.E. 1984. *Witchcraft, Oracles and Magic among the Azande*. Oxford: Clarendon Press.

Fawcus, Peter (with Alan Tilbury). 2000. *Botswana: The Road to Independence*. Gaborone: Pula Press.

Ferguson, James. 1990. *The Anti-Politics Machine. "Development," Depoliticization and Bureaucratic Power in Lesotho*. Cambridge: Cambridge University Press.

———. 2006. *Global Shadows. Africa in the Neo-Liberal World*. London: Duke University Press.

Fortes, M. and E.E. Evans-Pritchard (eds.). 1940. *African Political Systems*. London: International Institute for African Languages and Cultures.

Foucault, Michel. 1978. 'Governmentality'. *Ideology and Consciousness* 6(6): 5–21.

———. 1980. *Power/Knowledge*. Brighton: Harvester Press.

———. 1981. *The Will to Knowledge. The History of Sexuality Volume 1*. London: Pelican.

———. 1982. 'Afterword. The Subject and Power'. In Hubert L. Dreyfus and Paul Rabinow (eds.), *Michel Foucault. Beyond Structuralism and Hermeneutics*, pp. 208–226. London: Harvester Wheatsheaf.

———. 1988. *Technologies of the Self*. Edited by L.H. Martin, H. Gutman and P.H. Hutton, Amherst: University of Massachusetts Press.

———. 1990. *Michel Foucault. Politics, Philosophy, Culture*. Edited by L.D. Kritsman. London: Routledge.

Frank, L. 1981. 'Khama and Jonathan: Leadership Strategies in Contemporary Southern Africa'. *Journal of Development Areas* 15: 173–98.

Friedman, John T. 2011. *Imagining the Post-Apartheid State. An Ethnographic Account of Namibia*. Oxford/New York: Berghahn Books.

Fuller, Chris. 1994. 'Legal Anthropology, Legal Pluralism and Legal Thought'. *Anthropology To-Day* 10: 9–12.

Gabasiane, Odirile and Athalia Molokomme. 1987. 'The Legislative Council'. In F. Morton and J. Ramsey (eds.), pp. 161–71.

Geertz, Clifford. 1980. *Negra. The Theatre State in Nineteenth-Century Bali*. Princeton, NJ: Princeton University Press.

Geschiere, Peter. 1998. 'Globalization and the Power of Intermediate Meaning: Witchcraft and Spirit Cults in Africa and East Africa.' *Development and Change* 29: 811–37.

Gillett, Simon. 1973. 'The Survival of Chieftainship in Botswana'. *African Affairs* 72 (287): 179–85.

Gluckman, Max. 1949. 'Introduction' in M. Gluckman, J.C. Mitchell and J.A. Barnes, 'The Village Headman in British Central Africa'. *Africa* 19(2): 89–106.

———. 1963. *Order and Rebellion in Tribal Africa*. London: Cohen & West.

Goffman, Erving. 1963. *Stigma. Notes in the Management of Spoiled Identity*. Englewood Cliffs, NJ: Prentice Hall.

Good, Kenneth. 1992. 'Interpreting the Exceptionality of Botswana'. *Journal of Modern African Studies* 30 (1): 69–95.

———. 1993. 'At the Ends of the Ladder: Radical Inequalities in Botswana'. *Journal of Modern African Studies* 31(2): 203–30.

———. 1994. 'Corruption and Mismanagement in Botswana'. *Journal of Modern African Studies* 32 (3): 499–521.

———. 1996. 'Authoritarian Liberalism: A Defining Characteristic of Botswana'. *Journal of Contemporary African Studies* 14(1): 29–51.

———. 1999a. 'Enduring Elite Democracy in Botswana'. *Democratization* 6(1): 50–66.

———. 1999b. 'The State and Extreme Poverty in Botswana: The San and Destitutes'. *Journal of Modern African Studies* 37(2): 185–205.

———. 2002. *The Liberal Model and Africa: Elites against Democracy*. London: Palgrave.

———. 2008. *Diamonds, Dispossession and Democracy in Botswana*. Oxford: James Currey.

Good, Kenneth and Ian Taylor. 2005. 'Unpacking the 'Model': Presidential Succession in Botswana'. In R. Southall and H. Melbar (eds.), *Leadership Change and Former Presidents in African Politics*, pp. 51–72. Cape Town: HSRC Press.

Goody, Jack. 1974. *Technology, Tradition, and the State in Africa*. London: Hutchinson's University Library.

Government of Botswana. 1976. *The Rural Income Distribution Survey 1974/75*. Gaborone: Government Printer.

———. n.d. 'National Development Plan 1979–85'. Gaborone: Government Printer.

———. 2000. 'The Presidential Commission of Inquiry into Section 77. 78 and 79 of the Constitution of Botswana'. Gaborone: Government Printer.

Gramsci, Antonio. 1991. *Selections from the Prison Notebooks*. London: Lawrence and Wishart.

Grant, Sandy. 1984. 'The Revival of Bogwera in the Kgatleng—Tswana Culture or Rampant Tribalism?' *Botswana Notes and Records* 16: 7–18.

Griffiths, Anne M.O. 1997. *In the Shadow of Marriage: Gender and Justice in an African Community*. Chicago: University of Chicago Press.

Guenther, Mathias G. 1976. 'From Hunters to Squatters: Social and Cultural Change among the Farm San of Ghanzi, Botswana'. In R.I. Lee and I. De Vore (eds.), *Kalahari Hunter-Gatherers. Studies of the !Kung San and Their Neighbours*, pp. 120–33. Cambridge, MA: Harvard University Press.

Gulbrandsen, Ørnulf. 1980. *Agro-Pastoral Production and Communal Land Use. A Socio-Economic Study of the Bangwaketse*. Gaborone: Botswana Government Press.

———. 1986a. *When Land Becomes Scarce. Access to Agricultural Land and Communal Land Management in Eastern Botswana*. Bergen: Norse Publications.

———. 1986b. 'To Marry—or Not To Marry. Marital Strategies and Sexual Relations in a Tswana Society'. *Ethnos* 51(1): 7–28.

———. 1987. 'Privilege and Responsibility. On Transformations of Hierarchical Relations in a Tswana Society'. Department of Social Anthropology, University of Bergen, Norway.

———. 1991. 'On the Problem of Egalitarianism: The Kalahari San in Transition'. In R. Grønhaug, G. Haaland and G. Henriksen (eds.), *The Ecology of Choice and Symbol. Essays in Honour of Fredrik Barth*, pp. 81–110. Bergen: Alma Mater.

———. 1993a. 'Missionaries and Northern Tswana Rulers: Who Used Whom?' *Journal of Religion in Africa* 23(1): 44–83.

———. 1993b. 'The Rise of the North-Western Tswana Kingdoms: On the Sociocultural Dynamics of Interaction between Internal Relations and External Forces'. *Africa* 63(4): 550–82.

———. 1995. '"The King is King by the Grace of the People." Control and Exercise of Power in Subject-Ruler Relations'. *Comparative Studies in Society and History* 37(3): 415–55.

———. 1996a. *Poverty in the Midst of Plenty. Socio-Economic Marginalization, Ecological Deterioration and Political Stability in a Tswana Society.* Bergen: Norse Publications.

———. 1996b. 'Living Their Lives in Courts: The Counter-Hegemonic Force of the Tswana *Kgotla* in the Bechuanaland Protectorate'. In Olivia Harris (ed.), *Inside and Outside the Law*, pp. 125–56. London: Routledge.

———. 2001. 'Christianity in an African Context: On the Inadequacy of the Notion of a Sacred/Secular Divide'. *Journal of the Royal Institute for Inter-Faith Studies* 1: 31–59.

———. 2003. 'The Discourse of "Ritual Murder": Popular Reactions to Political Leaders in Botswana'. In Bruce Kapferer (ed.), *Beyond Rationalism: Rethinking Magic, Witchcraft and Sorcery*, pp. 215–33. New York: Berghahn Books. (Also published in *Social Analysis: Journal of Cultural and Social Practice* 46(3): 215–33.)

———. 2007. 'Town-State Formations on the Edge of the Kalahari. Socio-Cultural Dynamics of Centralization in Northern Tswana Kingdoms'. *Social Analysis: Journal of Cultural and Social Practice* 51(3): 55–77.

———. Forthc. 'For and against the State. Sardo/Italia and Tswana/Botswana compared'. In B. Kapferer (ed.), *Challenging the State*.

———. In prep. 'Ontologies of power and power abuse: Sardo and Tswana contrasted', paper presented at the Challenging the State Seminars., paper presented at the Challenging the State'. Ms. Department of Social Anthropology, University of Bergen.

Gulbrandsen, Ørnulf, Marit Karlsen and Janne Lexow. 1986. *Botswana's Remote Area Development Programme.* Bergen/Gaborone/Oslo: Government of Botswana, NORAD and SIDA.

Gunderson, G. L. 1970. 'Nation Building and the Administrative State: the Case of Botswana'. Ph.D. diss., Berkeley: University of California.

Gupta, Akhil and Aradhana Sharma 2006. 'Globalization and Postcolonial States'. *Current Anthropology* 47(2): 277–307.

Habermas, Jurgen. 1974. 'The Public Sphere'. *New German Critique* 3: 49–55.

———. 1992. *The Structural Transformation of the Public Sphere.* Cambridge: Polity Press.

Hailey, Lord. 1953. 'Native Administration in the British African Territories. Part V: The High Commission Territories Basutoland, Bechuanaland and Swaziland'. London: Her Majesty's Stationary Office.

Halperin, Daniel T. and Helen Epstein. 2004. 'Concurrent Sexual Partnerships Help to Explain Africa's High HIV-prevalence: Implications for Prevention'. *Lancet* 364: 4–6.

Hammond-Tooke, W.D. (ed.). 1974. *The Bantu Speaking Peoples of Southern Africa.* London: Routledge & Kegan Paul.

Hansen, Thomas Blom. 1999. *The Saffron Wave. Democracy and Hindu Nationalism in Modern India.* Princeton, N.J.: Princeton University Press.

Hansen, Thomas Blom and Finn Stepputat. 2005. 'Introduction'. In T.H. Blom and F. Stepputat (eds.), *Sovereign Bodies, Citizens, Migrants, and States in the Postcolonial World*, pp. 1–38. Princeton, NJ: Princeton University Press.

Hansen, Thomas and Finn Stepputat (eds.). 2001. *States of Imagination. Ethnographic Exploration of the Post-Colonial State.* Durham: Duke University Press.

Hardt, Michael and Antonio Negri. 2000. *Empire.* London: Harvard University Press.

———. 2005. *Multitude. War and Democracy in the Age of Empire.* London: Penguin.

Harvey, Charles and Stephen R. Lewis. 1990. *Policy Choice and Development Performance in Botswana.* London: Macmillan.

Harvey, Penelope. 2005. 'The Materiality of State-Effects: The Ethnography of a Road in the Peruvian Andes'. In C. Krohn-Hansen and K.G. Nustad (eds.), pp. 123–41.

Heald, Suzette. 2002. 'It's Never as Easy as ABC. Understandings of AIDS in Botswana'. *African Journal of AIDs Research* 1: 1–10.

———. 2006. 'Abstain or Die: The Development of HIV/AIDS Policy in Botswana'. *Journal of Biosocial Science* 38(1): 29–41.

Helle-Valle, Jo. 1996. 'Change and Diversity in a Kgalagadi Village, Botswana'. Ph.D. diss., Department of Social Anthropology, University of Oslo.

———. 1999. 'Sexual Mores, Promiscuity and "Prostitution" in Botswana'. *Ethnos* 64(39): 372–96.

———. 2002. 'Seen from Below: Concepts of Politics and the State in a Botswana Village'. *Africa* 72(2): 179–202.

———. 2003. 'Social Change and Sexual Mores: A Comparison Between Pre-20th-Century Norway and 20th-Century Botswana'. *History and Anthropology* 14(4): 327–47.

Herbst, Jeffrey. 2000. *States and Power in Africa: Comparative Lessons in Authority and Control.* Princeton, NJ: Princeton University Press.

Herzfeld, Michael. 1992. *The Symbolic Production of Difference.* Chicago: University of Chicago Press.

———. 1997. *Cultural Intimacy. Social Poetics in the Nation-State.* London: Routledge.

Hewitt, Adrian and Charles Stephens. 1981. 'The Second Lomé Convention'. In C. Stevens (ed.), *EEC and the Third World: A Survey,* pp. 30–58. London: Hodder & Stoughton.

Hillbom, Ellen. 2008. 'Diamonds or Development? A Structural Assessment of Botswana's Forty Years of Success'. *Journal of Modern African Studies* 46(2): 191–214.

Hitchcock, Robert K. 1978. *Kalahari Cattle Posts. A Regional Study of Hunter-Gatherers, Pastoralists, and Agriculturalists in the Western Sandveld Region, Central District, Botswana,* 2 vols. Gaborone: Government Printer.

———. 2002. '"We Are the First People": Land, Natural Resources and Identity in the Central Kalahari, Botswana'. *Journal of Southern African Studies* 28(4): 797–824.

Hobsbawm, Eric and Terence Ranger. 1983. *The Invention of Tradition.* Cambridge: Cambridge University Press.

Holm, John D. 1985. 'The State, Social Class and Rural Development in Botswana'. In Louis A. Picard (ed.), pp. 157–75.

———. 1988. 'Botswana: A Paternalistic Democracy'. in L. Diamond, J.J. Linz, and S.M. Lipset (eds.), *Democracy in Developing Countries,* pp. 182–98. Boulder, CO: Lynne Rienner Publisher.

Holm, John D. and Patrick Molutsi (eds.). 1989. *Democracy in Botswana,* Gaborone: Macmillan.

———. 1990. 'Monitoring the Development Democracy: Out Botswana Experience'. *The Journal of Modern African Studies* 26(3): 535–43.

Holm John D., Patrick P. Molutsi and Gloria Somolekae. 1996. 'The Development of Civil Society in a Democratic State: The Botswana Model'. *African Studies Review* 39 (2): 43–69.

Hubbard, Michael. 1986. *Agricultural Exports and Economic Growth. A Study of the Botswana Beef Industry.* London: Routledge Kegan Paul.

Ingstad, Benedicte. 1990. 'The Cultural Construction of AIDS and its Consequences for Prevention in Botswana'. *Medical Anthropological Quarterly* 4(1): 28–40.

Isaksen, Jan. 1981. *Macro-Economic Management: The Case of Botswana.* Uppsala: Scandinavian Institute of African Studies.

Jefferis, Keith. 1998. 'Botswana and Diamond-Dependent Development'. In W.A. Edge and M.H. Lekorwe (eds.), pp. 300–18.

Jeppe, W.J.O. 1974. 'Local Government in Botswana'. In W.B. Vosloo et al. (eds.), *Local Government in Southern Africa*, pp. 133–61. Cape Town: Academica.

Junod, Henri A. 1927. *The Life of a South African Tribe*. London: Macmillan.

ka-Mbuya, Titus and Fred Morton. 1987. 'The South'. In F. Morton and J. Ramsay, (eds.), pp. 147–60.

Kapferer, Bruce. 1988. *Legends of People. Myth of State. Violence, Intolerance, and Political Culture in Sri Lanka and Australia*. London: Smithsonian Institution Press.

———. 1997. *The Feast of the Sorcerer. Practices of Consciousness and Power*. Chicago: University of Chicago Press.

———. 2003. 'Introduction: Outside All Reason—Magic, Sorcery and Epistemology in Anthropology'. In B. Kapferer (ed.), *Beyond Rationalism: Rethinking Magic, Witchcraft and Sorcery*, pp. 1–32. New York: Berghahn Books.

———. 2008. 'The Crisis of Power and Reformations of the State in Globalazing Realities'. The Humboldt Lecture 2008.

Karlstrøm, Mikael. 1996. 'Imagining Democracy: Political Culture and Democratization in Buganda'. *Africa* 66(4): 485–505.

———. 1999. 'Civil Society and Its Presuppositions: Lessons from Uganda'. In John L. Comaroff and Jean Comaroff (eds.), pp. 104–24.

Kessel, Ineke van and Barbara Oomen. 1999. '"One Chief, One Vote": The Rival of Traditional Authorities in Post-Apartheid South Africa'. In E. Adrian B. van Rouveroy van Nieuwaal and Rijk van Dijk (eds.), pp. 155–80.

Kimble, David. 1953. *The Machinery of Self-Government*. Hammond-Worth: Penguin.

Klaits, Frederick. 1998. 'Making a Good Death: AIDS and Social Belonging in an Independent Church in Gaborone'. *Botswana Notes and Records* 30: 101–19.

———. 2005. 'The Widow in Blue: Blood and the Morality of Remembering in Botswana's Times of Aids'. *Africa* 75(1): 46–63.

———. 2010. *Death in a Church of Life. Moral Passion During Botswana's Time of Aids*. Berkeley: University of California Press.

Kooijman, Kunnie. 1978. *Social and Economic Life in a Tswana Village*. Leiden: Africa-Studiecentrum.

Krige, Eileen J. 1950. *The Social System of the Zulus*. Pietermaritzburg: Shuter & Scooter.

Krige, Eileen J. and Jacob D. Krige 1980. *The Realm of a Rain-Queen. A Study of the Pattern of Lovedu Society*. Johannesburg: Juta.

Krohn-Hansen, Christian and Knut G. Nustad. 2005. 'Introduction'. In C. Krohn-Hansen and K.G. Nustad (eds.), pp. 3–27.

Krohn-Hansen, Christian and Knut G. Nustad (eds.). 2005. *State Formation. Anthropological Perspectives*. London: Pluto Press.

Kunz, Frank A. 1991. 'Liberation in Africa. Some Preliminary Results'. *African Affairs* 90: 223–35.

Kuper, Adam. 1970. *Kalahari Village Politics. An African Democracy*. Cambridge: Cambridge University Press.

———. 1975. 'The Social Structure of the Sotho-Speaking Peoples of Southern Africa'. *Africa* 45(1): 67–81, 45(2): 139–49.

———. 1982. *Wives for Cattle*. London: Routledge and Kegan Paul.

Kyed, Helen M. and Lars Buur. 2007. 'Introduction. Traditional Authority and Democratization in Africa'. In L. Buur and H.M. Kyed (eds.), pp. 1–28.

Ladley, Andrew. 1991. 'Just Spirits? In Search of Tradition in the Customary Law Courts in Zimbabwe'. In *Proceedings of the VIth International Symposium of the Commission on Folk Law and Legal Pluralism*, Ottawa, 14–18 August 1990, pp. 584–604.

Landau, Paul. S. 1995. *The Realm of the World. Language, Gender, and Christianity in a Southern African Kingdom*. London: James Currey.

Leach, Edmund. 1954. *Political Systems of Highland Burma*. Boston: Beacon Press.

Leith, J. Clark. 2005. *Why Botswana Prospered*. Montreal: McGill-Queens University Press.

Lentz, Carola. 1998. 'The Chief, the Mine Captain and the Politician: Legitimating Power in Northern Ghana'. *Africa* 68(1): 46–67.

Livingston, Julie. 2005. *Debility and the Moral Imagination in Botswana*. Bloomington: Indiana University Press.

Livingstone, David. 1857. *Missionary Travels in South Africa*. London: Ward, Lock & Co.

Lloyd, E. 1895. *Three Great African Chiefs*. London: T. Fisher Unwin.

Machel, Samora. 1974. *Mozambique. Sowing the Seeds of Revolution*. London: Committee for Freedom in Mozambique, Angola and Guine.

Machiavelli, Niccolo. 1977. *The Prince*. London: Norton.

Mackenzie, J. 1871. *Ten Years North of the Orange River, from 1859–1869*. London: Frank Cass & Co. Ltd. (Reprinted 1971.)

———. 1883. *Day-Dawn in Dark Places: The Story of Wanderings and Work in Bechuanaland*. London: Cassell & Co. (Reprinted 1968, New York: Universities Press.)

———. 1975. *Papers of John Mackenzie*, selected and edited by A. J. Dachs. Johannesburg: Witwatersrand Univ. Press for Africa Studies Center.

Macpherson, C.B. 1964. *The Political Theory of Possessive Individualism*. Oxford: Oxford Paperbacks.

Magang, David. 2008. *The Magic of Perseverance*. Cape Town: Centre for Advanced Studies of African Society.

Makepe, Patricia M. 2005. 'Agriculture and Rural Development in Botswana'. In H.K. Siphambe et al. (eds.), pp.149–69.

Makgala, Christian J. 2005. 'The Relationship between Kenneth Koma and the Botswana Democratic Party, 1965–2003'. *African Affairs* 104/415: 303–23.

———. 2006. *Elite Conflict in Botswana. A History*. Pretoria: Africa Institute of South Africa.

———. 2010. 'Limitations of the British Territorial Control in Bechuanaland Protectorate, 1918–1953'. *Journal of Southern African Studies* 36(1): 57–71.

Mamdani, Mahmood. 1996. *Citizen and Subject. Contemporary Africa and the Legacy of Late Colonialism*. Princeton, NJ: Princeton University Press.

Masire, Quett K.J. 2006. *Very Brave or Very Foolish? Memoirs of an African Democrat*. Edited by Stephen R. Lewis, Jr. Gaborone: Macmillan.

Massow, Valentine von. 1983. 'On the Impacts of EEC Preferences for Kenya and Botswana'. *Quarterly Journal of International Agriculture* 22(3): 216–34.

Maundeni, Zibani. 2001. *Civil Society, Politics and the State in Botswana*. Gaborone: Medi Publishing.

———. 2002. 'State Culture and Development in Botswana and Zimbabwe'. *Journal of Modern African Studies* 40(1): 105–32.

Maylam, Paul. 1980. *Rhodes, the Tswana, and the British: Colonialism, Collaboration, and the Conflict in the Bechuanaland Protectorate, 1885-1899*. Westport, Conn.: Greenwood Press.

Mazonde, Isaac. 1994. *Ranching Enterprise in Eastern Botswana. A Case Study of Black and White Farmers*. London: Edinburgh Univ. Press for the International African Institute.

———. 2002. 'The San in Botswana and the Issue of Subjectivities—National Disintegration or Cultural Diversity'. In I.N. Mazonde (ed.), pp. 57–71.

Mazonde, Isaac (ed.). 2002. *Minorities of the Millennium. Perspectives from Botswana*. Gaborone: Lightbooks.

Mbabazi, Pamela and Ian Taylor. 2005. 'Botswana and Uganda as Development States (?)'. In P. Mbabazi and I. Taylor (eds.), pp. 1–15.

Mbabazi, Pamela and Ian Taylor (eds.). 2005. *The Potentiality of 'Developmental States' in Africa. Botswana and Uganda Compared*. Dakar: Council for the Development of Social Science Research in Africa.

Mbembe, Achille. 1992. 'Provisional Notes on the Postcolony'. *Africa* 62(1): 3–37.

Mgadla, Themba. 1987. 'The North-East and the South-East'. In Fred Morton and Jeff Ramsay (eds.), pp. 134–46.

Mgadla, Part T. and Alec Campbell. 1989. 'Dikgotla, dikgosi and protectorate administration'. In J. Holm and P. Molutsi (eds.), pp. 48–56.

Mitchell, Timothy. 1999. 'Society, Economy, and the State Effect'. In G. Steinmetz (ed.), *State/Culture: State-formation after the Cultural Turn*, pp. 76–97. Ithaca, NY: Cornell University Press.

Mockford, Julian, 1950. *Seretse Khama and the Bamangwato*. London: Staples Press.

Moffat, Robert. 1842. *Missionary Labours and Scenes in Southern Africa*. London: Snow.

Mogalakwe, Monageng. 1997. *The State and Organized Labour in Botswana: 'Liberal Democracy' in Emergent Capitalism*. Aldershot: Ashgate.

———. 2006. 'From Pre-Colony to Post-Colony. Continuities and Discontinuities in Political Power Relations and Governance in Botswana'. *Journal of African Elections* 5(2): 5–20.

Molokomme, Athaliah. 1994. 'Customary Law in Botswana: Past, Present and Future'. In S. Brothers, J. Hermans and D. Nteta (eds.), *Botswana in the 21ˢᵗ Century*, pp. 347–74. Gaborone: Botswana Society.

Molutsi, Patrick. 1989a. 'The Ruling Class and Democracy in Botswana'. In J. Holm and P. Molutsi (eds.), pp. 103–15.

———. 1989b. 'Whose Interests Do Botswana's Politicians Represent?' In J. Holm and P. Molutsi (eds.), pp. 120–31.

Molutsi, Patrick P. and John D. Holm. 1990. 'Developing Democracy When Civil Society Is Weak: The Case of Botswana'. *African Affairs* 89 (356): 323–40.

Morton, Fred, Andrew Murray and Jeff Ramsay. 1989. *Historical Dictionary of Botswana*. London: The Scarecrow Press.

Morton, Fred and Jeff Ramsay (eds.). 1987. *The Birth of Botswana. A History of the Bechuanaland Protectorate*. Gaborone: Longman.

———. 1994. *The Making of a President, Sir Ketumile Masire's Early Years*. Gaborone: Pula Press.

Motzafi-Haller, Pnina. 1995. 'Liberal Discourses of Cultural Diversity and Hegemonic Construction of Difference: Basarwa in Contemporary Botswana'. *Political and Legal Anthropology Review* 18(2): 91–104.

———. 2002. *Fragmented Worlds, Coherent Lives. The Politics of Difference in Botswana*. Westport, CT: Bergin and Garvey.

Murray, Andrew. 1987. 'The Northwest'. In F. Morton and J. Ramsay (eds.), pp. 110–22.

Nader, Laura. 1990. *Harmony Ideology: Justice and Control in a Zapotec Mountain Village*. Stanford, CA: Stanford University Press.

Nengwekhulu, Randwezi. 1979. 'Some Findings on the Origin of Political Parties in Botswana'. *Pula, Botswana Journal of African Studies* 1(2): 47–76.

Ngcongco, Leonard. 1977. 'Aspects of the History of the Bangwaketse to 1910'. Ph.D. dissertation, Dalhousie University, Nova Scotia.

———. 1989. 'Tswana Political Tradition: How Democratic?' In J. Holm and P. Molutsi (eds.), pp. 42–47.

Noppen, Dolf. 1982. *Consultation and Non-Commitment. Planning with People in Botswana.* Leiden: African Studies Centre.

Nteta, Doreen, Janet Hermans and Pavla Jezkova (eds.). 1997. *Poverty and Plenty. The Botswana Experience.* Gaborone: Botswana Society.

Nyamnjoh, Francis B. 2003. 'Chieftaincy and the Negotiation of Might and Right in Botswana Democracy'. *Journal of Contemporary African Studies* 21(2): 233–49.

———. 2004. 'Reconciling "the Rhetoric of Right" with Competing Notions of Personhood and Agency in Botswana'. In H. Englund and F.B. Nyamnjoh (eds.), pp. 33–63.

Nyati-Ramahobo, Lydia. 2001. 'Linguistic and Cultural Domination: The Case of Wayeyi of Botswana'. In B. Smieja and B.H. Batibo (eds.), *Minority Languages in Botswana*, pp. 217–34. Essen: Peter Lang.

———. 2002. 'From a Phone Call to the High Court: Wayeyi Visibility and the Kamanakao Association's Campaign for Linguistic and Cultural Rights in Botswana'. *Journal of Southern African Studies* 28(4): 685–709.

Odell, Macolm. 1985. 'Local Government: Traditional and Modern Roles of the Village Kgotla'. In Louis A. Picard (ed.), pp. 61–83.

Okihiro, Gary Y. 1976. 'Hunters, Herders, Cultivators and Traders: Interaction and Change in the Kgalagadi Nineteenth Century'. Ph.D. dissertation, Department of History, University of California, Los Angeles.

Oomen, Barbara. 2005. *Chiefs in South Africa. Law, Power & Culture in the Post-Apartheid Era.* Oxford: James Currey.

Otlhogile, Bojosi. 1993. 'Criminal Justice and the Problems of Dual Legal System in Botswana'. *Criminal Law Forum* 4(3): 521–33.

Owusu, Maxwell. 1986. 'Custom and Coups: A Juridical Interpretation of Civil Order and Disorder in Ghana'. *Journal of Modern African Studies* 24(1): 69–99.

———. 1997. 'Domesticating Democracy. Culture, Civil Society and Constitutionalism in Africa'. *Comparative Studies in Society and History* 39: 120–52.

Parry, Jonathan. 1974. 'Egalitarian Values in a Hierarchical Society'. *South Asian Review* 7(2): 95–124.

Parson, Jack. 1984. *Botswana. Liberal Democracy and Labour Reserve in Southern Africa.* London: Westview Press.

Parson, Jack (ed.).1990. *Succession to High Office in Botswana.* Athens: Ohio University Center for International Studies.

Parsons, Q. Neil. 1973. 'Khama III, the Bangwato, and the British, with Special Reference to 1895–1923'. Ph.D. dissertation, University of Edinburgh.

———. 1977. 'The Economic History of Khama's Country in Botswana, 1844–1930'. In Q. Neil Parsons and Robert Palmer (eds.), *The Roots of Rural Poverty in Central and Southern Africa*, pp. 113–43. Berkeley: University of California Press.

———. 1982. 'Settlement in Eastern-Central Botswana. C. 1800–1920'. In R. Renee Hitchcock and Mary R. Smith (eds.), *Settlements in Botswana*, pp. 115–28. Gaborone: Botswana Society.

———. 1985. 'The Evolution of Modern Botswana: Historical Revisions'. In Louis A. Picard (ed.), pp. 26–40.

————. 1987. 'The Central District: The BaNgwato Crisis 1948–1956'. In Fred Morton and Jeff Ramsay (eds.), pp. 123–33.

————. 1993. 'Botswana: An End to Exceptionality?' *The Round Table* 325: 73–82.

————. 1998. *King Khama, Emperor Joe and the Great White Queen. Victorian Britain through African Eyes*. Chicago: University of Chicago Press.

————. 2006. 'Unravelling History and Cultural Heritage in Botswana'. *Journal of Southern African Studies* 32(4): 667–81.

Parsons, Neil and Michael Crowder (eds.). 1988. *Monarch of All Land I Surveyed. Bechuanaland Diaries 1929–37 by Sir Charles Rey*. London: James Currey.

Parsons, Neil, Willie Henderson and Thomas Tlou. 1995. *Seretse Khama 1921–1980*. Gaborone: Macmillan.

Peters, Pauline E. 1994. *Dividing the Commons. Politics, Policy, and Culture in Botswana*. London: University Press of Virginia.

Picard Louis A. 1980. 'Bureaucrats, Cattle, and Public Policy. Land Tenure Changes in Botswana'. *Comparative Politics Studies* 13(3): 313–56.

————. 1987. *The Politics of Development in Botswana. A Model for Success*. London: Lynne Rienner Publishers.

Picard Louis A. (ed.) 1985. *The Evolution of Modern Botswana*. London: Rex Collings.

Pitcher, Anne, Mary H. Moran, and Michael Johnston. 2009. 'Rethinking Patrimonialism and Neopatrimonialism in Africa', *African Studies Review* 52 (1): 125–156.

Pitso, Joseph M.N. and Gordon A. Carmichael. 2003. 'Premarital Childbearing in Thamaga Village, Botswana'. *Journal of Population Research* 20(2): 187–202.

Poulantzas, Nicos. 1978. *State, Power, Socialism*. London: NLB.

Proctor, J. 1968. 'The House of Chiefs and the Political Development of Botswana'. *Journal of Modern African Studies* 6 (1): 59–79.

Radcliffe-Brown, A.R. 1940. 'Preface'. In M. Fortes and E.E. Evans-Pritchard (eds.), *African Political Systems*. London: Oxford University Press.

————. 1950. 'Introduction'. In E. E. Evans-Pritchard and D. Forde (eds.), *African Systems of Kinship and Marriage*, pp. xi–xxiii. Oxford: Oxford University Press.

Ramsay, Jeff. 1987. 'The Neo-Traditionalist: Sebele II of the Bakwena'. In Fred Morton and Jeff Ramsay (eds.) pp. 30–44.

————. 1998. 'Twentieth Century Antecedents of Decolonising Nationalism in Botswana'. In W.A. Edge and M.H. Lekorwe (eds.), pp. 101–17.

————. n.d. 'The Fall and Decline of the Kwena Monarchy'. Ms. Gaborone: Legae Academy.

Rathbone, Richard. 2000. *Nkrumah and the Chiefs. The Politics of Chieftaincy in Ghana 1951–60*. Oxford: James Curry.

Ray, Donald I. and E. Adrian B. van Rouveroy van Nieuwaal. 1996. 'The New Relevance of Traditional Authorities in Africa'. *Journal of Legal Pluralism* 37/38: 1–38.

Redfern, John. 1955. *Ruth and Seretse: A Very Disputable Transaction*. London: Victor Gollancz.

Reno, Williams, 1999. *Warlord Politics and African States*. London: Lynne Rienner Publishers.

Roberts, Simon. 1972. 'The Survival of Traditional Courts in the National Legal System of Botswana'. *Journal of African Law* 6(2): 103–29.

————. 1979. *Order and Dispute*. Harmondsworth: Penguin.

————. 1985. 'The Tswana Polity and "Tswana Law and Custom" Reconsidered'. *Journal of Southern African Studies* 12(1): 75–87.

————. 1991. 'Tswana Government and Law in the Time of Seepapitso, 1910–1916'. In K. Mann and R. Roberts (eds.), *Law in Colonial Africa*, pp. 167–82. London: James Carry.

Robins, Eric. 1967. *A White Queen in South Africa*. London: Robert Hale.

Rouveroy van Nieuwaal, E. Adrian B. van. 1999. 'Chieftaincy in Africa: Three Facts of a Hybrid Role'. In E. Adrian B. van Rouveroy van Nieuwaal and Rijk van Dijk (eds.), pp. 21–49.

Rouveroy van Nieuwaal, E. Adrian B. van and Rijk van Dijk (eds.). 1999. *African Chieftaincy in a New Socio-Political Landscape*. London: Lit Verlag.

Sahlins, Marshall. 1978. *Culture and Practical Reason*. Chicago: Chicago University Press

———. 1999. *Waiting for Foucault and Other Aphorism*. Charlottesville: Prickly Pear Pamphlets.

———. 2000. *Culture in Practice*. New York: Zone Books.

Samatar, Abdi I. 1999. *An African Miracle. State and Class Leadership and Colonial Legacy in Botswana Development*. Portsmouth, NH: Heinemann.

Samatar, Abdi I. and Sophie Oldfield. 1995. 'Class and Effective State Institutions: The Botswana Meat Commission'. *Journal of Modern African Studies* 33(4): 651–68.

Sansom, Basil. 1974. 'Traditional Rulers and Their Realms'. In W.D. Hammond-Tooke (ed.), *The Bantu Speaking Peoples of Southern Africa*, pp. 246–83. London: Routledge & Kegan Paul.

Saugestad, Sidsel. 1998. *The Inconvenient Indigenous: Remote Area Development in Botswana, Donors Assistance, and the First People of the Kalahari*. Uppsala: The Nordic African Institute.

Schapera, Isaac. 1935. 'The Social Structure of a Tswana Ward'. *Bantu Studies* 9(2): 203–24.

———. 1940. 'The Political Organization of the Ngwato in Bechuanaland Protectorate'. In M. Fortes and E.E. Evans-Pritchard (eds.), pp. 56–82.

———. 1942a. 'A Short History of the Bangwaketse'. *African Studies* 1(1): 1–26.

———. 1942b. 'A Short History of the Bakgatla-bagaKgafela of Bechuanaland Protectorate'. *Communications from the School of African Studies*, New Series no. 3, Cape Town: University of Cape Town.

———. 1943a. *Native Land Tenure in the Bechuanaland Protectorate*. Alice, South Africa: Lovedale Press.

———. 1943b. *Tribal Legislation among the Tswana of Bechuanaland Protectorate. A Study in the Mechanism of Cultural Change*. London: Percy Lund, Humphries & Co.

———. 1947a. *Migrant Labour and Tribal Life: A Study of Conditions in the Bechuanaland Protectorate*. London: Oxford University Press.

———. 1947b. *The Political Annals of a Tswana Tribe*. Cape Town: Communications for the School of African Studies (n.s.), no. 18, University of Cape Town.

———. 1952. *The Ethnic Composition of Tswana Tribes*. London: London School of Economics Monographs on Social Anthropology, no.11.

———. 1956. *Government and Politics in Tribal Societies*. London: C.W. Watts & Co.

———. 1957. 'Marriage of Near Kin among the Tswana'. *Africa* 27(2): 139–59.

———. 1963. 'Agnatic Marriage in Tswana Royal Families'. In I. Schapera (ed.), *Studies in Kinship and Marriage*, pp. 103–13. Occasional Paper No. 16. London: Royal Anthropological Institute.

———. 1965. *Praise-Poems of Tswana Chiefs*. Oxford: Clarendon Press.

———. 1966. 'Tswana Legal Maxims'. *Africa* 36(1): 121–33.

———. 1970. *Tribal Innovators: Tswana Chiefs and Social Change 1795–1940*. London: Athlone Press.

———. 1971a. *Rainmaking Rites of Tswana Tribes*. Leiden: Afrika-Studiecentrum.

———. 1971b. *Married Life in an African Tribe*. Harmondsworth: Penguin. (First publ. by Faber & Faber 1940.)

————. 1978. *Bogwera. Kgatla Initiation*. Mochudi, Botswana: Phuthadikobo Museum.

————. 1984. *A Handbook of Tswana Law and Custom*. London: Oxford University Press for the International African Institute (first publ. in 1938).

Schapera, Isaac (ed.). 1960. *Livingstone's Private Journals 1851–1853*. London: Chatto & Windus.

Schapera, Isaac and D.F. v.d. Merwe. 1945. *Notes on Tribal Groupings, History and Customs of the Bakgalagadi*. Communications from the School of African Studies. Capetown: University of Capetown.

Schapera, Isaac and Simon Roberts. 1975. 'Rampedi Ward Revisited: Another Look at a Kgatla Ward'. *Africa* 45: 258–79.

Schatzberg, Michael G. 1988. *The Dialectics of Oppression in Zaire*. Bloomington: Indiana University Press.

Scott, James C. 1990. *Domination and the Arts of Resistance. Hidden Transcripts*. New Haven, CT: Yale University Press.

————. 1998. *Seeing Like A State. How Certain Schemes to Improve the Human Condition Have Failed*. New Haven: Yale University Press.

Sebudubudu, David. 2005. 'The Institutional Framework of the Development State in Botswana'. In Pamela Mbabazi and Ian Taylor (eds.), pp. 79–89.

Sebudubudu, David with Patrick Molutsi 2009. 'Leaders, Elites and Coalitions in the Development of Botswana'. Research Paper 02, Leaders, Elites & Coalitions Research Programme, http://www.lecrp.org.

Sentsho, Joel. 2005. 'Growth and Performance in the Mining Sector'. In H.K. Siphambe et al. (eds.), pp. 138–49.

Silberbauer, George B. 1965. *Report to the Government of Bechuanaland on the Bushman Survey*. Gaberones (Gaborone): Bechuanaland Government.

Sillery, Anthony. 1954. *Sechele. The Story of an African Chief*. Oxford: George Roald.

————. 1965. *Founding a Protectorate: History of Bechuanaland 1885–1895*. The Hague: Mouton.

————. 1974. *Botswana. A Short Political History*. London: Methuen.

Siphambe, Happy K. 2003. 'Understanding Unemployment in Botswana'. The South African Journal of Economics 71 (3): 480–95.

————. 2005. 'Poverty and Unemployment in Botswana'. In H.K. Siphambe et al. (eds.), pp. 203–15.

Siphambe, Happy K. et al. (eds.). 2005. *Economic Development of Botswana. Facets, Policies, Problems and Prospects*. Gaborone: Bay Publishing.

Skalnik, Peter. 1996. 'Authority versus Power. Democracy in Africa Must Include Original African Institutions'. *Journal of Legal Pluralism* 37/38: 109–21.

————. 2004. 'Chiefdom: A Universal Political Formation?' *Focaal-European Journal of Anthropology* 43: 76–98.

Sklar, Richard L. 2005. 'The Premise of Mixed Government in African Political Studies'. In Ofuemi Vaughan (ed.), *Tradition and Politics. Indigenous Political Structures in Africa*, pp. 13–32. Asmara: African World Press.

Solway, Jacqueline S. 1986. 'Commercialization and Social Differentiation in a Kalahari Village, Botswana'. Ph.D. dissertation, University of Toronto.

————. 1994. 'From Shame to Pride: Politicized Ethnicity in the Kalahari, Botswana'. *Canadian Journal of African Studies* 28(2): 254–74.

————. 2004. 'Reaching the Limits of Universal Citizenship: 'Minority' Struggles in Botswana'. In Bruce Berman, Dickson Eyoh and Will Kymlicka (eds.), pp. 129–48.

————. 2009. 'Human Rights and NGO "Wrongs": Conflict Diamonds, Culture Wars and the "Bushman Question"'. *Africa* 79(3): 321–45.

Solway, Jacqueline S. and Richard B. Lee. 1990. 'Foragers, Genuine or Spurious: Situating the Kalahari San in History'. *Current Anthropology* 31(2): 109–45.

Solway, Jacqueline S. and Lydia Nyati-Ramahobo. 2004. 'Democracy in the Process: Building a Coalition to Achieve Political, Cultural and Linguistic Rights in Botswana'. *Canadian Journal of African Studies* 38(3): 603–21.

Somolekae, Gloria M. and Mogopodi H. Lekorwe. 1998. 'The Chieftaincy System and Politics in Botswana, 1966–95'. In W.A. Edge and M.H. Lekorwe (eds.), pp. 186–99.

Staugård, Frants. 1985. *Traditional Healers*. Gaborone: Ipeleng Publishers.

Taussig, Michael. 1997. *The Magic of the State*. New York: Routledge.

Taylor, Charles. 1990. 'Modes of Civil Society'. *Public Culture* 3(1): 95–117.

———. 1992. *Multiculturalism and "The Politics of Recognition"*. Princeton, NJ: Princeton University Press.

———. 1999. *Hegel and the Modern Society*. Cambridge: Cambridge University Press.

———. 2004. *Modern Social Imaginaries*. Durham, NC: Duke University Press.

———. 2007. *A Secular Age*. Cambridge, Mass: Harvard University Press.

Taylor, Ian. 2003. 'As Good as It Gets? Botswana's Democratic Development'. *Journal of Contemporary African Studies* 21(2): 215–31.

———. 2005. 'The Development State in Botswana: The Case of Botswana'. In P. Mbabazi and I. Taylor (eds.), *The Potentialities of 'Development States in Africa. Botswana and Uganda Compared*, pp. 44–57. Dakar: Council for the Development of Social Science Research in Botswana.

Hartland-Thunberg, Penelope. 1978. *Botswana an African Growth Economy*. Boulder, Colorado: Westview Press.

Tlou, Thomas. 1977. 'Servility and Political Control: Botlhanka among the Batawana of Northwestern Botswana, c. 1739–1906'. In S. Miers and I. Kopitoff (eds.), *Slavery in Africa: Historical and Anthropological Perspectives*, pp. 367–90. Madison: Madison University Press.

———. 1973. 'The Batawana of North-Western Botswana and Christian Missionaries, 1877-1906'. *Transafrican Journal of History* 3 (1&2): 112–28.

———. 1985. *A History of Ngamiland, 1750–1906*. Gaborone: Macmillan Botswana.

Tlou, Thomas and Alec Campbell. 1984. *History of Botswana*. Gaborone: Macmillan.

Trotha, Truz von. 1996. 'From Administrative to Civil Chieftaincy. Some Problems and Prospects of African Chieftaincy'. *Journal of Legal Pluralism* 37/38: 79–107.

Trouillot, Michel-Rolph.1990. *State against Nation: The Origins and Legacy of Duvalierism*. New York: Monthly Review Press.

———. 2001. 'The Anthropology of the State in the Age of Globalization: Close Encounters of the Deceptive Kind'. *Current Anthropology* 42 (1): 125–38.

Tselaetsele, Benjamin M. 1987. 'BaKgatla Ba-Ga-Mmanaana'. BA dissertation thesis, University of Botswana, Gaborone.

Tsie, Balefi. 1996. 'The Political Context of Botswana's Development Performance'. *Journal of Southern African Studies* 22(4): 599–616.

UNAIDS and World Health Organization. 2008. *Sub-Saharan Africa. AIDS Epidemic Update*.

Valeri, Valerio. 1985. *Kingship and Sacrifice. Ritual and Society in Ancient Hawaii*. Chicago: The University of Chicago Press.

Vaughan, Olufemi. 2003. *Chiefs, Power, and Social Change: Chiefship and Modern Politics in Botswana, 1880s-1990s*. Trenton, NJ: Africa World Press.

Vaughan, Olufemi (ed.). 2005. *Tradition and Politics. Indigenous Political Structures in Africa*. Trenton, NJ: Africa World Press.

Velsen, Jaap van. 1967. *The Politics of Kinship*. Manchester: Manchester University Press.

Vengroff, Richard. 1972. 'Local-Central Linkages and Political Development in Botswana'. Ph.D. dissertation, Syracuse University, NY.

―――. 1977. *Botswana. Rural Development in the Shadow of Apartheid*. London: Associated University Press.

Weber, Max. 1978. *Economy and Society*. 2 vols. edited by G. Roth and C. Wittich. Berkeley: University of California Press.

Warmelo, N.J. van. 1974. 'The Classification of Cultural Groups'. In W.D. Hammond-Tooke (ed.), pp. 56–84.

Werbner, Pnina. 2009. 'The Hidden Lion: Tswapong Girls' Puberty Rituals and the Problem of History'. *American Ethnologist* 36(1): 441–58.

―――. 2010a. 'The Politics of Infiltration: An Anthropological Case Study of Factionalism and Party Politics in the Manual Workers Union of Botswana,' *Critical African Studies*, Issue 3 (online).

―――. 2010b. 'Appropriating Social Citizenship: Woman's Labour, Poverty, and Entrepreneurship in the Manual Workers Union of Botswana,' *Journal of Southern African Studies* 36: 693–710.

Werbner, Richard. 1980. 'The Quasi-Judicial and the Experience of the Absurd: Remaking Land Law in North-Eastern Botswana'. *Journal of African Law* 24(1): 131–51.

―――. 1989. *Ritual Passage—Sacred Journey. The Process and Organization of Religious Movements*. Manchester: Manchester University Press.

―――. 1993. 'For Heartland to Hinterland: Elites and Geopolitics of Lands in Botswana'. In T. Bassett and D.E. Crummey (eds.), *African Agrarian Systems*, pp. 101–27. Madison: University of Wisconsin Press.

―――. 1996. 'Introduction. Multiple Identities, Plural Arenas'. In R. Werbner and T. Ranger (eds.), *Postcolonial Identities in Africa*, pp. 1–25. London: Zed.

―――. 2002a. 'Introduction: Challenging Minorities, Difference and Tribal Citizenship in Botswana'. *Journal of Southern African Studies* 28(4): 672–84.

―――. 2002b. 'Cosmopolitan Ethnicity, Entrepreneurship and the Nation: Minority Elites in Botswana'. *Journal of Southern African Studies* 28(4): 731–53.

―――. 2004. *Reasonable Radicals and Citizenship in Botswana. The Public Anthropology of Kalanga Elites*. Bloomington: Indiana University Press.

Williams, Susan. 2007. *Colour Bar. The Triumph of Seretse Khama and His Nation*. London: Penguin Books.

Willoughby, W.C. 1909. 'Notes in the Initiation Ceremonies of Becwana'. *Journal of the Royal Anthropological Institute* 39: 228–45.

―――. 1923. *Race Problems in the New Africa*. Oxford: Clarendon Press.

―――. 1928. *The Soul of the Bantu. A Sympathetic Study of the Magico-Religious Practices and Beliefs of the Bantu Tribes of Africa*. New York: Doubleday.

Wilmsen, Edwin. N. 1989. *Land Filled with Flies. A Political Economy of the Kalahari*. Chicago: University of Chicago Press.

Wilson, Richard. 2001. *The Politics of Truth and Reconciliation in South Africa. Legitimizing the Post-Apartheid State*. Cambridge: Cambridge University Press.

Wily, Elisabeth. 1979. *Official Policy towards San (Bushmen) Hunter-Gatherers in Modern Botswana: 1966–1978*. Gaborone: National Institute of Research.

―――. 1981. *The TGLP and Hunter-Gatherers: A Case Study in Land Politics*. Gaborone: National Institute of Research.

Wiseman, John A. 1998. 'The Slow Evolution of the Party System in Botswana'. *Journal of Asian and African Studies* 33(3): 241–64.

Wylie, Diana. 1990. *A Little God. The Twilight of Patriarchy in a Southern African Chiefdom*. London: Wesleyan University Press.

INDEX

Gillett, S., 66
Gluckman, M., 10, 33
globalization, 1, 3, 5, 7, 17–8, 39, 61, 133, 307–10, 313–4, 316
    See also beef export, diamonds, postcolonial state
Gobuamang I, *Kgosi* of the Bakgatla-baga-Mmanaana, 178
Gobuamang II, *Kgosi* of the Bakgatla-baga-Mmanaana (2001–), 177–78.
Goffman, E., 211
Good, K., 2, 117, 127–8, 140, 213, 229–31, 249, 283, 296, 302, 307
Goody, J., 33
governmentality
    and biopower, 260
    governmentalization of the state, 24, 255–60
    as historical transformation, 257–8
    and 'new techniques and tactics', 258, 260–1, 263, 274
    and pastoral power, 264, 280
    and positive power, 258, 260
    and rationality, 256, 258
    selfgovernment, 256–7, 261, 266, 280
    as state intervention, 256–7, 259, 261–70, 274–80
    and subjection, 271, 279
    and subjectivity, 257, 262, 264, 269–70, 273, 276–9
Gramsci, A., 19, 244, 256
Grant, S., xv, 148–50, 167–8,
Griffiths, A. M.O., 169
Guattari, F. *See* Deleuze
Guenther, M.G., 213
Gupta, A., 274

H
Habermas, J., 250, 254
Hailey, L., 74–5
Halperin, D. T., 266
Hansen, T. B., 2, 3, 112
Hardt, M., 8, 257, 282, 317
harmony ideology, 245
Hartland-Thunberg, P., 2
Harvey, Charles, 2, 8, 125–6, 255
Heald, S., 266
heat. *See mogote*
hegemony, 19–20, 176, 258, 299
    and authority, 19, 244–7
    and class, 192
    discourse of development as, 199–201
    and Tswana domination, 20, 30, 54, 57, 62, 176, 180, 191

to win, 19–20, 23, 62, 192, 199, 207, 223–4, 249
    See also ethnicity, postcolonial state
Helle-Valle, J., xv, 212, 242, 248, 266–7, 269
Herzfeld, Michael, 194, 222
Hewitt, A., 115
Hitchcock, Robert K., 128, 213
HIV/AIDS
    and abstention from sex, 267
    and blood, 267–8
    and condoms, 267
    and national interests, 270
    and existential significance of sex, 267–9
    and 'promiscuity' (*bobolete*), 269
    and resistance to state intervention, 267–9
    and sexual practices, 266–8
    and state intervention, 261–6
    statistics, 264, 266, 269
    See also postcolonial state
Hobsbawm, E., 309
hola, go (to heal, become cool), 173–6, 267–9. *See also mogote*
Holm, J. D., 2, 135, 229, 231, 243, 246, 250–1
hot. *See mogote.*
House of Chiefs (*Ntlo ya Dikgosi*), 99–104, 107, 137, 139, 151, 170, 178, 184, 216, 219–20, 228
Hubbard, M., 82, 115

I
indirect rule, 16, 49, 55, 60, 62, 66, 69, 75, 77, 105
individual accumulation, 206, 224, 279
    See also common good, liberalism
individualism, 12, 23–4, 63, 113, 120, 130, 193, 195, 204, 207, 257, 276, 280, 284–5, 297, 305, 315–6
    See also common good, liberalism
Ingstad, B., 266–7
intelligence service, 51, 161, 307
Isaksen, J., 2, 118

J
Jefferis, K., 125–6
Jeppe, W.J.O., 73
Johnston, Michael, 11–3
Junod, Henri A., 198

K
ka-Mbuya, T., 74
kagisano (make harmony/peace), 194